COMMENTARIES

ON THE

LAW OF BAILMENTS,

WITH

ILLUSTRATIONS

FROM

THE CIVIL AND THE FOREIGN LAW

BY

JOSEPH STORY, LL. D.,

DANE PROFESSOR OF LAW IN HARVARD UNIVERSITY.

Leges autem a me edentur non perfectæ (nam esset infinitum), sed ipsæ
summæ rerum, atque sententiæ. — CIC. DE LEGIBUS.

THE LAWBOOK EXCHANGE, LTD.
Clark, New Jersey

ISBN 978-1-58477-778-6

Lawbook Exchange edition 2007, 2025

The quality of this reprint is equivalent to the quality of the original work.

THE LAWBOOK EXCHANGE, LTD.

33 Terminal Avenue
Clark, New Jersey 07066-1321

*Please see our website for a selection of our other publications
and fine facsimile reprints of classic works of legal history:*

www.lawbookexchange.com

Library of Congress Cataloging-in-Publication Data

Story, Joseph, 1779-1845.
  Commentaries on the law of bailments : with illustrations
from the civil and the foreign law / by Joseph Story.
    p. cm.
  Originally published: Cambridge: Hilliard and Brown,1832.
  Includes bibliographical references and index.
  ISBN-13: 978-1-58477-778-6 (cloth : alk. paper)
  ISBN-10: 1-58477-778-8 (cloth : alk. paper)
  1. Bailments--United States. I. Title.
  KF940.S76 2007
  346.7302'5--dc22   2006036096

Printed in the United States of America on acid-free paper

COMMENTARIES

ON THE

LAW OF BAILMENTS,

WITH

ILLUSTRATIONS

FROM

THE CIVIL AND THE FOREIGN LAW

BY

JOSEPH STORY, LL. D.,

DANE PROFESSOR OF LAW IN HARVARD UNIVERSITY.

Leges autem a me edentur non perfectæ (nam esset infinitum), sed ipsæ
summæ rerum, atque sententiæ. — Cic. DE LEGIBUS.

CAMBRIDGE:

HILLIARD AND BROWN,

BOOKSELLERS TO THE UNIVERSITY.

1832.

CAMBRIDGE:
E. W. METCALF AND COMPANY,
Printers to the University.

TO THE

HONORABLE NATHAN DANE, LL. D.,

DISTINGUISHED ALIKE

FOR PURITY, SIMPLICITY, AND DIGNITY

IN HIS PRIVATE LIFE;

FOR

TALENTS, LEARNING, AND FIDELITY

IN HIS PROFESSION;

AND FOR

PUBLIC LABOURS IN THE STATE AND NATIONAL COUNCILS,

WHICH

HAVE CONFERRED ON HIM AN IMPERISHABLE

FAME

AS A STATESMAN AND PATRIOT: —

THIS WORK,

THE FIRST FRUITS OF THE PROFESSORSHIP

FOUNDED BY HIS BOUNTY,

IS RESPECTFULLY DEDICATED

BY HIS OBLIGED FRIEND AND SERVANT,

THE AUTHOR.

PREFACE.

THE following work has been prepared in the discharge of a part of the duties belonging to the chair of the Dane Professorship of Law in Harvard University. The Essay of Sir William Jones on the same subject is in the hands of every scholar and jurist, and deserves great praise for its elegant diction, its various research, and its abundant learning. Still it is but a mere outline ; and it must be admitted to be very imperfect in details, and occasionally quite erroneous in its principles. The author was (as every one perceives) deeply versed in the juridical antiquities of ancient and modern nations, and he indulged himself in a not unbecoming admiration and reverence of the civil law. He has everywhere manifested an extreme solicitude to make the principles of this branch of jurisprudence, as administered at Rome, appear in harmony with the common law, as administered in Westminster Hall. And this circumstance has sometimes appeared to mislead his judgment, and sometimes has disturbed the clearness of his reasoning. For the other defects of his work a still more satisfactory apology may be found in the actual state of the English Law of Bailments at the time when he wrote his Essay. Few and scanty were the materials, which could be gathered from any other sources than the jurisprudence of continental Europe. Lord Holt's celebrated judgment in the case of *Coggs* v. *Bernard* [1] constituted at that period almost the only attempt to arrange the principles of the Law of Bailments in a scientific order. It was a prodigious effort, in which, however, he was greatly assisted by Bracton, and still more by the civil law, from which Bracton had

---

[1] 2 Ld. Raym. R. 909.

drawn his own materials. In the Commentaries of Sir William Blackstone the title of Bailments occupies little more than two pages ; and even these contain some incorrect statements. Yet the Law of Bailments is of vital importance in a large class of commercial transactions.

Sir William Jones, if not the first, was at any rate among the first, to call the attention of English lawyers to the extraordinary merit of the treatises of Pothier upon the principal branches of commercial law. Nor is his eulogy upon this great man, warm and vigorous as it is, too strongly coloured. Few works have ever appeared in the jurisprudence of any country, in which the qualities of " luminous method, apposite examples, and a clear, manly style," are more perfectly exhibited, than they are in the writings of Pothier.

But while a just commendation is given to this eminent jurist, it should not be forgotten, that an equally high tribute is due to his predecessor and real master, Monsieur Domat, whose work, entitled " The Civil Law in its Natural Order," considering the age and the circumstances, in which it was written, is a truly wonderful performance. His method is excellent, and his matter clear, exact, and comprehensive. Pothier (as well as other continental jurists) has drawn largely upon him to assist his own labours.

My design in the present Commentaries has been to present a systematical view of the whole of the common law in relation to Bailments, and to illustrate it by, and compare it throughout with, the civil law, and the modern jurisprudence of continental Europe. I have treated every branch of the subject (at the hazard of some repetitions) as a distinct and independent subject; believing, that for elementary instruction such a course would be found more convenient, as well as more satisfactory, than the common method of reference to other heads. In this, as well as in many other respects, I have availed myself of the example of Pothier and Domat. I have not scrupled to follow in a very great measure the method and arrangement of these authors; and I have endeavoured to incorporate into my text every position to be found in their treatises, which could be of the slightest use, either in a practical or a theoretical view, to a student of the common law ; so that the reader, if he is disinclined to go over the pages of those authors, will, I trust, find at hand whatever is valuable in their collective labours. I have, in like manner, availed myself of the writings of other distinguished civilians and commentators on the civil law, as far as their labours appeared to me to afford any new lights in the exposition of my subject.

Perhaps some apology may be thought necessary for my having, in a treatise on the English Law of Bailments, borrowed so largely from foreign sources. My reasons are as follows : — In the first place, the learned founder of the Dane Professorship, with that spirit of professional liberality, which has always characterized him, suggested to me at an early period the propriety of my presenting, in all my labours upon commercial law, a full view of the corresponding portions of the commercial jurisprudence of continental Europe. To advice so given it was impossible not to listen with the utmost respect ; and the wisdom of it has appeared more and more strongly to my mind, as it has been contemplated in all its bearings. In the next place, I have long entertained the belief, that an enlarged acquaintance with the continental jurisprudence, and especially with that of France, would furnish the most solid means of improvement of commercial law, as it now is, or hereafter may be, administered in America. Mr. Chancellor Kent has already led the way in this noble career ; [1] and has, by an incorporation of some of the best principles of the foreign law into ours, infused into it a more benign equity, as well as a more persuasive cogency and spirit. The English common lawyers (it must be acknowledged with deep regret) have hitherto generally exhibited an extraordinary indifference to the study of foreign jurisprudence ; an indifference, as little reputable to their characters as jurists, as it is to their judgments as men. Doctor Strahan, in the Preface to his translation of Domat, has spoken on this subject

---

[1] 1 Kent Com. § 23, p. 481 *et seq.*

in language of such freedom and force, as entitle it to respect.
I know not, whether one ought to be most struck with the
calmness of its rebuke, or with the mortifying severity of
its truth. "I was surprised," says he, "to find, in a country [England], where all arts and sciences do flourish and
meet with the greatest encouragement, that one of the noblest of the human sciences, and which contributes the
most to cultivate the mind, and improve the reason of man,
as that of the civil law does, should be so much disregarded,
and meet with so little encouragement. And I observed, that
the little regard, which has of late years been shown in this
kingdom to the study thereof, has been in a great measure
owing to the want of a due knowledge of it, and to the being
altogether unacquainted with the beauties and excellences
thereof; which are only known to a few gentlemen, who have
devoted themselves to that profession; others, who are perfect
strangers to that law, being under a false persuasion, that it
contains nothing, but what is foreign to our laws and customs.
Whereas, when they come to know, that the body of the civil
law, besides the laws peculiar to the Commonwealth of Rome,
which are there collected, contains likewise the general principles of natural reason and equity, which are the fundamental rules of justice in all engagements and transactions
between man and man, and which are to be found no where
else in such a large extent, as in the body of the civil law,
they will soon be sensible of the infinite value of so great a
treasure." Such is the language used by an English civilian
more than a century ago. It is lamentable to say, that it
may be applied, with but little mitigation, to the general
state of the profession of the common law in our day.*

There is a remarkable difference in the manner of treating
juridical subjects, between the foreign and the English jurists.
The former, almost universally, discuss every subject with

---

* I take pleasure in referring the reader to an excellent article on
the civil law, published in "The American Jurist" for July, 1829, p. 39
et seq. It is written with all the sound judgment and practical sense of
its learned author.

an elaborate, theoretical fulness, and accuracy, and ascend to
the elementary principles of each particular branch of the
science. The latter, with few exceptions, write what they
are pleased to call *practical* treatises, which contain little
more than a collection of the principles laid down in the adjudged cases, with scarcely an attempt to illustrate them by
any general reasoning, or even to follow them out into collateral consequences. In short, these treatises are but little
more than full Indexes to the Reports, arranged under appropriate heads; and the materials are often tied together by
very slender threads of connexion. They are better adapted
for those, to whom the science is familiar, than to instruct
others in its elements. It appears to me, that the union of
the two plans would be a great improvement in our law treatises; and would afford no inconsiderable assistance to students in mastering the higher branches of their profession.

In the present work I do not pretend, in any suitable manner, to have accomplished such a plan, as is here proposed.
More learning and more leisure, than are within my reach, are
requisite for such a task. I have, however, endeavoured to
bring together the products of my own imperfect studies. As
the work is principally designed for students, I have not
hesitated to repeat the same train of remark, whenever, from
a new connexion, it might be useful to explain a difficulty,
or to illustrate a new position or authority. I have also
availed myself occasionally of the freedom belonging to a
commentator to express a doubt, or deny a doctrine. But I
have rarely done so, except when the point has been purely
speculative, or the Common Law authorities justified me in the
suggestion. Whatever is in this respect propounded, is to be
considered as submitted to the judgment of the reader, as matter worthy of further examination. If I have done any thing
to lighten the labours of any ingenuous youth, who are strug-
gling for distinction, or to attract abler minds to a more pro-
found investigation of this branch of Contracts, I shall reap
all the reward, which, beyond the mere fulfilment of duty,
I have ever proposed to myself. I throw myself on the

b

candour of a profession, from which I have uniformly received indulgence ;· and offer these Commentaries to the public in that spirit of subdued confidence, which invites examination, and, at the same time, is not unconscious of the real difficulties, with which a work of this nature is attended.

January, 1832.   J. S.

ERRATUM.

The dictum of Mr. Justice Cottesmore, p. 225, should read thus : — " If I grant goods to a man to keep for my use, if the goods, by his *default*, (*mesgarde*, i. e. inattention,) are stolen, he shall be chargeable to me for the same goods ; but if he is *robbed* of the same goods, he is excusable by law." The correction is important to the understanding of the context.

TABLE OF CONTENTS.

CHAPTER I.

ON BAILMENTS IN GENERAL.

CHAPTER II.

ON DEPOSITS.

CHAPTER III.

ON MANDATES.

CHAPTER IV.

GRATUITOUS LOANS.

c

CHAPTER V.

ON PAWNS OR PLEDGES.

CHAPTER VI.

CONTRACTS OF HIRE.

ART. VIII. COMMON CARRIERS.

d

ART. X.   SPECIAL OR QUASI BAILEES FOR HIRE.

INDEX TO CASES CITED.

COMMENTARIES.

CHAPTER I.

ON BAILMENTS IN GENERAL.

SECT. 1. THE Law of Bailments lies at the foundation of many commercial contracts, and therefore is entitled to receive an independent consideration. It is of perpetual though tacit reference in the law of shipping and factorage, and a just understanding of it seems preliminary to a full discussion of those, as well as of many other important heads in our jurisprudence.

§ 2. The term, Bailment, is derived from the French word, *bailler*, which signifies to deliver.[1] It is a compendious expression to signify a contract resulting from delivery. Sir William Jones has defined bailment to be " a delivery of goods on a condition express or implied, that they shall be restored by the bailee to the bailor, or according to his directions, as soon as the purpose, for which they are bailed, shall be answered." [2] He has again, in the closing summary of his Essay, defined it in language somewhat different, as " a delivery of goods in trust on a contract expressed or implied, that the trust shall be duly executed, and the

---

[1] 2 Bl. Com. 451; Jones's Bailm. 90.   See 1 Danc's Abr. ch. 17, art. 2.
[2] Jones's Bailm. 1.

1

goods redelivered, as soon as the time or use, for which they were bailed, shall have elapsed or be performed." [1] Each of these definitions seems redundant and inaccurate, if it be the proper office of a definition to include those things only, which belong to the genus or class. Both these definitions suppose, that the goods are to be restored or redelivered; but in a bailment for sale, as upon a consignment to a factor, no redelivery is contemplated between the parties. In some cases, no use is contemplated by the bailee; in others, it is of the essence of the contract; in some cases, time is material to terminate the contract; in others, time is necessary to give a new accessorial right.

Mr. Justice Blackstone has defined a bailment to be "a delivery of goods in trust upon a contract expressed or implied, that the trust shall be *faithfully* executed on the part of the bailee;"[2] and in another place, as a "delivery of goods to another person for a particular *use.*"[3] It may perhaps be doubted, whether (though generally true) a *faithful* execution, (if by faithful be meant a *diligent* execution,) or a particular *use*, (if by use be meant an actual *user* by the bailee,) constitutes an indispensable ingredient in all cases of bailment. Mr. Chancellor Kent, in his excellent Commentaries,[4] has blended, in some measure, the definitions of Jones and Blackstone.

Without professing to enter into a minute criticism, it may be said, that a bailment is a delivery of a thing in trust for some special object or purpose, and upon a contract, express or implied, to conform to the object or purpose of the trust.

---

1 Jones's Bailm. 117.　　　　2 2 Bl. Com. 451.

3 2 Bl. Com. 395.　　　　4 2 Kent, Com. lect. 40, p. 437

§ 3. Bailments are properly divisible into three kinds. 1. Those, in which the trust is for the benefit of the bailor. 2. Those, in which the trust is for the benefit of the bailee; and, 3. Those, in which the trust is for the benefit of both parties. The first embraces deposits and mandates; the second, gratuitous loans for use; and the third, pledges or pawns, and hiring and letting to hire.

§ 4. A DEPOSIT is commonly defined to be a naked bailment of goods to be kept for the bailor without recompense,[1] and to be returned when the bailor shall require it. The appellation and the definition are both derived from the civil law.[2] "Depositum est, quod custodiendum alicui datum est."

§ 5. A MANDATE is commonly defined to be a bailment of goods without reward, to be carried from place to place, or to have some act performed about them.[3] This appellation also is derived from the civil law. "Mandantis tantum gratiâ intervenit mandatum," is the language of the Institutes;[4] "Mandatum nisi gratuitum nullum est," is that of the Pandects.[5]

§ 6. A LOAN FOR USE, called in the civil law *commodatum*, is a bailment of goods to be used by the bailee for a limited time without reward.[6]   The same defini-

---

[1] Jones's Bailm. 36, 117. See also 1 Bell's Com. 257; 1 Dane's Abr. ch. 17, art. 2, § 3.

[2] Just. Inst. Lib. 3, tit. 15, § 3; Pandect. Lib. 16, tit. 4, l. 1; Domat. Civ. Law, B. 1, tit. 7, § 1; Pothier, tit. Traité du Contrat de Deposit. art. prelim.; Wood's Inst. Civ. Law, B. 3, ch. 2, p. 216; Vinnius in Inst. Lib. 3, tit. 15; Heinec. Elem. Jur. Lib. 3, tit. 15, § 1791.

[3] Jones's Bailm. 36, 117. See also 1 Bell's Com. 259; 1 Dane's Abr. ch. 17, art. 5.

[4] Inst. Lib. 3, tit. 1, § 1.

[5] Dig. Lib. 17, tit. 1, l. 1. See also Domat. B. 1, tit. 15, § 1; Pothier, Traité du Mandat. art. prelim.; Wood. Civ. Law, B. 3, ch. 5, p. 242.

[6] Jones's Bailm. 36, 117. See also 1 Bell's Com. 255; 1 Dane's Abr. ch. 17, art. 2.

tion is given in the civil law: "Commodata autem res tunc proprie intelligitur, si nullâ mercede acceptâ vel constitutâ res tibi utenda data est — gratuitum enim debet esse commodatum."[1] It differs from what is called in the civil law a *mutuum* in this, that in a commodatum the goods are lent to be specifically returned; in a mutuum the goods are to be consumed, and are to be repaid in property of the same kind.[2] Thus corn or wine delivered to one to be consumed, and to be repaid in kind, is a case of *mutuum*; but if a horse be gratuitously lent for a journey, it is a case of *commodatum*.

§ 7. A PLEDGE, or PAWN, is a bailment of goods to a creditor as security for some debt or engagement.[3] In the civil law, that was properly called a *pignus* (pledge), where the thing was delivered to the creditor; if it remained with the debtor, though pledged as security, it was called an *hypotheca* (hypothecation.) "Proprie pignus dicimus, quod ad creditorem transit; hypothecam cum non transit nec possessio ad creditorem." [4]

§ 8. A HIRING, called in the civil law *locatio-conductio*, is a bailment always for a reward or compensation. It is divisible into four sorts.   1. The hiring of a thing for use, (locatio rei.)   2. The hiring of work and labour, (locatio operis faciendi.)   3. The hiring of care and services to be performed or bestowed on the thing delivered, (locatio custodiæ.)   4. The hiring of the carriage of goods (locatio operis mercium vehendarum) from

---

[1] Inst. Lib. 3, tit. 15, § 2 ; Pothier, Traité du Pret. a usage, art. prelim. ; Wood, Civ. Law, B. 3, ch. 1, p. 215; Dig. Lib. 13, tit. 6; Domat. B. 1, tit. 5, § 1.

[2] Inst. Lib. 3, tit. 15, § 2 ; Wood, Civ. Law, B. 3, ch. 1, p. 212; Pothier, Traité de Pret de Consumption, art. prelim.

[3] Jones's Bailm. 36, 117 ; Inst. Lib. 3, tit. 15, § 4 ; Wood, Civ. Law, B. 3, ch. 2, p. 218. See also 2 Bell's Com. 20, 22 ; 1 Dane's Abr. ch. 17, art. 4, §.1.

[4] Dig. Lib. 13, tit. 7, l. 9, § 2 ; Lib. 20, tit. 1 ; Domat. B. 3, tit. 1, § 1.

one place to another.[1] The three last are but subdivisions of the general head of hire of labour and services.

These divisions, it will at once be perceived, are borrowed from the civil law; and they have been transferred into our law by the elaborate opinion of Lord Holt, in the case of *Coggs* v. *Bernard*, 2 Ld. Raym. 909, and by the elegant genius of Sir William Jones, in his Essay on Bailments.[2]

§ 9. It must be obvious, upon the slightest consideration, that these various classes of bailments admit, or may admit, of very different obligations on the part of the bailee, both as to the nature and the extent of his responsibility. Where, indeed, he enters into an express contract, there may not, in point of morals, *in foro conscientiæ*, be any difference in relation to the extent of his duty, or the fidelity to be exacted of him in its performance. But law, as a practical science, although it endeavours never to violate any moral duty, is compelled, on many occasions, to leave that duty wholly to the conscience of the party, without any attempt to enforce it by compulsive process. It is, for instance, a rule of the common law, which has its foundation also in other codes, not to enforce contracts made between parties, where there is no valuable consideration for the act to be done. If the act is left undone, the party, though his promise may be ever so direct, is not compellable to perform it. If, for instance, a person has gratuitously promised to give another money, the law

---

[1] Jones's Bailm. 36, 117; Wood's Civil Law, B. 3, ch. 5, p. 235; Inst. Lib. 3, tit. 25; Dig. Lib. 19, tit. 2; Pothier, Traité de Louage, ch. 1, § 1; Domat. B. 1, tit. 4, § 1. See also 1 Bell's Com. 452; 1 Dane's Abr. ch. 17, art. 4.

[2] See Ayliffe's Pandect. B. 4, tit. 7, 10, 11, 16, 17, 18, 20; 1 Bell's Com. 452, 455, 458, 459, 461, 465.

will not oblige him to perform his promise, for it is
deemed a nude pact (nudum pactum), a naked promise,
not clothed with a valuable consideration to support it;
and its maxim is, "Ex nudo pacto non oritur actio." If,
on the other hand, the money has been paid, the law
will not enable the party to recover it back, because it
has been paid in discharge of a moral obligation. But,
if a party, undertaking to do a thing, does it so ill, that
the other party suffers an injury thereby, there the law
will, in many cases, allow the injured party to recover
a compensation to the extent of the injury. In respect,
therefore, to gratuitous contracts lying in fesance, such
as mandates, the party may escape all responsibility by
a simple refusal to do the act promised. This distinction has been long settled in our law upon principles of
general policy; and though it may seem somewhat artificial, it is probably well founded in public convenience.
It is generally true, in gratuitous contracts, that for *nonfesance*, even when the party suffers a damage thereby,
no action lies; but for *misfesance* an action will lie.
Sir William Jones,[1] indeed, supposes, that in each case,
if there is a special damage, an action for that damage
may be maintained. But he is certainly mistaken.[2]
The reason of this distinction may probably be, that in
cases of nonfesance it was the party's own folly to trust
to a promise, which had no legal obligation; but that in
cases of misfesance, the other party had no right to excuse a wrongful *act* by setting up the defence, that he
was not bound to do any thing. But upon this subject
more will be said, when we come to the consideration
of the Law of Mandates.

---

[1] Jones's Bailm. 56, 100, 101.

[2] *Elsee* v. *Gateward*, 5 T. R. 143; *Coggs* v. *Bernard*, 2 Ld. Raym.
909, 919, 920; 11 Hen. 4, 33.

§ 10. But to return. The law in respect to bailments is generally founded upon the absence of any positive engagements between the parties, (for the express contract of the parties may vary or supersede those derived from the law;) and, therefore, the question arises, what obligations may, with reference to public policy and general convenience, be implied by law in the absence of such positive engagements. Natural justice would hardly persuade us, that the same obligations and the same duties ought to arise in all classes of bailments; and if it did, the general interests of society and the indulgence to involuntary error and mistake, which a sense of mutual infirmity insensibly produces, would soon introduce a relaxation of the rigid rule, and fix a practical exposition, which would invite rather than repel mutual confidence. It would be very difficult, indeed, to persuade any civilized community, that a depositary should be liable for every loss, and bound to the same vigilant care of the deposit, as a borrower for his own exclusive benefit; or that a mandatary, who from mere kindness gives his services to his friend, should have the same responsibility fastened on him, as the carrier for hire, who stipulates and receives a suitable and adequate reward at once for his services and his vigilance. And it will accordingly be found, that in the most polished, as well as in the least refined of ancient, as well as of modern nations, distinctions of responsibility have been adopted in these cases with a surprising uniformity. It is not our puspose to dwell on them; but many of them will be found collected in the beautiful Essay of Sir William Jones, which, with all its defects, will always constitute a gratifying study to every jurist and scholar.

§ 11. Before entering, however, upon the particular consideration of the distinctions of the common law, with the view of ascertaining the precise nature and extent of the obligations of the bailee in the various sorts of bailment, it may be of use to say a few words on the subject of the various degrees of care or diligence, which are recognised in that law.

It has been justly said, that there are infinite shades of care or diligence from the slightest momentary thought to the most vigilant anxiety; but extremes in this case, as in most others, are inapplicable to practice.[1] There may be a high degree of diligence, a common degree of diligence, and a slight degree of diligence; and these, with a view to the business of life, seem all that are necessary to be brought under review. Common or ordinary diligence is that degree of diligence, which men in general exert in respect to their own concerns. It may be said to be the common prudence, which men of business and heads of families usually exhibit in affairs, which are interesting to them. Or, as Sir William Jones has expressed it,[2] it is the care, which every person of common prudence, and capable of governing a family, takes of his own concerns.[3] It is obvious, that this is adopting a very variable standard; for it still leaves much ground for doubt, as to what is common prudence, and who is capable of governing a family. But the difficulty is intrinsic in the nature of the subject, which admits of an approximation only to certainty. And, indeed, it is less matter of law than of fact; and in every community must be judged of by what is the actual state of society, the habits of busi-

---

1 Jones's Bailm. 5.   2 Jones's Bailm. 6.
3 *Tompkins* v. *Saltmarsh*, 14 Surg. & Rawle, 275.

ness, the general usages of life, and the dangers, as well as the institutions peculiar to the age. So that, although it may not be possible to lay down a very exact rule, applicable to all times and circumstances; yet that may be said to be common or ordinary diligence in the sense of the law, which men of common prudence generally exercise in their affairs in the country and age, in which they live.

§ 12. It will thence follow, that in different times and in different countries, the standard is necessarily variable with respect to the facts, although uniform with respect to the principle. So that it may happen, that the same acts, which in one country, or in one age, may be deemed negligent acts, may at another time, or in another country, be justly deemed an exercise of ordinary diligence.

§ 13. It is important to attend to this consideration, not merely to deduce the *implied* obligations of a party in a given case ; but also to possess ourselves of the true measure, by which to fix the application of the general rule. Thus, in times of primitive or pastoral simplicity, when it is customary to leave flocks to roam at large by night, it would not be a want of ordinary diligence to allow a neighbour's flock, which is deposited with us, to roam in the same manner. But, if the general custom were, at night, to pen them in a fold, it would doubtless be a want of such diligence, not to do the same with them. In many parts of our country, especially in the interior, where there are, comparatively speaking, few temptations to theft, it is quite usual to leave barns, in which horses and other cattle are kept, without being locked by night. But in cities, where the danger is much greater, and the temptations more pressing, it would be deemed a great want of

2

caution to do the same. If a man were to leave his
friend's horse in his field, or in his barn, all night, in
many country towns, and the horse were stolen, it
would not be imagined, that any responsibility was incurred. But if in a large city the same want of precaution were shown, it would be deemed in many
cases gross neglect. If robbers were known to frequent a particular district of country, much more precaution would be required, than in districts, where robberies were of very rare occurrence. What then is
usually done in a country in respect to things of a like
nature, whether more or less in point of diligence, than
is exacted in another country, becomes, in fact, the
general measure of diligence.

§ 14. And the customs of trade, and the course of
business also, have an important influence. If, in the
course of a particular trade, particular goods, as for instance coals, are usually left on a wharf without any
guard or protection during the night, and they are stolen, the wharfinger or other person having the custody
might not be responsible for the loss, although for a like
loss of other goods, not falling under a like predicament,
he might be responsible. If a chaise were left during
the night under an open shed, and were stolen, the
bailee might not be liable for the loss, if such was the
usual practice of the place; and yet he would be, if
other precautions were usually taken. In short, diligence is usually proportioned to the degree of danger
of loss, and that danger is, in different states of society,
compounded of very different elements. Men entrusted with money might in some cases be required to go
armed; when, in other times, such a precaution would
be deemed wholly unnecessary.

§ 15. And what constitutes ordinary diligence, may also be materially affected by the nature, bulk, and value of the articles.[1]   A man would not be expected to take the same care of a bag of oats, as of a bag of dollars ; of a bale of cotton, as of a box of diamonds or other jewelry ; of a common load of wood, as of a box of rare paintings; of a rude block of marble, as of an exquisitely sculptured statue.   The value, especially, is an ingredient to be taken into consideration upon every question of negligence ; for that may be gross negligence in the case of a parcel of extraordinary value, which in the case of a common parcel would not be so. The degree of care, which a man may reasonably be required to take of any thing, must, if we are at liberty to consult the dictates of common sense, essentially depend upon the quality and value of the thing, and the temptation thereby afforded to theft.   The bailee, therefore, ought to proportion his care to the injury, or loss, which is likely to be sustained by any improvidence on his part.[2]   But this, as well as some other considerations touching the degree of diligence, will properly find place in other parts of our inquiry.

§ 16. Having thus ascertained the nature of ordinary diligence, we may be prepared to decide upon the two other degrees.   High, or great diligence, is of course extraordinary diligence, or that, which very prudent persons take of their own concerns; and low, or slight diligence is that, which persons of less than common prudence, or indeed of any prudence at all, take of their own concerns.   Sir William Jones considers the latter to be the exercise of such diligence, as a man of common

---

[1] Jones's Bailm. 38.
[2] *Batson* v. *Donovan*, 4 Barn. & Ald. 21, 36, 42.

sense, however inattentive, takes of his own concerns.[1]
Perhaps, this is expressing the measure a little too
loosely; for a man may possess common sense, nay, uncommon sense, and yet be so grossly inattentive to his
own concerns, as to deserve the appellation of having
no prudence at all. The measure is rather to be drawn
from the diligence, which men, habitually careless, or of
little prudence, (not "however inattentive" they may
be,) generally take in their own concerns.

§ 17. Having, then, arrived at the three degrees of
diligence, we are naturally led to those of negligence,
which correspond thereto; for negligence may be ordinary, or less, or more than ordinary. Ordinary negligence may be defined to be the want of ordinary diligence, as slight negligence may be of the want of great
diligence, and gross negligence may be of the want of
slight diligence. For he, who is only less diligent, than
very careful men, cannot be said to be more than slight-
ly inattentive; he, who omits ordinary care, is a little
more negligent than ordinarily men are; and he, who
omits even slight diligence, fails, in the lowest degree,
of prudence, and is grossly negligent.[2]

In strictness of speech, as has been well observed by
Pothier,[3] negligence is not permitted in any contract;
but a less rigorous construction prevails in some cases,
than in others. The law considers diligence to be, in
some sort, a relative term; and it must be judged of
from the nature of the bailment, and all other ingredients, which may fairly be presumed to enter into the
contemplation of the parties. He, who asks a favour, has
no right to expect to be absolved from a proportionate
care; and he, who accepts a burthen, has a right to

---

1 Jones's Bailm. 8. I have not been able to find the original passage
in my own edition of Pothier.
2 Jones's Bailm. 8, 9.   3 Jones's Bailm. 30.

demand, that he shall not be required to be as scrupulously exact, as if he received a benefit.

§ 18. The view, which has thus been taken of the various degrees of diligence required by the common law, is in perfect conformity to that, which the civilians have laid down.   And, indeed, it is almost impossible to escape from the conclusion, that our law is but a derivative from a common source.   In the civil law, there are three degrees of diligence, *ordinary* diligence (diligentia), *extraordinary* diligence (exactissima diligentia), and *slight* diligence (levissima diligentia); and, in like manner, the three degrees of fault or neglect are, *lata culpa*, gross neglect; *levis culpa*, slight fault or neglect; *levissima culpa*, very slight fault or neglect; and the definitions of these degrees are precisely the same with those in our law.[1]   "Qui enim eam non adhibent diligentiam quam solent patres familias ad rem attentissimi culpam *levissimam;* qui omittunt diligentiam a frugi patre familias adhiberi solitam, *levem ;* qui denique ne ea quidem diligentia, quâ omnes, etiam dissoluti homines uti solent, utuntur, *latam* committere dicuntur."[2]

§ 19. In respect to gross negligence, it is often said, that it is equivalent to fraud, or is evidence of fraud. That it may, in certain cases, afford a presumption of fraud, and, indeed, that in very gross cases it may approach so near, as to be almost undistinguishable from it, may be admitted, especially when the facts seem hardly consistent with any honest intention.   But, that generally gross negligence and fraud are convertible terms, is a doctrine not supported by any just inference from the authorities in the common law.

---

1 Wood's Inst. B. 1, ch. 1, p. 106; Halifax, Civ. Law, ch. 14, p. 61.

2 Heinec. Elem. Jur. Lib. 3, tit. 14, § 787 ; Dig. Lib. 50, tit. 16, §§ 223, 226 ; Dig. Lib. 19, tit. 2, § 25, 7; Vinnius ad Inst. Lib. 3, tit. 15. §§ 12, 13.

§ 20. Sir W. Jones, indeed, in various passages of his Essay, seems to inculcate a different doctrine, and to put gross negligence by the side of fraud, and as equivalent to it. Thus, he speaks of *ordinary* negligence, as "a mean between *fraud* and accident;"[1] of gross negligence being inconsistent with good faith;[2] and of a bailee, without reward, being "answerable only for fraud, or for gross neglect, which is considered evidence of it."[3] There are other passages, again, in which he seems to indicate a clear distinction between them,[4] though the general course of his reasoning leans the other way. His great respect for the civil law, and his desire to assimilate the doctrines of the common law to it, may, perhaps, somewhat have warped his judgment. In the civil law, he admits, that "gross neglect, *lata culpa*, as the Roman lawyers accurately call it, *dolo proxima*, is in practice considered as equivalent to *dolus*, or fraud itself."[5] And he is well warranted in this remark; for the civilians, in their definitions of the words *dolus, culpa*, and *casus*, leave no room to doubt, that such is the true meaning of *dolus* in the Roman code. "Dolus est omnis calliditas, fallacia, machinatio ad decipiendum, fallendum, circumveriendum, alterum adhibita. Culpa, factum inconsultum, quo alter laeditur, vel quod, quum à diligente provideri potuerit non sit provisum. Casus est eventus a divina providentia profectus, cui resisti non potest."[6]

---

[1] Jones's Bailm. 8.   [2] Jones's Bailm. 10, 46, 119.
[3] Jones's Bailm. 46.   [4] Jones's Bailm. 8, 9, 47.
[5] Jones's Bailm. 22; Id. 14, 15.
[6] Heinec. Elem. Jur. Lib. 3, tit. 14, § 784; Wood's Inst. B. 1, ch. 1, p. 100; Dig. Lib. 50, tit. 16, §§ 223, 226; Dig. Lib. 11, tit. 6, l. 1, § 1; Vinn. ad Inst. Lib. 3, tit. 15, § 12.

§ 21. If, however, Sir William Jones is to be understood, as maintaining, that the doctrine of the common
law is the same, as the civil law on this subject, the
error requires correction, since many cases may arise,
in which the difference is material. One is put by Sir
William Jones himself; that if a depositor commit a
gross neglect in regard to his own goods, as well as
those, which are bailed, by which both are lost or damaged, he cannot be said to have violated good faith;
and the bailor must impute to his own folly the confidence, which he reposed in so improvident and thought-
less a person.[1] So, where a cartoon was left in the
hands of an auctioneer, without any particular agreement to take care of it, or redeliver it safe, and without
any agreement for a reward, and it appeared, that the
painting was upon paper pasted on canvas, and that the
bailee kept it in a room next to a stable, in which there
was a wall, which had made it damp and peal, it was
held gross neglect, and the bailee made responsible,
although there was no imputation of fraud.[2]

§ 22. These cases sufficiently show, that the doctrine, that gross negligence is equivalent to fraud, cannot be maintained as a general result of the common
law authorities. On the contrary, gross negligence is,
or, at least, may be, entirely consistent with good faith
and honesty of intention. And it would be a most
mischievous error to confound it with fraud; for, then,
unless a jury should believe the party guilty of fraud,
no laches would come up to the legal notion of gross
negligence, so as to entitle the sufferer by the loss to
a recovery. A man may leave a casket of jewels, or a

---

[1] Jones's Bailm. 47.

[2] *Mytton* v. *Cock*, 2 Str. 1099. See also *Batson* v. *Donovan*, 4 Barn.
& Ald. 21 ; *Clarke* v. *Earnsham*, 1 Gow. R. 30.

purse of gold, upon the table of a public room at an inn, or may leave a large package of bank bills in a great coat in the common entry of an inn, from pure thoughtlessness; and a jury might be well satisfied, that it was gross negligence. But if fraud were a necessary ingredient, the very statement of the case would negative a right of recovery. The law, however, does not necessarily include, in the notion of gross negligence, any admixture of fraud, although in argument that is sometimes urged, with a view to relieve the defence from the pressure of other facts.

§ 23. Having, then, ascertained the various degrees of diligence, and negligence, it is next to be considered, in what manner the law applies them to the different sorts of bailments. And, here, the doctrine adopted seems at once rational, just, and convenient. When the bailment is for the sole benefit of the bailor, the law requires only *slight* diligence on the part of the bailee, and of course makes him answerable only for *gross* neglect. When the bailment is for the sole benefit of the bailee, the law requires *great* diligence on the part of the bailee, and makes him responsible for *slight* neglect. When the bailment is reciprocally beneficial to both parties, the law requires *ordinary* diligence on the part of the bailee, and makes him responsible for *ordinary* neglect.[1]

§ 24. A like division of the degrees of responsibility is to be found in the civil law. " In contractibus," says Heineccius, "in quibus penes unum commodum, penes alterum incommodum est, *ille*, ordinarie culpam etiam levissimam; *hic*, non nisi latam, præstat. Ubi par utriusque contrahentis commodum atque incommodum est,

---

[1] Jones's Bailm. 10, 119; *Coggs* v. *Bernard*, 2 Ld. Ray. 909.

culpa etiam levis ab utroque præstanda est."[1] The same rules are found in the French law;[2] and the Scotch law;[3] and may be deemed the general result of the jurisprudence of Continental Europe.

§ 25. It follows, as a natural consequence from these principles, that bailees in general are not responsible for losses resulting from inevitable accident, or irresistible force, although they may become so liable by special contract, or (as we shall hereafter see) by some positive policy of law. By *inevitable accident*, commonly called the act of God, is meant any accident produced by physical causes, which is irresistible; such as a loss by lightning and storms, by the perils of the seas, by inundations and earthquakes, or by sudden death or illness. By *irresistible force* is meant such an interposition of human agency, as is, from its nature and power, absolutely uncontrollable. Of this nature are losses occasioned by the inroads of a hostile army, or, as the phrase commonly is, by the king's enemies, that is, by public enemies. In the same manner, losses occasioned by pirates are deemed hostile,[4] for pirates are deemed the enemies of the whole human race, (hostes humani generis;) and by the common consent of nations, they are every where, when taken, punished with death.[5] By the law of nations they are esteemed outlaws, and their crimes, against whomsoever committed, are punishable in the courts of any nation, within whose criminal jurisdiction they are brought.

---

1 Heinec. Elem. Jur. Lib. 3, tit. 14, § 778; Wood's Inst. B. 1, ch. 1, p. 107 ; Vinn. ad Inst. Lib. 3, tit. 15, § 12.

2 Pothier, Oblig. P. 1, ch. 2, art. 1, § 1, n. 141, 142.

3 Ersk. Inst. B. 3, tit. 1, § 21, p. 488; 1 Bell's Com. 453.

4 Abbott on Ship. P. 3, ch. 4, §§ 2, 3.

5 *U. States* v. *Smith*, 5 Wheat. R. 153, 161, & note, id. 163.

§ 26. Robbery by force is also deemed irresistible.
Robbery (rapina) is in the civil law defined to be, the
violent taking from the person of another of money or
goods, for the sake of gain.[1] The definition of the
common law does not materially differ; for, in that law,
it is defined to be the felonious taking from the person
of another, or, in his presence, against his will, of goods
or money to any value, by force or violence, or putting
him in fear.[2] And, whether such robbery be by robbers on the highway, or by breaking open a house, and
assaulting the inmates, makes no difference.   The acts
of such banditti are considered irresistible.[3] In like
manner, in cases of insurance, the maritime law deems
a loss by robbers, or pirates, to be a loss by irresistible
force. " Si furtum committatur in mari per piratas et
latrones, tunc inter casus fortuitos connumeratur," is
the language of Roccus.[4] We shall have occasion,
hereafter, to notice an exception, not to the principle
of the rule, but to its application by the common law, in
the case of carriers.

§ 27. But a loss by a mere private, or secret theft, is
not considered irresistible;[5] and whether it excuses
the party, or not, depends upon the nature of the bailment, and the particular circumstances of the case.[6] If
the proper degree of diligence has been used by the
bailee, and notwithstanding that, a loss by such theft
ensues, he is not responsible.   There are exceptions,

---

1 Halifax, Anal. Civ. Law, ch. 23, p. 79; Inst. Lib. 4, tit. 2; Wood,
Inst. Civ. Law, B. 3, ch. 7, p. 257.

2 4 Bl. Com. 243; 2 East, Pl. Cr. ch. 16, § 124, p. 707.

3 Jones's Bailm. 44, 119; 10 Hen. 6, 21, (5).   See also Jones's Bailm.
40, 29; Lib. Assisarum, 28.

4 Roccus de Assecur. n. 41.

5 Roccus de Assecur. n. 42; Marsh. Insur. B. 1, ch. 7, § 4, p. 243.

6 *Clarke* v. *Earnshaw*, 1 Gow. N. P. Rep. 30.

also, to this rule, which will also be taken notice of hereafter.[1]

§ 28. Whether a loss, occasioned by the forcible breaking open of a house by robbers, or bandits, during the temporary absence of the family, would be deemed a loss by irresistible superior force, does not appear to have been directly settled in our law. Bonion's case,[2] whether it be law or not, does not come up to the doctrine. And Sir William Jones[3] states, that, in case of a *burglary*, no bailee can be responsible without a very special undertaking; but he cites no authority on the point. He doubtless intends to speak of that crime in its technical sense, which supposes an actual occupation of the house, as a mansion, or, at least, if the family is absent, that it is so *animo revertendi*.[4] Pothier considers a loss by forcibly breaking open a house to be a loss by irresistible force.[5]

§ 29. Our own Bracton (Lib. 3, ch. 2, p. 99,) enumerates among casualties, fire, internal decay, shipwreck, robbery, and hostile incursions; for, speaking of certain cases, in which a bailee may be responsible for casualties, he says, " Si forte incendio, ruinâ, naufragio, aut latronum vel hostium incursu consumpta fuerit vel deperdita, subtracta, vel ablata."

§ 30. In the civil law, in which parties are not generally liable for accidents, unless they expressly stipulate to be so liable, there are included, under the head of accidents, not only losses by lightning, inundation,

---

1 See Marshall on Insur. B. 1, ch. 7, § 4, p. 243; Roccus de Assecur. note, 42.

2 Mayn. Year Book, 275; Fitz. Abr. Detinue, 59.

3 Jones's Bailm. 39.

4 4 Bl. Com. 223; 2 East, Pl. Cr. ch. 15, § 11, p. 496.

5 Pothier, Traité du Pret. à Usage, art. 53.

torrents, shipwreck,[1] and other perils of the sea, but
also fire, robbery, hostile incursions, insurrections, and
piracies.[2] "Animalium, vero," (says the Digest,) "casus,
mortes, quæque sine culpâ accidunt, fugæ servorum,
qui custodiri non solent, rapinæ, tumultus, incendia,
aquarum magnitudines, impetus prædonum a nullo
præstantur."[3] Vinnius enumerates them somewhat
more in detail. "Casus fortuiti varii sunt, veluti a vi
ventorum, turbinum, pluviarum, grandinum, fulminum,
æstus, frigoris, et similium calamitatum, quæ cœlitus
immittuntur. Nostri vim divinam dixerunt; Græci ϑεοῦ
βίαν. Item naufragia, aquarum inundationes, incendia,
mortes animalium, ruinæ ædium, fundorum chasmata,
incursus hostium, prædonum impetus, &c., fugæ servorum, qui custodiri non solent. His adde damna om-
nia a privatis illata, quæ quo minus inferrentur, nullâ
curâ caveri potuit. Ad casus autem fortuitos non sunt
referendi illi casus, qui cum culpâ conjuncti esse solent;
cujusmodi sunt furta. Quamobrem, qui rem furto amis-
sam, vel incendio, verbi causâ servorum negligentiâ orto,
consumptam dicit, *is diligentiam suam probare debet.*
Quod vero incendium in alienis ædibus obortum occupat
ædes vicinas, aut quod fulmine excitatur aut a grassa-
toribus vel incendiariis immittitur, *id inter casus fortuitos numerari debet.*[4]

§ 31. These principles, both in the civil and in the
common law, are to be understood with this limitation,
that there is no subsisting contract between the parties,
which varies the general obligation resulting from them;
for, if there be such a contract, that governs the case,
unless it be against public policy, or positive law.

---

1 Dig. Lib. 4, tit. 9, l. 3, 1.   2 Id.
3 Dig. Lib. 50, tit. 17, l. 23; Dig. Lib. 13, tit. 6, l. 5, § 4.
4 Vinn. ad Inst. Lib. 3, tit. 15, § 5.

§ 32. In respect to cases of losses by fraud, there is a salutary principle belonging both to our law and the civil law. It is, that the bailee can never protect himself against responsibility for losses occasioned by his own fraud; nay, not even by a contract with the bailor, that he shall not be responsible for such losses. For the law will not tolerate such an indecency and immorality, as that a man shall contract to be safely dishonest; and it therefore declares all such contracts utterly void; and holds the bailee liable in the same manner and to the same extent, as if no such contract ever existed.[1] "Non valet, si convenerit, ne dolus præstitur," says the Digest.[2] So says Heineccius. "Dolus semper et in omni contractu præstandus, nec conveniri potest in antecessum, ut ne dolus præstetur.[3] Now, it will occur at once to the reader, that if the law be so, and gross negligence were equivalent to fraud, there could be no defence set up by the bailee founded, either on his own conduct in respect to his own goods, as well as those deposited, or on a special contract not to be liable for gross negligence. But there is no principle in our law, that would prevent a depositary from contracting not to be liable for any degree of negligence, in which fraud is really absent. The maxim of our jurisprudence is, that "modus et conventio vincunt legem," and it applies to all contracts not offensive to sound morals, or to positive prohibitions by the legislature.

§ 33. And here it may be proper to state, that as the legal responsibility of a bailee may be narrowed by

---

[1] Jones's Bailm. 11, 48 ; Doct. & Stud. Dial. 2, ch. 38.

[2] Dig. Lib. 50, tit. 17, § 23; Wood's Inst. B. 1, ch. 1, p. 107. · Vinn. ad Inst. Lib. 3, tit. 15, § 12.

[3] Heinec. Elem. Jur. Lib. 3, tit. 14, § 785.

any special contract either express or implied, so it may in like manner be enlarged. Thus, if a depositary should specially contract to keep the deposit *safely*, he might be liable for ordinary negligence, although the law would otherwise hold him liable only for gross negligence. Upon this ground Southcote's case, (4 Co. R. 83, b. 1 Inst. 89, a. b.,) may perhaps be maintained to be good law; and is not liable to the objection made against it in *Coggs* v. *Bernard*.[1] If, indeed, it proceeded upon the ground asserted by Lord Coke, that a bailment upon a contract *to keep*, and *to keep safely*, is the same thing, it is certainly not law; and was overruled in *Coggs* v. *Bernard.* But from the report it would seem, that the bailment was there *to keep safe;* and if so, then upon the special contract the party might have been held responsible, although he could not otherwise be by the general law. This was the doctrine maintained by all the judges in the case of *Coggs* v. *Bernard*,[2] which case proceeded mainly upon that ground.[3] And in a later case the same distinction was adopted by the court; and it was held, that if a depositary should accept to keep *safely*, he would be responsible for losses by robbery or theft, although not otherwise responsible upon the general principles of law.[4]

§ 34. The rule of the civil law is on this point conformable to ours. "Si quid nominatim convenit," is the language of that law, "vel plus vel minus in singulis contractibus, hoc servabitur, quod initio convenit; legem enim contractus dedit."[5]

---

[1] 2 Ld. Raym. 909, 911.
[2] 2 Ld. Raym. 909.
[3] Jones's Bailm. 42 to 45.
[4] *Kettle* v. *Brumsale*, Willes R. 118, 121.
[5] Jones's Bailm. 48; Dig. Lib. 50, tit. 37, 1. 23.

§ 35. To what extent a special agreement varies the obligations of the bailee resulting from the general principles of law must in a great measure depend upon the true exposition of the terms of the agreement. The general rule in such cases would seem to be, not to expound the contract unfavourably to the bailee beyond the obvious scope of its terms. Sir William Jones thinks,[1] that a depositary would not be liable for a loss of the goods by *robbery*, " without a most express agreement." St. German also holds, that if a depositary promise to restore the goods *safe*, at his peril, he is not responsible for casualties; but it would be otherwise if he is to receive a reward.[2] Lord Holt, in *Coggs* v. *Bernard*, (2 Ld. Raym. 909, 915, 918,) was of opinion, that upon a promise by a bailee without reward to keep or carry *safely*, he is not responsible for injuries or losses occasioned by the acts of *wrong-doers*;[3] and, *a fortiori*, that he is not responsible for a theft not caused by his own neglect. Robbery would of course in his opinion exempt him from liability. Mr. Justice Powell in the same case thought, that robbery would not be an excuse; and of course that theft would not;[4] because the bailee would have a remedy over against the robber. Mr. Justice Powys and Mr. Justice Gould seem to have agreed with Lord Holt.[5] Sir W. Jones holds, that in such a case the bailee would be responsible for a loss by *theft*, but not for a loss by *robbery*.[6] He founds himself manifestly upon the distinction taken in the civil law, that the attack of robbers is an irresistible force; but that of thieves may be guarded against by

---

1 Jones's Bailm. 44, 97, 98.   2 Doct. & Stud. Dial. 2, ch. 38.
3 Dig. Lib. 13, tit. 6, 1. 19.   4 2 Ld. Raym. 911.
5 2 Ld. Raym. 909, 914.   6 Jones's Bailm. 43, 44, 45, 98, 103.

vigilance : "Impetus predonum a nullo præstantur."[1] Lord Chief Justice Willes, however, seems to have thought, that upon such a special undertaking even robbery would not be an excuse.[2] The civil law does not appear to go so far as to make a bailee liable for robbery upon such a contract,[3] though he would be liable for theft. Its language is, "Non enim dubitari oportet, quin is, qui *salvum fore* recipit, non solum a *furto*, sed etiam a damno reddere videatur."[4]

§ 36. In respect to losses occasioned by inevitable accident, as by lightning, tempests, inundations, &c. there are very respectable authorities, that notwithstanding a special contract or undertaking to keep *safely*, the bailee will not be responsible for such losses. Sir W. Jones manifestly supported this doctrine.[5] It is sanctioned also by St. German in the passage above cited ;[6] and was avowed by the court in *Coggs* v. *Bernard.*[7] There are many cases in our law, where if a contract or condition, possible at the time it was made, become afterwards impossible by the act of God, or of the law, the obligation or condition is discharged.[8] There are others again, where a different doctrine is inculcated.[9] It is not easy to recon-

---

[1] Jones's Bailm. 44 ; Goth. Com. in LL. Contractus, p. 145, cited in note, ibid. id. ; Dig. Lib. 50, tit. 17. 1. 23.

[2] *Kettle* v. *Bromsale*, Willes R. 121.   [3] Code, Lib. 4, tit. 24, l. 6.

[4] Dig. Lib. 4, tit. 9, 5, 1.   [5] Jones's Bailm. 43, 44, 45.

[6] Doct. & Stud. Dial. 2, ch. 38.   [7] 2 Ld. Raym. 909, 911, 915.

[8] Powell on Contr. 446 ; Com. Dig. Condition D. 1, L. 12, 13 ; Co. Litt. 206 ; 1 Roll. Abrid. Condition I ; *Willams* v. *Hide*, Palmer R. 548, 550 ; W. Jones R. 179 ; Com. Dig. Assumpsit G. ; Bac. Abridg. Condition D. 1, 2 ; Noy. Max. 35 ; *Harrington* v. *Dennie*, 13 Mass. R. 93 ; *Badlam* v. *Tucker*, 1 Pick. 284.

[9] 1 Roll. Abr. Condition G., 8, 9, 10 ; Com. Dig. Assumpsit G. ; *Baylies* v. *Fettyplace*, 7 Mass. R. 325 ; *Phillips* v. *Stevens*, 16 Mass. R. 238 ; 2 Saund. 422, note by Williams (2) ; 6 T. R. 750.

cile the cases, or to point out the different reasonings, on which they proceed. In Aleyne's R. 27, this distinction is taken: "Where the law creates a duty or charge, and the party is disabled to perform it without any default in him, and he hath no remedy over, there the law will excuse him; but when the party by his own contract creates a duty or charge upon himself, he is bound to make it good, if he may, notwithstanding any accident by inevitable necessity; because he might have provided against it by his contract." This distinction has the countenance of highly respectable authorities.[1] But in the present state of the law it does not seem possible to lay down any general rule on the subject, as to what casualties will excuse in cases of a special contract.

§ 37. The general rule of the civil law is that stated by Heineccius, that a bailee is never responsible for casualties, unless there has been unjustifiable delay, or the party has taken upon him the risk of the casualty, or he is at the same time guilty of neglect. "Casus nunquam præstatur, nisi vel in morâ sit debitor, vel casum in se ultro susceperit, vel culpam simul admiserit."[2] A bailee, therefore, may render himself responsible for casualties, if he chooses to contract against them, even though he be a mere depositary. "Si convenit, ut in deposito et culpa præstetur, rata est conventio; contractus enim legem ex conventione accipiunt."[3] But it does not seem precisely laid down, what cases, or rather what special contracts shall be deemed

---

[1] 6 T. R. 750; *Hadley* v. *Clarke*, 8 T. R. 259, 267.

[2] Heinec. Elem. Jur. Lib. 3, tit. 14, § 785; Domat, B. 1, tit. 1, § 3, art. 10, and tit. 7, § 3, art. 6; Vinn. ad Inst. Lib. 3, tit. 15.

[3] Dig. Lib. 2, tit. 14. l. 7, § 15; Dig. Lib. 16, tit. 3, l. 1, § 6; Domat, B. 1, tit. 7, § 3, art. 7; Pothier, Oblig. P. 1, ch. 2, art. 1, § 142.

to include the risk of casualties. The general rule of
the civil law would seem to be, that the risk of casualties is never included under the general terms of a
contract. And however general the undertaking may
be, it includes only such risks, as might be foreseen,
and not those, which there could be no room to apprehend. Pothier[1] deduces this doctrine from the civil
law; and the Code seems to countenance it. "Quæ
fortuitis casibus accident, cum prævideri non potuerint,
(in quibus etiam aggressura latronum est) nulli bonæ
fidei judicio præstantur."[2] The Code of France adopts
into its positive regulations most, if not all, the rules of
the civil law on this subject. It considers the obligation extinguished, when the thing, which is the object
of the obligation, is extinguished, or has perished without the default of the obligee, unless he has agreed to
be charged with accidents.[3] And the same was the
antecedent rule, as we learn from Pothier.[4] Pothier,
in another place, says, that if by his contract the thing
is to be at the *risk* of the hirer during the period of
the bailment, by these terms the hirer is responsible
for the slightest negligence, but not for casualties, or the
vis major.[5]

§ 38. In respect to *theft* Sir William Jones has
given an opinion, that a loss by private *theft* is *presumptive* evidence of ordinary neglect.[6] And he cites with
manifest approbation the commentary of Gothofred on
the Pandects, where he says, "Alia est furti ratio; id

---

1 Pothier, Oblig. P. 3, ch. 6, art. 3, § 633; Pothier, Traité du Cont. de
Louage, P. 3, ch. 1, art. 3, § 5.

2 Code, Lib. 4, tit. 24, 1. 6.

3 Code Civ., B. 3, tit. 3, § 6, art. 1302, 1303.

4 Pothier, Oblig. P. 1, ch. 2, art. 1, § 1, art. 142, 143.

5 Pothier, Louage, n. 192.

6 Jones's Bailm. 43, 44, 119, 76, 77, 78, 109, and n. 9.

enim non casui, sed *levi culpæ* fermè ascribitur. Adversus *latrones* parùm prodest custodia; adversus *furem* prodesse potest, si quis advigilet." And the civil law seems well to warrant this distinction.[1] Pothier, too, has adopted it; but he considers the presumption of neglect in case of theft to be open to be rebutted by proof of due care.[2]

§ 39. There does not seem to be any such rule adopted into our law, as Sir William Jones supposes. If the theft has been caused by negligence, it is without doubt, that the bailee will be responsible, where the nature of the bailment would make such a negligence a breach of his implied obligation. But, abstractly speaking, there is nothing in the case of theft, from which we have a right to infer, that because a loss has happened by it, there must have been some neglect.[3] On the contrary, no degree of vigilance will always secure a party from losses by theft. A store may be broken open, however securely locked; a person may be robbed while riding in a stage coach, or while asleep; a servant may be faithless and betray the confidence reposed in him; a person may be seized with a sudden fit, or alienation of mind, and the theft committed without any consciousness on his part. In these and in many other cases there would not be any presumption of neglect. And the civil law itself supposes, that in such cases the bailee might repel the imputation of negligence.[4] By our law in many cases

---

1 Dig. Lib. 17, tit. 2, 52, 53; Wood, Inst. B. 1, ch. 1. p. 107; Domat, B. 1, tit. 4, § 8, art. 3; Just. Inst. Lib. 3, tit. 15, §§ 2, 3; Jones's Bailm. 44, n. *o.*

2 Pothier, Traité du Pret. a Usage, art. 53.

3 See *Vere* v. *Smith*, 1 Vent. 121; S. C. 2 Lev. 3; Jones's Bailm. 98.

4 Dig. Lib. 13, tit. 6, 1. 19, 20, 21; Domat, B. 1, tit. 4, § 8, art. 3; Inst. Lib. 3, tit. 15, § 3.

a bailee is excusable, when the loss is by theft; but never, when that theft is occasioned by gross negligence. So long ago as the reign of Edward the Third, (29 Assisarum, 28), it was held, that, if a person bail his goods to keep, and they are stolen, the bailee is excused. The reasoning of the court, in *Coggs* v. *Bernard*,[1] shows, that the court did not consider theft as *primâ facie* presumptive of negligence. In short, our law considers theft, like any other loss, to depend for its validity as a defence upon the particular circumstances of the case, and to be governed by the general nature of the bailment, and the responsibility attached thereto. It neither imputes the theft to the neglect of the party, nor, on the other hand, exempts him from responsibility from that fact alone. But, it decides upon all the circumstances, as leading to the conclusion, that there has, or has not, been a due degree of care used.[2]

§ 40. There is another topic, which may be properly considered in this preliminary view of the general doctrine of bailments, inasmuch as it seems applicable to every species of them. An allusion is here intended to the subject of the confusion of property by the bailee, so that the bailor's property cannot be distinguished from his own. Mr. Justice Blackstone has correctly stated the general rule, and truly said, that the English law partly agrees with, and partly differs from, the civil law. "If," says he,[3] "the intermixture be by consent, I apprehend, that in both cases, the proprietors have an interest in common, in proportion to their respective

---

[1] 2 Ld. Ray. 909. See 1 Vent. 121.

[2] *Finicune* v. *Small*, 1 Esp. N. P. C. 315; 2 Kent. Com. 449, 452.

[3] 2 Bl. Com. 405.

shares.[1] But if one wilfully intermixes his money,
corn, or hay, with that of another man, without his approbation or knowledge, or casts gold, in like manner,
into another's melting pot or crucible, the civil law,
though it gives the sole property of the whole to him,
who has not interposed in the mixture, yet allows a
satisfaction to the other, for what he has so improvident-
ly lost.[2] But our law, to guard against fraud, gives the
entire property, without any account, to him, whose
original dominion is invaded, and endeavoured to be
rendered uncertain without his consent."[3] But there
may be a case, neither of consent nor of wilfulness, in
the confusion of goods; as, where the bailee, by negligence or unskilfulness, or inadvertence, mixes up his
own goods of the same sort with those bailed; and
there may be a confusion arising from mere accident
and unavoidable casualty. Now, in the latter case of
accidental intermixture, the civil law deemed the property to be held in common, whether the mixture produced a thing of the same sort, or not, as if the wine of
two persons were mixed by accident.[4] Our law is
not, probably, different.[5] But, in cases of mixture by
unskilfulness, negligence, or inadvertence, a different
rule prevails in our law. In cases of this nature, the
true principle seems to be, that, if a man, having undertaken to keep the property of another distinct from,
mixes it with his own, the whole must, both at law
and in equity, be taken to be the property of the other,
until the former puts the subject under such circum-

---

1 Vinn. ad Inst. Lib. 2, tit. 1, p. 169 ; Inst. Lib. 2, tit. 2, § 27 ; Ayliffe's
Pand. B. 3, tit. 3, p. 291.
2 Vinn. ad Inst. Lib. 2, tit. 1, p. 170; Inst. Lib. 2, tit. 1, § 28.
3 See *Hart* v. *Ten Eyck*, 2 Johns. Ch. R. 62; 2 Kent. Com. 297, 298.
4 Vinn. ad Inst. Lib. 2, tit. 2, § 28.
5 Dane's Abr. ch. 76, art. 5, § 19.

stances, that it may be distinguished as satisfactorily, as it might have been, before that unauthorized mixture on his part. This rule was laid down by Lord Eldon, in *Lupton* v. *White;* [1] and by the Court of Exchequer, in *Panton* v. *Panton.* [2]   In the former case, Lord Eldon said, "What are the cases, in the old law, of a mixture of corn and flour? If one mixes his corn or flour with that of another, and they were of equal value, the latter must have the given quantity. But, if articles of different value are mixed, producing an aggregate of both, and, through the fault of the person mixing them, the other party cannot tell, what was the original value of his property, he must have the whole."   And Mr. Chancellor Kent has acted upon a similar principle, holding, that if a person, having charge of the property of another, so confounds it with his own, that it cannot be distinguished, he must bear all the inconveniences of the confusion. If he cannot distinguish and separate his own, he will lose it. [3]   The conclusion to be drawn from these decisions, and other authorities, [4] seems to be, that, in cases of negligent and inadvertent mixtures, (perhaps even of wilful mixtures) if the goods can be easily distinguished, and separated, then no change of property takes place, and each party may lay claim to his own. If the goods are of the same nature and value, though not capable of an actual separation by identifying each particular; yet, if a division can be made of equal value, (as in the case of a mixture of corn, or coffee, or tea, or wine, of the same kind and quality,) there each may claim his aliquot part. But,

---

[1] 15 Ves. 432, 436, 439.   [2] Cited 15 Ves. 440.

[3] *Hart* v. *Ten Eyck*, 2 Johns. Ch. R. 62.

[4] See *Bond* v. *Ward*, 7 Mass. R. 123; Dane's Abr. ch. 76, art. 3, § 15.

if the mixture is undistinguishable, and a new ingredient is formed, not capable of a just appreciation and division, according to the original rights of each, there the party, who occasions the wrongful mixture, must bear the whole loss.[1]

---

[1] See Ayliffe's Pand. B. 3, tit. 3, pp. 291, 292; Erskine, Inst. B. 2, tit. 1, § 17.

CHAPTER II.

ON DEPOSITS.

§ 41. A DEPOSIT is usually defined to be a naked bailment of goods, to be kept for the bailor without reward, and to be returned when he shall require it.[1]

§ 42. Pothier defines it to be a contract, by which, one of the contracting parties gives a thing to another to keep, who is to do so gratuitously, and obliges himself to return it, when he shall be requested.[2] In the Spanish Partidas, it is thus defined; "When one man gives any thing to another, in whom he has confidence, to keep it for him." [3]

§ 43. The word is derived from the Latin, *depositum*, which Ulpian informs us is compounded of *de* and *positum*. "Depositum est quod custodiendum alicui datum est. Dictum ex eo quod positum; prepositio enim, *de*, auget depositum. Ut ostendat totum fidei ejus commissum, quod ad custodiam rei pertinet." [4]

It is also sometimes called *commendatum*, for " commendare nihil aliud est quam deponere." [5]

§ 44. Deposits, in the civil law, are divisible into two kinds; necessary and voluntary. A necessary deposit is such as arises from pressing necessity, as for instance, in case of a fire, a shipwreck, or other overwhelming calamity; and thence it is called *miserabile*

---

[1] Jones's Bailm. 36, 117; 1 Bell Com. 257. See also 1 Dane's Abr. ch. 17, art. 1, § 3.

[2] Pothier, Traité de Depot. See Cod. Napol. art. 1915.

[3] Moreau & Carlton's Partidas, 5th, tit. 3, l. 1.

[4] Dig. Lib. 16, tit. 3, l. 1; Heinec. Pand. Lib. 16, § 217.

[5] Dig. Lib. 5, tit. 16, § 186.

depositum. A voluntary deposit is such as arises without any such calamity, from the mere consent and agreement of the parties.[1]

This distinction was material in the civil law, in respect to the remedy; for in voluntary deposits the action was only *in simplum;* in the other, *in duplum,* or two fold, whenever the depositary was guilty of any default.[2] The common law has made no such distinction; and, therefore, in a necessary deposit the remedy is limited to damages coextensive with the wrong.[3]

§ 45. Deposits are again divided in the civil law into *simple deposits,* and *sequestrations;* the former is, when there is but one party depositor, (of whatever number composed,) having a common interest; the latter is, where there are two or more parties depositors, having each a different and adverse interest. In this last case, the deposit is to be delivered to him, who is adjudged ultimately to have the right.[4]

§ 46. These distinctions are also found adopted in the French law;[5] and they give rise to very different considerations in point of responsibility and rights. Hitherto they do not seem to have been incorporated into our law; though if cases should arise, the principles applicable to them would scarcely fail of receiving general approbation, at least so far, as they affect the rights and the responsibilities of the parties. Cases of judicial sequestrations and deposits, especially in courts of chancery and admiralty, may hereafter require the

---

[1] Dig. Lib. 16, tit. 3, § 2; 1 Pothier, Pand. Lib. 16, tit. 3, § 1; Heinec. Elem. Pand. Lib. 16, tit. 3, § 219.

[2] Dig. Lib. 16, tit. 3, §§ 2, 3, 4.   [3] Jones's Bailm. 48.

[4] Dig. Lib. 16, tit. 3; Ayliffe's Pand. B. 4, tit. 17.

[5] Pothier, Traité de Dépôt, art. prelim; & ch. 1, art. 1, ch. 4, art. 84, &c. Code de France, B. 3, tit. 11, §§ 1920, 1921, 1949; Moreau & Carlton, Partidas 5, tit. 3, 1. 1.

subject to be fully investigated. At present there
have fortunately been few cases, in which it has been
necessary to consider, upon whom the loss should fall,
when the property has perished in the custody of the
law.

§ 47. A *deposit* differs from what is called in the
civil law a *mutuum*, for there the identical thing lent is
not to be returned, but another thing of the same kind,
quality, nature, or value.[1] In the latter case, the property passes immediately to the *mutuary*. But in the
case of a mere depositary, the property is not, as we
shall hereafter see, transferred or alienated; but it remains in the depositor; and the depositary has the
mere custody of the thing.[2]

§ 48. In the civil and French law, as in our law, the
principles, which regulate the contract of deposits, are
the deductions from natural law, and do not depend
upon any positive regulations. Pothier boasts, that
such is the foundation of the whole system: "Il n'est
assujetti," (says he,) "par le droit civile à aucune règle,
ni à aucune forme." He classes it, in his formal divisions, as a contract of natural law (*droit naturel*); as a
contract of beneficence; as a *real* contract in the sense
of the civil law, by which is meant such a contract as
takes effect by the delivery of the thing itself; and as
a synallagmatical or bilateral contract; though imperfectly so, as the obligation of the depositary is the principal, and that of the depositor is a mere incident.[3]

---

1 Inst. Lib. 3, tit. 15; Ayliffe's Pandect. B. 4, tit. 17; 1 Bell's Com.
257, 258.

2 Pothier, Traité de Dépôt, ch. 1, art. 2, § 2, n. 12; Dig. Lib. 16, tit. 3,
l. 17; Flor. Lib. 7; Ayliffe's Pand. B. 4, tit. 17; *Hartop* v. *Hoare*, 3 Atk.
43; S. C. 2 Str. 1187; 1 Wils. R. 8; 1 Bell's Com. 257, 258.

3 Pothier, Traité de Dépôt, ch. 1, art. 3, n. 18, 19, 20, 21; Pothier,
Oblig. ch. 1, art. 2, n. 9

These divisions are not usually found in the treatises of the common law, although they have a just foundation in every system aiming at entire accuracy.

§ 49. In considering the definition of a deposit, we are naturally led to the consideration of the persons, by and between whom it may be made; the subject matter of it; what is of its essence; when it is perfected; and lastly, the obligations, which arise from it.

§ 50. In respect to the persons, by and between whom it may be made, it is only necessary to state, that it is not distinguishable from other contracts in this respect. Infants, married women, and other persons labouring under personal disability, cannot be bound as depositors, or depositaries, though other persons may be so bound to them. If an infant receives a deposit, he is bound by the general principles of law to restore it, if it is in his possession or control; but he is not responsible, if he loses it. He may become responsible for any wrong he does to it; but he is not responsible upon the contract, unless it be a necessary contract, and manifestly for his benefit. Such, also, is the doctrine of the civil law, and the French law.[1]

§ 51. In respect to the subject matter, it is in our law limited to personal property, and is inapplicable to real property. The civil law, and the French law (which follows it), confine the bailment to corporeal property; and do not admit its application to incorporeal property, such as choses in action and debts. But the title deeds of such debts and credits, *ipsa instrumentorum corpora*, may become the subject of such a bailment.[2] The distinction is nice; but as the loss of

---

1 See Pothier, Traité de Dépôt, ch. 1, art. 1, n. 2; Pothier, Oblig. P. 1, ch. 1, art. 4, § 49.

2 Pothier, Traité de Dépôt, ch. 1, art. 1, n. 1.

the instrument will entitle the party to a recompense adequate to the injury done him, it is unimportant in practice.[1] In the common law, and in the Scotch law, debts, choses in action, and other instruments, may become the subject of deposit, properly so called.[2]

§ 52. It is not essential, that the depositor should have an absolute title in the thing, in order to make it a valid deposit. It is sufficient, that the party has a special property, or even a possession of it.[3] Nay, even a person, who holds property by wrong and without title, may lawfully deposit the same; and he is entitled to recover back the same against every one but the rightful owner.[4] By the civil law the owner may recover his property from any one, into whose hands he may trace it. If there has been a second bailment, he may, at his election, proceed directly against the second bailee; and if he recovers it against the latter, the right of his own first bailee is extinguished.[5] In the common law, also, where there has been a tortious conversion or possession, the owner may follow his property wherever he can find it.[6] Where there has been an original bailment by the owner, and a subsequent bailment by his bailee, if an action of *detinue* be brought by the owner against the last bailee, the latter may, in some cases, compel the owner and the first bailee to inter-

---

1 Com. Dig. Trover, C. ; *Arnold* v. *Jefferson*, 1 Ld. Raym. 275 ; 1 Roll. Abr. 5. K. 3.

2 1 Bell's Com. 258.

3 *Armorie* v. *Delarmirie*, 1 Str. 505 ; *Rooth* v. *Wilson*, 1 Barn. & Ald. 59; Com. Dig. Case-Trover, B. D. ; 2 Saund. 47, & note by Williams.

4 Ayliffe's Pand. B. 4, tit. 17, p. 522 ; Dig. Lib. 16, tit. 3, l. 1, § 30. Id. § 31, l. 1.

5 Ayliffe's Pand. B. 4, tit. 17, p. 522.

6 *Hartop* v. *Hoare*, 3 Atk. 43; *Taylor* v. *Plumer*, 3 M. & Selw. 562.

plead, and thus escape the dangers of a double recovery.[1] This remedy was given in the old common
law ; and it has been materially enlarged by the benefi-
cent operation of the jurisdiction of courts of equity.[2]
But this subject will more properly find a place in a
subsequent discussion.

§ 53. If by mistake or otherwise the real owner receives his own property on deposit, his obligation to
return it is extinguished, unless another person has acquired, as against him, some right, interest, or lien, which
he is bound to respect. " Qui rem suam deponi apud se
patitur, vel utendam rogat, nec depositi nec commodati
actione tenetur." [3] And the same principle will apply,
where he has subsequently become entitled as owner.[4]

§ 54. It is said in the civil law, that by a delivery of
the principal thing, that, which is assessorial, does not
pass. As if a slave with his clothing on is deposited ;
or a horse with his halter ; neither the clothes, nor the
halter are deposited.[5] But this doctrine, if true at all
in our law, must be received with many qualifications.
It must always depend upon the intent of the parties.
And even in the civil law Pothier seems to consider
the text as including no more than the proposition, that
the clothing and the halter cannot be demanded in a
separate action of deposit, but only as an accessory in
the principal action for the slave or horse ; at least, unless the slave or horse have perished.[6]

---

[1] *Rich* v. *Aldred,* 6 Mod. R. 216; 1 Roll. Abr. Interpleader, 2 Viner,
Bailment, E., § 32 ; Id. Interpleader.

[2] Bac. Abr. Bailment, D. ; Com. Dig. Chancery, Interpleader,
2 Bulstrode R. 313.

[3] Dig. Lib. 16, tit. 3, 1. 15 ; Pothier, Traité de Dépôt, ch. 1, art. 1,
§ 1, n. 4.

[4] Id.

[5] Dig. Lib. 16, l. 1, tit. 3, l. 1, § 5.

[6] 1 Pothier, Pand. Lib. 16, tit. 3, art. 3, § 1, p. 46. See also Pothier,
Traité de Dépôt, ch. 2, § 1, art. 2, § 1, n. 44.

§ 55. As to what is of the essence of the contract of deposit. The civil law has expounded this with minute accuracy. In the first place, the thing must be actually delivered to the bailee, if he has it not already in his possession. A mere contract, where the thing has never really or constructively passed, does not amount to a deposit.[1] In this sense it is a *real* contract. But the delivery, both by our law and the civil law, is complete, whether given personally by the bailor, or by his order or approbation, when and as soon as it is received by the bailee, or by another for him, or with his privity and approbation. When it is received by another person, it must clearly appear, that the delivery is not on his own account, but on account of the party, who is charged as bailee. A delivery to a servant, acting in the business of his master, is a delivery to the master, and binds the latter. Therefore, the delivery of a special deposit to the cashier of a bank, usually entrusted with that duty, is a delivery to the bank itself. But it would be otherwise, if the receipt were by a servant not entrusted with that duty, or if the receipt were clandestine, and in fraud of the master, and without his presumed privity or consent.[2] And in respect to implied or constructive deliveries, any circumstances, which establish, that the bailee assents to hold the property for another, although the same may not be in his actual possession, are sufficient for this purpose. As if a creditor, holding a pledge, assent, after payment of the debt, to hold it for the benefit of his debtor, it becomes a deposit. So if a thing be hired, and the purpose has been executed, and the property still remains

---

[1] Dig. Lib. 16, tit. 3, 1. 26, § 2.
[2] *Foster* v. *Essex Bank*, 17 Mass. R. 479, 498.

with the hirer with the assent of the lender, it becomes
a virtual deposit.[1]

§ 56. In the next place it is said, that the principal
end of the delivery must be *to keep the thing* ; if it be
not, then it becomes a different species of contract. As
if the delivery be for a donation, a transfer of title, &c.
it cannot be technically called a *deposit*. Another example put is, where title-deeds are delivered to an
attorney or solicitor to enable him to defend my cause ;
there it is not a case of *deposit*, but of *mandate*. So, if
A delivers a thing to B, that if Titius will not receive it,
B shall keep it ; or A directs B to keep a thing, which
is in the custody of another for A ; both of these
are deemed cases of mandates and not of deposits ;
for "uniuscujusque contractûs initium spectandum et
causa." [2] These distinctions seem unimportant in our
law, however they may be (as they are said to be) important in the civil law.

§ 57. In the next place the custody must be gratuitous ; which results indeed from the very definition
already given.[3] And care should be taken not to confound cases, where a compensation is allowed, with
cases of pure deposit. Sometimes a compensation
may be given to the party *diverso intuitu*, and yet the
contract be a pure deposit ; and sometimes the case
may be of a mixed nature. As, if A desires to hire the
use of my barn, in common with me, for his chaise, for
a specific price, to which I agree ; and I keep my own
carriage in the same barn ; and he desires me to take

---

[1] Dig. Lib. 16, tit. 3, § 14 ; Pothier, Traité de Dépôt, ch. 1, art. 2, § 1,
n. 8.

[2] Dig. Lib. 17, tit. 1, l. 8 ; Dig. Lib. 16, tit. 3, 1, 1, §§ 11, 12, 13 ;
Pothier, Traité de Dépôt, ch. 1, art. 2, § 2, n. 9.

[3] Dig. Lib. 16, tit. 3, l. 1, §§ 8, 9 ; Pothier, Traité de Dépôt, ch. 1, art.
2, § 3, n. 9.

care of his chaise when in the barn; there, I am a mere depositary of the chaise. But, if the contract were, that for the hire I should take care of the chaise; there it would be a case of lucrative contract, and not of mere deposit.[1]

§ 58. In the next place, the deposit must ordinarily be to some other person than the owner; for if he receives his own property, as we have already seen, he generally receives it discharged of the bailment.[2] There may, however, arise cases of deposit, where a bailee of the owner, having an interest in the property, delivers the same to the owner for a limited time to be redelivered to the bailee on request, or at the end of the term.

§ 59. And, in the last place, there must be a voluntary consent of the parties in entering into the contract. If, on either side, there is a real mistake as to the contract and its purport, it is obligatory on neither as a deposit; though other obligations, founded upon conscience and right, may be substituted by law, where an actual delivery of the thing has passed. But a mere mistake of the quality or nature of the thing, or of the person of the bailor or bailee, will not render it less obligatory upon the bailee as a deposit, unless fraud or intentional imposition has intervened.[3]

§ 60. In every case, however, there must be a voluntary undertaking; for it is not in the power of a bailor to force upon another person any custody of his goods; but it must be voluntarily assumed. Direct proof, indeed, is not indispensable; but consent may be inferred

---

1 See *Finucane* v. *Small*, 1 Esp. R. 315; 2 Kent. Com. 441.

2 Dig. Lib. 16, tit. 3, l. 31, § 1; Pothier, Traité de Dépôt, ch. 1, art. 1, § 1, n. 4.

3 Pothier, Traité de Dépôt, ch. 1, art. 2, § 4. n. 16.

from circumstances. And where servants and clerks are allowed to receive deposits, and especially if the practice is general and unlimited, it will bind their principals as depositaries. But it will be otherwise, if the deposit is received by the servants or clerks clandestinely, and without any consent, express or implied, on the part of the principals.[1] And a person, to whom a valuable picture is sent as a depositary, will not be answerable, if he has no knowledge of the fact, and has not assented to receive it.[2]

§ 61. We now pass to the consideration of the obligations arising on the part of the depositary from the fact of deposit. It consists of two things; first, that he shall keep it with reasonable care; secondly, that he shall, upon request, return it to the depositor.[3]

§ 62. As to the first, the natural inquiry is; — What is to be deemed reasonable care. Being a bailee without reward, the depositary is bound, of course, upon principles already stated in the introductory chapter, to *slight* diligence only; and he is not, therefore, answerable, except for gross neglect.[4] But in every case, good faith requires, that he should take reasonable care; and what is reasonable care, must materially depend upon the nature and quality of the thing, the circumstances, under which it is deposited, and sometimes upon the character and confidence, and particular dealing of the parties.[5] The degree of care and diligence is not altered by the fact, that the depositary is joint owner of the goods with the depositor; for in such

---

1 *Foster* v. *Essex Bank*, 17 Mass. R. 479, 498.
2 *Lethbridge* v. *Phillips*, 2 Stark. R. 544.
3 1 Dane's Abr. ch. 17, art. 1 & 2 ; 2 Bl. Com. 452.
4 1 Dane's Abr. ch. 17, art. 2.
5 See *Tompkins* v. *Saltmarsh*, 14 Searg. & R. 275.

a case, if the possessor is guilty of gross negligence,
he will still be responsible, in the same manner as a
common depositary, having no interest in the thing.[1]

§ 63. It is often laid down in our books, that the
depositary is bound to take the same care of the deposited goods, as he takes of his own; and it is thence
deduced, as a corollary, that if he commits a gross neglect in regard to his own goods, as well as in regard
to those bailed, by which both are lost, he is not liable,
and the depositor must impute it to his own folly to
have trusted so improvident a person.   Sir Wm. Jones
seems, in some places, so to understand the doctrine.[2]
Thus, in his commentary on the case of *Mytton* v. *Cook*,
(2 Str. 1099,) where a painted cartoon, pasted on canvas, had been deposited, and the bailee kept it so near
a damp wall, that it peeled and was much injured, and
the verdict was for the plaintiff; he says, "If it had
been proved, that the bailee had kept his own pictures
of the same sort in the same place and manner, and
they too had been spoiled, a new trial would, I conceive, have been granted."[3]   And our own Bracton
(Lib. 3, 99, *b*,) lays down the same rule: "Is apud
quem res deponitur, re obligatur, et de eâ re quam
accepit restituendâ tenetur; et etiam ad id, si quid in
re depositâ dolo commiserit.   Culpæ autem nomine
non tenetur, scilicet, desidiæ vel negligentiæ, *quia* qui
negligenti amico rem custodiendam tradit, sibi ipsi et
propriæ fatuitati hoc debet imputare."   In this, he
does no more than copy the very words of the Insti-

---

1 Jones's Bailm. 82, 83.
2 Jones's Bailm. 46, 47; but see id. 82, 83, 122, 123; 1 Dane's Abr.
ch. 17, art. 1, § 3.
3 Jones's Bailm. 122, 123.

tutes;[1] and he is supported by the clear result of the Pandects.[2] Lord Holt, too, has given the doctrine the authority of his own great name.[3] Pothier implicitly adopts it,[4] and he is followed by Mr. Chancellor Kent[5] and other learned Judges.[6]

§ 64. Notwithstanding the weight of these authorities, they seem to me not to express the general rule in its true meaning. The depositary is, as has been seen, bound to slight diligence only; and the measure of that diligence is that degree, which persons of less than common prudence, or indeed of any prudence at all, take of their own concerns.[7] The measure, abstractly considered, has no reference to the character of the individual, but looks to that, which belongs to a whole class of persons;[8] and so Sir William Jones has intimated on some occasions.[9]

§ 65. Cases may, indeed, occur, in which the character of the individual may be important, for the purpose, not of furnishing a general rule, but an exception to that rule.[10] In the civil law it is natural, that there should be very great stress laid upon the habits and character of the depositary. In that law, gross negligence and fraud are considered as exactly equivalent

---

1 Just. Inst. Lib. 3, tit. 15, § 3.

2 Dig. Lib. 16, tit. 3, 1. 32; Domat, Lib. 1, tit. 7, § 3, n. 2.

3 *Coggs* v. *Bernard*, 2 Ld. Ray. 909, 914; S. P. 1 Ld. Ray. 655.

4 Pothier, Traité de Dépôt, ch. 2, § 1, art. 1, n. 27.

5 2 Kent. Com. 438.

6 *Foster* v. *Essex Bank*, 17 Mass. R. 479, 499; *Gibbon* v. *Paynton*, 4 Burr. 2298.

7 *Tompkins* v. *Saltmarsh*, 14 Searg. & Rawle, 275; Jones's Bailm. 8, 118, 119.

8 See Jones's Bailm. 82, 83; *Tompkins* v. *Saltmarsh*, 14 Searg. & Rawle, 275.

9 Jones's Bailm. 82, 83, 88.   10 *The William*, 6 Rob. 316.

to each other.[1]   Hence the depositary is not made responsible for any loss, which does not carry with it a
just presumption of fraud.   Now, if the depositary did
in fact take the same care of the bailed property as of
his own, it would go far to repel the presumption of
fraud; for no person, however careless, would desire
the loss of his own property.   On the other hand, if
the depositary took better care of his own property
than of that bailed, the presumption of fraud would be
strengthened.   And the principle, on which this presumption rests, is the same, whether the party is a very
careless or a very careful person in his own affairs;
and it is applicable to other bailments, as well as to deposits.[2]   The French law has adopted the same line of
reasoning; and therefore Pothier follows it; and the
cases put by him by way of illustration are of this nature.[3]   If a slave is deposited, and he is delivered
back to a person, who is supposed to be his master,
and is not; the depositary is not liable.[4]   So, in case of
a fire in the house, where the goods are lodged, if the
depositary omits to remove them, supposing them to
be safe, especially if his own goods perish also, he is
not responsible for any loss by the fire.   But if he
should remove his own goods, and not the others, then
he would be responsible; for there would arise a presumption of fraud, unless the other circumstances of
the case repelled it.   The presumption would be still
stronger, if the goods saved were of little value, and

---

1 Dig. Lib. 16, tit. 3, l. 32; Id. Lib. 50, tit. 17, l. 23; Lib. 13, tit. 6, l. 5,
§ 2; Just. Inst. Lib. 3, tit. 15, § 3.

2 *Clark* v. *Erninshaw*, 1 Gow. R. 30; Jones's Bailm. 46; 2 Ld. Ray.
914, 915; *Foster* v. *Essex Bank*, 17 Mass. R. 479, 498.

3 Pothier, Traité de Dépôt, ch. 2, § 1, art. 1.

4 Id. n. 28; Dig. Lib. 16, tit. 3, l. 1, § 32.

those lost were of great value.[1]   Pothier puts a case as
of clear responsibility for gross negligence, where the
party, having a deposit of money, diamonds, or other
precious jewels, which are ordinarily kept under lock,
leaves them in an ante-chamber or vestibule of a house,
exposed to all persons going and coming, and they are
stolen by thieves.[2]   Yet upon his own principles, if the
party left his own in the same situation, and they also
were stolen, it would repel the imputation of fraud.   After
all, he is compelled to admit, that, practically speaking,
the particular character of the depositary can rarely
enter into discussions of this nature, and that the presumption of good faith is usually made in his favour.[3]

§ 66. Our law upon the subject of gross negligence
differs from that of the civil law; for gross negligence,
though it may sometimes be presumptive of fraud, and
undistinguishable from it, may consist with perfect innocence of intention.   Hence it is no defence to a depositary, that he has acted with good faith, if in truth
he has been guilty of gross negligence.   In the case of
the diamonds above put, the depositary would be liable
for gross negligence, even though his own were left in
the same place; since such articles are usually kept in
more secure places; and every depositary must be presumed to undertake for reasonable care with reference
to the nature of the things bailed.   Sir William Jones[4]
admits this; and Domat deduces this as the true exposition of the civil law.[5]   Cases may, indeed, be put, in
which the circumstances are so strong of extreme rash-

---

1 Pothier, Traité de Dépôt, ch. 2, § 1, art. 1, n. 34.
2 Pothier, Traité de Dépôt, ch. 2, § 1, art. 1 ; Id. n. 27.
3 Id. ch. 2, § 1, art. 1, n. 28; Jones's Bailm. 30, 46, 82, 83; 1 Domat,
B. 1, tit. 7, § 3, n. 5.
4 Jones's Bailm. 38.   5 Domat, B. 1, tit. 7, § 3, n. 5.

ness on the part of the depositor, as justly to create an exception to the general rule of law, or rather a dispensation with it. As, if he should knowingly trust his diamonds or other valuables with a man notoriously weak and infirm in judgment, or to a minor without any experience or discretion, or to a man grossly negligent and prodigal in his affairs, or subject to an absence of mind bordering on derangement, or to a person given to habitual intoxication; and from these known infirmities, the thing bailed should innocently be lost; there might be strong ground to presume, that the depositor was content to trust the party with all his faults and infirmities, and to take upon himself the responsibility of all losses not arising from actual fraud.[1]   At least, it might fairly be put to a jury to presume a special contract in such a case, that the depositary should take the same care as he did of his own property, and that he should not be responsible, except for fraud.[2]   But these cases do not impugn the general rule. They turn upon circumstances, which imply a waver of it, or a substitution of a different contract.

§ 67. The doctrine here stated has also the sanction of adjudged cases in its support. Thus, where a gratuitous bailee put a horse of his brother into a pasture with his own cattle in the night time, and by reason of a defect of fences the horse fell into a neighbouring field and was killed; it was thought, that he was responsible to the owner, because it was gross negligence to put the horse into a dangerous pasture, to which he was unused.[3]   So, in the case of the painting, (which has been before referred to,) where it appeared, that it was injured by being kept in a damp room

---

[1] Domat, B. 1, tit. 7, § 3, n. 5.   [2] *The William*, 6 Rob. 316.
[3] *Rooth* v. *Wilson*, 1 Barn. & Ald. 59.

next to a stable, it was held, that the party was liable for gross negligence; and that the law, in the case of a deposit, will raise an implied promise, that the party will not grossly neglect or abuse the deposit.[1] In other words, the depositary is bound to reasonable care. The true way of putting cases of this nature is, to consider, whether the party has omitted that care, which bailees without reward usually are understood to take of property of the like nature. Therefore, where a person had a deposit of money, and put it with his own in a valise on board a steamboat, and left it there in an exposed situation all night, and it was stolen, and his own money was left, he was held responsible for gross negligence. But if he had left it for a moment only, under ordinary circumstances, and no pressing danger, it would have been otherwise.[2] Lord Stowell, in a case of justifiable capture, where the captors are held responsible for due (that is, for reasonable) diligence, has expressed himself with great clearness on this subject. "On questions of this nature" (says he) "there is one position sometimes advanced, which does not meet with my entire assent; namely, that captors are answerable only for such care, as they would take of their own property. This, I think, is not a just criterion in such case; for a man may, with respect to his own property, encounter risks from views of particular advantage, or from a natural disposition of rashness, which would be entirely unjustifiable in respect to the custody of the goods of another person, which have come to his hands by an act of force. Where property is confided to the care of a particular person by

---

[1] *Mytton* v. *Cook*, 2 Str. 1099.
[2] *Tracey* v. *Wood*, 3 Mason R. 132.

one, who is, or may be supposed to be, acquainted with his character, the care, which he would take of his own property, might, indeed, be considered as a reasonable criterion."[1]   Certainly it might, if such character was known, and the party under the circumstances might be presumed to rely, not on the rule of law, but on the care, which the party was accustomed to take of his own property in making the deposit.   But unless he knew the habits of the bailee, or could be fairly presumed to trust to such care, as the bailee might use about his own property of a like nature, there is no ground to say, that he has waived his right to demand reasonable diligence.

§ 68. Lord Coke has adopted a doctrine somewhat different.   In his Institutes, he says, that in cases of deposit the engagement of the bailee is to keep safely; " for if goods are delivered to one to be *kept* and to be *safely kept,* it is all one in law."[2]   Hence he concludes, that if goods are delivered a man to be safely kept, and afterwards those goods are stolen, this shall not excuse him, because by the acceptance he undertook to keep them safely, and therefore he must keep them at his own peril.   But if the goods are delivered to him to keep, as he would keep his own, there, if they are stolen from him without his default or negligence, he shall be discharged.[3]   And he recommends, on this account, to those, who receive goods, that they should receive them in a special manner, viz. to be kept as their own, or at the peril of the owner.[4]

§ 69. Lord Coke considered this as the settled law in his time; and he mainly relies for its support upon

---

1 *The William*, 6 Rob. 316.

2 Co. Lit. 89, *b* ; 1 Dane's Abr. ch. 17, art. 1, § 3.

3 Co. Lit. 89, *b*.   4 See 2 Bl. Com. 452.

Southcote's case.[1] That case, according to his report, was as follows. Southcote brought detinue against Bennet for certain goods, and declared, that he delivered them to the defendant *to keep safe;* the defendant confessed the delivery; and pleaded in bar, that after the delivery, one J. S. stole them feloniously out of his possession; the plaintiff replied, that the said J. S. was the defendant's servant, retained in his service, and demanded judgment; and upon a demurrer in law, judgment was given for the plaintiff. And the reason and cause of the judgment was, because the plaintiff delivered the goods to be safe kept, and the defendant had taken it upon him by the acceptance upon such delivery, and therefore he ought to keep them at his peril; although, in such case, he should have nothing for his safe keeping. This is the whole of the case; and Lord Coke, in the sequel, proceeds to expound his own views of the general doctrine, as above stated, with that superabundance of learning, for which he was so remarkable.

§ 70. The decision in Southcote's case has been subjected to much minute criticism; but it is far from being clear, that Lord Coke misunderstood the case, or the principles, upon which the court decided it. The decision may itself be correct, although in the reasoning of the court principles may have been avowed, which cannot now be supported. And in his first Institute, Lord Coke declares, that all these cases were resolved and adjudged in the king's bench in Southcote's case.[2] * The real point of decision in this case

---

[1] 4 Rep. 83, *b.* 84.   [2] Co. Litt. 89, *b.*

* The report of the same case in Cro. Eliz. 815, confirms Lord Coke's statement of the point decided; but goes no farther.

was, that upon a bailment to keep safely, the bailee was responsible for a loss occasioned by theft, whether the theft was by his servants, or by others.[1] Now this depends, as has been before stated, not upon any general principle of law, but upon the import and effect of an undertaking to *keep safely.* Lord Holt manifestly dissented from Southcote's case; two other judges seem to have agreed with him in that dissent.[2] There are also earlier authorities, which countenance a different doctrine.[3] But the latest case in England seems to admit the general correctness of Southcote's case in the point actually in judgment.[4]

§ 71. A strong doubt is, however, thrown over the decision by a very elaborate judgment in one of our own courts.[5] The learned judge, who delivered the opinion of the court on that occasion, seemed to think, and there is much to warrant the suggestion, that in a case where the bailment is to keep safely, the depositary would not be liable for a loss by theft, unless it should arise from his own negligence and want of due diligence and care.[6] Blackstone (2 Comm. 452) seems to hold a similar modified opinion; he says, that "if he" (the bailee) "undertakes specially to keep the goods safely and securely, he is bound to the same care as a prudent man would take of his own;" that is, he is bound to ordinary diligence. Sir William Jones,[7] as

---

1 1 Dane's Abr. ch. 17, art. 1, § 4; art. 11, § 3.

2 *Coggs* v. *Bernard,* 2 Ld. Ray. 909, 914, 915.

3 Doct. & Stud. Dial. 2, ch. 38; *Williams* v. *Lloyd,* 1 Jones, 179; S.C. Palmer R. 549; 22 Assisarum, 41.

4 *Kettle* v. *Bromsale,* Willes R. 118.

5 *Foster* v. *The Essex Bank,* 19 Mass. R. 479, 500. But see Noy. Maxims, c. 43.

6 1 Dane's Abr. c. 17, art. 11, § 3, is to the same effect.

7 Jones's Bailm. 43, 44, 119.

we have already seen, thinks, that theft is presumptive
proof of ordinary negligence ; but he admits, that upon
proof of ordinary diligence, the bailee in such a case
would not be chargeable.

§ 72. But all the later authorities explode the doctrine,
that an undertaking to keep, and an undertaking to
keep safely, amount to the same thing. It was expressly overruled in *Coggs* v. *Bernard.*[1] And in a
very early case in the Year Books, (29 Assisarum,
28,) it was held, that if goods be bailed to a party to
keep, and he puts them among his own goods, and they
are stolen, he is not chargeable with the loss.[2] This, of
course, must be subject to the exception, that the theft
is not by gross neglect.

§ 73. The general doctrine, however, of Lord Coke,
that if a man accepts goods · to keep as his own, he is
not responsible for losses by theft, is confirmed by later
authorities. It is treated, however, as he treats it, not
as an undertaking resulting from the general law of
deposits, but as a special undertaking ; and limiting the
common responsibility.[3] In many cases this consideration may become important ; and especially, where the
bailee is notoriously very careless and indifferent about
his own affairs ; in which case the depositor might
fairly be presumed to trust to such care as the bailee
takes of his own goods.

§ 74. In like manner, if the depositor agree, that the
goods may be kept in a particular place, as in a ship's
cabin, he cannot afterwards object, that the place is
not a safe one ; for his assent amounts either to a qual-

---

[1] *The King* v. *Hertford,* 2 Show. R. 172, [184.]

[2] Brook, tit. Bailments, 7. See 1 Dane's Abr. c. 17, art. 7.

[3] *Southcote* v. *Bennet,* Cro. Eliz. 815; 4 Rep. 84 ; *Kettle* v. *Bromsale,*
Willes R. 118; *Coggs* v. *Bernard,* 2 Ld. Ray. 909. Powell's opinion.

ification of the contract for safe custody, or to an agreement, that for all the purposes of the deposit it shall be deemed sufficiently safe. But if the depositary should in such a place expose the deposit to undue perils, or be guilty of gross negligence, whereby it is stolen, he will be responsible for the loss. Thus, if a deposit of money is made with the master of a ship, with an assent, that he may place it in his cabin for safe custody; and he does so; but he afterwards exposes the place, where the money is concealed, in the presence of suspicious persons, and enables them to know the fact, that money is there; or if he leaves the cabin wholly unguarded during a considerable portion of the night under circumstances calling for more precaution, and the money is stolen, he will be deemed guilty of gross negligence, and responsible for the loss.[1]

§ 75. There is a question often treated of under this head, which is not merely curious but important; and that is, how far a depositary is responsible for the loss of articles contained in a package, the contents of which are unknown to him.[2] If, for instance, a sealed box or locked casket, containing jewels, be deposited, and the depositary has no knowledge, that it contains jewels, how far will he be responsible for any losses of the jewels. The Roman lawyers discussed this question with a good deal of acuteness and ability. In the Pandects we find the following case and reasoning. If a sealed box is deposited, is the box only to be demanded in action, or may the articles contained in it be comprehended? Trebatius says, that the box only, and not the particular things, is to be sued for as a deposit. But if the contents are shown, and then

---

1 *Bradish* v. *Henderson*, 1 Dane's Abr. c. 17, art. 11, § 4.
2 See 1 Dane's Abr. ch. 17, art. 6.

deposited, the contents are to be added. But Labeo says, that he, who deposits the box, seems to deposit the contents also; and therefore he should sue for the contents. What then, if the depositary is ignorant what the contents are? It is not of much consequence, since he has accepted the deposit. And I am of opinion, (says Ulpian,) that he has a right to sue for the deposit of the contents, although the sealed box was deposited.[1] Domat adopts the doctrine of Trebatius.[2] The Scotch law arrives at the same conclusion.[3] The case, as put in the Pandects, seems principally to have reference to the nature of the suit, or the form of the libel; but it is obvious, that the difference of opinion among the Roman jurists was not confined to these merely technical points.[4]

§ 76. Bonion's case in the Year Books[5] may be supposed to bear upon this question. It is as follows. Bonion brought his writ of detinue for certain goods, to wit, seals, plate, and jewels, against M. The defendant pleaded, that Bonion bailed to him the chest under lock to keep, and took away the key, and that he did not know, that the jewels and other things were therein; and thieves came in the night, and broke open the chamber of the defendant, and carried away the chest into the field and broke it open, and at the same time took and carried away the goods of the defendant with the other goods. The plaintiff replied, that the jewels &c. were delivered not locked up (*hors d'enclosure*) to be returned at his pleasure; and upon this issue was

---

1 Jones's Bailm. 38; Dig. Lib. 16, tit. 3, l. 1, § 41.
2 1 Domat, B. 1, tit. 7, § 1, p. 17.
3 Erskine's Inst. B. 3, tit. 1, § 27, p. 490.
4 Jones's Bailm. 38.
5 Mayn. Year Book, Edw. 2, p. 275, Fitz. Abr. Detinue, 59.

joined. The case is a little differently reported by Fitzherbert, in his Abridgment, who says, the party was driven to reply, that the goods were not carried away by thieves. Sir William Jones seems to suppose this case to be wholly incomprehensible,[1] and incapable of any rational explanation. If the case, however, turned upon the point of the issue suggested by Fitzherbert, namely, that the loss was not by thieves, there is nothing in it, which is not sound law. For if the plea was falsified in a material fact, the action was clearly maintainable. It is true, that the compiler of the Table to the Year Book relies on a distinction, that "if a casket sealed be delivered to me, in which there are jewels, and thieves in the night rob me and take them, I am not answerable ; but that it is otherwise, if the jewels were delivered to me and I put them into a chest."[2] But this distinction has no foundation in the case. And even if the account in the Year Book be the correct one, it shows no more, than that the plaintiff chose to put his case upon an immaterial issue. Fitzherbert in his Abridgment refers to another case,[3] which shows, that the received law then was, that if a party receives goods to keep, and he keeps them as his own, he is not chargeable, even in a case of theft.

§ 77. The question, however, which divided the Roman lawyers, would, in our law, admit of different determinations, according to circumstances. If the bailee knew, that the box or casket contained jewels, although the bailor took away the key, he would be bound to a degree of diligence proportioned to the value of the contents. In other words, the same degree of care, which would ordinarily be required to be taken of such

---

[1] Jones's Bailm. 39.   [2] Jones's Bailm. 39, 40.
[3] Fitz. Abr. Accompt, 11 ; 9 Edw. 4, 40.

valuables when deposited, would be exacted of him. If he had no ground to suppose, that the box or casket contained any valuables whatsoever, he would be bound only to such reasonable care, as would be required of depositaries in cases of articles of common value. And under such circumstances, if he were guilty of gross negligence, he would be held responsible for the loss, at least to the extent of what he might fairly presume to be the value of the contents. If, on the other hand, there was a meditated concealment of the contents of the box or casket from the bailee, with a view to induce him to receive the bailment, and he would not have received it, or have exposed it, as he did, if he had been made acquainted with the facts, then the transaction would be deemed a fraud upon him; or, at least, the loss would be deemed one occasioned by the bailor's own folly or laches; and the bailee would not, even in a case of gross negligence, be responsible beyond the value of the box or casket itself, without the contents.

§ 78. The two first of these propositions may be deduced from the comments of Lord Holt in the case of *Coggs* v. *Bernard.* The last seems established by the prevailing doctrine in respect to carriers, who give notices, and thereby limit their responsibility, when packages are entrusted to them, the contents of which are unknown or concealed, upon which we shall have occasion to enlarge hereafter, when we come to that highly important branch of bailments.[1] And there is sound reason for the distinctions thus made, in point of responsibility, in the different cases. No person has a right, by practising concealment or fraud, to impose a duty

---

[1] *Batson* v. *Donovan*, 4 B. & Ald. 21; *Sleat* v. *Fogg*, 5 B. & Ald. 342; *Bradley* v. *Waterhouse*, 1 Mood. & Malk. R. 154; *Gibbon* v. *Paynton*, 4 Burr. 2298.

upon another, which he would not otherwise knowingly
have undertaken.   On the other hand, no person knowing or having reason to presume the contents of a
box to be of very high and tempting value, has a right
to excuse himself from a just responsibility, because the
contents have not been formally communicated to him,
and a request formally made, that he will undertake the
custody of the whole; since he may naturally presume,
that such is the intention of the depositor, notwithstanding the security of a lock or seal; and good faith requires him, under such circumstances, not to disappoint
the just confidence of the party.   But, if he has no reason to suppose the contents to be of more than ordinary value, then he may fairly discharge himself by such
care, as belongs ordinarily to trusts of that sort, and there
is nothing communicated, which calls for superior vigilance.

§ 79. The general rule, then, being, that the depositary is bound to reasonable care, proportioned, indeed,
to the nature and value of the article and the danger of
loss; and the measure of that care being slight diligence,
the result is, that he is generally liable for gross negligence only.   If he takes the same care of the goods
bailed, as of his own, that ordinarily will repel the presumption of gross negligence; but he may still be
chargeable, if the negligence is such as even persons
of slight diligence would not be guilty of.   In short, he
must exert the common diligence used by, and required
of, depositaries in general; and he cannot exempt himself
from the consequences of omitting such diligence, unless he can deduce a more limited liability from all the
circumstances of his own particular case.[1]   He may
make a special contract, either to enlarge or to narrow

---

[1] Jones's Bailm. 82, 83.

his general responsibility. And then, in case of a loss, it will be incumbent on the party, who seeks to avail himself of the benefit of such contract, to establish it by suitable proofs. It will be rare, that such a contract can be expressly proved. It is usually implied from collateral circumstances, which afford presumptions varying almost infinitely in cogency and strength. We have already seen, that the depositary's own character for diligence or carelessness may sometimes form an ingredient in the case, to negative, or to support a presumption. The proof must be strong, which will justify an inference, that the bailee is at liberty to take less care of the thing bailed, than of his own. And in many cases, a higher diligence may properly be exacted, than the bailee is accustomed to take of his property, especially if his character, in this respect, is not most thoroughly known to the bailor.

§ 80. Some exceptions to the general rule of diligence in cases of deposits are laid down by elementary writers. But, where the case is in strictness a deposit, they all resolve themselves into two, viz. 1. Cases, where there is a special contract; 2. Cases, where there is a spontaneous and officious offer by the depositary to keep the deposit.

§ 81. The first exception requires no commentary; the last is deserving of much consideration. Sir William Jones[1] states it to be a rule of our law, that the depositary is liable for losses, where he has made an officious offer; though he does not cite any authority in support of it. The rule certainly existed in the civil law. The Pandects adopt the doctrine of Julian on this subject. "Sed, et si se quis deposito obtulit (idem

---

[1] Jones's Bailm. 48, 50.

Julianus scribit) *periculo* se depositi illigâsse; ita, tamen, ut non solum dolum, sed etiam culpam et custodiam, præstat; non tamen casus fortuitos." [1] So, that
the party was liable, not merely for fraud, but for negligence, or at least for ordinary negligence. Domat[2]
says he is liable not only for gross mistakes, but for
other faults. For the depositor might, but for such
officiousness, have chosen another depositary, who
would have been more careful. Pothier adopts the
Roman rule without comment or question. He holds,
that in such a case of an officious offer without request,
the party is bound to keep the deposit with all possible
care, since he has thereby prevented the depositor from
delivering it to a person, who would have been more
careful than himself.[3]

§ 82. The rule is certainly *strictissimi juris*; and
its incorporation into our law ought not readily to be
admitted. A voluntary offer of kindness to a friend,
even when importunately urged, ought hardly to carry
with it such penal consequences; since it is generally
the result of strong affection, a desire to oblige, and
often of a sense of duty, especially in cases of imminent
peril or sudden emergency. The reason assigned for
the rule is not satisfactory. It might, with at least as
much force, be said, that he, who trusts such a deposit
to a friend at his urgent request, confides it to him, as a
proof of his personal confidence, and requires no more
than, that he should guard it, as he guards his own, or
at least as men ordinarily guard deposits. He does not
mean to place a burthen on his friend, by which extraordinary responsibility is to be incurred; but to mani-

---

1 Dig. Lib. 16, tit. 3, l. 1, § 35; Ayliffe's Pand. B. 4, tit. 17.
2 1 Domat, B. 1, tit. 7, § 3, n. 8; Vinn. Lib. 3, tit. 15, § 12.
3 Pothier, Traité de Dépôt, ch. 2, § 1, art. 1. p. 30.

fest a personal confidence in the character and caution of his friend. Sir W. Jones has himself quoted, with apparent approbation, the opinion of Labeo, in the stronger case of a *negotiorum gestor*,* in which Labeo requires no more than good faith of him, when he interferes officiously, but from pure kindness, to act in my affairs ; " affectione coactus, ne bona mea distrahantur, negotiis se meis obtulerit." [1] The good sense of this, as a general rule, interpreting the offer of the party in its fair intendment, would seem more to belong to the manliness of the common law, than the rule promulgated by Julian, even with all the authority of imperial wisdom. The modern code of France introduces a mitigated form of the rule ; for, having announced, that a depositary must bestow, in keeping the thing deposited, the same care, which he bestows in keeping his own, it proceeds to declare, that the rule thus promulgated, " is to be applied with more rigour, if the depositary has himself offered to receive the deposit." [2] It seems thus to insist upon somewhat more watchfulness, without changing the ordinary obligations arising from deposits ; that is, it requires more watchfulness in the discharge of duty, but not a different kind of diligence.

§ 83. In respect to cases of necessary deposits, that is, such as are suddenly and almost involuntarily made in cases of extraordinary peril and difficulty, such as in

---

[1] Jones's Bailm. 49.   [2] Cod. Civ. art. 1927, 1928.

* The *Negotiorum Gestor* in the civil law[1] is one, who spontaneously, and without authority, undertakes to act for another during his absence, in his affairs. Of course, as his acts are wholly without the assent of the owner, the case is much stronger than that of a depositary, who officiously interferes in another's affairs with his consent.

[1] Dig. Lib. 3, tit. 5; 1 Bell's Com. 269.

cases of fire, shipwreck, inundations, insurrections, at-
tacks by mobs, and other casualties and pressing emer-
gencies, our law does not seem to vary the responsibility of the bailee from that arising in ordinary circumstances.[1] Nor indeed does the civil law, as to the
degree of diligence required; but it only inflicts a
double compensation for any misconduct of the bailee,
upon the ground, that public policy requires, that perfidy
in such cases should be punished, so as to suppress the
temptation to commit wrong.[2] Our law contents itself
with an ample compensation for the actual injury or
loss, leaving the additional moral infamy, which attaches
to cases of extraordinary perfidy, to be punished by the
severe judgment of public disgrace, which inevitably
follows it. The French law does not, in principle,
differ from ours in cases of necessary deposits, applying the general rule of responsibility to them.[3]
The only circumstance in that law, in which a necessary deposit differs from a common deposit, is, that
proof by witnesses is admitted, whatever may be the
value of the necessary deposit, whereas in other cases
no deposit beyond a limited value can be proved but
by writing.[4]

§ 84. There is another class of deposits noticed by
Pothier, and called by him *irregular* deposit. This
arises, when a party having a sum of money, which he
does not think safe in his own hands, confides it to
another, who is to return to him not the same money,

---

[1] Jones's Bailm. 48, 49; Domat, B. 1, tit. 7, § 5.

[2] Dig. Lib. 16, tit. 3, 1. 3, §§ 1, 2, 3, 4; 1 Domat, B. 1, tit. 7; prel.
art. and tit. 7, § 5.

[3] Cod. Civ. B. 3, tit. 11, art. 1949, 1950; Pothier, Traité de Dépôt,
ch. 3, § 1, p. 75; Domat, B. 1, tit. 7, § 5, art. 3.

[4] Pothier, Traité de Dépôt, ch. 3, § 1, n. 75; Cod. Civ. B. 3, tit. 11,
art. 1924, 1950.

but a like sum, when he shall demand it.[1] It differs from a mutuum simply in this respect, that the latter has principally in view the benefit of the receiver, and in the former the benefit of the bailor. In the civil law the obligations springing from these contracts were different; for in cases of mutuum the party borrowing was not held to pay interest upon the money lent; but in cases of irregular deposit interest was due to the depositary, both *ex nudo pacto* and *ex morâ*.[2] These distinctions are not recognised, at least not practically, in the French law; nor, as it is believed, in the common law. In both cases interest is by the French law due *ex morâ*.[3] In the common law the payment of interest is not generally fixed by positive rules; but interest is usually allowed upon money lent, if detained beyond the proper period, at which it ought to be repaid. And whether the case is a strict loan, or an improper deposit, if there is an unreasonable delay in the repayment, our courts would generally, if not invariably, allow interest *ex morâ*.

§ 85. There is a kind of deposit, which may, for distinction's sake, be called a *quasi* deposit, which is governed by the same general rule, as common deposits. It is, where a party comes lawfully to the possession of another person's property by finding. Under such circumstances the finder seems bound to the same reasonable care of it, as any voluntary depositary *ex contractu*. St. German[4] says, "If a man finds goods of another, if they be after hurt or lost by wilful negligence, he shall be charged to the owner. But if they

---

[5] Pothier, Traité de Dépôt, ch. 3, § 3, n. 82, 83.

[1] Digest, Lib. 16, tit. 3, l. 24; Pothier, Traité du Dépôt, ch. 3, § 3, n. 83.

[2] Pothier, Traité de Dépôt, n. 83.

[3] Doct. & Stud. Dial. 2, ch. 38.

be lost by other casualty, as if they be laid in a house, that by chance is burned, or if he deliver them to another to keep, that runneth away with them, I think he be discharged." [1]

§ 85. In Bacon's Abridgment it is laid down, that "if a man find goods and abuse them, or if he find sheep and kill them, this is a conversion. But if a man find butter and by his negligent keeping it putrify; or if a man find garments and by negligent keeping they be moth eaten, no action lies. So it is, if a man find goods and lose them again." [2] And the reason of the difference is there stated to be this : " Where a man only finds the goods of another, the owner did not part with them under the caution of any trust or engagement ; nor did the finder receive them into his possession under any obligation ; and therefore the law only prohibits a man in this case from making an unjust profit of what is another's. But the finder is not obliged to preserve these goods safer than the owner himself did ; for there is no reason for the law to lay such a duty on the finder in behalf of the careless owner. And it seems too rigorous to extend the charity of the finder beyond the diligence of the proprietor. It is therefore a good mean to punish an injurious act, namely, the conversion of the goods to his own use ; but not to punish a negligence in him, when the owner is guilty of a much greater one." [3]

§ 86. The doctrine here laid down is very unsatisfactory. Surely, a thing may be lost without any negligence of the owner ; and if the owner is negligent in losing it, it furnishes no very good reason, why the

---

[4] See *Mosgrave* v. *Agden*, Owen R. 141; 2 Ld. Raym. 909, per Gould J.; Noy's Maxims, ch. 43, p. 92.

[2] 1 Bac. Abridg. Bailment, D.   [3] Id.

finder should apologize for his own negligence by
setting up that of the owner. If it were meant only to
be said, that the finder is not liable for any thing but
gross negligence, that would be intelligible. But the
proposition is not so limited in the text. On the contrary it supposes, that no degree of negligence would
make him chargeable; which is directly against the
doctrine laid down in the Doctor and Student in the
passage above stated.[1] The only authorities relied on
by the author of Bacon's Abridgment are in Owen's,
Bulstrode's, and Leonard's Reports. The case in Owen
decides no more, than that the finder of six barrels of
butter was not liable *in trover* for a conversion, when
the butter was impaired and decayed, *ratione negligen-
tis custodiæ ;* for the court said, that he, who finds
goods, is not bound to preserve them from putrefac-
tion; but if the goods were used and by usage made
worse, the action would lie. For aught appearing in
the case there may not have been any but ordinary
or even slight negligence. And there is a clear difference between a conversion of a thing, and negligence
in keeping it. Trover lies only in the case of a conversion. The same case is reported in Cro. Eliz. 219,
and in 1 Leon. R. 224. In the former report it is
stated, that the case came on upon a demurrer to the
declaration, the count alleging only, that the finder
tam negligenter custodivit, that the property became
of little value. And the court were of opinion, that the
action did not lie ; for negligence was no conversion.
Lord Chief Baron Comyns, in his Digest,[3] understands
this to be the sole point of the case. The court, how-

---

1 Doct. & Stud. Dial. 2, ch. 38.

2 *Musgrave* v. *Agden,* Oweñ, 141.

3 Com. Dig. Trover, E.

ever, is reported to have said, that "No law compelleth him, that finds a thing, to keep it *safely* ; as if a man finds a garment and suffers it to be moth eaton ; or if one finds a horse and gives him no sustenance ; but if a man finds a thing and useth it, he is answerable, for it is a conversion" &c. ; — "but for negligent keeping no law punisheth him." In 1 Leon R. 224, the court is reported to have said, "A man that comes to goods by trover is *not bound to keep them so safely*, as he, who comes to them by bailment." And Walmsley J. said, "If a man find my garments, and suffereth them to be eaten with moths by the negligent keeping of them, no action lieth ; but if he weareth my garments, it is otherwise ; for the wearing is a conversion." The whole of this doctrine was clearly extrajudicial ; for the only point before the court was, whether there was any conversion or not. The case cited from Leonard's Reports [1] turned on a point of pleading ; and Mr. Justice Anderson there said, *arguendo*, "When a man comes to goods by trover, there is not any doubt, but by law he hath liberty to take possession of them. But he cannot abuse them, kill them, or convert them to his own use, or make any profit of them ; and if he do, it is great reason, that he be answerable for the same. But if he lose such goods afterwards, or they be taken from him, then he shall not be charged ; for he is not bound to keep them." This is the only *dictum* in the case bearing on the doctrine ; and it may be correct, when understood with the natural limitations belonging to it, namely, that the finder has not been guilty of gross negligence. But if the learned judge meant to say, that if the goods are lost by the gross negligence of the

---

[1] *Vandrink* v. *Archer*, 1 Leon R. 221.

finder, he is not answerable for the loss; such a doctrine would require some authority beyond a mere incidental dictum to support it.

§ 87. At the time, when these opinions were promulgated, the law of bailments was not as well defined, as
it is at present; and therefore they would be entitled
to less weight, than is usually given to judicial determinations, even if they stood without any contradiction.
But at a later period we have an elaborate judgment
of Lord Coke directly against the doctrine. In *Isaac
v. Clarke*,[1] that great judge deliberately declared,
that "if a man finds goods, an action on the case lies
for his ill and negligent keeping of them, but not trover
or conversion, because this is but a nonfesance." And
this seems the true doctrine of the law; for though a
finder may not be compellable to take goods, which he
finds, as it is a mere deed of charity for the owner; yet
when he does undertake the custody, he ought to exercise reasonable diligence in preserving the goods.
And the least degree of care known to our law, that is
slight diligence, may well be required of him, being that,
which is applied to gratuitous acts of kindness. This
is conformable to the rule laid down, as has been already seen, in the Doctor and Student,[2] and seems incidentally recognised in other authorities.[3] So, that
there seems no just foundation in our law for any distinction, as to responsibility, though there may be as to
remedy, between cases of conversion and misfesance
by the finder of goods, and cases of negligence, if the

---

[1] 2 Bulst. 306, 312; S. C. 1 Roll. R. 125, 130.
[2] Dial. 2, ch. 38.
[3] S. P. Gould J., in *Coggs* v. *Bernard*, 2 Ld. Ray. 909. See 2 Ld.
Ray. 917; Noy. Maxims, ch. 43, p. 92.

loss has arisen from that degree of negligence, for which gratuitous bailees would ordinarily be liable.

§ 88. In ordinary cases of deposits of money with banking corporations, or bankers, the transaction amounts to a mere *loan* or *mutuum*, and the bank is to restore, not the same money, but an equivalent sum, whenever it is demanded. But persons are sometimes in the habit of making, what is called, a special deposit of money or bills in a bank, where the specific money, as silver or gold coin, or bills, are to be restored, and not an equivalent. In such cases the transaction is a genuine deposit; and the banking company has no authority to use the money so deposited, but is bound to return it *in individuo* to the party. A case of great interest has been recently decided upon this subject. Such a special deposit of gold coin was made in a bank, and the money was deposited in the vaults of the corporation, under the care of the cashier of the bank, who also had the custody of the money of the corporation in the same vaults, and kept the keys thereof. He was unfaithful in the discharge of his duty, and embezzled the special deposit, as well as other property belonging to the bank. The Court, before which the cause was heard, in a very elaborate judgment, decided, that in such a case the banking corporation was liable only in case of gross negligence; that the receipt of the deposit by the cashier must be deemed obligatory upon the corporation; but, that the corporation was not liable in this case, because there was no gross negligence on its part; for the same care was taken of this as of other deposits, and of the property belonging to the corporation. The fraud and embezzlement, being by the cashier, did not, under such circumstances, vary the case; but its responsibility was the same, as if the theft had been committed by a stranger; for there was no want of diligence on its part in selecting proper officers, and the act of embezzlement was not within the scope of the duty of the cashier, as agent of the corporation. If goods deposited are stolen by the servants of a private depositor, without gross negligence on his own part, he is not chargeable any more than he would be, if the theft were by a stranger; and the same rule must be applied to banking corporations.[1] In this case, the cashier had given a written acknowledgment, that the gold was deposited for "*safe keeping*"; but this was not thought to vary the application of the general rule, as the paper imported no more, than was ordinarily implied in all such cases; and a special contract was not within the scope of the authority of the cashier.[2]

§ 89. In respect to the mode of keeping the deposit, and the authority of the depositary over it, a question often arises, how far the depositary is at liberty to use the thing deposited. In general it may be laid down, that a depositary has no right to use the thing deposited. This is the clear result of the civil law,[3] and the French law,[4] and it has been incorporated into ours.[5] But, this proposition must be received with many qualifications. There are certain cases, in which the use of the thing may be necessary for the due preservation of the deposit. There are others, again, where it would be mischievous; and others, again, where it would be,

---

[1] *Foster* v. *Essex Bank,* 17 Mass. R. 479. See also *Finucane* v. *Small,* 1 Esp. R. 315.

[2] Id. 17 Mass. R. 505.

[3] Dig. Lib. 16, tit. 3, 1. 29; 1 Domat, B. 1, tit. 7, § 3, n. 15; Ayliffe, B. 4, tit. 17, p. 519.

[4] Pothier, Traité de Dépôt, ch. 2, § 1, art. 1, n. 34.

[5] Bac. Abr. Bailm. D; Jones's Bailm. 81, 82; 1 Dane's Abr. ch. 17, art. 11, § 2.

if not positively beneficial, at least indifferent. If a bailment were made of a horse, the depositary would certainly be at liberty to use him, so far, at least, as to preserve his health; and if he should die from gross negligence in this particular, the depositary might be chargeable with the loss; for every person, in such a case, contracts for reasonable care.[1] If a milch cow be deposited, the milking of the cow, to say the least of it, would not subject the depositary to an action, for it would not injure, but might promote the health of the animal.[2] The Roman and the French law, in such a case, would justify the act; but would require the depositary to account for the value of the milk, deducting the reasonable charges for her nourishment.[3] On the other hand, if diamonds and jewels were deposited, it might be deemed an abuse of the trust to wear them, or to suffer them to be worn by the family of the depositary, even though the use might be of no injury.[4]

§ 90. The best general rule on the subject, (for every case must be governed by its own particular circumstances), is to consider, whether there may, or may not be an implied consent, on the part of the owner, to the use. If the use would be for the benefit of the deposit, the assent of the owner may well be presumed; if to his injury, or perilous, it ought not to be presumed; if the use would be indifferent, and other circumstances do not incline either way, the use may be deemed not allowable.[5] If money is deposited, especially if locked

---

[1] Jones's Bailm. 81, 82.

[2] Ibid; *Moses* v. *Conham*, Owen R. 123, 124; Anon. 2 Salk. 522; 2 Kent Com. 450.

[3] Pothier, Traité de Dépôt, ch. 2, § 1, art. 2, § 1, n. 47; Dig. Lib. 16, tit. 3, 1. 29, § 1; Jones's Bailm. 81, 82; Pothier, Nantissement, n. 35.

[4] Jones's Bailm. 81, 82.   [5] Jones's Bailm. 80, 81.

up in a chest, or enclosed in a bag, the right to use it could scarcely be presumed to have been within the intention of the parties.[1]   The same rule would apply to other valuables, as jewelry, for they would be subject to extraordinary perils.   If books are lodged in a trunk, and locked up, the use of them would seem to be impliedly prohibited, especially if the key is kept by the bailor.   But, if the books are in an open chest, or book-case, or are left generally accessible, Pothier supposes, that a consent to the use of them by the depositary may be fairly presumable.[2]   But, if this be true, the right to lend them to other persons would not be presumed.   And if the books are very valuable, and have very expensive plates in them, which would be injured by use, a consent to use them would scarcely be presumed.   A deposit of valuable paintings would not justify a general use of them for purposes of show, or parade, which would expose them to injury; but a modified use of them might be fairly presumed, as an ornament of a private room, if they were left open in their frames.   A deposit of a library of law books in the library of a friend, who is a lawyer, would almost carry with it the implication of a right for him to use them for private consultation.   Many other cases might be put to show the application of the principle of presumption.[3]   Pothier puts one, of the use of a setting dog, where the use might be fairly presumed for game;[4] and the same may apply to hounds for the chase.[5] The French code expresses the true sense of the law

---

1 Pothier, Traité de Dépôt, ch. 2, § 1, art. 1, n. 37.
2 Pothier, Traité de Dépôt, ch. 2, § 1, art. 1, n. 37.
3 Ayliffe's Pand. B. 4, tit. 17; Jones's Bailm. 79, 80, 81.
4 Pothier, Traité de Dépôt, ch. 2, § 1, art. 1, n. 37.
5 Jones's Bailm. 79, 80, 81.

on this subject. The depositary cannot make use of the thing deposited, without the express or presumed permission of the depositor.[1]

§ 91. The Roman law treated the use of the thing deposited, without any express or implied consent of the owner, to be a gross breach of trust, and involving the criminality of theft. " Qui rem depositam, invito domino, sciens prudensque in usus suos converterit, etiam furti delicto succedit." [2] Our law deems it a mere breach of private confidence, unless in very special cases, which might demonstrate a felonious intent, or, as it is technically called, *animus furandi.*

§ 92. It follows from what has been said, that it is a gross breach of trust, which gives to the injured party a just cause of action, for a bailee to break open a locked chest, or a sealed package, which is deposited with him. *A fortiori* the depositary has no authority to sell, or pledge them ; and if he does, the owner may reclaim them from any person, who is found in possession of them.[3] The Roman law, also, gave a right of action to a testator, who trusted another with his will, to be kept for him, if he discovered the contents of it to any other persons.[4] Our law does not, as far as I know, provide any redress in such a case ; unless, at least, some positive injury results from it ; but it is as aggravated a breach of trust, as can well be conceived, and may often be attended with serious mischiefs. The French law has followed the reasonable doctrine of the civil law ; [5] and one cannot but wish, that the

---

1 Cod. Civ., B. 3, tit. 11, art. 1930.

2 Code, Lib. 4, tit. 34, l. 3 ; Dig. Lib. 16, tit. 3, l. 29.

3 *Hartop* v. *Hoare*, 3 Atk. 43 ; S. C. 1 Wils. 8, 9 ; 2 Str. 1187.

4 Dig. Lib. 16, tit. 3, l. 1, § 38.

5 Pothier, Traité de Dépôt, ch. 2, § 1, art. 2, § 1, n. 39.

common law had animadverted on it in some form, either of civil or of criminal prosecution, which should add a legal, to what now seems a mere moral sanction upon the conscience of a testamentary depositary.

§ 93. It is often laid down in our books, that a depositary has a special property in the deposit. There is no doubt, that in certain kinds of bailment the bailee has a special property; but, that he possesses it in a case of mere deposit, is matter of serious doubt. Blackstone, in his Commentaries,[1] lays down the doctrine as follows: " In all these instances (i. e. in *all classes* of bailment) there is a special qualified property transferred from the bailor to the bailee, together with the possession. It is not an absolute property, because of his contract for restitution; the bailor having still left in him the right to a chose in action, grounded upon such contract. And on account of this qualified property of the bailee, he may, as well as the bailor, maintain an action against such as injure, or take away the chattels." For the full extent of this proposition, he mainly relies on Heydon & Smith's case, (13 Rep. 67, 69,) which certainly does not support it. Sir William Jones also lays down the doctrine in equally general terms; "for," (says he,) "every bailee has a temporary qualified property in the things, of which possession is delivered to him; and has, therefore, a possessory action, or an appeal in his own name, against a stranger, who may damage, or purloin them."[2] And for this he relies on a case in the Year Books, (21 Hen. 7, 14, *b.*) which, it must be admitted, seems full to the point. Mr. Justice Fineux there said, (and it was an action of replevin brought by a bailee, for aught that appears, upon a general bailment,) " In this

---

[1] 2 Bl. Com. 452.   [2] Jones's Bailm. 80.

case, the bailee has a property in the thing against a stranger, for he is chargeable to the bailor; and for this reason he shall recover against a stranger, who takes the goods out of his possession." And judgment was accordingly given for the plaintiff. Now, an action of replevin will lie only, where the party hath a general or a special property in the thing.[1] There can be no doubt, that if the bailee, in that case, was a pawnee, or factor, he might maintain the action. What sort of bailee he was, does not appear in the report. There are other cases, which hint at the same doctrine, as that in the Year Book.[2] But, the doctrine generally maintained by the better authorities is, that a depositary has no property whatsoever in the deposit, but a custody only. It was so adjudged, upon very full consideration by the Court, in *Hartop* v. *Hoare*,[3] where the point was directly in judgment; and Southcote's case (4 Co. 83, 84,) was relied on as supporting it.[4] There is nothing in the case of *Sutton* v. *Buck*, (2 Taunt. R. 301,) which, properly considered, affects that decision. There, a party, who was the purchaser of a ship, and had taken possession, but whose title was not completed by any proper registry, or by any regular conveyance, sued in trover for the recovery of certain portions of the ship against a wrong-doer, by whom he had been dispossessed; and it was held, that he was entitled to recover against the defendant. The ground of the opinion was, that his possession alone, under such circumstances, was a

---

1 Co. Lit. 145, *b.*; Com. Dig. Replevin, B.

2 *Rich* v. *Aldred*, 6 Mod. 216; 2 Ld. Ray. 912, per Powell J.; 2 Saund. R. 47, *b.* note; *Holliday* v. *Camsell*, 1 T. R. 658; 2 Bl. Com. 451, 452, 453.

3 3 Atk. 49.

4 Anon. Godbolt. R. 160, pl. 224; *Arnold* v. *Jefferson*, 1 Ld. Ray. 275; 1 Dane's Abr. ch. 17, art. 8, § 9.

good title against a mere wrong-doer. The doctrine of that case has been since affirmed; and it has been held, that a simple or naked bailee has a sufficient interest to sue in trover.[1] Indeed, the like doctrine was held by Lord Coke as long ago, as the case of *Isaac* v. *Clarke*, (2 Bulst. R. 306, 311,) where, in delivering his opinion as Chief Justice, he said, "Bailment makes a privity. If one hath goods as a bailee, where he hath only a possession, and no property, yet he shall have an action for them." The case of *Rooth* v. *Wilson* (1 B. & Ald. 59) goes no farther; and only shows, that the depositary may maintain an action for any wrong done to the deposit, for which he is responsible; but not that a special property passes to him. Such a right of action may exist without a special property in the thing.[2] There is, however, a very recent case, arising under another class of gratuitous bailments, which seems somewhat at variance with the doctrine here spoken of, and which may, perhaps, be thought to admit of some question in point of principle. A person was entrusted with a parcel, containing a bank note, for the purpose of having it booked, to go by a common coach to London; — Instead of doing so, being himself about to go to London by the same coach, he put it into his own bag. The bag was stolen by some of the servants of the coach-owner, in the course of the journey. An action was brought by the passenger against the coach-owner for the loss of his bag and its contents, and

---

[1] *Burton* v. *Hughes*, 2 Bing. R. 173; Best C. J. See also *Oughton* v. *Lepping*, 1 Barn. & Adolp. 241, & 2 Saund. R. 47, *a* & *b*., & note of Williams Edit. of Patterson & Williams; 2 Bl. Com. 452, 453; 2 Kent Com. 456; 1 Dane's Abr. ch. 17, art. 8 & 9; *Waterman* v. *Robinson*, 5 Mass. R. 503.

[2] Bac. Abr. Bailm. D, cites 13 Co. Rep. 69.

among other things, of the packet so entrusted to him. But the Court held, that no recovery in damages could be had by him in that action for the loss of such parcel, although he was responsible over to the owner of it. The ground of the decision seems to have been, that as the delivery to the party was for a special purpose, which was not complied with, he had neither a general, nor a special property in the parcel, and therefore was not entitled to recover damages, notwithstanding, by his misconduct, he had become responsible to the bailor.[1] We may have occasion to advert again to this case, when we come to the subject of mandates.[2]

§ 94. There is no doubt, however, that, notwithstanding a deposit, the general owner may, upon the ground of his general ownership, maintain a suit against strangers for any injury, or conversion of it.[3] In such a case a recovery by him will bar any redress by the depositary, even when, by reason of his responsibility over, he might otherwise be entitled to an action for the same injury or conversion.[4]

§ 95. The doctrine of the civil law coincides with what is here stated to be the common law on this point. By the civil law the property of the thing remains in the depositor; and at most the possession only passes to the depositary. "Rei depositæ proprietas apud deponentem manet, sed et possessio (nisi apud sequestrem) deposita est."[5] Pothier states the doctrine quite as strongly. "In a true deposit," (says

---

[1] *Miles* v. *Cattle*, 6 Bing. R. 743; S. C. 1 Lloyd & Welsby R. 353.
[2] Post, §§ 148, 149, 262, 263.
[3] 2 Bl. Com. 453; Bac. Abr. Bailm. A, B, C; Id. Trespass, C; Trover, C; *Thorp* v. *Burling*, 11 Johns. R. 285; *Brownell* v. *Manchester*, 1 Pick. 232.
[4] Bac. Abr. Ibid.
[5] Dig. Lib. 16, tit. 3, l. 17, § 1; Ayliffe's Pand. B. 4, tit. 17.

he,) " he, who has deposited any pieces of gold or silver, remains the proprietor of them, and he even continues the possessor of them, the depositary detaining in the name of him, who has made the deposit.[1] In the Scotch law it would seem, that though the property and possession are in some sort severed by the deposit, the former belonging to the depositor, and the latter to the depositary, yet the possession of the deposit is deemed for all effective purposes to remain with the depositor.[2] Perhaps, after all, the distinction here pointed out is not materially different from what is recognised in common law. The possession of the depositary is certainly for many purposes deemed the possession of the depositor in our law, both as to rights and remedies. And it could scarcely have been the intention of the civil law to declare, that possession did not, in fact, pass to the bailee by the delivery of the deposit. It meant only to affirm, that the possession was not exclusive of that of the bailor; but rather in subordination to it.

§ 96. We may now pass to the consideration of another part of the duty of the depositary, and that is, his obligation to return the deposit, when it is required of him.[3]

§ 97. In the first place the deposit is to be returned *in individuo*, and in the same state, in which he received it. If it is lost, or injured, or spoiled by his fraud, or gross negligence, he is responsible to the extent of the loss or injury.[4] If he has kept the deposit with the

---

[1] Pothier, Traité de Dépôt, ch. 3, § 3, n. 82 ; ch. 1, art. 2, § 2, n. 12.

[2] 1 Bell's Com. 257, 258.

[3] 1 Bell's Com. 257 ; Jones's Bailm. 36, 46.

[4] Jones's Bailm. 36, 46, 120 ; *Foster* v. *Essex Bank*, 17 Mass. R. 479; *Stanton* v. *Bell*, 2 Hawk. N. Car. R. 145; 1 Dane's Abr. ch. 17, art. 1 and 2.

same care, as his own goods of the same kind, this will ordinarily repel the presumption of fraud and gross negligence. Still, however, it must be under this reserve, that he has not omitted those common precautions, which other persons would not omit; such, for instance, as keeping money under lock and key.[1] "Latæ culpæ finis est, non intelligere id, quod omnes intelligunt."[2] It follows, of course, that where the deposit is lost, or perishes, or is injured, either by accident, or inherent defects, or its own perishable quality, or even from slight or ordinary neglect of the depositary, he is not chargeable.[3] If part is lost and part remains, the latter is to be restored. If to save a perishable deposit it has been sold by the bailee, the money is to be paid to the owner; for a necessary sale is good and for his benefit.[4]

§ 98. Although the obligation to restore a deposit seems to flow from the first principles of the contract, as well as from natural justice ; yet, strange as it may seem, it was held in the reign of Queen Elizabeth, as Sir William Jones has not scrupled to declare, against common sense and common honesty, that no action would lie for a non-delivery of the deposit. But this decision was soon afterwards overruled and the present doctrine firmly established.[5]

§ 99. The depositary is also bound to restore not only the thing deposited ; but any increase or profits,

---

[1] 1 Domat, B. 1, tit. 7, § 3, n. 3, 4.

[2] Dig. Lib. 50, tit. 16, l. 223 ; *Mytton* v. *Cook*, 2 Str. 1099. See *Rooth* v. *Wilson*, 1 Barn. & Ald. 59.

[3] 1 Domat, B. 1, tit. 7, § 3, n. 5, 6 ; Jones's Bailm. 10, 46 ; 1 H. Bl. 162 ; Pothier, Traité de Dépôt, ch. 2, § 1, art. 2, § 1, p. 42, 43, 44.

[4] Pothier, Traité de Dépôt, ch. 2, § 1, art. 2, § 1, n. 44, 45.

[5] Jones's Bailm. 51 ; Yelv. R. 4, 50, 128 ; *Wheatley* v. *Low*, Cro. Jac. 668.

which may have accrued from it. If an animal deposited brings forth young, the latter are to be delivered to the owner.[1] And by the civil and French law, if interest has been made upon money deposited, this also should be given up to the depositor.[2] If the depositary has used the money wrongfully, this seems a just, or at least a moderate compensation for the wrong. If the right to let the money, or to use it followed from the bailment, it would cease to be a deposit, and fall under some other denomination.[3]

§ 100. If the depositary had sold the deposit, and afterwards repurchased it, he was by the civil law bound to restore the value, even if it afterwards was lost without his default; and the reason assigned is, that the original sale was a fraud upon the owner, and could not be purged away, but by a delivery of the thing itself to the owner.[4] Our law would say in such a case, that the party should not be permitted to take advantage of his own wrong; and that the sale being a conversion of the property, the right of action of the owner was then complete, and could not be varied, except as to the extent of the damages, even by a subsequent restitution to the owner.[5]

§ 101. Cases are also put in the civil and French law, how far the heir or administrator of a deceased bailee is liable, if in ignorance of the bailment he sells the thing. It is held, that he is liable, not as in case of a tort, but for the price, which he has received, and only

---

[1] Dig. Lib. 16, tit. 3, l. 1, §§ 23, 24; 1 Domat, B. 1, tit. 7, § 3, n. 9.

[2] Pothier, Traité de Dépôt, ch. 2, § 1, art. 2, § 1, n. 41, 47, 48; Dig. Lib. 16, tit. 3, l. 29, § 1; Ayliffe's Pand. B. 4, tit. 17, p. 519, 523.

[3] 1 Bell's Com. 257.

[4] Pothier, Traité de Dépôt, ch. 2, § 1, art. 2, § 1, n. 43; Dig. Lib. 16, tit. 3, l. 1, § 25.

[5] 1 Roll. Abr. 5, L. pl. 1.

when he has received it.[1] Our law would probably
treat the case as one of conversion; and give the
owner the value of the thing so sold; or enable him in
most cases, at his election, to proceed against the vendee for restitution.[2]

§ 102. The next inquiry is, To whom is restitution
to be made? Generally speaking, it is to be made to
the bailor; though there may be special cases, in which
that would not be required, or justified. As, for instance, if goods have been deposited by a thief, who
has been convicted, and the owner reclaims them, he
alone is entitled to receive them.[3] A question has
often been raised, whether an innocent bailee is generally responsible to any other person, than him, from
whom he has received the goods, or in case of his
death, to his legal representatives. It was formerly
held, that if the goods of A are bailed by B to C, C
must redeliver them to B; for (it was said) C cannot,
as bailee, be allowed to remove or alter that possession,
which has been committed to him, in order to restore
it to the right owner; for the right of restitution must
be demanded of the bailor B, that did the injury, of
which the bailee has no pretence to judge; and therefore it would be downright treachery in him to deliver
them to any other person, than the bailor.[4] But it
was said, that in such a case, if B, the bailor, dies, there
his executors are chargeable only to C, who has the

---

1 Dig. Lib. 16, tit. 3, l. 1, § 47, l. 2; Pothier, Traité de Dépôt, ch. 2,
§ 1, art. 2, § 1, n. 45, 46.

2 2 Saund. R. 47, *b*, note by Williams.

3 Dig. Lib. 16, tit. 3, l. 31; Pothier, Traité de Dépôt, ch. 2, § 1, art.
2, § 1, n. 51; Cod. Napol. art. 1937, 1938.

4 Bac. Abr. Bailment, A; 3 Reeve's Hist. 449–453; 1 Roll. Abr. 606,
607, Detinue, C; Fitz. N. B. 138, M; Bro. Trespass, 216, 295; 2 Saund.
47 *b*, Williams's note; 6 Mod. 216.

right; for the executors came to the possession by the law, and therefore must deliver it to those persons, in whom the law has established the property.[1] This doctrine, however, even in regard to the bailee himself, was probably limited to cases, where the bailor came to the possession of the goods by right; for if he came to them by wrong, it would seem, that the owner might reclaim them from any person, in whose possession they were found.[2] But the doctrine itself may now be justly deemed overruled; and the right of the owner to recover his property in all cases, against a person having no title, whether a bailee or not, and whether a first or a second bailee, seems now fully established in our law; for the reason, that the bailee can never be in a better situation than his bailor. If the latter has no title, the real owner is entitled to recover the property, in whose hands soever it may be.[3] Recent cases have also decided, that if a bailee of goods for a particular purpose transfers them in contravention of that purpose, even although it be to a *bonâ fide* vendee without notice, the latter cannot resist the claim of the owner.[4] And, *a fortiori*, if the bailee has obtained the goods upon a claim of ownership not made out, and under an agreement, that if the claim is unfounded, they shall be restored, the bailee cannot retain them against the true owner.[5]

§ 103. If a bailor, after a deposit, transfers to another person his right to the thing deposited, the latter

---

[1] Id. ibid.; 9 Hen. 6, 58.

[2] *Taylor* v. *Plumer*, 3 M. & Selw. 562.

[3] Id. ibid.; *Wilson* v. *Anderton*, 1 Barn. & Ald. 450; *Ogle* v. *Atkinson*, 5 Taunt. R. 759.

[4] *Wilkinson* v. *King*, 2 Camp. R. 335; *Loeschman* v. *Machin*, 2 Stark. R. 311.

[5] *Hurd* v. *West*, 7 Cowen R. 752.

cannot (it is said) compel a delivery of it to himself;
but the bailee, if he chooses, may deliver it to the
person, to whom it is transferred; and it will be a
justification.[1] But if A delivers goods to B to be delivered over to C, there C hath the property, and may
demand the goods; for B undertakes to make the
delivery to C, and hath no interest or claim but for
that purpose.[2] But in such cases there must be a
clear assent on the part of B to such undertaking; for
the mere receipt of the goods will not always be sufficient to establish such assent. It has been settled by
several modern decisions, that in case of a remittance of
a bill to an agent or banker with directions to apply a part
of it to the payment of a debt due to a third person,
the mere fact of a receipt of the remittance does not,
unless the remittee assents to such disposition of the
proceeds, and agrees to pay over the same to the creditor, amount to such an appropriation of the proceeds,
as will enable such creditor to recover the same against
the remittee. And the same principle has been applied
to a consignment of goods for sale, with direction to
make payment of a debt out of the proceeds.[3]

§104. It has been further asserted to be law, (though
it is open to much question,) that if goods are delivered to a bailee, to be delivered over to another, and
afterwards an action be brought against him by one,
who hath a right to the goods, the defendant may,
pending the action, deliver over the goods to the per-

---

[1] *Rich* v. *Aldred*, 6 Mod. 216. *Quære*, and see post, §§ 264, 265.

[2] Bac. Abr. Bailment, D; 2 Bulst. 68; Roll. Abr. Detinue, C. 606;
9 H. 6, 58.

[3] *Williams* v. *Everett*, 14 East R. 582; *Yates* v. *Bell*, 3 Barn. & Ald.
643; *Stewart* v. *Fry*, 7 Taunt. R. 339; *Grant* v. *Austin*, 3 Price R. 58;
Wedlake v. *Hurley*, 1 Lloyd & Wellsby, 330; *Tiernan* v. *Jackson*, 5 Pet.
Sup. R. 580.

son, to whom upon the bailment they were deliverable, and he will be discharged.[1] But a bailor, where the delivery over is not for a valuable consideration, may at any time countermand his bailment; and after such countermand the delivery over by his bailee will not be good.[2]

§ 105. If a bailee delivers the goods to a second bailee, the first bailee may demand and recover the same from the second bailee, because the latter hath the possession of the former, and undertakes for the custody; — But the original bailor may also demand and recover the same from either bailee, because he has the property, and both are bound to answer to him.[3] A like action is given to the bailor by the civil law in the case of a second bailment.[4] If the second bailee has delivered the goods to the original bailor, it is said, that it is no bar to a suit by the first bailee against him.[5] But this doctrine seems at all times to have been questionable.[6] And it may be now considered as entirely exploded, both in England and America, by the recent authorities.[7] If the bailee should lose the goods bailed, and a stranger, finding them, should deliver them to the bailor, there the finder would not be liable to the bailee; for he does not come in in privity under the bailment.[8] But it is said,

---

[1] Fitz. N. B. 138, M; Bac. Abr. Bailm. D; Roll. Abr. Detinue, D, 607.

[2] Bac. Abr. Bailm. D.

[3] Isaac v. Clarke, 2 Bulst. 306, 312, per Coke C. J.; Bac. Abr. Bailm. D; Roll. Abr. Detinue, C, p. 606; 9 Hen. 6, 58; see Gosling v. Burnie, 7 Bing. R. 339.

[4] Pothier, Traité de Dépôt, ch. 2, § 1, art. 3, n. 63.

[5] Roll. Abr. Detinue, C, 606; 9 Hen. 6, 58.

[6] See Flewellin v. Rave, 1 Bulst. 69.

[7] Ogle v. Atkinson, 5 Taunt. 759; Willson v. Anderton, 1 Barn. & Adolp 430; Whittier v. Smith, 11 Mass. R. 211.

[8] Roll. Abr. Detinue, C, 606, 607.

that if a recovery is had by a third person against a stranger, so finding goods, he will still be liable to the true owner of them in an action; for it is no answer to the owner, that another has recovered from the finder, what he had no right to.[1]   Whenever such a question shall again arise, it may probably be thought worthy of farther consideration, especially if the finder has had no notice of the true ownership.

§ 106. Where a deposit has been made by a servant in behalf of his master, the goods are to be redelivered to the master, especially if he gives notice, that they should not be redelivered to the servant.   But a delivery back to the servant would, in many cases, and especially where there was no reason to suspect impropriety, be a good discharge.[2]

§ 107. No right of action, however, accrues in any case against the bailee, unless there has been some wrongful conversion or loss by the gross negligence of the bailee, until after a demand made upon him, and a refusal by him to redeliver the deposit.   A demand and refusal is ordinarily evidence of a conversion; unless the circumstances constitute a just excuse, or a justification of the refusal.[3]

§ 108. The civil law and the French law coincide in many respects with ours in the particulars above mentioned.   In the civil law the depositary was generally bound to restore the goods to the depositor.   But if the right owner appeared, he might deliver them to him;[4] and especially if they were stolen from the

---

1 Roll. Abr. Detinue, C, 607; Bac. Abr. Bailm. D.

2 1 Domat, B. 1, tit. 7, § 3, n. 6; Pothier, Traité de dépôt, ch. 2, § 1, art. 2, § 2, n. 49.

3 *Brown* v. *Hotchkiss,* 9 Johns. R. 361.

4 Dig. Lib. 16, tit. 3, l. 31; Ayliffe's Pand. B. 4, tit. 17, p. 522; Cod. Civ. art. 1937, 1938.

owner. If the ownership was doubtful, or the right was disputed by the depositor, the depositary had a right to detain the property, until the right was ascertained, and thus became, as it were, pending the dispute, a judicial depositary or sequestrator.[1] And the real owner, who in ignorance of his rights became a depositary, might always retain them, unless some superior right attached to the depositor.[2] The French law does not, in these respects, materially differ from the civil law.[3] In case of theft the Code of France requires, that the bailee should give notice to the owner, and if the owner fails to claim the goods in a limited time, he may safely redeliver them to the depositor. But, generally in other cases, the depositary is bound to deliver the goods to the party, on whose account he received them, whatever may be the claims of other persons.[4] And this rule, it seems, will apply to a bailment by a servant of his master's property, where it has been bailed in his own name, and not in the name of his master.[5]

§ 109. Where a deposit is made by a party in a special character, as in the character of guardian, or executor, or trustee; there, if the trust has terminated, as if the guardianship has ceased, or the executor been removed and a new administrator appointed, the delivery should be to the party entitled of right to the property. As if an infant has come of age, the delivery should be to him; or in case of a new administrator, the

---

1 Domat, B. 1, tit. 7, § 3, n. 5, 6; Ayliffe's Pand. B. 4, tit. 17, p. 520.

2 Dig. Lib. 16, tit. 3, l. 31; Pothier, Pand. Lib. 16, tit. 3, § 1, art. 1, § 9; Cod. Civ. art. 1946.

3 Pothier, Traité de Dépôt, ch. 2, § 1, art. 2, § 2, p. 49, 50, 51, 52, &c. Id. ch. 2, § 1, art. 3, p. 67.

4 Cod. Civ. B. 3, art. 1937, 1938; Pothier, Traité de Dépôt, n. 51.

5 Pothier, Traité de Dépôt, ch. 2, § 1, art. 2, § 2, n. 49.

delivery should be to him.[1]   And the like rule applies, where a third person has by forfeiture or otherwise succeeded to the right of property;[2] as in case of a forfeiture for crimes ; or the subsequent marriage of a feme bailor ; or the guardianship of a person, who has since the bailment become *non compos mentis.*   The French law furnishes a similar rule;[3] and, indeed, it is so consonant to common sense, that it would seem to be a principle of universal justice.

§ 110. It may be asked, What is to be done by a bailee, where different persons claim the same thing from him under different titles ? Is he to be subject to the action of each, and thus to run the chance of a double recovery against him ? Or may he protect himself by any legal proceedings ? We have already seen, that he may in certain cases compel the adverse parties to litigate the right by interpleading at law, or in equity.[4]   But this right is principally limited to cases of privity between the parties, as for instance, between the bailor and a second bailee, who may compel the first bailee to interplead.   But where the parties claim in absolutely adverse rights, not founded in any privity of title, or common contract, there the bailee must defend himself as well as he may ; for, generally speaking, he cannot compel mere strangers to interplead with each other, and especially if any tort has intervened.[5]

---

1 Pothier, Traité de Dépôt, ch. 2, § 1, art. 1, § 1, n. 50.

2 Id. n. 52 ; Bac. Abr. Bailm. B.

3 Cod. Civ. B. 3, tit. 11, art. 1940, 1941.

4 *Rich* v *Aldred,* 6 Mod. 216, Coop. Eq. 45–50; *Isaac* v. *Clarke,* 2 Bulst R. 306, 313.

5 Vin. Abr. Enterpleader, L, M, N, &c; see *Rich* v. *Aldred,* 6 Mod. R. 216; 3 Reeves' Hist. of the Law, 450, 451, 452, 453 ; 7 Dane's Abr. ch. 226, art. 9, § 4.

§ 111. Although the subject of interpleader in cases of this sort belongs properly to another branch of law, it may not be without use to add here some explanations of it. In cases of bailments (as we have had occasion to state) the common law in certain cases enabled the bailee, if sued, to call upon the other proper parties, who were interested in the property, to appear and contest the title between themselves, and thus to exonerate him from responsibility. Thus, by the common law, if two persons deposited deeds or chattels with a third to be redelivered according to the terms of an agreement, and one of them brought an action of detinue against the depositary, the latter might, upon a suitable allegation, by a proceeding called *garnishment*, which is in effect a notice of the suit, compel the other depositor to appear and become defendant in the action in his stead. And if a person was sued in separate actions of detinue by two depositors upon such a deposit, or by any two persons claiming to be the owners of the goods, which he had found, he might in like manner allege the deposit, or finding on the record, and compel them to interplead. But, as these proceedings by garnishment and interpleader were not allowed in any personal action, except that of detinue,[1] (a form of action, which has of late fallen into much disuse,) no practical advantage has been derived from them in modern times. The only course now resorted to for the relief of a person sued, or in danger of being sued by several claimants is that of filing a bill to compel the parties, by the authority of a court of equity, to interplead at law.

---

1 3 Reeves' Hist. of the Law, 449.

§ 112. From this description of interpleader at the common law, it is obvious, that, with the exception of cases of finding goods, it is confined to cases, where there is a privity between the parties. So, that the remedy is not only restricted to actions of detinue, but falls far short of adequate relief, even in actions of that sort. Courts of equity are more liberal in granting relief, not only when suits are brought at law, but when they are threatened. But the relief even here is not, perhaps, in all cases, coextensive with the mischief; for the claim in each case must be of the same nature, or for the same duty, and founded in privity ; — At least, the claim must grow out of some transaction, in which the defendant is a mere stake-holder or bailee, and disconnects himself from any tort in regard to the conflicting titles.[1] *

§ 113. It would seem, that the civil law and the French law do not exactly limit the rights of the bailee in the same manner as our law, in cases requiring an interpleader by third persons. On the contrary, where-ever an adverse right is set up, and especially if the property is arrested in the hands of the depositary, he is not bound to deliver it to either party, until the title is

---

[1] Eden on Injunctions, p. 339 et seq. 342; 2 Vesey jr., 101; 1 Vez. & B. 334; 1 Merivale R. 405; 3 Madd. R. 277, 564; 5 Madd. R. 47; 1 Montague Pl. in Equity, 232, &c.; 2 Mont. Pl. in Eq. 380, &c., 397, &c.; Hinde. Pr. 26; Cooper Eq. Pl. 45 to 50; Bridgman's Pr. Index, Bill 9, Interpleader; *Wilson* v. *Anderton*, 1 Barn. & Adolp. R. 450, 456.

* This account of the proceedings by garnishment is copied verbatim from a recent Report made to Parliament by the Common Law Commissioners, and ordered to be printed by the House of Commons, on the 8th of March, 1830, p. 25. For further information, the reader is referred to 3 Reeves' Hist. of the Law, 448 to 453; Eden on Injunctions, 335 et seq.; Cooper, Eq. Pl. 45 to 50; 1 Montague Pl. in Eq. 232; 2 Montag. Pl. in Eq. 380, 382, note, X, P; Vin. Abr., Enterpleader, L, M, N.; Bac. Abr. Bailm. D.

established; or, at all events, until one party, after notice, has refused to proceed,[1] so as to decide in a fit suit the title to the property.

§ 114. Another inquiry may be, What is the duty of a depositary in cases, where there has been a joint bailment to him? Generally speaking, he is not bound to redeliver the deposit, without the consent of all the parties to the bailment.[2] But this rule applies in strictness to those cases only, where the bailment has been joint; and not where the interest in the deposit is joint, but there has been a delivery by one of the joint owners, without any consent or privity of the other owners.[3] And there may also be a joint deposit, where a several delivery to each person of his share is expressly provided for in the original contract; and in such a case, a several action will accrue to each owner upon a demand of his own share.[4] If the property deposited belongs jointly to the depositor and depositary, this, as we have seen, in no respect varies the ordinary obligations of law, as to the care, which he is bound to take of it.[5] But in cases of joint deposit, where there are many owners, and the depositary is one, it seems, that if either of the other owners gets the deposit out of his possession against his will, he is remediless; for it has been decided, that in such a case he cannot recover back the deposit, although the delivery is upon a special trust for all the owners, and although he has

---

[1] 1 Domat, B. 1, tit. 7, § 1, n. 5, 6; Pothier, Traité de Dépôt, ch. 2, § 1, art. 2, § 4, n. 59; Ayliffe's Pand. B. 1, tit. 7, p. 519, 520; Cod. Civ. art. 1937, 1944; Ersk. Inst. B. 3, tit. 1, § 27.

[2] 2 Kent Com. 442, 443.

[3] *May* v. *Harvey*, 13 East. R. 197. See Roll. Abr. Enterpleader E; Brook. Abr. Bailm. pl. 4.

[4] Dig. Lib. 16, tit. 3, l. 1, § 44.

[5] Jones's Bailm. 82, 83.

given a bond for the safe custody of it.[1]   If this decision be correct, it is full of hardship and inconvenience.
It is full of hardship ; for it takes away from the depositary the means of preserving his exclusive possession
and safe custody ; and yet does not seem to exonerate
him from responsibility for such safe custody under his
bond. It is full of inconvenience; for it disables joint owners, in case of any personal distrust, from protecting their
several rights by a mutual deposit, for the benefit of all,
in the custody of one, enjoying the respect and confidence of all.   It enables one owner, in violation of his
contract, by fraud or stratagem, to put at hazard the
joint property, or even to apply it to purposes wholly
against the objects, for which it is held.   It deserves
consideration, whether in such a case the bailee, in
virtue of his special undertaking, might not fairly be
held to have a special interest, or property, or lien
in the thing, as an indemnity against his responsibility
upon his bond, in virtue of an implied contract to this
effect, evidenced by the very nature of the deposit.

§ 115. The civil law provided, that in cases of joint
deposits, restitution should be to all together, and not
to one or more of the joint owners.   This rule applied
with more force and strictness, where the thing was in-
divisible, or was deposited as one thing, than where it
was severable, or composed of different parcels.   However, if the thing were divisible, as a sum of money,
and the parties were agreed as to their shares, the depositary might divide it, and each was at liberty to receive his own.   And so in case of a joint deposit the
depositary was discharged by a delivery to any one, if
such was the special agreement of the parties at the

---

1 *Holliday* v. *Camsell*, 1 T. Rep. 658.

time of the deposit.[1]   The same general rule, as to the
necessity of joint restitution, was applied to the case of
co-heirs, where the depositor died.[2]   However, it would
seem, that the depositary might, if the thing were divisible, deliver the share of each heir to him personally ;
and in case of an insolvency of the depositary before
all the heirs had received their shares, the heir, who had
received his, would not be bound to contribution for the
loss of his co-heirs.[3]

If any dispute arose as to the shares, or title of the
co-heirs, the depositary was not bound to deliver up
the property without security, or until the title was
judicially ascertained.[4]   The old French law closely
followed the substance of these provisions ;[5] and they
stand incorporated into the present civil code of that
kingdom.[6]   If a deposit is bequeathed as a legacy, after
the assent of the executor to it, it may be delivered
over to the legatee; and after such assent, it is held to
the use of the legatee, though not before.[7]

§ 116.   Where there are two or more joint depositaries, they are each liable for the restitution of the whole
deposit.   And consequently each in effect becomes a
guarantor against the fraud and gross negligence of
the other.   Domat so understands the civil law ;[8] but

---

[1] 1 Domat, B. 1, tit. 7, § 3, n. 11, 12, 13; Dig. Lib. 16, tit. 3, 1. 1,
§ 36, 1. 14, — 1. 1, § 44.

[2] Id.

[3] 1 Domat, B. 1, tit. 7, § 3, n. 12; Dig. Lib. 16, tit. 3, 1. 14 ; Cod. Lib.
4, tit. 4, 1. 12.

[4] 1 Domat, B. 1, tit. 7, § 3, n. 11 ; Dig. Lib. 16, tit. 3, 1. 1, § 36.

[5] Pothier, Traité de Dépôt, ch. 2, § 1, art. 2, § 2, n. 54 ; Id. art. 3, n. 62.

[6] Cod. Civ. art. 1939.

[7] Pothier, Traité de Dépôt, ch. 2, § 1, art. 2, § 1, n. 55 ; Toller's Ex'rs,
B. 3, ch. 4, § 2.

[8] 1 Domat, B. 1, tit. 7, § 1, n. 14; Dig. Lib. 16, tit. 3, 1. 1, § 43.

Pothier thinks, that an exception lies in favour of the depositary, who is not guilty of fraud, at least when he has
not actually bound himself for the good conduct of the
other.[1]

§ 117. The next inquiry is, as to the place where
restitution is to be made. If a particular place is agreed
on between the parties, that of course is to regulate the
matter. If no place is agreed on, the property ought to
be restored in the place, where it is, or ought to be kept.
If it is fraudulently or improperly removed to another
place, the depositor is not bound to receive it there.[2]
On the other hand, the depositor cannot demand it at
an improper place, nor the depositary insist upon its
being received at such place. It is difficult to lay down
any general rule, as to the place of restitution, other
than, that ordinarily it may be at the place of deposit.[3]
If the deposit is of a nature to be kept at the domicil of
the depositary, that will ordinarily be the place, where
it is to be restored, even when his domicil has been
changed. But this, and indeed every other rule on the
subject, must admit of exceptions. Much must depend
upon circumstances, and the presumed intention of the
parties. It cannot, for instance, be presumed, that a
depositor could intend, that if the depositary removed
to another country, he should carry the deposit with
him.

§ 118. Whenever by the contract it was agreed, that
the deposit should be restored in any one of several
places, the civil law gave to the depositary the choice

---

1 Pothier, Traité de Dépôt, ch. 2, § 1, art. 3, p. 64.
2 Pothier, Traité de Dépôt, ch. 2, § 1, art. 2, § 3 ; Dig. Lib. 16, tit. 3,
l. 12, § 1 ; 1 Domat, B. 1, tit. 7, § 3, n. 8.
3 Cod. Civ. art. 1942, 1943.

of the place.[1] In our law it would depend upon the
particular structure of the agreement, or the presumed
intention of the parties deducible from all the circumstances of the case.   If the agreement did not expressly
give the choice of place to the depositor, the natural inference would be, that the choice was given to the depositary, as the law would not incline to impose a burthen
upon him, when his undertaking was wholly gratuitous.

§ 119. It is also laid down in the civil law, that if a
deposit is made to be restored at a future time, it may
immediately be demanded back by the depositor; for
as the depositary has no interest in the custody, he
can have no right to retain the thing against the will of
the depositor.   " Si sic deposuero apud te, ut post
mortem tuam reddas — possum mutare voluntatem,
et ante mortem tuam depositum repetere."[2]   This
rule seems not unreasonable in ordinary cases, and is
adopted into the French law.[3]   How far it would be
adopted into our law may admit of doubt ; for the general tendency of our law is to act upon the contracts
of parties, exactly as they have made them.   And
though cases may easily be imagined, in which the detainer might be deemed wholly inexcusable in point of
justice and reason ; yet other cases may be put, in
which the time might be very important as an inducement for the depositary to receive the deposit.

§ 120. There are certain other cases put in the
foreign law, which may constitute an excuse, or an
exception to the obligation of the depositary to deliver
the deposit when demanded.   If, for instance, the de-

---

1 1 Domat, B. 1, tit 7, § 3, n. 11 ; Dig. Lib. 16, tit. 3, l. 5, § 1.

2 Dig. Lib. 16, tit. 3, l. 1, § 45 ; Domat, B. 1, tit. 7, § 1, n. 7.

3 Pothier, Traité de Dépôt, ch. 2, § 1, art. 2, § 4, n. 58 ; Cod. Civ. art.
1944.

positary has it not at the place, where it is demanded,
Pothier seems to think, that time ought to be allowed
him, even though he is bound to deliver it there.[1]
Doubtless also by our law the demand must be made
at a reasonable time; and a reasonable time must be
allowed to redeliver the property. Another case of
exception or excuse is, where the property is arrested or attached; and this applies as well to our
law, as to the French.[2] If the property is lawfully
taken from the possession of the depositary by process
of law, without negligence on his part, as if taken in
execution, as the property of the bailor, the depositary
will be excused. So, if it is recovered from him by one,
who possesses a paramount title; for he is only liable
for a loss by gross negligence; and he cannot help a
recovery by law against him.[3] Another case of exception or excuse is, where a party, as heir or executor,
demands the property. In such a case the depositary
is not bound to deliver it, until the party has proved his
title or character.[4] And this is also true in our law; for
the party must give reasonable proof of his title.

§ 121. The depositary is generally entitled to be
reimbursed all the necessary expenses, to which he has
been subjected for the preservation of the deposit.
And by the civil and French law he is entitled to a
lien for all such expenses upon the deposit.[5] He has
not, however, any right to detain it for any other debt,

---

[1] Pothier, Traité de Dépôt, ch. 2, § 1, art. 2, § 4, n. 59.

[2] Id. Cod. Civ. art. 1944.

[3] *Edson* v. *Weston*, 7 Cowen R. 278; *Shelbury* v. *Scotsford*, Yelv. R. 23.

[4] Pothier, Traité de Dépôt, ch. 2, § 1, art. 2, § 4, n. 59; Cod. Civ. 1944.

[5] Ayliffe's Pand. B. 4, tit. 17, p. 521, 522; Domat, B. 1, tit. 7, § 2, n. 1, 2, 3; Pothier, Traité de Dépôt, ch. 2, § 1, art. 2, § 4, n. 59, ch. 2, § 3, n. 69, 74; Cod. Civ. art. 1948.

or on any other account, than for such expenses.[1] The
civil and French law also give the depositary a right
of indemnity for all losses occasioned by the deposit.[2]
Whenever he has a lien, he may of course detain the
deposit, until the lien is fully discharged.

§ 122. If the depositary improperly refuses to redeliver the deposit, when it is demanded, he henceforth
holds it at his own peril. If, therefore, it is afterwards
lost either by his neglect, or by accident, it is the loss
of the depositary ; for he is answerable for all defaults
and risks in such cases.[3] It is said, indeed, in the
civil law, that if the thing afterwards perishes from its
own inherent defect without any accident, and it would
have perished, although it had been restored to the
depositor, such a loss, not being the effect of the delay,
is not at the risk of the depositary.[4] If such a case
can exist, and be made entirely certain, it must be a
case of a very rare and extraordinary nature ; and any
attempt to get rid of a loss on such a ground ought to
be watched with great suspicion. Our law has not as
yet recognised any such distinction ; and as the non-
delivery after such a demand is a tortious conversion,
it seems difficult to see, how it could be maintained.

§ 123. And not only is the depositary, who is in
default, (*in morâ,* as it is called in the civil law,) liable
for all losses ; but the civil law imposes upon him the
duty of paying interest, or other compensation for the
use of it.[5] And this is with great justice. Our law
would doubtless allow a like compensation in the shape

---

[1] Domat, B. 1, tit. 7, § 3, n. 14.

[2] Cod. Civ. art. 1948, 1949 ; Pothier, Traité de Dépôt, ch. 2, § 1, art.
3, § 2, n. 70.

[3] Jones's Bailm. 70 – 121 ; Dane's Abr. ch. 17, art. 14.

[4] Dig. Lib. 16, tit. 3, l. 12, § 3, l. 14, § 1.

[5] Ayliffe's Pand. B. 4, tit. 17, p. 523.

of damages, where the circumstances of the case should call for any thing more, than a simple indemnity for the direct loss.

§ 124. There are certain cases of deposits made by public officers, which deserve to be brought under notice, before this subject is concluded. By the local jurisprudence of some of the New England states, and particularly of the states of Massachusetts, New Hampshire, and Maine, personal property (as well as real estate) may be attached upon mesne process to respond the exigency of the writ, and satisfy the judgment. In such cases of attachment it is a common practice for the officer to bail the goods attached to some person, who is usually a friend of the debtor, upon an express or implied agreement on his part to have them forthcoming on demand, or in time to respond the judgment, when the execution thereon shall be issued.

§ 125. Upon bailments of this sort it may not be without use to consider, what are the rights and duties of the officer or bailor, and what are the rights and duties of the bailee, commonly called the receiptor. In the first place, as to the rights and duties of the officer. The officer making an attachment on process acquires a special property in the goods attached,[1] which continues, until the attachment is legally dissolved. If during this period his possession is violated, he may maintain all the usual remedies, such as trover, trespass, and replevin against the wrong-doer.[2] If upon

---

[1] *Ladd* v. *North*, 2 Mass. R. 514 ; *Perley* v. *Foster*, 9 Mass. R. 112 ; *Whittier* v. *Smith*, 11 Mass. R. 211 ; *Bowker* v. *Miller*, 6 Johns. R. 195.

[2] Ibid. and *Ludden* v. *Leavitt*, 9 Mass. R. 104 ; *Warren* v. *Leland*, 9 Mass. R. 265 ; *Gibbs* v. *Chase*, 10 Mass. R. 125 ; *Gates* v. *Gates*, 15 Mass. R. 310 ; *Brownell* v. *Manchester*, 1 Pick. R. 232 ; *Badlam* v. *Tucker*, 1 Pick. 389.

the attachment being made, the goods are delivered into the hands of any bailee for custody, without any specific time for the return, the officer has a right to demand the possession of them at any time, at his pleasure, even before any judgment or execution in the suit ;[1] and upon the bailee's refusal the officer may maintain a suit against him for the goods, and also for damages.[2] And if no actual attachment has taken place, but the bailee has accepted the bailment, as if the goods were attached, and waived the formality of an actual attachment, the officer, if he has made return upon his precept of an attachment of the goods, is entitled, as against the bailee, to all the rights, which he would have possessed by an actual attachment.[3]

§ 126. The right of the officer to have restitution of the goods against his bailee is not affected by the fact, that the judgment in the suit, on which the attachment has been made, is satisfied by the debtor, if the officer still remains liable to the debtor for the goods, or to any subsequent attaching creditor.[4] But in case the officer is discharged from all liability over to any person, his right to maintain an action is gone, and the bailee will be discharged from his obligation to the officer.[5]

§ 127. If the bailee has actually delivered over the goods to the debtor, the officer may, at any time during the continuance of the attachment, retake them from

---

[1] *Phillips* v. *Bridge*, 11 Mass. R. 242.   [2] Ibid.

[3] *Jewett* v. *Torrey*, 11 Mass. R. 219 ; *Lyman* v. *Lyman*, 11 Mass. R. 317 ; *Bridge* v. *Wyman*, 14 Mass. R. 190.

[4] *Jenney* v. *Rodman*, 16 Mass. R. 464 ; *Whittier* v. *Smith*, 11 Mass. R. 211 ; *Knap* v. *Sprague*, 9 Mass. R. 258 ; *Jewett* v. *Torrey*, 11 Mass. R. 219.

[5] *Lyman* v. *Lyman*, 11 Mass. R. 317 ; *Jenney* v. *Rodman*, 16 Mass. R. 464.

the possession of the debtor; for his special property continues, notwithstanding such bailment and delivery over.[1]

§ 128. The officer, who has made an attachment upon goods, is considered as having the custody thereof as long as the attachment continues; and if he delivers them over to the bailee or to the debtor, and a loss ensues, he will be liable to the creditor, and the loss of the property is at his own peril.[2]

§ 129. The creditor in the suit has no property or interest whatsoever in the goods attached; and can maintain no action for any wrong or injury done to them by any person, who takes them or injures them, while in possession of the officer. His sole remedy is against the officer.[3] The officer is not bound to deliver up the goods to the creditor, who has obtained judgment and execution, that they may be levied on by another officer; for he is still accountable to the debtor for them.[4] And, notwithstanding any delivery of the goods to a bailee, the officer may attach them upon any subsequent process coming into his hands, while they remain in the hands of his bailee, and the bailee will be responsible for the goods; and it will furnish no defence to him, that he has subsequently delivered them up to the debtor.[5]

§ 130. The officer, then, being responsible over to the debtor for a due redelivery of the property at-

---

1 Bond v. Padelford, 13 Mass. R. 394.

2 Phillips v. Bridge, 11 Mass. R. 242; Tyler v. Ulmer, 11 Mass. R. 163; Congdon v. Cooper, 15 Mass. R. 10.

3 Ladd v. North, 2 Mass. R. 514.

4 Blake v. Shaw, 7 Mass. R. 505; Badlam v. Tucker, 1 Pick. 389.

5 Whittier v. Smith, 11 Mass. R. 211; Knap v. Sprague, 9 Mass. R. 258; Jewett v. Torrey, 11 Mass. R. 219; Lyman v. Lyman, 11 Mass. R. 317.

tached, in case of the dissolution of the attachment, or
a satisfaction of the creditor's claim in any way whatsoever, it behoves him to take care, that he does not
put it in jeopardy by any act of his own. If it is lost
by his negligence, he will be responsible therefor.[1]
But what degree of negligence will make him responsible does not seem to have been directly decided.
He would doubtless be responsible for gross negligence
and fraud; but whether for ordinary negligence, does
not appear to have been decided by any adjudged
case;[2] though, as he is a bailee for compensation, it
may be thought, that he is bound by the common rule
in such cases to ordinary diligence.

§ 131. In cases of attachment of property a question has often arisen, how, and by whom the officer is
to be indemnified for the expenses of keeping the
property. If, for instance, by direction of the creditor,
he attaches cattle, who is to discharge the necessary
expenses of their maintenance ? There were formerly
many doubts on the subject. The rule, as now settled,
is, that the debtor, whose cattle are attached, is bound
at his own risk and peril to provide suitable food for
them, and if they perish through the want of it, it is
his exclusive loss.[3] But the officer is bound, if the
debtor neglects it, to provide suitable food ; and if he
does, and a recovery is had against the debtor, the
expenses are a charge upon the property in the officer's hands, and may be deducted by him from the
proceeds of the sale on execution.[4] If no recovery is
had in the suit against the debtor, then the officer is

---

1 See *Jenner* v. *Jolliffe*, 6 Johns. R. 9.
2 See *Burke* v. *Trevitt*, 1 Mason's R. 96, 100, 101, 102.
3 *Sewall* v. *Mattoon*, 9 Mass. R. 537.
4 *Tyler* v. *Ulmer*, 12 Mass. R. 163, 168.

entitled to be reimbursed by the creditor, who has
directed the attachment.[1] If the officer does not
provide suitable food, and by his neglect the cattle
perish, he will be liable to the creditor for their full
value.[2]

§ 132. In the next place, as to the rights and duties
of the bailee. His duties are sufficiently apparent
from what has been already stated under the preceding head. He is bound to keep the property, and to
return it on demand to the officer, and to take reasonable care of it, while in his custody. For any omission
of duty in any of these particulars he will be responsible to the officer. But his obligation to return the
property to the officer is not in all cases absolute. If
the attachment is dissolved, and no other person has any
just claim upon the property, he may, by a restitution
of it to the owner, discharge himself from his obligation to the officer; for in such a case the special property of the officer is gone.[3] And if the officer has
wrongfully attached the goods of a third person, as the
property of the debtor, and has bailed them, the bailee
may, by a delivery of them to the true owner, protect
himself; for by such redelivery, the officer will be discharged from any liability for the goods to the creditor,
and the debtor, and the real owner.[4]

§ 133. The bailee has no property in the goods, but
a mere naked custody.[5] And, therefore, it has been
held in Massachusetts, that he cannot maintain any
action for them against any one, who shall take them

---

1 *Phelps* v. *Campbell,* 1 Pick. R. 59, 61.
2 *Sewall* v. *Mattoon,* 9 Mass. R. 537.
3 *Whittier* v. *Smith,* 11 Mass. R. 211; *Cooper* v. *Mowry,* 16 Mass. R. 5.
4 *Learned* v. *Bryant,* 13 Mass. R. 224.
5 *Norton* v. *People,* 8 Cowen's R. 137.

out of his possession.[1] But it deserves consideration, whether his possession would not be a sufficient title against a mere wrong-doer; and whether this responsibility over to the officer does not furnish a just right for him to maintain an action for injuries, to which such responsibility attaches.[2] It has, on the other hand, been decided upon full consideration in New Hampshire, that the bailee of the officer has a sufficient property to maintain an action against a stranger for any dispossession or injury of the goods attached.[3] In the French law, in cases of seizure or attachment of goods, the bailee is deemed to possess only a naked custody. But this is true in that law also, as to the attaching officer himself, in which respect it differs from our law.[4] But assuming, that the bailee has only a naked custody in the goods, it is agreed, that the bailee may retake them from the custody of the debtor, to whom he has delivered them, although he could not maintain an action for the possession of them either against him or a third person.[5]

§ 134. The French law upon the subject of the rights and duties of officers, attaching property under judicial process, and their bailees, is entitled to the attention of every lawyer, who is ambitious of acquiring a rational view of the subject.[6] The general obligation in that law is understood to be for ordinary diligence on the part of the officer. But a detail of all

---

[1] *Ludden* v. *Leavitt*, 9 Mass. R. 104; *Warren* v. *Leland*, 9 Mass. R. 265; *Commonwealth* v. *Morse*, 14 Mass. R. 217.

[2] See §§ 93, 153, 266, 267; *Waterman* v. *Robinson*, 5 Mass. R. 503.

[3] *Poole* v. *Symonds*, 2 New Hamp. R. 289; *Odiorne* v. *Colby*, 2 New Hamp. R. 70.

[4] Pothier, Dépôt, n. 91, 92, 93, 99.

[5] *Bond* v. *Padelford*, 13 Mass. R. 394.

[6] Pothier, Dépôt, n. 91 to n. 98.

the rights and duties springing out of such attachments in that law would lead us too far into collateral inquiries.

§ 135. It has been said, that by an attachment the general property of the debtor is in abeyance and suspended.[1]   This proposition, however, is to be received with some qualifications.   The debtor, during the existence of the attachment, is doubtless barred of any right to recover the same against the officer.   But, subject to the lien of the attachment, he retains the right to the property, and may alienate the same ; and his vendee upon discharging the attachment, or satisfying the debt, will be entitled to receive the same from the person, in whose custody it is.[2]

§ 136. Here we finish the consideration of the subject of deposits; a title, which has employed the learning, and exercised the ingenuity, of some of the proudest names in the annals of jurisprudence.

---

[1] *Ladd* v. *North,* 2 Mass. R. 514 ; Domat, B. 1, tit. 7, § 4.
[2] See the reasoning in *Bigelow* v. *Wilson,* 1 Pick. R. 485 ; see also Pothier, Dépôt, n. 93.

CHAPTER III.

ON MANDATES.

§ 137. We come next to the consideration of the contract, which in the civil law is called *mandatum*, and which Sir William Jones, for want of a more appropriate English word, has not scrupled to call a *mandate*. We are accustomed, indeed, in common parlance, to use this word in the sense of a judicial command or precept, which, however, he deems only a secondary and inaccurate usage of it.[1] And he defines a mandate to be, a bailment of goods without reward, to be carried from place to place, or to have some act performed about them.[2] In this definition, he seems mainly to have followed that of Lord Holt, in *Coggs* v. *Bernard,*[3] whose language is, that it is a delivery of goods or chattels to somebody, who is to carry them, or to do some act about them gratis, without any reward for such work or carriage. Perhaps this is more properly an enumeration of the various sorts of mandates, than a strict definition of the contract. At least, it may be more simply stated to be, at the common law, a bailment of personal property, in regard to which the bailee engages to do some act without reward. The civil law has defined it thus: "Mandatum est contractus, quo quis negotium gerendum committit alicui gratis illud suscipienti animo invicem contrahendæ obligationis."[4] Wood defines it to

---

[1] Jones's Bailm. 52.   [2] Jones's Bailm. 117.

[3] 2 Ld. Ray. 909, 913.

[4] Pothier, Pand. Lib. 17, tit. 1 ; Dig. Lib. 17, tit. 1 ; Cod. Lib. 35 ; Inst. Lib. 3, tit. 27 ; Ayliffe's Pand. B. 4, tit. 10, p. 476.

be a contract of the law of nations, by which an affair
is committed to the management of another, and by him
undertaken to be performed gratuitously.[1] This is substantially the definition of Pothier, adding, only, that it
is to be done at the risk and in the place of the bailor,
and that the bailee is to render to him an account.[2] Dr.
Halifax says, " A mandate, or commission, is a contract,
by which a lawful business is committed to the management of another, and by him undertaken to be performed without reward."[3] The Code of France declares,
that a mandate, or procuration, is an act, by which one
gives to another a power of doing something for the
mandant, and in his name.[4] Heineccius gives a still
more concise definition, "Mandatum (a manûs datione
dictum,*) est contractus consensualis, bonæ fidei, quo
alteri negotium, gratis gerendum, committitur, et ab alte-
ro suscipitur."[5] In the choice of definitions, none
strikes my mind to be more neat and distinct, than that
of Mr. Chancellor Kent. "A mandate" (says he) "is
when one undertakes, without recompense, to do some
act for another in respect to the thing bailed."[6]

§ 138. But, not to dwell further upon mere definitions, the person employing is called, in the civil law,
mandans or *mandator ;* (and hence, in the Scotch law,
he is called *mandant ;*)[7] and the person employed is

---

1 Wood, Civ. Law, B. 3, ch. 5, p. 242.

2 Pothier, Traité de Mandat, art. prélim. 1.

3 Halifax, Analysis of the Civ. Law, 70.

4 Cod. Civ. B. 3, tit. 13, ch. 1, art. 1984 ; Merlin. Repert. Mandat.
§ 1, art. prélim.

5 Hein. ad Pand. Pars 3, Lib. 17, § 230.   See Vinn. ad Inst. p. 684 ;
Partidas, B. 5, tit. 12, l. 20, &c. ; 1 Bell's Com. 259.

6 2 Kent Com. 443.   7 Ersk. Inst. B. 3, tit. 3, § 31.

* Noodt gives a similar derivation. See also Pothier, Contrat de
Mandat, art. prélim. ; Ayliffe's Pand. B. 4, tit. 10, p. 476.

called *mandatarius.* I shall not scruple to call the former, for want of a more appropriate word, the *mandator*;[1] and usage has already sanctioned the propriety
of calling the latter the mandatary.[2] *

§ 139. From the language of Dr. Halifax, it would
seem, that he supposed, that the contract of mandate
was not recognised in the common law. His words
are, "In the laws of England, the contract of mandatum is of no use;"[3] in which assertion he is under an
entire mistake. The common law may not, and, indeed, does not comprehend, under that appellation, all
the contracts of mandate according to the civil law.
But for the most part, the principles, applicable to all
the various classes of mandates, have a place in each
law, though they may be differently arranged, and may
have acquired a different appellation.

§ 140. The contract of mandate seems so nearly al-
lied to that of deposit, that it may properly be deemed
to belong to the same class. The great distinction between them is said to be this, that the former (at least
in one of its principal divisions) lies in *fesance,* and the
latter simply in *custody.*[4] Philosophically, or even technically speaking, it may be doubted, whether this distinction really exists. In cases of deposit, something
almost always remains to be done, besides a mere pas-

---

[1] 1 Brown, Civ. Law, 382; Halifax, Anal. Civ. Law, 70.
[2] Jones's Bailm. 53.
[3] Halifax, Anal. Civ. Law, 70, §§ 18, 19.
[4] Jones's Bailm. 53.

* In the French law, the former is called Le Mandant, the latter
Le Mandataire, or Procureur. Pothier, Traité de Mandat Art. prél.
Dr. Halifax calls the former Mandator, the latter Mandatee. I should
have followed him, if Mandatary had not been already naturalized.[1]

[1] Halifax, Analys. of Civ. Law, 70, §§ 16, 17.

sive custody. If the deposit is perishable, labour must be performed to keep it in proper order. If it is a living animal, as a horse, suitable food and exercise must be given to it. And these may properly be said to lie in fesance. In the next place, in mandates there is commonly custody; the possession of the thing being generally indispensable to the performance of the act intended by the parties. So, that in each contract there is custody, and labour, and service to be performed. The true distinction between them is, that in the case of a deposit, the principal object of the parties is the custody of the thing, and the service and labour are merely accessorial; in the case of a mandate, the labour and services are the principal objects of the parties, and the thing is merely accessorial. The distribution of the subject into different heads may, on this account, not be unjustifiable; and it is certainly convenient.

§ 141. The contract of mandate in our law is (as the definition imports) confined to mere personal property; and does not embrace, as it does in the civil law, real property. In general, the civil law makes few distinctions of rights, and duties, and remedies between the one species of property and the other. In our law the distinctions are very broad and important in all these respects. There is certainly no repugnance to any principles of our law in considering a gratuitous contract, to do an act in respect to real property, to be a mandate. It may involve obligations precisely the same, as it would in relation to personal property. But the definition of Sir William Jones, above stated, as well as the description of this sort of bailment by Lord Holt in *Coggs* v. *Bernard*, in which he constantly speaks of goods and chattels,[1] abundantly shows the habit of our law to be, to confine bailments to personal property. In the civil law a gratuitous engagement to clear out a ditch, or to cultivate or sell a farm of the person giving the direction, would be deemed a mandate.[2] In our law it would be treated merely as a special undertaking, without falling under that class of contracts.

§ 142. In the civil law the contract of mandate may also intervene, although there is no delivery of property by the mandator. Thus, all cases of gratuitous agency or procuration give rise to the obligations of a mandate in the civil law. As if A requests B to purchase a farm for him, or to buy stock, or to build a boat, or to write a deed or other instrument, without any recompense, express or implied, it will be deemed a mandate.[3] In our law we should treat it as a case of agency, and not of bailment. The obligations in point of law may, in many respects, be the same; but the classification would be different.

§ 143. It has been observed, according to known distinctions in the foreign and civil law, that the contract of mandate is one of the law of nations, (that is, one arising from the law of nature, common to nations,) that it is founded upon mere consent, express or implied; that it is a contract of mere kindness and beneficence; and that it belongs to the class called synallagmatical;

---

[1] 2 Ld. Raym. 909, 913, 918. See also Jones's Bailm. 1, 117; Bac. Abr. Bailment.

[2] 1 Pothier, Pand. Lib. 17, tit. 1, P. 1. art. 1, §§ 3, 4, 5; Dig. Lib. 17, tit. 1, l. 2; 1 Brown, Civ. Law, 381.

[3] 1 Domat, B. 1, tit. 15, § 1; Wood, Civ. Law, 242; 1 Pothier, Pand. Lib. 17, tit. 1, P. 1, § 1, art. 1, §§ 3, 5; Pothier, Contrat de Mandat, ch. 1, n. 1, 6, 7; Gaius's Institutes, Lib. 3, §§ 155–161; 1 Brown, Civ. Law, 321; Ayliffe's Pand. B. 4, tit. 10, p. 476.

that is, involving mutual and reciprocal obligations.[1]
But these distinctions are not material to be considered
in our law.

§ 144. From the very terms of the definition, three
things are necessary to create a mandate. First, that
there should exist something, which should be the
matter of the contract, "ut sit negotium, quod gerendum alter committat, alter suscipiat." Secondly, that
it should be to be done gratuitously; and thirdly, that
the parties should voluntarily intend to enter into the
contract.[2]

§ 145. In the first place, as to the matter of the contract. It must respect an act to be done *in futuro,*
and not one already complete, *ut sit gerendum, non jam
gestum.* Thus, it is said, that if A requests B to lend
C at his (A's) risk, a sum of money, and he lends it
accordingly, it is properly a mandate, and A is responsible accordingly. But if, unknown to A, B has already
lent C the sum, there the contract does not arise. So
says the civil law: "Si post creditam pecuniam mandavero creditori credendam, nullum esse mandatum."[3]
And the civil law would also class under the head of
mandate, a request from a third person to a creditor to
give time to his debtor at the risk of the mandator.[4]

§ 146. It must also respect some certain thing; for
if the thing be wholly uncertain, it is impossible, that
any contract can arise. The very vagueness of it

---

1 Pothier, Mandat, ch. 1, § 1, art. 1, 2, 3, 4, 5; Vinn. ad Inst. de
Mandat, Lib. 3, tit. 27.

2 Pothier, Pand. Lib. 17, tit. 1, p. 1, § 1; Pothier, Contrat de Mandat, ch. 1, § 2.

3 Pothier, Contrat de Mandat, ch. 1, § 2, art. 1, § 1, n. 6; Dig. Lib.
17, l. 12, § 14.

4 Pothier, Contrat de Mandat, ch. 1, § 2, art. 1, n. 6; Dig. Lib. 17,
l. 12, 14.

prevents the law from acting upon it. Thus, in the civil law, an example of a void mandate would be, where A charged B to buy something for him on a particular evening, or at a particular fair. There, as it is wholly uncertain what he is to buy, no contract arises.[1] An example in our law would be, where A requested B to take something for him to carry to C, and nothing was ever delivered, or designated to B to be carried.

§ 147. It must also be an act of a nature, that it may properly be deemed the act of the mandator, through the instrumentality of the mandatary, or his agent, according to the maxim, *qui mandat, ipse fecisse videtur.* Thus, if A directs B to take upon hire a sum of money from his bankers belonging to A, and B receives it, it is plain, that it is not a mandate, but a hiring; for A cannot lend to himself. This case may seem too clear for controversy; but the civil law has thought it important enough for a place in its text. "Si quis Titio mandaverit, ut ab actoribus suis mutuam pecuniam acciperet, mandati eum non acturum." [2]

§ 148. So the act to be done must be of a nature capable of being done, and not vain or absurd. A cannot create a contract of mandate with B by requesting B to buy for him his (A's) goods, for A cannot buy of himself; nor B's goods, for B cannot buy of himself. But if the act be possible, the contract may arise, although the mandatory may not have the proper skill or power to perform it well; for there is no absurdity in his undertaking it.[3]

---

1 Pothier, Contrat de Mandat, ch. 1, § 2, art. 1, n. 3.

2 Pothier, Contrat de Mandat, ch. 1, § 2, art. 1, § 4, n. 10; Pothier, Pand. Lib. 17, tit. 1, P. 1, § 4, art. 1, § 3.

3 Pothier, Contrat de Mandat, ch. 1, § 2, art. 1, § 5, n. 13, 14; Pothier, Pand. Lib. 17, tit. 1. p. 1, § 1, art. 1, §§ 4, 10.

§ 149. If the thing to be done concerns only the interest of the mandatary, it is equally plain, that no contract arises. As if I direct A to invest his money in a particular fund; for it is but mere advice or recommendation. " Si tuâ tantum gratiâ tibi mandem, supervacuum est mandatum, et ob id nulla ex eo obligatio nascitur." But if it concerns the interest of the mandator, as well as the interest of the mandatary, or another, the contract may arise; for there is nothing inconsistent in such a case in the mandatary undertaking to act for the mandator in respect to his interest. Therefore, it is said, in the civil law, " Mandatum inter nos contrahitur, sive meâ tantum gratiâ tibi mandem, sive meâ et tuâ, sive tuâ et alienâ."[1]

§ 150. In general, a mandatary cannot be said to have any special property in the thing, unless he has incurred expenses about it, for which he has a lien. In this respect he stands in the same situation as a depositary. But although neither of them has a special property in the thing bailed, it does not follow, as we shall presently see, that they may not have an action for any tort done to the thing while in their possession, especially if they are liable over to the bailor in such a case.[2]

§ 151. But it may be asked, whether it is necessary, that the act to be done should be for the benefit of the mandator, or whether he must have a right or interest

---

[1] Pothier, Cantrat de Mandat, ch. 1, § 2, art. 1, § 6, n. 15; Id. § 7; Dig. Lib. 17, tit. 1, l. 2 ; Pothier, Pand. Lib. 17, tit. 1, P. 1, § 1, art. 1, §§ 5, 11, 12, 13 ; Wood, Civ. Law, 242 ; 1 Domat, B. 1, tit. 15, § 1, n. 10, 11, 12 ; Halifax, Analys. Civ. Law, 70.

[2] 1 Barn. & Ald. 59 ; 2 Ld. Raym. 909, 911 ; Pothier, Pand. Lib. 17, tit. 1, P. 2, § 2, 30. But see Jones's Bailm. 80 ; *Miles* v. *Cattle,* 1 Lloyd & Wellsby, 353; S. C. 6 Bing. R. 743. See also 2 Bing. R. 173 ; 2 Taunt. 302.

in the thing itself. The civil law has answered this in the negative. If the act to be done be at the request of the mandator for the benefit of a third person, and the mandator might himself become liable, if it were not done, then the mandatary would be chargeable upon his undertaking. But if the mandator acts simply as an agent in giving the mandate, and incurs no personal responsibility, it would be otherwise. Thus, by the civil law, the rule is, that no one can contract, except for his own interest, " Nemo stipulari potest, nisi quod suâ interest." But the same law says, " Si tibi mandavero, quod meâ non interest, veluti ut pro Seio intervenias, vel ut Titio credas, erit mihi tecum actio mandati." And Pothier understands this doctrine to rest on the distinction above suggested.[1]

§ 152. The common law has not generally been supposed to be different. And where a mandatary delivers goods to another person, and they receive an injury, for which the mandatary would be liable over to the owner, there does not seem to be any objection, upon principle, to his right to recover for his own indemnity. At least, there are analogous cases, which approach very near to this doctrine,[2] even if others should be thought to question it. The ground of the doctrine has been before alluded to. The general principle of the common law is, that possession with an assertion of right, and in many cases possession alone, is a sufficient title to enable the possessor to maintain a suit against a mere wrong-doer for any wrong or injury done to the

---

[1] Pothier, Contrat de Mandat, ch. 1, § 2, art. 1, § 7, n. 17; Dig. Lib. 17, l. 6, § 4; Wood, Civ. Law, 242; 1 Domat, Civ. Law, B. 1, tit. 15, § 1, n. 11, 12; Halifax, Analys. Civ. Law, 70; Ayliffe's Pand. B. 4. tit. 10, p. 477; Pothier, Pand. Lib. 17, tit. 1, p. 2, § 1, art. 2, § 30.

[2] Bac. Abr. Bailm. D; Id. Trover, C; 2 Kent Com. 456; *Rooth* v. *Wilson*, 1 Barn. & Ald. 59; 2 Ld. Ray. 909, 911.

thing. However, in *Miles* v. *Cattle*,[1] (which has been already cited in another place,) this rule seems not to have been deemed applicable to the case of a mandatary, who had disobeyed the direction, under which a parcel had been entrusted to him, and thereby had made himself personally responsible to the owner; first, because he had no special property in the parcel, which was delivered to him for a particular purpose, which he had disobeyed; and secondly, because, by that act, he had deprived the defendants of the intended hire for the carriage of the parcel. Whether this case can be distinguished in principle from other decisions, which have been made in cases of deposits and gratuitous loans;[2] and whether, if not so distinguishable, it stands upon more satisfactory reasoning, and better analogies of the law, deserves the consideration of those, who shall hereafter be called upon to administer this branch of the law.

§ 153. Secondly. The contract must be gratuitous. And this is of the very essence of the contract; for if any compensation is to be paid, it passes into another contract, that is to say, the contract of hire. "Mandatum nisi gratuitum, nullum est." And it matters not, in this particular, whether the compensation is express, or implied; whether it is certain, or uncertain in amount. If, however, there is a mere honorary payment, not as a compensation, but as a mark of respect and favour, this will leave it still a mandate. So says Ulpian: "Si remunerandi gratiâ honor intervenit, erit mandati ac-

---

1 1 Lloyd & Welsby R. 353; S. C. 6 Bing. R. 740, 743.

2 2 Saund. R. 47 *b.*, Williams's note; *Sutton* v. *Buck*, 2 Taunt. 302; *Armorie* v. *Delamarie*, 1 Str. R. 505; *Barton* v. *Hughes*, 2 Bing. R. 173; *Hurd* v. *West*, 7 Cowen R. 752.

tio."[1] Thus, if a client upon employing an advocate
in his cause, promises to give him *ex honore* a valuable
book, it does not change the contract from that of a
mandate to a hiring of services; for it is not understood between the parties, as a compensation for services.   In England, counsel are understood not to be at
liberty to make any charge for their services in argu-
ing a cause, or for advice; and they cannot recover in a
suit for such services.   The compensation, given to
them, is, therefore, deemed a gratuity, *quiddam honora-
rium.*   And their employment, in the civil law, would
be called a mandate.   But it is different in respect to
attorneys.   They are entitled to compensation, and
therefore are strictly engaged under a contract for
hire.

§ 154. But although a mandatary, as such, is not
entitled to any compensation for his services, his actual
disbursements and expenses about the thing may, nevertheless, be recoverable.   This is naturally implied in
the undertaking; because a gratuitous act would otherwise become a burthen.

§ 155. Thirdly.   There must be a voluntary intention on the part of both parties, to enter into the contract.   If there be any constraint or duress, any substantial mistake, any fraud or imposition, any miscon-
ception of the real intention on either side, the contract
does not arise.   Thus, in the civil law a mere recommendation, and so *bonâ fide* intended, cannot amount
to a mandate.   But care must be taken in using language, that a contract of mandate be not implied from
the purport of the expressions.   For, if the language

---

[1] Pothier, Contrat de Mandat, ch. 1, § 2, art. 3, n. 22, 23; Pothier,
Pand. Lib. 17, tit. 1, § 1, art. 2, § 15, 16; Dig. Lib. 17, tit. 1, l. 1, § 4,
l. 6; 1 Domat, B. 1, tit. 15, n. 1, 9; Ayliffe's Pand. B. 1, tit. 10, p. 477.

would naturally, even though unintentionally, create, on
the other side, a belief, that the party designed to raise
a contract of mandate, and not to give a mere recommendation; the civil law would deem it to be at the
risk of the party using it, and operating as an imposition upon the other party.[1]   But, with the exception
above stated, mere advice will not create the obligation
of a mandate, according to the known maxim, "Nemo
ex consilio obligatur."   However, if there is any fraud
intervening, there a right of action may arise for any
injury, although the contract of mandate may not strictly take effect.   The general rule of the civil law is,
"Consilii non fraudulenti nulla obligatio;" however in-
discreet the advice may be.   The exception is, where
there is fraud or bad faith; "Cæterum, si dolus et calliditas intercessit, de dolo actio competit."[2]

§ 156.   The common law would not treat these as
cases of mandates, but as cases of guaranty or fraudulent representation; and would administer a remedy
accordingly.

§ 157.   But the common law follows the civil law in
the other particulars, and would deem the contract of
mandate, properly so called, void, where there was a
substantial mistake, or fraud, or imposition, practised by
one party on the other.   So, if an article were left
without any express or implied assent of the mandatary
to perform the act.   A case affording a striking analogy, though not a mandate, has been decided.   A lent

---

1 Ayliffe's Pand. B. 4, tit. 10, p. 477, 478.
2 Pothier, Contrat de Mandat, ch. 1, § 2, art. 2, n. 18, 19, 20, 21; Dig.
Lib. 50, tit. 17, l. 47; Wood, Civ. Law, 243; 1 Domat, B. 1, tit. 15, § 1,
n. 13; 1 Pothier Pand. Lib. 17, tit. 1, § 1, art. 3, § 17, 18; Ayliffe's Pand.
B. 4, tit. 10, p. 477; *Clarke* v. *Russell,* 7 Cranch, 69.   See Fell on Guaranty, *passim.*

a picture to B, who wished to show it to C; B, without any communication with and unknown to C, sent the picture to C's house, where it was accidentally injured; it was held, that C was not liable for not keeping the picture safely, inasmuch as he had not voluntarily entered into any engagement to receive the picture.[1]

§ 158. Fourthly. In mandates, as in other species of contracts, it is indispensable, that the act to be done should be lawful and not against sound morals. This is a principle of universal justice, and is as fully recognised in the civil law, as in ours; "Rei turpis," (says the former,) "nullum mandatum est."[2] It matters not, whether it is against sound morals, or *malum in se*, or only against positive legislation, as *malum prohibitum*, though otherwise it might be licit. In all such cases the contract has no legal obligation. Thus, if a person is authorized by another to smuggle contraband goods belonging to the latter, it is a void mandate; and the party is neither bound to execute the commission, nor, if he does execute it, will he be entitled to recover the expenses incurred by him in the service. And no action will lie to compel the mandatary to account for such goods. In conscience there may be a moral obligation to restore the goods, and to account for the profits. But the law leaves the violaters of its precepts to their own remedies, and assists neither.[3] This is an example of a prohibition by positive law. But the rule is the same, if a person undertakes to carry poison for the purpose of poisoning another; or

---

[1] *Lethbridge* v. *Phillips*, 2 Stark. 544.

[2] 1 Pothier, Pand. Lib. 17, tit. 1, P. 1, § 1, art. 1, § 2; Dig. Lib. 17, tit. J, l. 3; Ayliffe's Pand. B. 4, tit. 10, p. 476, 477, 479.

[3] Pothier, Contrat de Mandat, ch. 1, § 2, art. 1, § 2, n. 7.

undertakes to do some act about goods for the purpose of having them used in a house of infamy.[1]

§ 159. But, suppose the case of an act lawful in itself, but not strictly lawful with reference to certain relations between the parties, or others. As, if a trustee authorizes another person to sell, or to carry away the goods of the *cestui que trust,* in violation of his trust, would a legal contract arise between the trustee and the mandatary? Pothier thinks, that in such a case the mandatary may properly refuse to execute the mandate. But if he does execute it, then it becomes a valid mandate to the extent of making him liable to account to the trustee. *A fortiori,* the mandator will not be permitted to set up its nullity in order to escape from the payment of the expenses of the mandatary. And Pothier distinguishes between those acts, which are positively forbidden by the law, or involve moral turpitude, and those acts, which the law forbids upon the policy of suppressing fraud.[2] In the common law the case would probably turn upon the question, whether it was an actual fraud, meditated by the parties to injure the *cestui que trust,* or only a constructive fraud, consistent with good faith, but inconsistent with the juridical policy, which governs in cases of trusts. In the latter case, at least, it might not be deemed utterly void, but only voidable at the election of the *cestui que trust.* If he ratified it, there would be no reason to consider it a mere nullity.

If the mandatary is ignorant of the illegality, he will of course be entitled to his action for an indemnity.[3]

---

[1] Ibid. Dig. Lib. 17, tit. 1, l. 12, § 11 ; 1 Pothier, Pand. Dig. Lib. 17, tit. 1, P. 1, § 1, art. 1, § 3.

[2] Pothier, Contrat de Mandat, ch. 1, § 2, art. 1, § 4, n. 11.

[3] 1 Pothier, Pand. Lib. 17, tit. 1, P. 1, § 1, art. 1, §§ 2, 4.

§ 160. Lastly. There is no particular form or manner of entering into the contract of mandate prescribed either by the common law, or by the civil law, in order to give it validity. It may be verbal, or in writing; it may be express, or implied; it may be in solemn form, or in any other manner.[1] The French law in certain cases requires it to be in writing; but this is matter of positive institution.[2] Our law has introduced no such positive restriction, though it has in many other cases of contract, by what is called the statute of frauds, required the solemnity of a writing to give them efficacy.

§ 161. The contract may be varied at the pleasure of the parties; it may be absolute or conditional; general or special; temporary or permanent.[3] In the sense of the civil and foreign law, a power of attorney to do any act or acts is a mandate or procuration, and is governed by the principles applicable to such a contract.[4] But in the common law, as has been already intimated, such cases are treated as cases of naked agency.

§ 162. The next inquiry naturally arising is, between what parties the contract may take effect. The general answer is, between all parties, who are capable, and willing to enter into contracts generally. Married women and minors may doubtless become mandataries.

---

[1] 1 Pothier, Pand. Lib. 17, tit. 1, P. 1, § 2.

[2] Pothier, Contrat de Mandat, ch. 1, § 3, n. 28–36; Merlin. Repert. Mandat, § 1, art. 7.

[3] Wood, Civ. Law, 242; 1 Domat, B. 1, tit. 15, § 1, 6, 7, 8; Pothier, Contrat de Mandat, ch. 1, § 3, n. 34, 35, 36.

[4] Ibid. Pothier, Contrat de Mandat, ch. 1, § 3, n. 30, 31; Cod. Civ. B. 3, tit. 13, ch. 1, art. 1984; Ayliffe's Pand. B. 4, tit. 10, pp. 476–480; Merlin. Repert. Mandat, § 1, art. 8; Pothier, Pand. Lib. 17, tit. 1, P. 1, §§ 2, 19.

But inasmuch as they are not capable of entering into contracts to bind themselves to any responsibility, there may not be the same remedy against them in many cases, as there is in respect to persons possessing full capacity. Their acts, when done, may bind the mandator; but it does not follow, that they would be liable for an imperfect, or ill execution of the thing committed to their charge. Thus, a married woman or a minor may become a mandator; but the mandatary may not have any remedy over against them upon the implied obligations of the contract; though they may have a remedy over against him. The principles, however, which are applicable to this subject, turn upon the general rights and authorities of married women and minors in respect to contracts generally, and therefore do not require any particular enumeration in this place.[1]

§ 163. The next inquiry is, what are the obligations arising in point of law, on each side, from the contract of mandate, when made between competent parties.

And first, as to the mandatary. Pothier lays it down,[2] that the mandatary incurs three obligations; first, to do the act, which is the object of the mandate, and with which the party is charged; secondly, to bring to it all the care and diligence, which it requires; and thirdly, to render an account of his doings to the other party. The Code of France has given a positive sanction to the same obligations.[3] The doctrines of each are directly derived from the text of the civil

---

[1] Merlin. Repert. Mandat, § 1, art. 9.

[2] Pothier, Contrat de Mandat, ch. 2, n. 37; Merlin. Repert. Mandat, § 2; Pardessus Droit Comm. tom. 2, §§ 558 – 560.

[3] Cod. Civ. B. 3, tit. 13. art. 1991 et seq.

law.[1] It may be well to consider, how far these principles have been engrafted into the common law ; and
the limitations and qualifications, with which they are
received in each law.

§ 164. And here the first point, which meets us, is,
how far the mandatary is under an obligation to perform the act, which he has undertaken to do. The
general principle of the civil law certainly is, that
though a bailee is at liberty to reject a mandate, yet if
he chooses to accept it, he is bound to perform it
according to his engagement ; and if he fails so to do,
he will be liable for all damages sustained by the mandator by his neglect, in like manner as he would be
liable for any misfesance. The rule in the Digest is
thus laid down : "Sicut liberum est mandatum non
suscipere, ita susceptum consummare oportet ; si susceptum non impleverit, tenetur ; quod mandatum susceperit, tenetur etsi non gessissit."[2] Certain excuses,
however, for nonperformance were admissible in the
civil law ; such as ill health, and other just causes of
hindrance, among which were enumerated deadly en-
mities, (*capitales inimicitiæ*).[3] And if no loss or injury
was sustained by the mandator, or the mandatary re-
nounced it in a seasonable time to prevent injury, no
action lay.[4] "Mandati actio tunc competit, cum cœpit
interesse ejus qui mandavit. Cæterum, si nihil interest, cessat mandati actio, et eatinus competit, quate-
nus interest.[5] And if the neglect of the mandatary

1 1 Domat, B. 1, tit. 15, § 3, art. 1 et seq. ; Dig. Lib. 17, tit. 1, l. 5, l. 6,
l. 11, l. 22 ; Inst. Lib. 3, tit. 29, § 11.

2 Dig. Lib. 17, tit. 1, l. 5, l. 6, 1, l. 21, l. 11 ; Inst. Lib. 3, tit. 27,
l. 11 ; Pothier, Pand. Lib. 17, tit. 1, P. 2, § 1, art. 2, §§ 25, 26, 27, 28, 29.

3 Dig. Lib. 17, tit. 1, l. 23, 24, 25.

4 Ibid. tit. 1, l. 22, § 11, l. 27, § 2.

5 Ibid. tit. 1, l. 8, § 6.

were owing to the inability of the mandator to perform his implied obligations, as to furnish funds for the object, there the former was excused. " Iniquum est," (says the civil law,) " damnosum cuique esse officium suum."[1] The same rules governed in the old French law, as expounded by Domat and Pothier;[2] and they are now substantially incorporated into the modern Code of France. The Scotch law also recognises them in their full extent.[3]

§ 165. Sir William Jones has strenuously contended, that the same doctrine substantially belongs to the common law. He admits, indeed, what cannot be denied, that in the common law there is a clear distinction between cases of nonfesance and misfesance. In cases of nonfesance the mandatary is not generally liable, because his undertaking, being gratuitous, there is no consideration to support it, and it becomes a *nude pact ;* and the rule is, *Ex nudo pacto non oritur actio.* But in cases of actual misfesance, the common law gives a remedy for the injury done, and to the extent of that injury. But while he admits this distinction, and its consequences to be well settled, he contends, that the rule, as to nonfesance, applies only, where no special damage or injury accrues to the mandator; and that in cases of such special damage or injury an action will lie.[5]

§ 166. But this doctrine of Sir William Jones, however rational and equitable it may seem to be upon the

---

1 Pothier, Contrat de Mandat, ch. 2, art. 1, n. 41.

2 Domat, B. 1, tit. 15, §§ 3, 1, 12, §§ 4, 3, 4, 5; Pothier, Contrat de Mandat, ch. 2, art. 1, n. 38, &c.

3 Code of France, art. 1991 – 1997.

4 Erskine's Inst. B. 3, tit. 3, §§ 35, 40.

5 Jones's Bailm. 53, 57, 61, 120.

ground stated by the great Roman lawyer Paulus,
" Adjuvari quippe nos, non decipi, beneficio oportet ; " [1]
and however reprehensible it may be in morals to
break a deliberate promise of this sort, it cannot be
affirmed to constitute an actual element in the common law. The early cases in the Year Books, which
have been commented upon by Sir William Jones with
much ingenuity, and by Mr. Chief Justice Kent with
admirable fulness and accuracy, may not be thought
entirely satisfactory or conclusive upon the point. But
the modern cases of *Elsee* v. *Gatward* (5 T. R. 143)
in England, and of *Thorne* v. *Deas* (4 Johns. R. 84)
in America, which were very deliberately argued and
considered, appear to conclude the question, so far as
judicial reasoning goes, in both countries.[2] Mr. Chancellor Kent, in his Commentaries, upon a very full
review, has given the doctrine of these cases his entire approbation.[3] If the question were now open for
controversy, it might not be uninstructive to examine
the decisions at large, and the reasoning, by which
they are supported. But, it is believed, that the
authorities already referred to, contain all, that is material ; and it would be a waste of time to subject
them to a critical analysis, for purposes of mere speculative argument.

§ 167. The grounds, upon which this doctrine of
the common law is founded, have often been matters
of inquiry by ingenuous minds. There is so much
apparent equity in allowing compensation for injuries

---

[1] Jones's Bailm. 57 ; Dig. Lib. 13, tit. 6, 1. 17, 3.

[2] See also *Coggs* v. *Bernard*, 2 Ld. Raym. 909, 919, 920; *Rutgers* v.
Lucet, 2 Johns. Cas. 92; Doct. & Stud. Dial. 2, ch. 24, p. 210; *Wilkinson* v. *Coverdale*, 1 Esp. R. 74.

[3] 2 Kent Com. 443, 444.

resulting from a misplaced confidence in others, that it is not easily reconcilable with a sense of justice, to allow, that the contrary rule ought to prevail. Besides, there is an artificial refinement in the distinction between nonfesance and misfesance, which seems to be a little unphilosophical, and not quite agreeable to the dictates of common sense.

§ 168. It is not easy in all cases to give satisfactory reasons for doctrines, which are, nevertheless, firmly established in the jurisprudence of many countries. In some instances those doctrines were probably founded in accidental or temporary reasons; in others upon false theories; and in others again upon what may fairly be deemed a mere measuring cast of conflicting opinions. But whenever a doctrine is established in either way, it cannot, upon the theory of our judicial institutions, be broken in upon, without disturbing the certainty, as well as the harmony of the law. Perhaps it would have been better, if the distinction alluded to had never been recognised; and the broad principle of the Roman code, to give a remedy in cases of special damage, had been universally proclaimed.[1] It is not, however, difficult to perceive some of the reasons, upon which the common law has stopped at its present point, as that law generally aims more at practical good, than mere theoretical consistency.

§ 169. There are many rights and duties of moral obligation, which the common law does not even attempt to enforce. It deems them of imperfect obligation, and therefore leaves them to the conscience of the individual. And in a practical sense there is wisdom

---

[1] See Kent C. J. in 4 Johns. R. 84.

in this course; for judicial tribunals would otherwise be overwhelmed with litigation, or become scenes of the sharpest conflict upon questions of casuistry and conscience. It is a fundamental principle of the common law, that a valuable consideration is necessary to support every parol contract; and the importance of such a consideration is never lost sight of, except in solemn instruments under seal. A gratuitous contract, not under seal, is therefore absolutely void.[1] It has no legal existence or power. Now, a mandate is precisely a contract of this nature. What reason is there for excepting this particular class of contracts out of the general rule, any more than many or even all others? It may not involve more of good faith or confidence than many others. We must then either dispense with the general rule, or with exceptions, or draw an arbitrary line between them. The common law has adopted the former course, as the wisest and safest, both in principle and application. The rule being once known and established, there cannot be any real ground of complaint on the part of the mandator. He knew, or might have known, (and his ignorance of the law cannot constitute any better excuse in this, than in other cases,) that the contract was a nullity. It was his own folly or rashness to confide in it. If he trusted to it, he took the risk of non-fulfilment upon himself, and he has no right to complain, that he has suffered by that risk, which has been the result of his own overweening confidence.

§ 170. In regard to the distinction between nonfesance and misfesance, although it is nice, it may be

---

1 *Coggs* v. *Bernard*, 2 Ld. Raym. 909, 911, 919; *Elsee* v. *Gatward*, 5 T. R. 143; Doct. & Stud. Dial. 2, ch. 24, p. 210, 211.

accounted for in this way. The mandatary has his choice, to renounce the contract, or to perform it; to treat it as a nullity, or as a subsisting obligation.[1] If he choses to consider it in the latter light, and to act upon it as obligatory, why should he be permitted to separate the parts of the obligation, or to disjoin those, which were entered into as a whole? Besides, an injury accrues; and the mandator sues the other party for the wrong. The wrong is admitted, and the party sets up the contract in his defence. Ought the law to give him the benefit of the contract, as a subsisting obligation to protect him from being deemed a mere unauthorized wrong-doer; and yet, at the same time, to enable him to escape from its obligations, by proving, that he has violated the fundamental terms of that very contract? The common law has deemed it unreasonable, that he should have such an indulgence. It has left him free to act, or not to act; if he chooses to act, it is at his own peril. He is not at liberty to commit a tort, and then shift his defence upon the imperfect obligation of a contract, under which the tort was done. It is difficult to affirm, that there is any thing positively inequitable or unjust in this; and it is not inconsistent with the general rule, as to void pacts, that the common law should give a remedy for injuries occasioned by an unskilful or mischievous execution of the trust.

§ 171. Whether this reasoning is entirely satisfactory or not, it furnishes the key to the doctrine now under consideration; and if the result is thought to be inconvenient, it exclusively belongs to the legislative power to apply the proper remedy. It may, how-

---

[1] *Elsee* v. *Gatward*, 5 T. R. 143.

ever, be observed, that it is generally a favorite policy of the common law to prompt men to vigilance and care in their own concerns, and not to an over confidence in others. The maxim of *caveat emptor* rests on this foundation; and it has not hitherto been thought wrong in principle, or found inconvenient in practice.

§ 172. The same rule, which is applied by the common law to cases of malfesance, governs also cases of negligent execution of a gratuitous trust or agency. As, for instance, if a gratuitous agent undertakes to procure a policy of insurance, which is in his own name, to be renewed, and assigned to a party, who has become a purchaser of the property insured, and he proceeds to procure a renewal of the policy, but makes no assignment thereof, so that, upon a subsequent loss of the property, no recovery can be had by the purchaser, he will be responsible for the loss; although, if he had done nothing, he would have been exonerated from all responsibility.[1]

§ 173. 2. In the next place, what is the degree of care or diligence, which the mandatary is bound to apply in respect to the thing committed to his charge? It is not perhaps very easy to ascertain from the texts of the civil law, what was the degree of diligence exacted by that law in all cases of mandataries. The language in Ulpian's famous law is, that in mandates the party is liable for deceit and neglect, (*dolum et culpam mandatum*).[2] In other passages something more would seem to be required, and even a very

---

[1] *Wilkinson* v. *Coverdale*, 1 Esp. Rep. 7; Marsh. Insur. B. 1, ch. 8, § 2, p. 299.
[2] Dig. Lib. 50, tit. 17, 1. 23.

high degree of diligence. Thus, in the Code it is said, that a Procurator is liable for fraud, and every neglect (*dolum et omnem culpam.*)[1] The treatise of Sir William Jones abundantly shows, that civilians are not agreed among themselves as to the true interpretation of the Roman law on this point.[2] And Domat is manifestly perplexed in his own attempt to explain it.[3] Heineccius, one of the most exact of jurists, seems to adopt the conclusion, that, by the civil law, a mandatary is liable not only for deceit, but for neglect, although very slight. " Ut non solum dolum, sed et culpam, etiam levissimam, præstare debeat." [4] Pothier asserts the true principle to be, as well in the civil, as in the French law, that the mandatary is not only bound to good faith, but is also bound to bestow on the matter, with which he is charged, all the care and all the diligence, which the proper execution of it requires.[5] And he holds the mandatary liable, not merely for faults of commission, or misfesance, but also for faults of omission, or negligence. According to him every mandatary engages himself for every thing necessary to accomplish his undertaking ; and consequently for all the care and diligence required by it. " Spondet diligentiam et industriam negotio gerendo parem." If, therefore, the mandatary exerts himself to his utmost capacity ; and yet he has not sufficient to accomplish the undertaking, he is, according to Pothier, still responsible ; for he should not have engaged

---

1 Cod. Lib. 4, tit. 35, l. 13; Pothier, Pand. Lib. 17, tit. 1, P. 2, § 1, art. 1, §§ 2, 36.

2 Jones on Bailm. 14, &c.

3 1 Domat, Civ. Law, B. 1, tit. 15, § 3, n. 4, 5; see also Ayliffe, Pand. B. 4, tit. 10, p. 478.

4 Hein. Elem. Pand. Lib. 17, tit. 1, § 233.

5 Pothier, Contrat de Mandat, ch. 2, art. 2, n. 46.

in the undertaking.[1] Pothier does not, indeed, insist, that in all cases he shall exert the same care and diligence, that the most diligent and attentive men do. But he holds him liable even for the slightest neglect (*levissimâ culpâ*) in affairs requiring extraordinary diligence; and in affairs requiring only ordinary diligence for slight neglect, (*levi culpâ*.)[2] He allows indeed some indulgence, where the mandatary has been pressed into the service, because a competent person could not be found;[3] and he exempts the mandatary from all responsibility for losses from mere accidents and superior force, unless he has entered into some stipulation to the contrary.[4] And, on the other hand, the mandatary is at liberty to exempt himself from all responsibility, except for fraud, by an exceptive stipulation. The modern Code of France does not speak so definitely on this subject, as it might; but it seems silently to pursue the lead of Pothier.[5]

§ 174. Let us now proceed to the consideration of the manner, in which the common law has treated this subject. According to the general principles, which have been already stated, a mandatary, as the contract is wholly gratuitous, and for the benefit of the mandator, is bound only to slight diligence, and of course is responsible only for gross neglect. And this, it is conceived, is the doctrine of the common law, universally applied to mandates.

§ 175. Sir William Jones, however, has taken distinction, and maintained, that there is a difference of principle in respect to the two classes, into which he

---

1 Pothier, Contrat de Mandat, ch. 2, art. 2, n. 48.
2 Pothier, Id. n. 49. 3 Id. n. 49. 4 Id. n. 50.
5 Cod. Civ. B, 3, tit. 13, ch. 2, art. 1992; Merlin, Repert. Mandat, § 2, art. 3.

divides mandates; (1.) A mandate to do work about
goods ; (2.) A mandate to carry goods from place to
place.[1] In respect to the latter, he adopts, without
hesitation, the doctrine, that the party is bound only to
good faith, and slight diligence, and is responsible only
for gross neglect.[2] But in respect to the former, he
holds the mandatary, as engaging to use a degree of
diligence and attention adequate to the performance of
the undertaking. It may be well to give his reasoning
in his own words. "The great distinction then," (says
he,) "between one sort of mandate and a deposit is,
that the former lies in fesance, and the latter simply in
custody, whence, as we have already intimated,[3] a
difference often arises between the degrees of care
demanded in the one case and the other. For a mandatary being considered as having engaged himself to
use a degree of diligence and attention adequate to the
performance of his undertaking, the omission of such
diligence may be, according to the nature of the business, ordinary or slight neglect ; although a bailee of
this species ought regularly to be answerable only for
a violation of good faith. This is the common doctrine
taken from the law of Ulpian. But there seems in
reality to be no exception in the present case from the
general rule ; for since good faith itself obliges every
man to perform his actual engagements, it of course
obliges the mandatary to exert himself in proportion to
the exigence of the affair in hand ; and neither to do
any thing, how minute soever, by which his employer
may sustain damages, nor omit any thing, however
inconsiderable, which the nature of the act requires.

---

1 Jones's Bailm. 53, 62, 117, 120.
2 *Coggs* v. *Bernard*, 2 Ld. Raym. 909.   3 Jones's Bailm. 22.

Nor will a want of ability to perform the contract be any defence for the contracting party; for though the law exacts no impossible things; yet it may justly require, that every man should know his own strength, before he undertakes to do an act; and that, if he deludes another by false pretensions to skill, he shall be responsible for any injury, that may be occasioned by such delusion. If, indeed, an unskilful man yield to the pressing instances of his friend, who could not otherwise have his work performed, and engage reluctantly in the business, no higher degree of diligence can be demanded of him, than a fair exertion of his capacity."[1] And in other passages he enlarges on the same point.[2]

But, he adds, in another place, "a bailment without reward to carry from place to place is very different from a mandate to perform work. And there being nothing to take it out of the general rule, I cannot conceive, that the bailee is responsible for less than gross neglect, unless there be a special acceptance, &c. Every thing, therefore, that has been expounded in the preceding article concerning deposits, may be applied exactly to this sort of bailment, which may be considered as a subdivision of the second species."[3]

§ 176. If this distinction, taken by Sir William Jones, is clearly settled in the common law, it ought to be acquiesced in, even if the reasons, on which it is built, should not be thought entirely satisfactory. But the inquiry naturally presents itself, whether it is thus firmly established. Sir William Jones has cited no authority in support of it; and none has been found, in my researches, which directly recognises it.

---

[1] Jones's Bailm. 53.   [2] Ibid. 22, 61, 98, 120.
[3] Ibid. 62, 63.

§ 177. It is worthy of remark, that the whole reasoning of Sir William Jones on the point is exclusively
derived from the views taken of the civil law by the
able commentators already referred to. But they apply
it to all cases of mandates whatsoever, and by no
means limit it to cases, where work is to be performed.
So far as their authority goes, then, it repudiates the
distinction; and so far as their reasoning goes, it proceeds on a basis applicable to every species of mandate.[1] And, indeed, it is very difficult to perceive in
common sense or in legal principles any ground, upon
which the distinction can be maintained. A mandate
to carry a thing from one place to another may properly enough be deemed a mandate to perform work;
and it imports, just as much as a mandate to do work,
an engagement to perform the undertaking, and to
exercise due diligence and care about it. If A undertakes gratuitously to carry B's goods from one
place to another, does not good faith oblige him to
perform his undertaking, and to exert proper diligence
in proportion to the exigence of the affair? Does not
the bailor trust to his fidelity in performing it with as
much confidence, as when he undertakes to do work,
strictly speaking, upon the same goods? Why should
he not be under the same obligation to carry safely, as
to do the work well? When he undertakes to carry,
does he not, by necessary implication, engage, that he
has ability to do so, and that he will exercise all reasonable diligence to accomplish his undertaking? To
do work on goods is not, or may not be, more important, than to carry them to another place. To carry

---

[1] Pothier, Contrat de Mandat, ch. 2, art. 2, n. 46, 47, 48, 49; Partidas 5, tit. 12, l. 20 – 25.

jewels safely may be a far more valuable service, and require far more vigilance, than to clean the gold, which enchases them. The same reasoning, then, seems applicable to each class of mandates; and it is applied in the text of the civil and foreign law, from which it is borrowed, indiscriminately to all. Where the act to be done requires skill, and the party, who undertakes it, either has the skill, or professes to have it, there he may well be made responsible for the want of due skill, or for the neglect to exercise it. In such cases the undertaking may well be deemed a special undertaking to exercise due skill; and the omission of it imports, in all such cases, at least ordinary negligence; and in many cases, operating, as it must, as a fraud upon the party, may well be deemed gross negligence. But this class of cases stands, not as an exception from the general law, but as a qualification of it from the implied engagement of the mandatary. It is only deciding, that the parties may vary the responsibility implied by law by an express or implied contract for this purpose. Sir William Jones himself puts a case, which shows the propriety of admitting this doctrine; for he agrees, that if an unskilful man, who is known to be so, does the work at the solicitation of a friend, with such ability, as he possesses, he stands excused, although it is unskilfully done; for it is the mandator's own folly to trust to him, and the party engages for no more than a reasonable exertion of his capacity.[1] It is apparent, then, that the fact of skill or want of skill, as known or unknown to the bailor, or professed or not professed by the bailee, constitutes a material ingredient in construing the engagement; and qualifies, or enlarges it. In other terms, it varies the

---

1 Jones's Bailm. 53, 98.

17

presumption, as to the actual contract, according to the express or implied intention of the parties. It is not so much an exception from the common rule, as a waiver or limitation of it.

§ 178. If there be no authority in support of the distinction suggested by Sir William Jones, and none has been produced, let us next inquire, whether there are not authorities, which lead the other way. In the great case of *Coggs* v. *Bernard,* (2 Ld. Raym. 909,) where all the antecedent authorities were reviewed, and where Lord Holt expounds the nature and responsibility arising from every kind of bailment, no such distinction is hinted at. Yet that was the case of a mandate to carry goods; and Lord Holt says, this undertaking obliges the undertaker to diligent management. The reasons, he says, are, because in such a case, a neglect is a deceit to the bailor, who trusts the bailee upon his undertaking to be careful; and the latter puts a fraud upon the former by being negligent. And Lord Holt puts, by way of illustration of his doctrine, the case of a mandate of the other sort, namely, an action against a man, who had undertaken to keep one hundred sheep, and he was held liable for letting the sheep be drowned by his default. He afterwards puts the case of a carpenter, who unskilfully builds a house, without reward; and suggests no difference between that case and a mandate to carry.[1] From these considerations it may fairly be deduced, that as Lord Holt, in treating on the express point, suggests no such distinction, none was, in his judgment, furnished by the common law. Mr. Justice Gould in the same case said, "If a man takes upon him ex-

---

[1] 2 Ld. Raym. 909, 919, 920.

pressly to do such a fact [act] *safely* and *securely*, if the thing comes to any damage by his miscarriage, an action will lie. If it be only a general bailment, (that is, without such express undertaking,) the bailee will not be answerable without a gross neglect." [1] So that the difference he insists on, is between a special contract, and the general obligation implied by law, from the nature of the bailment.

§ 179. The case of *Moore* v. *Mourgue*, (Cowp. R. 480,) probably decided the very question under consideration, if that case was a gratuitous undertaking. There, an agent having written orders for the purpose, procured a policy of insurance to be made ; but in the policy there was an exception of a risk common in the policies of other offices, but not in those used by this office ; and the loss arose from that risk ; and the same premium was given in all the offices, without any increase on account of such risk. It was held by the Court, that the agent was not liable, as he had acted *bonâ fide*, and to the best of his judgment, and without gross negligence. There is, however, nothing on the face of the report, which absolutely settles it to have been a gratuitous undertaking, though the structure of the case would lead to that conclusion.

§ 180. But the case of *Shiells* v. *Blackburne* (1 H. Bl. 158) seems directly in point, against the distinction of Sir William Jones. There, a merchant had undertaken gratuitously to enter certain goods of the plaintiff at the custom-house, with his own goods of the like kind ; and by mistake he entered them by a wrong name, so that all the goods were seized and lost, both the plaintiff's and his own. An action was brought by the plaintiff to

---

[1] Ld. Raym. 909.

recover damages for this misfesance; and upon full
consideration the Court held, that as there was not
any gross negligence, the action would not lie. Now,
this was the very case of a mandate to do an act,
in contradistinction to one to carry goods. And
if the contract did, *per se,* imply an engagement to
use all the care and diligence, which were necessary
to the performance of the act, namely, to make a proper entry at the custom-house, and the bailee omitted
so to do, he ought to have been held liable, even if
there was not gross negligence. The Court, however, put the case upon the true ground of a general
mandate, where there is no special undertaking for
skill. Mr. Justice Heath there said, " the defendant
was not guilty either of gross negligence or fraud. He
acted *bonâ fide.* If a man applies to a surgeon to
attend him in a disorder for a reward, and the surgeon
treats him improperly, there is gross negligence, and
the surgeon is liable to an action. The surgeon would
also be liable for such negligence, if he undertook
gratis to attend a sick person, because his situation
implies skill in surgery. But if the patient applies to
a man of a different employment, or occupation, for his
gratuitous assistance, who either does not exert all his
skill, or administers improper remedies to the best of
his ability, such person is not liable. It would be attended with injurious consequences, if a gratuitous
undertaking of this sort should subject the person, who
made it, and who acted to the best of his knowledge, to
an action." Mr. Justice Wilson said, " where the undertaking is gratuitous, and the party has acted *bonâ
fide,* it is not consistent either with the spirit or the
policy of the law to make him liable to an action. A
wrong entry at the custom-house cannot be considered

as gross negligence, when, from the variety of laws &c., reliance must be placed on the clerks in the office." Lord Loughborough said, " I agree with Sir William Jones, that where a bailee undertakes to perform a gratuitous act, from which the bailor is alone to receive benefit, there the bailee is only liable for gross negligence. But if a man gratuitously undertakes to do a thing to the best of his skill, where his situation or profession is such as to imply skill, an omission of that skill is imputable to him as gross negligence.[1] If in this case a ship broker, or clerk in the custom-house, had undertaken to enter the goods, a wrong entry would in them be gross negligence, because their situation and employment necessarily imply a competent degree of knowledge in making such entries. But when an application under the circumstances of this case is made to a general merchant to make an entry at the custom-house, such a mistake as this is not to be imputed to him as gross negligence." So that the whole Court held, that a mandatary was not liable, except for gross negligence ; and that an express or implied warranty of skill was necessary, under such circumstances, to impute to him gross negligence.

§ 181. The doctrine of the case of *Shiells* v. *Blackburne* has never been impeached; and it is incidentally confirmed in other analogous cases.[2] So far as the American authorities have gone,[3] they appear to pro-

---

[1] See Jones's Bailm. 53, 34, 98.

[2] See *Neilson* v. *McIntosh*, 1 Stark. R. 237 ; *Rooth* v. *Wilson*, 1 Barn. & Ald. 59.

[3] *Stanton* v. *Bell*, 2 Hawk. N. C. Rep. 146 ; *Foster* v. *Essex Bank*, 17 Mass. R. 459 ; *Tracey* v. *Wood*, 3 Mason R. 132 ; *Tompkins* v. *Saltmarsh*, 14 Serg. & Rawle, 275.

ceed on the same principles, and to deem the mandatary, like the depositary, liable only for gross negligence.*

§ 182. Dr. Paley, in his treatise on Moral Philosophy, has, with his usual practical good sense, put the case of mandates upon a reasonable ground. " Whoever " (says he) " undertakes another man's business, makes it his own, that is, promises to employ upon it the same care, attention, and diligence, that he would do, if actually his own ; for he knows, that the business is committed to him with that expectation. And he promises no more than this." [1] According to Mr. Bell, the Scottish law makes the mandatary responsible only for his actual misfesances [intromissions], and for such diligence as he employs in his own affairs.[2]

§ 183. *Prima facie*, in cases of a general mandate, the fact, that the party did the work on the bailment with the same care, that he did the work on like goods of his own, would repel the imputation of any negligence.[3] But, without doubt, the presumption may be overcome by proofs of actual negligence,[4] or of conduct, which though applied to his own goods, as well as those bailed, would be deemed negligent in bailees without hire of ordinary prudence.[5]

§ 184. Sir William Jones has put a case, aptly illustrating the former position.[6] " If Stephen desire Philip to

---

1 Paley's Moral Phil. B. 3, P. 1, ch. 12.   2 1 Bell's Com. 481.
3 *Lane* v. *Cotton*, 2 Ld. Raym. 655 ; *Kettle* v. *Bromsall*, Willes 121.
4 *Rooth* v. *Wilson*, 1 B. & Ald. 59.
5 *Tracy* v. *Wood*, 3 Mason's R. 132 ; 1 Brown, Civ. Law, 383, note.
6 Jones's Bailm. 62.

* Mr. Chancellor Kent, in his Commentaries, has adopted the text of Sir William Jones on this subject. But the reasonableness of the distinction does not seem to have undergone any deliberate examination by his learned mind.

carry a diamond ring from Bristol to a person in London, and he put it with bank notes of his own into a letter case, out of which it is stolen at an inn, or seized by a robber on the road, Philip shall not be answerable for it, although a very careful, or perhaps a commonly prudent man would have kept it in his purse at the inn, and have concealed it somewhere in the carriage. But if he were to secrete his own notes with peculiar vigilance, and either leave the diamond in an open room, or wear it on his finger in the chaise, he would be bound, in case of a loss by stealth or robbery, to restore the value of it to Stephen." The case of a robbery may perhaps admit of some qualification; for if the robbery were by force, and if every thing found on Philip's person, including his purse, were stolen, then if the exposure of the ring did not afford any additional temptation, nor aid the loss, it might perhaps be thought, that the bailee out to be excused.[1]

§ 185. The other position is illustrated by a case, which has passed into actual judgment.[2] A undertook, gratuitously, to carry two parcels of doubloons for B, from New York to Boston, in a steam-boat, by the way of Providence. A, in the evening, (the boat being to sail early in the morning,) put both bags of doubloons, one being within the other, into his valise with money of his own, and carried it on board the steam-boat, and put it into a birth in an open cabin, although notice was given to him by the steward, that they would be safer in the bar-room of the boat. A went away in the evening and returned late, and slept in another cabin, leaving his valise, where he had put it. The next morning,

---

1 See 1 Brown, Civ. Law 383, note 73.
2 *Tracey* v. *Wood*, 3 Mason's R. 132.

just as the boat was leaving the wharf, he discovered, on opening his valise, that one bag was gone ; and he gave an immediate alarm, and run up from the cabin, leaving the valise open there with the remaining bag, his intention being to stop the boat. He was absent for a minute or two only, and on his return the other bag also was missing. An action being brought against him by the bailor for the loss of both bags, the question was left to the jury, whether there was not gross negligence, although the bailee's own money was in the same valise. The jury were directed to consider, whether the party used such diligence, as a gratuitous bailee ought to use under such circumstances. They found a verdict for the plaintiff for the first bag lost, and for the bailee for the second.

§ 186. It scarcely requires to be stated, that the degree of care, which a mandatary may be required to exert, must be materially affected by the nature and value of the goods, and their liability to loss or injury. That care and diligence, which would be sufficient as to goods of small value, or of slight temptation, might be wholly unfit for goods of great value, and very liable to loss and injury. In the former case the same acts might be deemed slight neglect only, which, in respect to the latter, might be justly deemed gross neglect. Illustrations of this rule have already been presented in another place. Lord Stowell in the case of *The Rendsberg*, (6 Rob. 142, 155) put a case in point. " If " (said he) " I send a servant with money to a banker, and he carries it with proper care, he would not be answerable for the loss, if his pocket were picked in the way. But if instead of carrying it in a proper manner, and with ordinary caution, he should carry it openly in his hand, thereby exposing valuable property, so as to invite the snatch of any person he might meet in the crowded population of this town, he would be liable, because he would be guilty of the *negligentia malitiosa*, in doing that, from which the law must infer, that he intended the event, which has actually taken place." Perhaps the best general test is to consider, whether the mandatary has omitted that care, which bailees without hire, or other mandataries of common prudence, are accustomed to take of property of the like description.[1]

§ 187. It may not be unfit at the close of this discussion on the point of the mandatary's responsibility for gross negligence only again to remark, that the Scottish law has deserted the Roman doctrine on this subject, and holds the mandatary liable only for actual intromissions, or for such diligence, as he employs in his own affairs.[2]

§ 188. The rule in respect to the mandatary's liability applies only to cases, where he is in the actual performance of some act or duty, entrusted to him in regard to the property. For if he violates his trust by a misuser of the property, or does any other act inconsistent with his contract, or in fraud of it, he will be clearly liable for all losses and injuries resulting therefrom. He is not bound to suggest wise precautions against accident or loss; but he is not at liberty to expose the property to injury or loss by hazards inconsistent with his duty.[3] And in cases of misuser, especially such, as might amount to evidence of a conversion, it may perhaps be true, that every subsequent

---

[1] *Tracy* v. *Wood*, 3 Mason's R. 132.
[2] Erskine's Inst. B. 3, tit. 3, § 36; 1 Bell's Comm. 481.
[3] Jones on Bailm. 101, 114, 115, 116.

loss and injury, whether by accident or otherwise, would be at the risk of the mandatary.[1] This is certainly the rule of the civil law; and it has been incorporated into many, perhaps into all the systems of foreign law derived from it.[2]

§ 189. There is a class of mandates arising in the civil law, which does not seem to have any place in our law, at least not under the same appellation. This class arises under what is called the *Quasi contract* of *Negotiorum gestorum,* where a party spontaneously, and without the knowledge or consent of the owner, intermeddles with his property, as to do work, or to carry it to another place, &c. In cases of this sort, as he acts wholly without authority, there can, strictly speaking, be no contract; but the civil law raises a *quasi* mandate by implication for the benefit of the owner in many of such cases.[3] Nor is an implication of this sort wholly unknown to the common law, where there has been a subsequent ratification of acts of this sort by the owner; and sometimes, where unauthorized acts are done, positive presumptions are made by law for the benefit of particular parties. Thus, if a person enters upon a minor's lands, and takes the profits, the law will oblige him to account to the minor for the profits, as his bailiff, in many cases.[4] Whoever wishes for more exact information upon this title of the civil law (*negotiorum gestorum*), will find it treated

---

1 *De Tollenere v. Fuller,* 1 So. Car. Const. R. 121; *Ulmer* v. *Ulmer,* 2 Nott & McCord, 489; *Catlin* v. *Bell,* 4 Camp. 183; 2 Kent Com. 481.

2 Pothier, Contrat de Mandat, ch. 2, art. 3, § 1, n. 51; Erskine's Inst. B. 3, tit. 3, § 37; Merlin Repert. Mandat, § 2; Pothier, Pand. Lib. 17, tit. 1, P. 2, § 1, art. 2, 28, 29; Vinn. ad Inst. l. 3, tit. 27, 8.

3 Pothier, Appx. Negot. Gest. Mandat, n. 167, &c.

4 Dane Abr. ch. 8, art. 2, § 10; 1 Bac. Abr. Account; 1 Com. Dig. Accompt, A 3.

with uncommon fulness and accuracy by the learning of Pothier. But it is so remote from the jurisprudence of the common law, that it does not seem important to review it in this place with its various distinctions.

§ 190. There is a case, which has undergone decision in our law, which approaches very near to that of *negotiorum gestorum.* A master of a ship had gratuitously taken charge of and received on board of his vessel a box, containing doubloons and other valuables, belonging to a passenger, who was to have worked his passage, but was accidentally left behind. During the voyage the master opened the box in the presence of the passengers, to ascertain its contents, and whether there were contraband goods in it; and he took out the contents and lodged them in a bag in his own chest in his cabin, where his own valuables were kept. After his arrival in port, the bag was missing. The master was held responsible for the loss on the ground, that he had imposed upon himself the duty of carefully guarding against all perils, to which the property was exposed by means of the alteration in the place of custody, although, as a bailee without hire, he might not otherwise have been bound to take more than a prudent care of them; and that he had been guilty of negligence in guarding the goods.[1]

§ 191. We come, in the next place, to the implied obligation of the mandatary to render an account. And here the common law and the civil law recognise the same doctrine, and proceed *pari passu.* The mandatary is bound to render to the mandator upon request a full account of his proceedings; to show, that the trust has been duly performed; or, if not perform-

---

[1] *Nelson* v. *Macintosh,* 1 Stark. R. 237 [188.]

ed, to offer a justification or legal excuse for the non-performance. If the property is to be restored to the bailor after the work is done, then such restitution is included in the mandatary's duties. If by his fraud, or gross negligence, or misuser, the mandatary has made himself liable in damages, he must pay these damages. Of course the form and mode, in which the remedies of the bailor are to be enforced, in case of noncompliance by the mandatary, depend upon the municipal law of the particular country. In the civil law and the foreign law derived from it, the remedy would ordinarily be *actio mandati directa*, which is one of the nominate forms of that law.[1] In the common law it would be either an action founded on the contract, as an action of assumpsit, or founded on tort, as an action on the case for misfesance, or negligence, or conversion.

§ 192. It has been asked, whether the mandatary can recoup or set off in damages the benefits, which the mandator has received on one mandate, against the losses he has sustained on another. Pothier decides the question in the same manner, that it is presumed the common law would decide it, that he cannot.[2] But if, upon the same mandate of goods, a part be injured, and extraordinary profit be made upon the rest by extraordinary diligence, it might deserve consideration, whether the damage should exceed, what, upon an average of the whole, might be deemed the fair profit, which would have accrued by the mandatary's using ordinary care and diligence.

§ 193. Of course, in rendering an account, the mandatary is entitled to deduct and receive an allowance for all expenses and charges, to which he has been

---

1 Pothier, Contrat de Mandat, ch. 2, art. 4, n. 61 – 66.
2 Id. ch. 2, art. 3, § 1, n. 52.

necessarily subjected in performing the trust. But the consideration of this will fall more properly under another head.

§ 194. In making restitution of the property bailed, when that constitutes a part of the trust, the mandatary is not only bound to restore the thing specially, but the increment, earnings, and gains, derived from it. If animals are to be restored, their young also belong to the bailor. If gold or silver has been delivered to be made interest of, and to be specifically returned, the interest is to be accounted for, as well as the principal. If a vehicle has been delivered to be let for hire, the mandatary must account for the hire earned, as well as for the vehicle.[1] These principles are found in the civil law, and seem of general applicability in the common law.

§ 195. If there are joint mandataries, each is responsible for the whole *in solido.* If there are joint mandators, the account must be rendered to them jointly. But these are points of pleading and practice in the common law, and more properly belong to a general treatise on parties, than to one on a single branch of contracts.[2]

§ 196. We come next to the consideration of the obligation of the mandator, arising from the contract of mandate. And here little more remains, than to state the doctrines of the civil and continental law, the common law having, as yet, furnished no decisions, which go to the point. What is here stated can, therefore, be relied on only, as the reasoning of learned minds on a similar sub-

---

[1] Pothier, Contrat de Mandat, ch. 2, art. 3, § 2, n. 58, 59.

[2] Jones's Bailm. 51, 52; Pothier, Contrat de Mandat, ch. 2, art. 4, n. 63; Domat, B. 1, tit. 13, § 2, n. 5; Pothier, Pand. Lib. 17, tit. 1, P. 2, art. 1, § 2, n. 21; Ersk. Inst. B. 3, tit. 3, § 34.

ject, which, in the absence of all positive adjudications, may not be unfit to be submitted to the consideration of the professors of the common law. The mandator, then, contracts to reimburse the mandatary for all expenses and charges reasonably incurred in the execution of the trust; and also in respect to all contracts, which arise incidentally in the proper discharge of his duty. This is called in the civil law *obligatio mandati contraria*, because it is reciprocal, and incidental to that of the mandatary, which is *obligatio mandati directa*.[1]

§ 197. First, in relation to expenses. It is obvious, that if the bailor contemplates any thing to be done on his goods, by which the mandatary must or may incur expenses, he is bound to reimburse him; for it can never be presumed, that a gratuitous trust is designed to be a burden on the party. Thus, if a party requests a friend to receive his goods, and enter them at the custom-house, and pay the duties thereon, an implied obligation arises to reimburse the amount of duties, and other incidental expenses and charges upon the entry. If a party requests a friend to carry goods for him in a stage-coach to another town, for which goods carriage-hire is usually paid, a like duty to pay the bill is presumed. And even if the expenses should exceed what the owner himself would have paid, still if they are such, as were reasonably incurred, he is liable therefor; and under particular circumstances he may also be compellable to pay interest thereon.[2] And it will make no difference, that the mandator has not derived the expected benefit from the execution of the trust,

1 Pothier, Contrat de Mandat, ch. 3, art. 1, § 1, n. 68, art. 3, n. 82.
2 Domat, B. 1, tit. 15, § 2, 1. 2, 3; Dig. Lib. 17, tit. 1, l. 10, § 9, 1. 27, § 4, l. 12, § 9; Pothier, Contrat de Mandat, ch. 3, § 1, art. 1, § 1, n. 69, § 3, n. 78, 79.

if it be not occasioned by the default of the mandatary.[1]
It follows of course from what has been said, that if the
expenses be unnecessary or extravagant, or arise from
the gross negligence or fraud of the mandatary, they
are not reimbursable.[2]

§ 198. Secondly, as to indemnity for incidental contracts made by the mandatary. This is obviously
founded on the same general principles of justice, and
the presumed intention of the parties, as the reimbursement of expenses. If A requests B to take a
package of goods with him gratuitously in a ship, in
which B is bound from Liverpool to Boston, and B
engages with the master to pay the freight thereof,
A is bound to indemnify B for entering into the contract.
So, if B in the same case gives a bond at the custom-
house for the duties. So, if A requests B to carry his
chaise to Boston, and procure it to be repaired there
by some proper artisan, and B contracts to pay the
repairs, A is bound to indemnify him. But in all such
cases the contract must be reasonably and properly
entered into by the mandatary; and no presumption
must arise from the circumstances, that no indemnity is
expected or intended between the parties. For the
parties are at liberty to waive such compensation, or
to decline entering into a stipulation of indemnity. If
a father says to his son, I will take your chaise to
Boston, and have it repaired at my own expense, no
contract to indemnify the father arises. But if the
right to compensation or indemnity exists, then it is not
material, that by some accident the mandator has not

---

[1] Domat, B. 1, tit. 15, § 2, 1. 2; Cod. Lib. 4, tit. 35, 1. 4; Cod. Civ. art.
1999.

[2] Domat, B. 1, tit. 15, § 2, 1. 2; Pothier, Contrat de Mandat, ch. 3, § 1,
art. 1, § 2, n. 3, 78, 79.

derived the proper benefit; as if his chaise is burnt up before it is returned to him.[1]

§ 199. It follows from the like considerations, that all contracts made with third persons by the mandatary, in the execution of his agency, and within the scope of his authority, are binding upon the bailor, and must be fulfilled by him, when he is made a contracting party. Pothier has under this head discussed many questions as to the extent, scope, and limits of the agency, and how far the acts of the agent bind the bailor.[2] But discussions of this nature more properly fall, in our law, under the head of agency generally, than under the particular contract of bailment.

§ 200. Thirdly. Another question is, how far the bailor is bound to indemnify the mandatary for any losses or injuries sustained by him in the execution of the trust. Now upon this subject the civil and foreign law contain some very nice distinctions. The general rule seems to be, that the bailor is bound to indemnify the mandatary against all losses and injuries, the *cause* of which can be directly traced to the execution of the mandate; but not for losses and injuries, of which the mandate was the *occasion*. Thus, in the civil law it is said, that if A is plundered by a slave, whom he has been requested by B to buy and bring to him, B is responsible for the loss, although he was ignorant, that the slave was a thief, if the loss was not occasioned by any default of the mandatary.[3] Pothier says, that the distinction between the *cause* and the *occasion* of

---

1 Pothier, Contrat de Mandat, ch. 3, § 1, art. 2, n. 80, 81; Dig. Lib. 17, tit. 1, l. 45.

2 Pothier, Contrat de Mandat, ch. 3, § 1, 2, n. 90–100.

3 Dig. Lib. 47, tit. 2, l. 61, § 5; Pothier, Contrat de Mandat, ch. 3, § 1, art. 1, § 2, n. 75.

a loss is most important to be attended to; and he puts several cases to illustrate it. Some of these cases furnish matter of much nice and curious reasoning; and deserve the attention of critical jurists. But it will be sufficient to illustrate his meaning by a few obvious cases. If A undertakes to carry money gratuitously for B to another place, and the journey is undertaken wholly on B's account, and A is robbed of his own money, as well as of B's, on the journey, there the loss must be borne by B, for the mandate is the cause of the loss. So, if A were going the same journey by another road less infested by robbers, and he takes a particular road solely for B's accommodation, there B must bear the loss. But if A were making the same journey on his own account, or were bound to the same place, and there was no choice of roads, there the loss must be borne by A; for there it is not the cause, but the occasion of the loss. So in a case of shipwreck, if it happens in the passage of a river, which the mandatary is accustomed to make on his own business, there it cannot be said, that the execution of the mandate, with which he is entrusted at the same time, is the cause of the loss, which is sustained by the shipwreck. It is but the occasion. " Hoc casibus imputari oportet." But if the loss happens in the course of a navigation, to the risk of which the mandatary is solely exposed in the execution of the trust, and to which he would not otherwise be exposed, there the mandate is to be considered the cause of the loss. But even in such cases those losses only are to be repaid, which are of goods or things indispensable for the voyage or journey, and not such as are carried for the mere pleasure or profit of the mandatary.[1]

---

[1] Pothier, Contrat de Mandat, ch. 3, § 1, art. 1, § 2, n. 75, 76, 77;

19

§ 201. How far any of these doctrines are, or would be adopted into our law, cannot be satisfactorily answered by adjudged cases; for none can be found. Doctor Paley has, however, discussed the point; and it seems fit, in the absence of all authorities, to lay before the reader the opinion of this eminent divine. "The agent" (says he) "may be a sufferer in his own person or property by the business he undertakes. As where one goes a journey for another, and lames his horse, or is hurt himself by a fall on the road; can the agent in such case claim a compensation for the misfortune? Unless the same be provided for by express stipulation, the agent is not entitled to any compensation from his employer on that account. For where the danger is not foreseen, there can be no reason to believe, that the employer engaged to indemnify the agent against it. Still less, where it is foreseen; for whoever knowingly undertakes a dangerous employment, in common construction takes upon himself the danger and the consequences. As where a fireman undertakes for a reward to rescue a box of writings from the flames, or a sailor to bring off a passenger from a ship in a storm." [1] In such a case, however, one would incline to say with Pothier, that if there is no legal obligation to indemnify, there is a strong moral claim upon the party from propriety and humanity to do so.[2]

§ 202. We next come to the inquiry, in what manner the contract of mandate may be dissolved. (1.) And in the first place, it may at the common law

---

1 Domat, B. 1, tit. 15, § 2, l. 6; Cod. Civ. B. 3, tit. 13, art. 2000. See also Heinec. Pand. Lib. 17, § 234.

1 Paley's Moral Phil. B. 3, P. 1, ch. 12.

2 Pothier, Contrat de Mandat, ch. 3, § 1, art. 1, § 2, n. 76.

be dissolved by the mandatary at any time, before he has entered upon its execution; though the rule of the civil and foreign law is, (as we have seen,) under some circumstances, different. But in this case, as indeed in all others, where the contract is dissolved before the act is done, which the parties intended, the property bailed is to be restored to the mandator.[1] (2.) In the second place it is, or may be dissolved by the death of the mandatary; for being founded in personal confidence, it is not presumed to pass to his representatives, unless there is some special stipulation to that effect. But this principally applies to cases, where the mandate remains wholly unexecuted; for if it be in part executed, there may, in some cases, arise a personal obligation on the part of the representatives to complete it.[2] As, for example, if A has bought books for B at his request to be sent to B at Washington, and the books are bought, and before they are sent to Washington A dies, the representative of A is bound to send them on. At least, such is the doctrine of the civil and foreign law.[3] If there are joint mandataries, the death of one of them dissolves the contract as to all, according to the French law.[4] At the common law the rule would be the same, whenever the trust was of a nature, which required the united advice, confidence, and skill of all, and might therefore be deemed a joint personal trust to all. The general rule of the common law is, that an authority to two cannot be executed except by both, and if one refuse, or die, the authority is gone; for in such cases the authority

---

1 See also Pothier, Contrat de Mandat, ch. 2, art. 1, n. 38 – 46.

2 2 Kent Com. 504, § 4.

3 Pothier, Contrat de Mandat, ch. 4, § 1, n. 101.

4 Id. n. 102.

is construed strictly. Therefore, generally, an authority given to A, B, and C to sell a thing, is gone by the
death of either of them.[1] But, suppose goods are sent
to a partnership at Boston to be by them sent to New
Orleans, and they gratuitously undertake to forward
them, and then one of the partners dies; is the mandate
at an end, it being an act in its own nature requiring
no peculiar personal confidence or skill? Suppose
goods sent to a partnership to sell gratis, and one
partner dies; is the power to sell necessarily gone, or
may it be construed, by implication, to survive? These
questions are put merely for consideration; as they do
not appear to have been decided by any direct authority.[2]

§ 203. The death of the mandator, in like manner,
puts an end to the contract; the rule of the common
law being, on this point, coincident with that of the
civil law, *mandatum, re integrâ morte domini finitur*.[3]
And in like manner, if a power of substitution be allowed by the original mandate, the substitution ceases
with the death of the mandatary, who made it, unless,
indeed, the nature of the substitution provided for be
such, that the substitute becomes the direct agent of
the mandator, in lieu of the mandatary.[4]

§ 204. But, although an unexecuted mandate ceases
with the death of the mandator; yet if it is executed
in part at that time, it is binding to that extent, and his
representatives must indemnify the mandatary.   And

---

1 See. Co Litt. 112 *b*; Id. 181 *b*; Com. Dig. Attorney, C. 8; Bac.
Abr. Authority, C; 2 Kent's Com. 504.

2 See 2 Kent's Com. 494, 505, 507; *Wells* v. *Ross*, 7 Taunt. R. 403.

3 Cod. Lib. 4, tit. 35, l. 15; *Hunt* v. *Rousmaniere's Adm'r*, 2 Mason R.
342; 8 Wheaton R. 174; 2 Kent's Com. 507; 1 Domat, B. 1, tit. 15,
§ 4, n. 6, 7, 8; Pothier, Contrat de Mandat, ch. 4, § 2, n. 103.

4 Pothier, Contrat de Mandat, ch. 4, § 2, n. 105.

the civil law goes farther, and provides, that if the mandatary in good faith acts after the death of the mandator, and in ignorance of that fact, his acts are binding upon the representatives of the mandator.[1] And if the mandate be of a nature admitting of no delay, the mandatary may, in order to prevent a positive loss or injury, even with a knowledge of the death of the mandator, proceed to execute it, if there be no time to give notice to his representatives to act.[2] As, if fruit is ordered to be sold in a foreign port, and it would perish before the proper orders from the administrators could be obtained, the mandatary would be justified in making a sale. In such a case the common law may not, perhaps, differ; since factors are not obliged to sell goods in the name of their principal, as mere agents; but are clothed with an implied authority to sell them in their own names, as persons have a general right of disposal.[3]

§ 205. The common law, however, is in many respects different from the civil law on this subject; for, although by that law an authority coupled with an interest in the thing may survive; yet a mere naked power or authority dies with the party giving it. And there is no exception, even though the mandatary is ignorant of the death of the party.[4] This seems to be a very rigid rule; but it flows naturally from the doctrine, that the power to be executed can exist only while the party, in whose name it is to be done, is in

---

1 Pothier, Mandat, ch. 4, § 2, n. 106; Dig. Lib. 17, tit. 1, l. 26, l. 58; 1 Domat, B. 1, tit. 15, § 4, n. 7; Cod Civ. art. 2008.

2 Pothier, Mandat, ch. 4, § 2, n. 107.

3 Ibid.

4 2 Kent's Com. 507; 6 East R. 356; *Hunt* v. *Rousmaniere's Adm'r*, 2 Mason R. 244; 8 Wheat. R. 174; Willes, 101, 103; 2 Vez. & Beam. 51; 5 Esp. R. 118.

existence. A dead man can do no act. Whether the
civil law has not introduced a more equitable principle,
is a point fairly open for consideration, and upon which
much reasoning may be urged on both sides.

§ 206. In the third place, the contract of mandate
may be dissolved by a change of the state of the parties. As, if either party, being a female, marries before the execution of the mandate; or becomes insane;
or non compos mentis; or is put under guardianship.
Pothier puts the case only of the marriage of the mandator. But the same rule would seem, ordinarily, to
apply to the marriage of the mandatary, since her husband's rights may be affected by her conduct. The
civil law treats all these supervening disabilities as good
causes of dissolution, subject, however, to the same
exceptions, as it recognises in cases of death.[1] The
common law, in like manner, deems the marriage of a
woman to be a revocation of the antecedent authorities
conferred by her on other persons; for her acts may
be to the prejudice of the husband's rights.[2] But it
does not appear to have engrafted the same exceptions
upon the rule, as the civil law.

§ 207. The contract of mandate may also cease by
a revocation of the authority, either by operation of
law, or by the act of the mandator. It ceases by operation of law, when the power of the mandator ceases
over the subject matter. As, if he be a guardian, it
ceases, as to his ward's property, by the termination of
the guardianship.[3] So, if he sells the property, it ceas-

---

1 Pothier, Mandat, ch. 4, § 3, n. 111.

2 2 Roper, Husb. & Wife, 69, 73; Salk. 117; Bac. Abr. Baron &
Feme, E; 2 Kent Com. 506.

3 Pothier, Mandat, ch. 4, § 4, n. 112.

es upon the sale, if it is made known to the mandatary.[1]

§ 208. By the civil law the contract of mandate also
ceases by the revocation of the authority by the mandator himself. In general, every mandator may revoke
a mere authority at his own will. "Extinctum est
mandatum finitâ voluntate."[2] And this revocation
may be implied or express. The former is quite as
effectual as the latter, if it be clearly manifested. As
if a mandator appoints another person to do the same
act, this is an implied revocation.[3] So an authority to
act, during the absence of a party, is revoked by implication by his return, although it is not expressly limited
to such return by its terms, if the intention be clear.[4]
But, in such cases, the revocation is not complete until
notice is given to the mandatary, whose acts still bind
until such notice.[5] But, if the mandate is partly executed at the time, to that extent it is obligatory. Nay,
by the civil law in such case, the mandatary may, notwithstanding the revocation, go on to do whatever necessarily follows from the antecedent part of the execution.[6]

§ 209. The common law, in many of these respects,
coincides with the civil law. In general, the party giving an authority is entitled to revoke it. But if it is
given as a part of a security, as if a letter of attorney is
given to collect a debt, as a security for money advanc-

---

1 7 Vez. jr. 276.

2 Dig. Lib. 17, tit. 1, 1. 12, § 16; Cod. Nap. B. 3, tit. 13, art. 2003 to
2008.

3 6 Pick. R. 198.

4 Pothier, Mandat, ch. 4, § 5, n. 115 to 119.

5 Id. § 120; *Salt* v. *Field*, 5 T. R. 215; Wallace's R. 126; 5 Binn. R.
316; Cod. Nap. art. 2005.

6 Ibid. § 121 ; 2 Kent Com. 505, 506.

ed, it is irrevocable by the party, although revoked by
his death.[1]

§ 210. In cases of bailment, where the thing is to be
delivered to a third person, if the latter has no interest
in it, the bailor may revoke the bailment at any time.[2]
And whenever a revocation takes place by the act of
the party, it suspends, by the common law, all future
operations of the mandatary, under the power previously confided to him.

§ 211. Bankruptcy of the mandator, also, generally
operates as a revocation of the authority of the mandatary, by the common, as well as by the civil law.[3] And
bankruptcy of the mandatary is, in like manner, a revocation by the civil law.[4] *

§ 212. There still remain a few points to be considered before we close the subject of mandates. One
is, upon whom the burthen of proof lies in cases, where
the bailor sues the mandatary on the ground of gross
negligence. In respect to different sorts of bailees,
different rules seem to be adopted by the common law
on this point.[5] The present remarks will, therefore, be
confined to the case of mandataries.

---

1 *Hunt* v. *Rousmaniere's Adm'r*, 2 Mason R. 342 ; 8 Wheat. 174 ; 2
Esp. R. 565 ; 7 Vez. 28 ; 2 Vez. & B. 51 ; 1 Stark. R. 121 ; 4 Camp. R.
272.

2 1 Dane's Abr. ch. 17, art. 4, § 10.

3 *Merrett* v. *Forrester*, 4 Taunt. 541 ; *Parker* v. *Smith*, 16 East, 382 ;
2 Kent Com. 506.

4 Pothier, Mandat, ch. 4, § 5, n. 120.

5 Jones's Bailm. 96, 98 ; *Bennett* v. *Sneller*, 5 T. R. 276, per Buller J. ;
Finucane v. *Small*, 1 Esp. R. 316 ; 3 Munf. R. 239 ; 4 Binn. 127 ; 6
Johns. R. 160 ; *Harris* v. *Packwood*, 3 Taunt. 264 ; 5 Barn. & Cres. 322 ;
1 T. R. 33 ; *Platt* v. *Hibbard*, 7 Cowen R. 497 & 500, note ; 2 Salk. 255.

* The Scotch law, on the whole subject of revocations, seems a mere
transcript from the civil law.   Erskine's Inst. B. 3, tit. 3, § 40.

§ 213. It may be proper to remark, that something may depend on the form of the action, and upon the posture of the evidence at the trial, as well as the stage of the cause, at which the question arises. It may possibly be different, where a *primâ facie* case, to support an action of trover, is made out at the trial, from what it would be in an action of assumpsit, or an action of the case founded on negligence. In the latter actions, the plaintiff must make out his case *primâ facie*, as he charges it; in the former, he may rely on an apparent conversion, or a demand and refusal of the property, and thus put the other side on the defence. But, waiving all considerations of this sort, it seems a general principle of the common law, that every person is to be presumed to do his duty, until the contrary is established; and on this account, in many cases, the burthen is on the plaintiff to negative this presumption by appropriate proofs.[1] How far this principle ought to govern in cases of bailment generally, deserves consideration. That gross negligence by a gratuitous bailee is a very reprehensible neglect of duty, will scarcely be doubted. And it was accordingly deemed infamous in the Roman law.[2] Under such circumstances, it may not be thought unreasonable, that the burthen of proof of such negligence should be thrown on the plaintiff.

§ 214. A case of a somewhat anomalous character was once put by Lord Ellenborough, and deserves notice in this place. Suppose a chattel, as a boat, belonging to another person, be taken to do an act of charity, (as to extinguish a fire,) or to do an act of

---

[1] *Williams* v. *East India Comp'y*, 3 East R. 192.

[2] Jones's Bailm. 62; Pothier, Mandat, ch. 2, § 2, art. 4, n. 65.

kindness to the party, who is the owner of it, (as to save his other property from the flames,) and an injury or loss happens to the thing, unintentionally, in the use of it for this purpose; how far would the party be responsible to the owner for such loss or injury? Lord Ellenborough was of opinion, that he would not be responsible in any manner for it.[1]

§ 215. There are certain exceptions usually enumerated under the head of Mandates, in which the responsibility of the bailee for neglect is different from that, which is ordinarily implied by law. Such are the cases of a special contract or engagement; an officious voluntary offer by the mándatary; or an interest accruing to both parties from the particular bailment.[2] These cases do not, however, properly constitute exceptions from the general law, but they rather furnish grounds for excluding its operation; and what has been already said respecting them, under the head of Deposits, applies with equal force here, and need not be repeated.

§ 216. A case, falling practically under the last class of exceptions, deserves attention. A conversation took place between A and B relative to the purchase of a slave of A by B; and it was agreed between them, that B should have the slave for a particular price, if on trial and keeping him he liked him. B accordingly received the slave, and suffered him to go to a neighbouring village the same evening, when the slave ran away. The question was, whether this permission, on the part of the bailee, was such a negligence, as rendered him liable to the bailor. The Court thought, that it was

---

1 *Drake* v. *Shorter*, 4 Esp. R. 165.
2 Jones's Bailm. 63.

not, any more than it would have been to suffer him to go on an errand for the bailee.[1] This case seems one of mutual interest, rather than one of gratuitous bailment.

§ 217. But, suppose a slave should be put into the custody of a friend, to be carried in a vessel from one port to another, and he should run away during the voyage; would the friend be responsible, unless there had been gross negligence on his part, even if he did not take, as he might have done, greater precautions to prevent his escape? Looking to the analogy furnished by other cases, it would probably be held, that he would not be responsible for the loss.[2]

§ 218. Here end these commentaries on the subject of Mandates, a contract, on which, Sir William Jones has remarked, actions are very uncommon, for a reason not extremely flattering to human nature; because it is very uncommon to undertake any office of trouble without compensation.[3] Perhaps a large survey of human life might have furnished a more charitable interpretation of this absence of litigation; first, because from the great facilities of a wide and cheap intercourse in modern times, there is the less reason to burthen friends with the execution of such trusts; and secondly, because in cases of loss there is an extreme reluctance, on the part of bailors, to make their friends the victims of a meritorious, though it may be, a negligent kindness.

---

1 *De Fonclear* v. *Shottenkirk*, 3 Johns. R. 170.
2 *Beverly* v. *Burk*, 2 Wheat. R. 100.
3 Jones's Bailm. 57.

CHAPTER IV.

ON GRATUITOUS LOANS.

§ 219. THE next class of Bailments to be considered is that, which, in the civil law, is called COMMODATUM, and which, for the want of a more appropriate term, Sir William Jones has, after the French jurists, called a LOAN FOR USE (*Prêt à Usage*), to distinguish it from a *mutuum*, or loan for consumption.[1] He defines it to be a bailment of a thing for a certain time, to be used by the borrower without paying for it.[2] In the civil law it is defined to be a grant of a thing to be used by the grantee gratuitously for a limited time, and then to be specifically returned.[3]

§ 220. Lord Holt has defined this bailment to be, when goods or chattels, that are useful, are lent to a friend gratis, to be used by him; and it is called *commodatum*, he adds, because the thing is to be restored in specie.[4] Mr. Chancellor Kent, with his usual neatness, defines it to be a bailment or loan of an article for a certain time, to be used by the borrower without paying for it.[5]

§ 221. It is unfortunate, that our language has no word, which exactly expresses the meaning of the Roman word; for the term, *loan*, is often employed to

---

[1] Jones's Bailm. 64.

[2] Jones's Bailm. 118.

[3] Ayliffe's Pand. B. 4, tit. 16, p. 516; Inst. Lib. 3, tit. 15, § 2; Dig. Lib. 13, tit. 6, l. 1, 17, 3; Domat, B. 1, tit. 5, § 1, n. 1; Wood's Inst. B. 3, ch. 1, p. 215; Hein. Pand. Lib. 13, tit. 6, n. 96.

[4] *Coggs* v. *Bernard*, 2 Ld. Raym. 909, 913.

[5] 2 Kent Com. 446, 447.

signify a lending upon interest, or a lending to be returned in kind.[1] It would have been well, if Sir William Jones had not scrupled to naturalize the name by calling it a *commodate*, (as he has called *mandatum* a mandate,) and thus to have made it as familiar in our law, as *commodate* is in the Scottish law to express the same contract.[2] Ayliffe, in his Pandects, has gone farther, and terms the bailor the *commodant*, and the bailee the *commodatary*,[3] thus avoiding those circumlocutions, which, in the common phraseology of our law, have become almost indispensable.

§ 222. In the subsequent remarks on this subject, this contract will be designated by the term "loan," and the bailor will be called the *lender*, and the bailee the *borrower*, according to the known usage of our language.

§ 223. It follows, from the definition above stated, that several things are essential to constitute this contract. First. There must be a thing which is lent; and this, according to the civil law, may be either a thing movable, as a horse, or an immovable, as a house or land, or goods, or even a thing incorporeal.[4] But in our law, the contract seems confined entirely to goods and chattels, or personal property, and not to extend to real estate. This is sufficiently apparent from the definition of Lord Holt.[5] It must be a thing lent, in contradistinction to a thing deposited, or sold, or entrusted to another for the purposes of the owner.

---

1 Doct. & Stud. D. 2, ch. 38.

2 Erskine's Inst. B. 3, tit. 1, § 20 ; 1 Bell's Com. 225.

3 Ayliffe's Pand. B. 4, tit. 16, n. 517.

4 Ayliffe's Pand. B. 4, tit. 16, n. 517 ; Dig. Lib. 13, tit. 6, l. 1, § 1; Pothier, Prêt à Usage, ch. 1, § 2, art. 2, n. 14 ; Domat, B. 1, tit. 5, § 1, n. 5.

5 2 Ld. Raym. 913.

§ 224. Secondly. It must be lent gratuitously; for if any compensation is to be paid in any manner whatsoever, it falls under another denomination, that of hire.[1] Therefore, if A lends B his oxen for a week, under an engagement, that B shall lend A his oxen in return for another week, this is not a *commodatum*, but a contract for hire.[2]

§ 225. Thirdly. It must be lent for use, and for the use of the borrower. It is not material, whether the use be exactly that, which is peculiarly appropriate to the thing lent, as a loan of a bed to lie on, or a loan of a horse to ride. It is equally a loan, if the thing is lent to the borrower for any other purpose, as to pledge as a security on his own account. But it is said in the civil law not to be a loan, if the lender, at the request of the borrower, pledges the property to a creditor of the borrower, as security for his debt; for then it is properly a mandate.[3] This, at least in our law, may often turn upon a nice question of evidence, as to the intent of the parties, whether it be to create a loan, or a mandate. And the use must be a principal object, and not merely accessorial; for a pawnee, or depositary, may be at liberty to use the thing bailed, or even bound so to do, if necessary for its due preservation.

§ 226. If the use be jointly for the benefit of the borrower and lender, it is no longer a loan. As if A and B are about to make a common entertainment for their mutual friends at their joint expense at B's house, and A lends a service of plate to B for the occasion; it is not strictly a loan, but an innominate contract, where

---

1 Ayliffe's Pand. B. 4, tit. 16, n. 516.
2 Pothier, Prêt à Usage, ch. 1, art. 1, n. 2, 3, art. 2, n. 11.
3 Pothier, Prêt à Usage, ch. 1, § 1, art. 1, n. 2 ; Dig. Lib. 13, tit. 6, l. 5, 12.

ordinary diligence only is required.[1]   So, if the goods are lent for the sole benefit or gratification of the lender, the borrower will not be liable, except for gross neglect, as if a person passionately fond of music, for his own gratification at a concert, were to lend his own instrument to a player, and it were injured without gross negligence or wantonness by the player, he would not be liable for the injury; but if lent for their joint benefit and gratification, then he would be bound to ordinary diligence at least, and he would be liable for ordinary neglect.[2]

§ 227. But the rights of the borrower are strictly confined to the use actually or impliedly agreed to by the lender, and cannot be lawfully exceeded.[3]   The use may be for a limited time, or for an indefinite time. If it is for an indefinite time, at the pleasure of the lender, it would, in the civil law, fall under the denomination of a *precarium*, or a bailment at will;[4] but it would, in our law, still remain a loan.

§ 228. Fourthly. The property must be lent to be specifically returned to the lender at the determination of the bailment; and in this respect it differs from a *mutuum* or loan for consumption, where the thing borrowed, such as corn, wine, money, is to be returned in kind.[5]   It follows, that a loan can never be of a thing,

---

[1] Jones's Bailm. 72; Ayliffe's Pand. B. 4, tit. 16, n. 517; Dig. Lib. 13, l. 6, 18; Domat, B. 1, tit. 5, § 1, n. 12; Pothier, Prêt à Usage, ch. 2, § 2, art. 2, n. 51.

[2] Jones's Bailm. 73; 1 Dane's Abr. ch. 17, art. 2, § 2.

[3] Pothier, Prêt à Usage, ch. 1, § 1, art. 1, n. 5.

[4] Ayliffe's Pand. B. 4, tit. 16, n. 516; Dig. Lib. 43, tit. 26, l. 1; Domat, B. 1, tit. 5, § 1, n. 2.

[5] Jones's Bailm. 64; Pothier, Prêt à Usage, ch. 1, § 1, art. 1, n. 4, art. 3, n. 10, § 2, art. 2, n. 17, art. 3; Ayliffe's Pand. B. 4, tit. 16, 517; 2 Kent Com. 447; Domat, B. 1, tit. 5, § 1, n. 3 & 6; 1 Dane's Abr. ch. 17, art. 11.

which is to be consumed by the use, as if wine is lent to be drunk at a feast, even if no return in kind is intended, unless, perhaps, so far as it is not drunk; for as to all the rest, it is strictly a gift.

§ 229. As to the persons, between whom it may be contracted. In general, it may be said to arise between any persons, who have a legal capacity to contract. But in respect to idiots, lunatics, and married women, it cannot arise, unless, in the latter case, it is with the consent of her husband; in which event it binds him, but not her. In respect to minors the contract is not absolutely void, but it is voidable at his election. The contract must also be of a legal nature; for if it is immoral, or against law, it is utterly void. But on these points we need not dwell, since they belong to the law of contracts generally.

§ 230. It is not necessary, that the lender should be the absolute proprietor of the thing; it is sufficient, if he have either a qualified or a special property, or a lawful possession of it.[1] And though a man cannot generally be a borrower of his own goods, so as to bind himself by the contract, whether known or unknown to him at the time; yet, where the lender has a special property or a lien on them, he may lend them to the general owner for a particular use; and the contract of loan, with its accessorial obligation to return it, will arise.[2]

§ 231. In the next place, let us consider, what are the rights, which the contract of loan confers on the borrower. In general it may be said, that the borrower has the right to use the thing during the time and for the purpose, which was intended between the parties.

---

[1] Domat, B. 1, tit. 5, § 1, n. 7.

[2] Pothier, Prêt à Usage, ch. 1, § 2, art. 2, n. 19; 1 Atk. 235; 8 T. R. 199; *Roberts* v. *Wyatt*, 2 Taunt. 268.

and during this period and continuance of the use, the lender, according to the civil law, was bound to suffer it to remain in the possession of the borrower.[1] Of this, more will be said hereafter.

§ 232. But the right of using the thing bailed is strictly confined to the use, expressed or implied in the particular transaction.[2] And the borrower, by any excess, will make himself responsible. If, therefore, A lends B his horse to ride from Boston to Salem, B has no right, however urgent his business may be, to ride with the horse to Newburyport.[3] And in such a case, if he rides the horse to Newburyport, and any accident occurs to the horse, though it be by inevitable casualty, he will be responsible for the loss. This rule is equally the result of the common law and the civil law.[4]

§ 233. Lord Holt has put several cases to illustrate this doctrine. If a man lends another a horse to go westward, or for a month; and the bailee goes northward, or keeps the horse above a month, if any accident happens on the northern journey, or after the expiration of the month, the bailee will be chargeable; because (says he) he has made use of the horse contrary to the trust he was lent under; and it may be, if the horse had been used no otherwise, than he was lent, that accident would not have befallen him.[5] Bracton inculcates the like

---

[1] Pothier, Prêt à Usage, ch. 2, § 1, n. 20.

[2] Id. ch. 2, § 1, n. 21.

[3] Jones's Bailm. 68 ; *Wheelock* v. *Wheelwright*, 5 Mass. R. 104.

[4] Jones's Bailm. 68, 69 ; Cro. Jac. 244 ; 2 Ld. Raym. 909, 916; Ayl. Pand. B. 4, tit. 16, 517 ; Domat, B. 1, tit. 5, § 2, n. 10, 11, 12; Dig. Lib. 13, tit. 6, 1. 18; Cod. Civ. art. 1881 ; Pothier, Prêt à Usage, ch. 2, § 1, n. 22 ; Id. art. 3, n. 58 ; *Isaac* v. *Clarke*, 2 Bulst. 306.

[5] *Coggs* v. *Bernard*, 2 Ld. Ray. 909, 915, 916; *Tollemere* v. *Fuller*, 1 Const. Rep. S. C. 121.

doctrine; and it seems, indeed, as old as the first rudiments of our law.[1]

§ 234. The loan is to be considered as strictly personal, unless from other circumstances a different intention may be presumed. Thus, if A lends B her jewels to wear; this will not authorize B to lend them to C to wear. So, if C lends D his horse to ride to Boston, this will not authorize D to allow E to. ride the horse to Boston. But if a man lends his horses and carriage for a month to a friend for his use; there a use by any of his family, or for family purposes, may be fairly presumed; though not a use for the mere benefit of strangers.

§ 235. The case of *Bringloe* v. *Morrice*[2] illustrates this doctrine. An action of trespass was brought for immoderately riding the plaintiff's horse. The defendant pleaded, that the horse was lent to him by the plaintiff, and license given to him to ride him, and that by virtue of the license the defendant, and *his servants*, alternately had ridden the animal. The plaintiff demurred. And the Court, on the demurrer, held, that the license was annexed to the person of the defendant, and could not be communicated to another; for this riding was matter of pleasure. And Lord Chief Justice North took a difference, where a certain time is limited for the loan of a horse, and where not. In the first case the borrower has an interest in the horse during that time; and in that case his servant may ride; but in the other case not. A difference was also taken between hiring a horse to go to York, and borrowing a horse. In the first place the party may

---

1 Bracton, Lib. 3, ch. 2, § 1, pp. 99, 100.
2 1 Mod. R. 210; S. C. 3 Salk. 271.

allow his servant to ride; in the second, not. The case is obscurely reported. But the real meaning of the Court seems to have been, that in cases of a mere gratuitous loan, the use is to be deemed strictly a personal favour, and confined to the borrower, unless a more extensive use can be implied from other circumstances.

§ 236. In the next place, as to the obligations of the borrower. These are, to take proper care of the thing borrowed; to use it according to the intention of the lender; to restore it at the proper time; and to restore it in a proper condition.[1]   These will be spoken of in their order.

§ 237. In the first place, as to the proper care of the thing. As the loan is gratuitous, and exclusively for the benefit of the borrower, he is, upon the common principles of bailment, already stated, bound to extraordinary diligence; and of course he is responsible for slight neglect in relation to the thing loaned.[2]   It is singular, that Lord Holt,[3] and after him Mr. Justice Blackstone,[4] should have considered, that the same degree of diligence, and the same degree of responsibility, attached to a bailee for hire, and to a borrower; for the contracts are wholly unlike in their nature and character. Sir William Jones is of opinion, that the borrower's incapacity to exert more than ordinary diligence, will not, even on the ground of impossibility, furnish a sufficient excuse for slight neglect; for he contends, that the borrower ought to have considered his own capacity, before he deluded his friend by en-

---

1 1 Domat, B. 1, tit. 5, § 2, n. 1.
2 Jones's Bailm. 64, 65.
3 *Coggs* v. *Bernard*, 2 Ld. Raym. 909, 916.
4 2 Bl. Com. 453.

gaging in the undertaking.[1] But this doctrine must be
received with some qualification and reserve; and confined to cases, where there is either an implied engagement for extraordinary diligence, or the lender has no
reason to suspect or presume a want of capacity. For
if the lender is aware of the incapacity of the borrower, he has no right to insist upon such rigorous diligence. He has a right to insist on that degree of diligence only, which belongs to the age, the character,
and the known habits of the borrower. Thus, if a
spirited horse is lent to a raw or rash youth, or to a
weak and inefficient person, who is known to be such,
the lender must content himself with such diligence as
they may be fairly expected to use; and he has no
right to insist upon the diligence or prudence of a very
thoughtful and experienced rider.[2]

§ 238. The language of the civilians on this subject
is very strong. "Exactissimam diligentiam custodien-
dæ rei prestare compellitur, nec sufficit ei eandem diligentiam adhibere, quam suis rebus adhibet, si alius dili-
gentior custodire poterit," is the language of the Pandects.[3] Pothier says, that "the borrower ought to
exert all possible care, such as the most careful persons apply to their own affairs; and that he is liable
not only for a slight fault, but for the slightest fault, *de
levissimâ culpâ.*"[4] This rule, however, applies only to
cases, where there is no special contract, express or
implied, varying the general obligation; or where the
loan is strictly for the benefit of the borrower; for, if it

1 Jones's Bailm. 65; 1 Dane's Abr. ch. 17, art. 12.
2 Jones's Bailm. 65; 2 Kent Com. 447; Pothier, Prêt à Usage, ch. 2,
§ 2, art. 2, n. 49; Bract. Lib. 3, tit. 2, § 1, 99 *b.*
3 Dig. Lib. 44, tit. 7, l. 1, § 4.
4 Pothier, Prêt à Usage, ch. 2, § 2, art. 2, n. 48.

is for the mutual benefit of borrower and lender, ordinary diligence only could be required.[1] An attempt has been made to engraft another exception upon the rule, viz. where the lender makes a voluntary or officious offer, before he is asked by the borrower. But Pothier justly considers, that such an offer, if accepted, ought not to change the responsibility of the borrower.[2]

§ 239. What will be deemed slight neglect, or want of extraordinary diligence, must depend upon the particular circumstances of each case. It has been before seen, that by the civil law, and foreign law, theft ordinarily constitutes no excuse, because, it is said, that it can scarcely arise without some default or negligence of the borrower. But this is merely presumptive evidence, which may be repelled by the borrower, and if the theft has been without any fault on his part, he will be excused.[3] Thus, if A borrows a silver ewer of B, and afterwards delivers it to a person of extraordinary fidelity and vigilance, to be returned to B, if it should be stolen from that person by thieves, without any neglect on his part, A would be excused.[4] *A fortiori*, the borrower would be excused, if the thing should be stolen by robbery with open force, or by burglary; for this is a case of the *vis major*.[5]

§ 240. The borrower is also exempted, generally, from all liability for losses by inevitable accident, or by casualties, which could not be foreseen and guarded against. This is equally true in the common and the

---

[1] Pothier, Ibid. n. 50, 51.   [2] Pothier, Ibid. n. 52.

[3] Dig. Lib. 13, tit. 6, l. 20 & 21, § 1; Pothier, Prêt à Usage, ch. 2, § 2, art. 2, n. 53.

[4] Dig. Ibid.; Pothier, Ibid.; Jones's Bailm. 66.

[5] Pothier, Prêt à Usage, ch. 2, § 2, art. 2, n. 53; Jones's Bailm. 69; 2 Ld. Raym. 909, 915, 916.

civil law. "Is, qui utendum accepit, si majore casu cui humana infirmitas resistere non potest, veluti incendio, ruinâ, naufragio, omiserit, securus est," is the language of the Pandects;[1] and our own Bracton announces the same doctrine.[2] And under the head of casualties may be enumerated, not only such as are abovementioned, viz. fire, the fall of ruins, shipwreck, and lightning; but all such as human prudence cannot by extraordinary diligence guard against, such as losses by pirates, by enemies, by mobs, by sudden inundations, by sudden sickness, and even by the frauds of strangers, against which the borrower could not guard himself.[3]

§ 241. But there is an implied exception to all these cases of casualty and accident, which is, that they shall be without any default on the part of the borrower; for if they are connected with his default, his responsibility remains.[4] Thus, if a borrower is imprudent enough to leave the high road and pass through some thicket or unfrequented path, or to travel at an unseasonable hour, or on a road notoriously frequented by robbers, without proper precautions, and a robbery takes place, he will nevertheless be liable for the loss. So, if he rides a borrowed horse on an improper road, and he falls and is killed by the accident; or if he puts the horse into an improper pasture, and he is stolen by robbers; for accident or irresistible force will not ex-

---

1 Dig. Lib. 44, tit. 7, l. 1, § 14.

2 Bract. Lib. 3, ch. 2, p. 99; Vin. Abr. Bailment, A.

3 Domat, B. 1, tit. 5, §§ 2, 6, p. 113; Dig. Lib. 13, tit. 6, l. 5, § 2, & 4; Pothier, Prêt à Usage, ch. 2, § 2, art. 3, n. 55; Jones's Bailm. 66, 67.

4 Pothier, Prêt à Usage, n. 55, 56, 57; Jones's Bailm. 67, 68, 69; Dig. Lib. 13, tit. 6, l. 5, § 4.

cuse his own rashness.[1] So, if a lady borrows jewels
to wear at a ball, and by her imprudence they are lost
by robbery; or if she exposes them to any other undue
perils, by leaving them in an improper place, the loss,
though by accident, will be her own.[2]

§ 242. But in a like case of borrowed jewels, if they
were lost by robbery, or by accident, and the borrower
used them in a suitable manner, and left them in suitable places only, then the loss must fall on the lender;
for although the lady's wearing them, or leaving them
in the particular place, may be said to be the occasion
of the loss, yet it was not the cause of the loss. And
this difference is deemed very material by Pothier in
solving questions of this nature.[3] My passing through
a forest with a borrowed horse may be the occasion of
my being robbed of him there; but in a just sense, if
the forest were necessary to be passed in my journey,
my passing could not be considered as the *cause* of the
loss, as I was guilty of no neglect. But the cause of
the loss is correctly to be referred to the robbery.[4]
So, that the borrower is responsible for the loss, not
only when he might have saved the thing by proper care
from the accident, but when his own neglect has been
the occasion of the accident.[5] If the borrower puts a
borrowed horse under a ruinous building, and it falls,
and kills or maims the horse, and the borrower might
have foreseen this, he is responsible. But if the fall is

---

[1] Jones's Bailm. 67, 68; Pothier, Prét à Usage, ch. 2, § 2, art. 2, n.
55, 56, 57.

[2] Jones's Bailm. 68, 69; Pothier, Ibid. n. 56, 57.

[3] Jones's Bailm. 67; Pothier, Prét à Usage, n. 55, 56, 57.

[4] Id. ibid.

[5] Pothier, ibid. n. 56, 57; Dig. Lib. 13, tit. 6, l. 5, § 4; Dig. Lib. 44,
tit. 7, l. 1, § 4.

caused by an unexpected storm, then he is not responsible, if, in ordinary cases, the place would have been safe.[1]

§ 243. Cases of fraud, also, are naturally and properly excepted, whether they are founded in positive misrepresentation, or in injurious concealment, *suppressione veri, aut allegatione falsi.* There may be a direct fraud practised by asking the loan under false pretences ; and there may be a tacit fraud by misleading the ignorance of the lender under circumstances raising the presumption of a different state of facts. Pothier, and after him Sir William Jones, puts a case in illustration of this doctrine. If a soldier were to borrow a horse of a friend for a battle expected to be fought the next morning, and were to conceal from the lender the fact, that his own horse was as fit for the service, if the borrowed horse were slain in the engagement, the borrower would be responsible ; for the natural presumption created by the concealment was, that the horse of the borrower was unfit, or that he had none. But if the borrower had frankly stated the fact, then the loss must have been borne by the lender.[2] A more simple case of tacit fraud would be, where the soldier had borrowed the horse for the next day, concealing the fact of any expected battle, or of any intended use for that purpose ; for the lender might be fairly presumed, in such case, to lend for a journey, or for common use, and not for war.[3]

§ 244. There are yet other cases, which also form, or rather, under peculiar circumstances, may form exceptions to the general rule, that the borrower shall not

---

[1] Pothier, ibid. n. 56 ; Jones's Bailm. 68 ; Doct. & Stud. D. 2, ch. 38.

[2] Pothier, Prêt à Usage, n. 59 ; Jones's Bailm. 70.

[3] Dig. Lib. 13, tit. 6, l. 5, § 7 ; 1 Domat, B. 1, tit. 5, § 1, n. 9.

be responsible for accidents. Thus, it is said, that if the thing lent perishes by an accident, against which the borrower might have guarded by employing a like thing of his own, he shall be responsible for the loss; for, it is said, that he ought not to have used it, except for want of his own.[1] But this doctrine, if true at all, is true only under such circumstances, as lead to a just imputation of negligence, or of an improper exposure of the thing borrowed. If A borrows the jewels of B for a ball, deeming them more brilliant or more pleasing than his own, and they are lost by a casualty without his default, it is difficult to perceive a sound reason, why he should be made liable for the loss. The use was contemplated; and if the lender knew, that the borrower also owned jewels, he must have meant to leave the choice to the borrower. If he did not know, that the borrower owned jewels, and there was no fraud or concealment practised upon him to encourage the loan, the same result would seem to follow. If A owns a horse, and B lends him his horse for a week, why may not A use the borrowed horse, as well as his own, for common purposes, not intending to expose him to undue labour, or peril? Suppose he should deem the exercise proper and beneficial for the borrowed horse, and he should perish by some accident, would it be his loss?

§ 245. Pothier and the Civilians have put a case under this head, which is somewhat nice and curious; and as Sir William Jones has commented on it, it may be well to state it in his own words. "If the house of Caius be in flames, and he, being able to secure one thing only, saves an urn of his own in preference to the

---

[1] 1 Domat, B. 1, tit. 5, § 2, n. 7.

22

silver ewer, which he had borrowed of Titius, he shall
make the lender a compensation for the loss; especially if the ewer is the more valuable, and would consequently have been preferred, had he been owner of
them both. Even if his urn is the more precious, he
must either leave it, and bring away the borrowed vessel, or pay Titius the value of that, which he has lost;
unless the alarm was so sudden and the fire so violent, that no deliberation or selection could be justly
expected; and Caius had time only to snatch up the
first utensil, that presented itself." [1] This is apparently the doctrine of the Pandects, the text of which is as
follows: "Si incendio vel ruinâ aliquid contigit, vel
aliquod damnum fatale, non tenebitur, nisi forte, quum
posset res commodatas salvas facere, suas prætulit." [2]
Pothier approves of the same doctrine; and assigns as
a reason, that the borrower is obliged to use the most
exact diligence in respect to the thing borrowed, and
he bestows less than his engagement imports, when he
uses less, than he applies to his own property, even
when he applies it to a case, where there is an impossibility of saving the borrowed property, as well as his
own.

§ 246. Three cases are put by Pothier, and may be
readily imagined; first, where the thing borrowed is of
greater value than the borrower's own property; secondly, where the things are each of the same kind and
value; thirdly, where the borrower's own are of the
greatest value. Pothier decides each of the cases
against the borrower, admitting the last to be of chief
difficulty. His reasoning on the last case is to this
effect. It is true, that the borrower cannot be re-

---

[1] Jones's Bailm. 69, 70.   [2] Dig. Lib. 13, tit. 6, l. 5, § 4.

proached with any want of fidelity; but still the borrower undertakes for extraordinary diligence, *tenetur adhibere exactissimam diligentiam,* and by the nature of his contract he engages for all risks, except losses occasioned by the *vis major.* " Præstat omne periculum præter casus fortuitos, seu vim majorem." Now, that alone is deemed to be *vis major,* which cannot be resisted, *vis major, cui resisti non potest.* Although the borrower could not save both his own and the borrowed goods; yet he could have saved the latter at the expense of his own; and therefore they could not be said to be lost by the *vis major.* He admits, that it would be otherwise, where the tumult is such, that the borrower has no choice, and saves what comes to his hands first, without any exercise of judgment.[1]

§ 247. It may seem rash to doubt the accuracy of the reasoning or conclusions of such distinguished minds, backed, as they are, by the positive text of the civil law. And, if the question were one of a practical nature, it might be fit to abstain from any commentary. But, as it is scarcely more than a speculative proposition, it may not be wholly useless to lay before the reader some considerations for doubt on the point.

§ 248. It is observable, that the question is not stated by the learned jurists as one of presumptive evidence, fit for the decision of a court or jury, as judges of the facts; but as a conclusion of law. If the thing borrowed is of very great value, as a casket of jewels, and the thing saved is of little proportionate value, there might be some foundation for a presumption of undue preference for the latter, and an undue inattention to the former. That, however, would be mat-

---

[1] Pothier, Prêt à Usage, n. 56.

ter of fact to be weighed under all the circumstances.
But the case, as put, goes much farther, and decides,
that even if the borrower's own property is of very
great value, nay, of the highest value, and the borrowed
property is of very subordinate value, the law is the
same; and *a fortiori* it is the same, if they are of equal
value. It is chiefly in relation to the case of the superior value of the borrower's property, that the reasoning is pressed, and to that our doubts may be now confined.

§ 249. The question, in our law at least, (and it
would seem, also, in the civil law,) is, whether the borrower has been guilty of slight negligence, which, of
course, is the omission of very exact diligence; for,
without that, he is not liable at all. The loss is confessedly by an "*inevitable mischance,*" (for so Sir William Jones[1] and Pothier put it;) and in such a case, no
responsibility can attach upon the borrower, unless
there has been some neglect on his own part. It is
not true, as Pothier suggests, that the borrower is responsible for all losses not occasioned by the *vis major*,
or fortuitous occurrences. Losses by theft without default of the borrower, and losses of all sorts, where he
exercises the proper degree of diligence, are to be
borne by the lender. It is not sufficient to show, that
the loss has not been absolutely fortuitous, or by the
vis major, in a strict sense. It is sufficient to show,
that there has been no negligence whatsoever in occa-
sioning the loss. The question, then, is, whether there
is any negligence in the case thus presented. It is not,
of course, sufficient to show, as Pothier suggests, that
the borrower has taken as good care of the borrowed

---

[1] Jones's Bailm. 69.

goods, as of his own; for that is not the extent of his
obligation, it being for very exact diligence. But, if the
party does, in fact, use very exact diligence in respect
to his own, then, if he uses the same diligence in regard
to the borrowed goods as his own, his obligation is fully
complied with. Now, if a man, in a case of fire, saves
of his own goods those, which are preeminently valuable, it would be against common sense to say, that he
did not use the utmost diligence in respect to all, when
it was impossible for him to save all. The very case
put by Pothier supposes, that it is impossible to save
both the lender's and the borrower's goods. In a case,
then, confessedly of extreme necessity, the borrower is
made responsible for an exercise of the natural right of
choice. He saves the most valuable, which would seem
to be a rational course, and yet he is bound to pay for
the loss of the other. Pothier does not pretend, that,
in such a case, there is any negligence imputable to the
borrower. His reasoning implies, that there is none.
But he assumes (what he does not prove), that if the
thing borrowed could by possibility have been saved,
at however great a sacrifice, the borrower is bound to
make that sacrifice. Nay, both he and Sir William
Jones seem to admit, that, if in such a case he might
have saved the borrowed goods, by abandoning his
own, and he leaves both to perish in the flames, he is
excusable. How can this be, if there is any negligence
in the case, arising from the mere fact of leaving the
borrowed goods? If a party suffers his own goods to
perish in the flames, it is no excuse for suffering the
borrowed goods to perish in the same manner. It may
afford some presumption against negligence, especially
if the borrower's own goods were of very superior
value. But, if he might have saved the borrowed goods

by uncommon diligence, where is his excuse in point of law?

§ 250. But it is not true, that a borrower is bound to make every possible sacrifice in order to save the borrowed goods. If a man borrows a friend's horses and carriage for a journey, he is not bound to carry with him a troop of horse to guard them against a possible robbery; nor is he bound to protect them at the risk of his own life, or to the imminent hazard of his own person, or other valuable property. If, finding himself unexpectedly beset by robbers, and not knowing their force, he abandons the horses and carriage, and he escapes with his servants, not choosing to hazard the possible chances of resistance, partly because he has very valuable treasures with him, and partly from fear of assassination, can he be held responsible for the loss, if there was a fair and honest exercise of judgment, and it was such conduct, as a very diligent and careful man ought to adopt? If a house is on fire, is a man bound to risk his life or limbs to save borrowed goods, even if, in the event, from unforeseen circumstances, or by great steadiness of purpose, it was possible, nay practicable, so to do? No doctrine has as yet gone to this extent. The reasoning, then, which we have been considering, turns upon a supposed superior duty in a common calamity, or accident, to save that, which is borrowed, in preference to that, which is one's own, whatever may be the value of the latter compared with the former. But the whole controversy turns upon the very question, whether there is any such superior duty.[1] It is not to be assumed, and then reasoned from. It must be established as a just infer-

---

[1] Jones's Bailm. 47; a similar case put of deposit.

ence from the principles of law applicable to the subject.

§ 251. The doctrine of our law is, that in every case of a loan, to charge the borrower, there must be some neglect of duty, some slight omission of diligence. If the highest possible diligence cannot save both the borrowed goods and the goods of the borrower, where is the rule to be found, which prescribes the choice in such a case, and compels a man to abandon his own for another's? Principles going much deeper into human feelings, and morals, and rights, have not insisted on such an overwhelming sacrifice of personal preference. If two men are on a plank at sea, and it cannot save both, but it may save one; it has never yet been held, that in a common calamity and struggle for life, either party was bound to prefer the other's life to his own. If a ship is capsized at sea, and the ship's boat is sufficient to save a part of the crew only, is there a known duty to prefer a common destruction of all to the safety of a part? If the crew of a foundered ship are dying from hunger at sea, are all to perish, or may they not cast lots for life or death to preserve the rest? These cases are put merely to show, that in a common calamity, the law does not look to mere heroism, or chivalry, or disinterested sacrifices. If it has furnished no rule for such cases, it is because they are incapable of any; for necessity has no law. And to say the least of it, the equity, as well as the policy, of any such rule as Pothier contends for, is as questionable, as any, which can be put in the dialectics of casuistry. The Code of France (art. 1882) has, however, adopted the doctrine of Pothier; and thus given it a sanction, which may, perhaps, be thought sufficient to silence any private doubts.

§ 252. Another exception may arise, where there is a special contract between the parties. As if the borrower undertakes for all perils, he will become chargeable for any loss covered by his engagement, although he would not be otherwise chargeable; for there is a sufficient consideration to support such an engagement.[1]

§ 253. A curious question has been much discussed by the Civilians, which Pothier mentions, and Sir William Jones has also commented on, as properly belonging to this head. It is, whether, in the case of a valued loan, or where the goods are estimated at a certain price, the borrower must be considered as bound, at all events, to restore either the things lent, or the value of them.[2] The controversy has grown out of some texts of the Pandects,[3] in one of which, it is said, " Si forte res æstimata data sit, omne periculum præstandum ab eo, qui æstimationem se præstaturum recepit;" and in another place, " Æstimatio periculum facit ejus, qui suscepit. "

§ 254. In the common law, the controversy would turn wholly upon the construction of the words of the particular contract. The mere estimation of a price would not, of itself, settle the point, whether the borrower took upon himself every peril, or any additional peril beyond the common rules of law; but it would be construed as a mere precaution to avoid dispute in case of a loss, unless some other circumstances raised a presumption, that the parties intended something more. If the lender were to pay to the borrower, on lending

---

1 Domat, B. 1, tit. 5, § 2, n. 8; Pothier, Prêt à Usage, ch. 2, § 2, art. 3, n. 61; Jones's Bailm. 72.

2 Jones's Bailm. 71.

3 Dig. Lib. 13, tit. 6, l. 5, § 3; Dig. Lib. 19, tit. 3, l. 1, § 1.

him a horse, " You know my horse is worth one hundred dollars, and you will be obliged to pay that sum,
if he should be lost by your negligence ; take therefore
the proper care of him ; " to which the borrower should
assent ; no one would imagine, that if the horse died on
the journey without any default of the borrower, he
would by our law be liable to pay for the loss.   But if
the borrower were to say to the lender, " Lend me your
horse to go to Oxford, and I will either return him to
you, or pay you his value, which is one hundred dollars," and the lender should assent; then it might
justly be inferred, that he took the peril upon himself.
So, that it would with us come to a matter of fact, what
the contract was, rather than a matter of law.   Such is
the opinion of Sir William Jones.[1]   Pothier holds a
like opinion, and supports it with strong reasons.[2]   It
is not of any great importance to perplex ourselves
with questions of this nature, as they seem purely
speculative, since a case can scarcely be imagined,
where some circumstance, giving a construction one
way or the other, would not be found to explain the
reason for fixing the price.   The Code of France has
however declared (art. 1883), that if the article is valued on the lending, the loss, which may happen even
by accident, is the borrower's, if there is no agreement to the contrary.   The fixing of a price, therefore,
raises a presumption of a contract on the part of the
borrower against all risks, which he may repel by
other proofs.

§ 254. In the next place, as to the proper use of
the thing by the borrower.   It is very clear, that the

1 Jones's Bailm. 71, 72.
2 Pothier, Prêt à Usage, ch. 2, § 2, art. 3, n. 62, 63.

lender has a right to prescribe the terms and conditions, on which the loan shall be made ; and the borrower is bound to follow them with all due fidelity.[1] If there is any excess in the nature, time, manner, or quantity of the use, beyond what may be fairly inferred to be within the intention of the parties, the borrower will (as we have already seen) be responsible, not only for any damages occasioned by such excess, but even for losses by accidents, which could not be foreseen or guarded against.[2] As, if a man lends his friend a service of plate for an entertainment in a city, and he, without the knowledge or assent of the lender, carries it into the country, and it is there lost by accident or otherwise, the borrower is responsible for the loss.[3]

§ 255. In respect to the use, what is, or is not within the scope of the bailment must depend upon a great variety of implications and presumptions, growing out of the circumstances of each particular case ; and no general rule can be laid down, which will govern all cases. In general it may be said, in the absence of all controlling circumstances, that the use intended by the parties is the natural and ordinary use, for which the thing is adapted.[4] In regard to time, if no particular time is fixed, a reasonable time must be intended, keeping in view the objects of the bailment. If a horse is lent for a journey, it is presumed to be a loan for the ordinary time consumed in such a journey, making

---

1 Domat, B. 1, tit. 5, § 1, n. 8.

2 Ante, p. 137; Noy. Max. ch. 43; 2 Ld. Raym. 909, 915, 916; Jones's Bailm. 68, 69; Bracton, Lib. 3, ch. 2. § 1, p. 99; Pothier, Prêt à Usage, ch. 2, § 1, n. 22, ch. 2, § 2, art. 3, n. 57, 58; Dig. Lib. 13, tit. 6, 1. 18; Code Civ. art. 1880, 1881.

3 Jones's Bailm. 69; Pothier, Prêt à Usage, n. 58.

4 Domat, B. 1, tit. 5, § 1, n. 8, 9, § 2, n. 11.

proper allowance for the ordinary delays and the ordinary objects of such a journey.[1] The place of the use must also be governed by circumstances. If A lends his horse to B to be used for a day, and both reside in the same town, it may be presumed, that the use is to be within that town, unless there are some circumstances creating a different presumption of intention.

§ 256. If in using the thing the borrower is put to any expense, this must be borne by himself.[2] But suppose, in consequence of the loan, the lender is in the mean time put to some trouble or expense; is the borrower to repay it? As if A lends his horse to B for a journey, and during the interval of his absence A is forced by some pressing business to hire another horse; is B responsible for the hire? Pothier thinks he is; and Sir William Jones has apparently adopted his reasoning.[3] No case in our law has decided such a point; and it would be extremely difficult to deduce it as an implication from the nature or obligations of the contract.

§ 257. As to the restitution of the thing loaned. This is a most material part of the obligations of the borrower. He is to make a return of the thing at the time, and in the place, and in the manner contemplated by the contract.[4] If no particular time is agreed on, then the party is to return it in a reasonable time. By the civil law, and the foreign codes derived from it, the borrower is not bound to return the thing, until he has had the proper use of it, or until the bailment has

---

1 Domat, B. 1, tit. 5, § 1, n. 10, § 2, n. 11.

2 Domat, B. 1, tit. 5, § 2, n. 14.

3 Pothier, Prêt à Usage, ch. 2, § 2, art. 3, n. 55; Jones's Bailm. 67.

4 Domat, B. 1. tit. 5, § 1, n. 11; Dig. Lib. 13, tit. 6, l. 5, l. 17, § 3 ; Id. l. 3, § 1.

terminated, although the thing is previously demanded by the lender. Nor is he then obliged to return it
in any other manner, than was originally contemplated
by the parties.[1] And this rule applies, although the
lender has in the mean time had a necessity of using
the same thing, if the occurrence might have been
foreseen. But if it is a sudden and unexpected necessity, then the thing may be demanded back before
the expiration of the time, unless the borrower will
furnish a proper substitute, and the return will be to
his injury.[2] And so, if the purpose of the loan is accomplished, although the time has not expired, it may
be demanded back again. As, if a manuscript is lent
for a week to be copied, and the copy is made in two
days, the lender may require the manuscript back, unless some other circumstance has intervened to justify
the full delay.[3] However, where the loan is by its nature or character precarious, it may by the civil law be
demanded at any time.[4]

§ 258. These principles are not supposed to have
any foundation in the common law ; in which the loan
is understood, as to its continuance, to rest upon the
good pleasure and good faith of the lender, and to be
strictly precarious. As the bailment is merely gratuitous,
the lender may terminate it, whenever he pleases.[5] But

---

1 Pothier, Prêt à Usage, ch. 2, § 2, art. 1, § 1, n. 24 ; Dig. Lib. 13, tit. 6,
l. 17, § 3 ; Domat, B. 1, tit. 5, § 1, n. 13, § 3, n. 1 ; Cod. Civ. art. 1888.

2 Pothier, ib. n. 25.

3 Pothier, ib. n. 26, 27.

4 Domat, B. 1, tit. 5, § 1, 2, n. 13, § 3, n. 2 ; Pothier, Prêt à Usage,
ch. 4, art. 1, n. 86, 87.

5 *Orser* v. *Storms*, 9 Cowen, 687 ; Viner Abr. Bailment D. ; Bac. Abr.
Bailment D. ; 2 Leon R. 30, 89 ; Dyer, 48 *b* ; Cro. Jac. 687 ; 2 Roll.
R. 440 ; Id. 38 ; 1 Str. R. 165 ; Vin. Abr. Countermand A ; Sheppard's
Epitome, Countermand ; *Taylor* v. *Linday*, 9 East R. 49 ; 1 Dane Abr.
ch. 17, art. 4, § 10.

if he does so unreasonably, and it occasions any injury or loss to the borrower, the latter may perhaps have a suit for damages, where the object of the bailment has been partly accomplished; or if he retains the thing, in a suit by the lender he may insist upon the unreasonableness of the demand, or the injury to himself, and thus perhaps may recoup in the damages, whatever he has lost, and repel any claim for a large compensation on account of his delay and refusal to return the thing bailed, when it was demanded of him.

§ 259. If the borrower does not return the thing at the proper time, he is deemed to be in default, or, as the civil law phrases it, *in morâ (en demeure),* and then he is responsible for all injuries, and even for all accidents.[1] Sir William Jones has put, as exceptions, (in which he is apparently supported by Pothier), " unless in cases, where it may be strongly presumed, that the same accident would have befallen the thing bailed, even if it had been restored at the proper time; or unless the bailee has legally tendered the thing, and the bailer has put himself *in morâ* by refusing to accept it." [2] The latter is a very clear case in the common law, as well as in the civil law. But in the former case the common law is different; for the refusal or delay is at the risk of the borrower; and it is deemed a misfesance or negligence on his part, which makes him liable for accidents.[3] And with this doctrine the Code of France (art. 1881) coincides, as well as the Scottish law.[4]

---

[1] Jones's Bailm. 70; Pothier, Prêt à Usage, ch. 2, § 2, art. 2, n. 60.

[2] Jones's Bailm. 70; Pothier on Oblig. n. 143.

[3] Noy's Maxims, ch. 43; Jones's Bailm. 68; *Coggs v. Bernard,* 2 Ld. Raym. 909, 915.

[4] Ersk. Inst. B. 3, tit. 1, § 22.

§ 260. And the thing borrowed is not only to be returned, but every thing, that is accessorial to it. Thus, the young of an animal, born during the time of the loan, are to be restored; and the income of stock, which has been lent to the borrower to enable him to pledge it as a temporary security, belongs to the lender.[1]

§ 261. In regard to the place, where the thing is to be returned, several rules are found in the foreign law. If no particular place is pointed out by the contract, it is to be returned to the lender at his usual dwelling-house, unless the thing properly belongs elsewhere. If the lender has in the meantime removed his domicil to another place, the borrower is not bound to follow it, and return the thing at the new residence; but only to return it to the former residence, unless, indeed, there is a trifling difference only in the distance between them. The common law seems not to have laid down any special rules on this subject; but has left the decision to be made upon the particular circumstances of each case, as it shall arise, according to the presumed intention of the parties.[2]

§ 262. It is wholly immaterial whether the thing is returned to the lender or to his authorized agent; or by the borrower or by his agent. But in each case the return must be completed in order to discharge the borrower.[3]

§ 263. Perhaps also a delay in the return of the thing may, in some cases, be excused by the imminent danger of loss, if it had been sent at the stipulated time; for there must be an exercise of due diligence

---

[1] Dig. Lib. 13, tit. 6, l. 5; Ayliffe, Pand. B. 4, tit. 16, n. 518; Pothier, Prêt à Usage, ch. 2, § 2, art. 4, § 2, n. 73, 74.

[2] Pothier, Prêt à Usage, ch. 2, § 2, art. 1, § 3, n. 36, 37.

[3] Pothier, Prêt à Usage, n. 41.

as to the time and manner of return ; and if the borrower
takes undue hazards by returning the thing punctually,
ad punctum temporis, he may be responsible for any
loss occasioned by his rashness.[1]   So, if his refusal is
solely to prevent the commission of a crime, he may
stand excused.   As, if the lender desires his pistols
to be returned in order to kill another person.[2]

§ 264. The borrower cannot detain the thing borrowed for any antecedent debt due to him.   And this
is the rule of the civil, as well as of the common law.[3]
The plain reason is, that it would be a departure from
the tacit obligations of the contract.   No intention to
give a lien for debt can be implied from the grant of a
mere favour.

§ 265. In regard to whom the thing is to be restored.
Generally speaking, it is to be restored to the lender,
unless it has been agreed, that the restitution shall be
to some other person.[4]   If the lender is dead, it is to be
restored to his personal representative, if known.   If
not known, or no administration is taken on his estate,
the borrower may detain the thing, until an administration is made known.   A restitution to or by an agent
is, of course, the same thing, as to the lender personally.   If the lender is a woman, and she afterwards
marries, restitution is to be made to her husband, and
not to her personally.   So, if the lender has been put
under guardianship, the return must be to his guardian.[5]
And if the lender has become *non compos mentis*, or a
lunatic, and has no guardian, a redelivery to him will
not be good ; but the thing must be kept, until a com-

---

1 Pothier, ibid. n. 42.   2 Pothier, ibid. n. 45.
3 Domat, B. 1, tit. 5, § 2, n. 13 ; Vin. Abr. Bailment, B 6.
4 Pothier, Prêt à Usage, ch. 2, § 2, art. 2, § 2, n. 29.
5 Pothier, ibid. n. 33.

petent party exists, to whom it may be delivered.[1]
But a redelivery to a minor would be good, if, in the
meantime, he has not had any guardian appointed over
him; and even if he has a guardian, if the thing has
been usually entrusted to the minor by his guardian.[2]

266. Even if the lender is not the owner of the
thing, the borrower must ordinarily restore it to him,
and has no right to set up the title of a mere stranger
against him; for the lender has, by his contract, a right
to be reinstated in his possession. However, if, in the
mean time, a recovery has been had against the borrower,[3] or if the thing has been attached in his hands
in an adverse suit, that will constitute a sufficient excuse.[4] And if the borrower actually restores the thing
to the true and real owner, without any injury or injus-
tice to the lender, he will no longer be liable to any
action.[5] In like manner, if the thing is taken out of
the possession of the borrower by the real owner;[6] or
if, upon a threat to sue by such owner, he has delivered up the thing to him, he will be discharged.[7]

§ 267. If the loan has been to several persons jointly, they are all responsible *in solido* for the return; and,
of course, a return by one is a discharge of all, as a
misuser by one is a misuser by all.[8]

§ 268. As to the state or condition, in which the thing
is to be restored. The borrower not being liable for

---

[1] Pothier, Ibid. n. 34.

[2] Pothier, Ibid. n. 35.

[3] *Edson v. Weston*, 7 Cowen R. 278; *Wilson v. Anderton*, 1 Barn. &
Adolp. R. 450.

[4] Pothier, Prêt à Usage, ch. 2, § 2, art. 1, n. 46.

[5] *Whittier v. Smith*, 11 Mass. R. 211.

[6] *Shelbury v. Scotchford*, Yelv. R. 23.

[7] *Wilson v Anderton*, 1 Barn. & Adolp. 450; Littledale J.

[8] Pothier, Prêt à Usage, n. 65; Cod. Civ. art. 1887.

any loss or deterioration of the thing, unless caused by his own neglect of duty, it follows, that it is sufficient, if he returns it in the proper manner, and at the proper time, however much it may be deteriorated from accidental or other causes, not connected with any such neglect.[1] It matters not, that the deterioration has arisen from the use made of it by the borrower, if that use is reasonable, and not beyond what was contemplated by the parties; for, by the loan, the lender has taken upon himself to bear the loss consequent upon such a use. Thus, if A lends B a cloak to wear on a journey from Boston to Washington and back again, the injury by the wear and tear of the journey must be borne by A. So, if A lends B his horse for a long journey; and, by the natural fatigues of such a journey, the horse is injured, it is A's own loss.[2]

§ 269. By the civil law, wherever the thing borrowed is returned in an injured or deteriorated state by the default of the borrower, the latter is responsible for all damages notwithstanding the return, at least, if there has not been an express or implied waiver of any damages by the lender. If the thing is materially damaged, the owner may refuse to receive it back; but it is otherwise, if the damage is inconsiderable.[3] By the common law, if the act, by which the injury is occasioned, is a mere negligence, the remedy would be by an action on the case, in which damages for the injury only would be recoverable.[4] But, wherever it amounts

---

1 Pothier, Prêt à Usage, ch. 2, § 2, art. 1. § 3, n. 38 ; Dig. Lib. 13, tit. 6, 1. 19.

2 Pothier, Ibid. n. 39 ; Dig. Lib. 13, tit. 6, 1. 23 ; Domat, B. 1, tit. 5, § 2, n. 6, 12.

3 Pothier, Prêt à Usage, ch. 2, § 2, art. 4, § 2, n. 69, 70, 71.

4 1 Selw. N. P. 425.

to a misfesance, and conversion of the property, there the owner is not bound to receive it back, but may recover the full value of it. If he does receive it back, he will still be entitled to damages for the injury.[1]

§ 270. In the next place, as to the obligations on the part of the lender. These, as the nature of a gratuitous loan would naturally lead us to presume, are few, and merely accessorial.

§ 271. In the civil law, the first obligation on the part of the lender is, to suffer the borrower to use, and enjoy the thing loaned during the time of the loan, according to the original intention, without any molestation or impediment, under the peril of damages. He is, at least, obliged "per se hæredemque suum non fieri quo minus commodatorio uti liceat."[2] We have already seen, that by the common law the bailment may be terminated at the pleasure of the lender, and that it is always deemed a precarious loan.[3]

§ 272. But if, during the time of the use, a stranger molests or disturbs the borrower in the use, there the remedy of the borrower is solely against the stranger, and not against the lender, unless the stranger derives a title from the lender, or does the act by his connivance; or unless the loan is made in bad faith by the lender, knowing, that the title is in the stranger, who will reclaim it.[4]

---

[1] *Bayliss* v. *Fisher*, 7 Bing. R. 153 ; Paley on Agency, 73, 74, n. (*e*); 4 T. R. 264; Peake N. P. R. 49 ; *Murray* v. *Burling*, 10 Johns. R. 172; *Gibbs* v. *Chase*, 10 Mass. R. 125 ; *Wheelock* v. *Wheelwright*, 5 Mass. R. 104.

[2] Pothier, Prêt à Usage, ch. 3, n. 75, 76, 77; Domat, B. 1, tit. 5, § 3, l. 1, 2 ; Dig. Lib. 13, tit. 6, l. 17, n. 3.

[3] Vin. Abr. Bailment, D ; Bac. Abr. Bailment, D.

[4] Pothier, Ibid. n. 79, 80.

§ 273. Another obligation of the lender, by the civil law, is to reimburse the borrower the extraordinary expenses, to which he has been put for the preservation of the thing lent. The borrower (as we have already seen) is compellable to bear the ordinary expenses, for the loan being for his benefit, he must be presumed to bear the burthen, as an incident to the use. But the extraordinary expenses are at the risk of the lender. Thus, if a horse is lent for a journey, the ordinary expenses of the horse on the journey are to be borne by the borrower. But, if the horse is taken sick, the extraordinary expenses of the hire are to be paid by the lender. So, if the horse is stolen, the extraordinary expenses of pursuit and recapture are to be paid by the lender.[1] And upon the same reasoning, if a coach is lent for a journey, the ordinary repairs of a slight nature during the journey would belong to the borrower; but those of an extraordinary nature, as procuring a new wheel for one, which had failed, would belong to the lender. And in all these cases the borrower would have a lien on the thing, and may detain it, until these extraordinary expenses are paid; and the lender cannot, even by an abandonment of the thing to the borrower, excuse himself from repayment; nor is he excused by the subsequent loss of the thing by accident; nor by a restitution of it by the borrower, without insisting upon repayment.[2]

§ 274. No case seems to have arisen in the common law, where this question has occurred in judgment. Probably, in such a case (for it cannot be asserted to be clear) in the absence of all countervening presump-

---

[1] Pothier, Ibid. n. 81.
[2] Pothier, Ibid. n. 82, 83; Dig. Lib. 13, tit, 6, l. 18, § 4.

tions, if the repairs had conferred a permanent benefit upon the thing loaned beyond the mere use for the journey, an obligation to reimburse the borrower to that extent might be implied. There might be more difficulty in regard to the cure of the sick horse, the expenses of which cure might be reasonably presumed, within the scope of the contract, to be a charge on the borrower, as necessary to his further use upon the journey.

§ 275. Another case of implied obligation on the part of the lender by the civil law is, that he is bound to give notice to the borrower of the defects of the thing loaned; and if he does not, and conceals them, and any injury occurs to the borrower thereby, the lender is responsible. One case put in the Roman law is, where a party lends an infected vase, and the wine put into it by the borrower is spoiled thereby from want of notice, the lender is answerable.[1] A more stringent case would be, where a vicious horse is lent to put into a chaise for a ride, with a concealment of his defects, and thereby the chaise is broken to pieces, and the borrower injured in his limbs. How our law would deal with such cases, where there is no fraud in the concealment, does not appear to have been decided.

§ 276. Another case of implied obligation on the part of the lender in the civil law is, where the thing has been lost by the borrower, and after he has paid the value to the lender, the thing has been restored to the lender. In such a case the lender must return to the borrower either the price or the thing; for by such payment of the loss the property is effectively transferred to the borrower.[2] And the result would be the

---

1 Pothier, ib. n. 84; Dig. Lib. 13, tit. 6, 1. 18, § 3.
2 Pothier, ib. n. 85; Dig. Lib. 13, tit. 6, 1. 17, § 5.

same, if a recovery of the full value should be had by
the lender in a suit against the borrower for an alleged
conversion of the thing.   In such a case the property,
by a satisfaction of the judgment, would be transferred
to the borrower.[1]   The common law seems to recognise the same principles, though it would not perhaps
be easy to cite a case on a gratuitous loan directly on
the point.

§ 277. We next come to the consideration of the
right or power of the lender to make a revocation of
the loan.   How far the lender may revoke the loan
at his mere pleasure, has been already incidentally
noticed; and it seems, that by the common law all
such loans are deemed precarious and during the mere
will and pleasure of the lender.[2]   But there are also
revocations implied by law, as by a change of the
state of the parties.   Thus, the death of the borrower will ordinarily operate as a revocation of the loan;
for it is presumed to be a personal confidence and
benefit.   But if such a presumption does not arise
from the nature and circumstances of the loan, the
civil law deems the death of the party no revocation.[3]
And the death of the lender does not by the civil
law operate as a revocation of the loan, unless it is
of the nature called precarious or during pleasure.[4]
The general analogy of the common law would lead
to the conclusion, that the death of either party would
amount to a revocation of the loan.   So, if a woman,
after a bailment made by her or to her, contracts mar-

---

1 Pothier, ib. ch. 2, § 2, art. 4, § 2, n. 68.
2 *Orser* v. *Storms*, 9 Cowen R. 687; 8 Johns. R. 432; 1 T. R. 480;
2 Camp. R. 464.
3 Pothier, Prêt à Usage, ch. 2, § 2, art. 1, § 1, n. 27.
4 Domat, B. 1, tit. 5, § 1, n. 13.

riage, that operates as a termination or revocation of the bailment.[1]

§ 278. In this class of bailments also the question may arise, upon whom, in case of any damage or loss to the thing loaned, the burthen of proof rests, whether on the lender to establish the neglect of the borrower, which renders him responsible, or upon the latter to establish his innocence, and to show, that the damage or loss has been without any neglect. Pothier in some passages seems to intimate, that the burthen of proof is on the borrower.[2] It is perhaps not easy to lay down any absolute rule on this subject, as the rule of the common law, which might not be subject to some exceptions. Where a demand of the thing loaned is made, the party must return it, or give some account how it is lost. If he shows a loss, the circumstances of which do not lead to any presumption of negligence on his part, there the burthen of proof might perhaps belong to the plaintiff to establish it. There are cases at least, in which it has been held, that the plaintiff must prove the negligence under special circumstances.[3] But where there is a demand of the thing loaned and a general refusal, without any special excuse stated or proved, at the time of the demand, there the burthen of proof would seem to be on the defendant to negative the *primâ facie* right of recovery thus made out by the plaintiff. And in many complicated cases of evidence, the burthen of proof may alternately shift from one party to the other in different stages of the trial.

---

1 Viner, Abr. Bailment, D.

2 Pothier, ib. n. 40, 41.

3 *Harris* v. *Packwood,* 3 Taunt. 264 ; Abbott C. J. in *Marsh* v. *Horne,* 2 B. & Cres. 322 ; *Platt* v. *Hibbard,* 7 Cowen R. 497, 500, note.

§ 279. There is another point, in respect to the rights of the lender and the borrower, which it may be of some importance to mention, although it has been already somewhat considered under other heads. It is, who is to be deemed the owner or proprietor of the thing during the period of the loan, or in other words, whether the borrower has a special property in it, or only a naked possession. By the civil law the lender still retains the sole proprietary interest, and nothing passes to the borrower but a mere right of possession and user of the thing during the continuance of the bailment. Nay, the possession of the borrower is deemed the possession of the lender. " Rei commodatæ et possessionem et proprietatem retinemus. Nemo enim commodando rem facit ejus cui commodat," is the doctrine of the Roman code, as well as of the continental jurisprudence founded on it in modern times.[1] And the same rule prevails in the common law ; so that an action for a trespass or conversion will lie in favour of the lender against a stranger, who has obtained a wrongful possession, or has made a wrongful conversion of the thing loaned. A mere gratuitous permission to a third person to use a chattel does not, in the contemplation of the common law, take it out of the possession of the owner.[2]

§ 280. But notwithstanding the borrower has no special property in the thing loaned, still it seems, that

---

[1] Dig. Lib. 13, tit. 6, l. 6, 8; Pothier, Prêt à Usage, ch. 1, § 1, art. 2, n. 5, art. 3, n. 9; Ayliffe's Pand. B. 4, tit. 16, p. 517; Domat, B. 1, tit. 5, § 1, n. 4.

[2] *Thorp* v. *Burling*, 11 Johns. R. 285; *Hurd* v. *West*, 7 Cowen R. 753; *Orser* v. *Storms*, 9 Cowen R. 687; 2 Saund. R. 47 *b*; Bac. Abr. Trespass, C. 2; id. Trover, C ; *Smith* v. *Mills*, 1 T. R. 480, Ashurst J.; *Lotan* v. *Cross*, 2 Camp. R. 464; *Putnam* v. *Wiley*, 8 Johns. R. 432; *Hoyt* v. *Gilston*, 13 Johns. R. 141, 561.

if the injury done by a stranger is of such a nature, that the bailee would be liable over to the lender for it, the latter may maintain an action of trespass, and even trover, founded upon his possession, to recover damages; for the mere possession of property without title is sufficient against a wrong-doer.[1] A simple bailee (said Mr. Chief Justice Best) has a sufficient interest to sue in trover.[2] The same doctrine is laid down in Blackstone's Commentaries in very strong and decided terms.[3]

§ 281. There is a very loose note in the case of *Rich v. Aldred* (6 Mod. R. 216), which contains two positions, said to have been laid down by Lord Holt, on the subject of bailments, which may seem to require notice. One is, that if A bails the goods of C to B, and C brings detinue against B, the latter may plead the bailment to him by A to be redelivered to A, and so bring in A as garnishee to interplead with C. It does not appear under what circumstances this opinion was expressed; and it is by no means clear, that in all cases such a plea would be good, even for the purposes of interpleader at the common law, however the case may be in equity. Generally speaking, a bailee cannot, as we have before seen, be in a better situation than the person, from whom he has re-

---

1 *Hurd v. West,* 7 Cowen, 753; Bacon Abr. Trespass, C. 2; *Burton v. Hughes,* 2 Bing. R. 172; *Sutton v. Buck,* 2 Taunt. R. 302; *Rooth v. Wilson,* 1 B. & Ald. 59; 2 Ld. Raym. 911; *Barker v. Miller,* 6 Johns. R. 195; *Badlam v. Tucker,* 1 Pick. R. 389, 395; *Waterman v. Robinson,* 5 Mass. R. 303; Bac. Abr. Bailment, D.; 2 Bl. Com. 453; 1 Dane's Abr. ch. 17, art. 9.

2 *Burton v. Hughes,* 2 Bing. R. 172, 175; see also *Ogle v. Atkinson,* 5 Taunt. 759; *Hurd v. West,* 7 Cowen R. 752; *Amory v. Delamirie,* 1 Str. R. 505.

3 2 Bl. Com. 453; see also ante, §§ 93, 150, 152.

ceived it. If the latter has no title to detain the property against the owner, he cannot do it; and his deten-
tion is a conversion.[1]

§ 282. The other position is, that if A bails goods to
C, and afterwards transfers his whole right in them to
B, B cannot maintain detinue for them against C, because the special property, that C acquires by the bailment, is not thereby transferred to B.[2] This position
also seems questionable. For if the bailment is a
naked bailment, no special property passes to C; and
what difficulty can there then be in A's transferring his
property to a thing in the possession of his agent or
bailee? Nothing is more common than a transfer
of property, by a principal, of goods in the hands of his
factor; and no one doubts, that it is a valid transfer,
subject only to any lien, which the factor may possess.
So, a transfer of goods, while at sea, in the possession
of the master of a ship, is deemed a valid transfer, and
if he refuses to deliver them, upon a due demand and
refusal the vendee may maintain a suit against him
for a recovery of them or their value. There is great
reason, therefore, to suspect the accuracy of the report
in both respects.

§ 283. We have already had occasion to notice the
distinction between a *mutuum* and a *commodatum*. In
the latter case no special property passes to the borrower. In the former case the absolute property
passes to the borrower, it being a loan for consumption, and he being bound to restore, not the same
thing, but other things of the same kind.[3] Thus, if

---

[1] *Wilson* v. *Anderton*, 1 Barn. & Adolp. 450; ante, § 102.

[2] Ante, § 103.

[3] Jones's Bailm. 64; 2 Ld. Raym. 916; 1 Dane's Abr. ch. 17, art. 11,
16; 1 Bell's Com. 255.

corn, wine, money, or any other thing, which is not intended to be re-delivered back, but only an equivalent
in kind, is lost or destroyed by accident, it is the loss of
the borrower, for it is his property, and he must restore the equivalent in kind.[1]   In a case in New York
the accuracy of this doctrine seems to have been
brought into doubt.   There, a person sent to a miller
a quantity of wheat, to be exchanged for flour, and
the miller mixed it with a mass of wheat of the same
quality, belonging to himself and others.   Before the
flour was delivered to the party, the mill with all its
contents was destroyed by an accidental fire, without
any fault or negligence of the miller.   It was held by
the Court, in a suit by the party, who sent the wheat,
that the miller was not responsible for the loss, and
was not obliged to deliver the flour.   The ground was,
that the contract was not a sale of the wheat, and
the property in it was not transferred to the miller.[2]
Now, in this case, if the flour to be returned was to
be that ground out of the specific wheat delivered, the
decision of the court stands upon acknowledged principles.   But if other flour only, equal to that, which
would be ground out of wheat of a like kind and quality, was to be returned, it was a clear case of *mutuum*;
and the defendant (the miller) was responsible; for
the wheat, on the delivery, became his property.   The
latter would seem to have been the actual posture of
the case; but the Court must have proceeded upon
the ground, that it was bailment of hire.   The case of
Slaughter v. *Green* (1 Rand. Virg. R. 3) must be
supported, if at all, upon the same ground.   The de-

---

1 Noy's Maxims, ch. 43; Jones's Bailm. 64, 102.
2 *Seymour* v. *Brown*, 19 Johns. R. 44.

cision in the former case has been pointedly disapproved of upon its circumstances by Mr. Chancellor Kent in his Commentaries, whose opinion is supported by a later decision in the same state.[1] The common law is coincident with the civil law on this point, as Sir William Jones has sufficiently pointed out.[2]

§ 284. In the Scottish law, there is a peculiar word, *fungible*, which is used to designate such articles as may be the subject of contracts of *mutuum*. A fungible, in that law, is defined to be any thing whatever, which consists in quantity and is regulated by number, weight, or measure, such as corn, wine, or money ; and it answers to the description in the civil law of things, of which there may be a *mutuum, res quæ pondere, numero, et mensurâ constant.*[3] *

§ 285. Here ends the intended commentary on the Contract of Gratuitous Loans, a subject of daily occurrence in the actual business of human life. It has, however, furnished very little occasion for the interposition of judicial tribunals, for reasons equally honorable to the parties, and to the liberal spirit of polished society. The generous confidence thus bestowed is rarely abused; and if a loss or injury unintentionally occurs, an indemnity is either promptly offered, or promptly waived.

---

[1] 2 Kent Com. 463, 464; *Hurd* v. *West*, 7 Cowen R. 752, 756, note; *Buffum* v. *Merry*, 3 Mason R. 478.

[2] Jones's Bailm. 102; Dig. Lib. 19, tit. 2, 1. 31 ; Pothier, Prêt à consumption ; Doct. & Stud. D. 2, ch. 38.

[3] 1 Bell's Com. 255, n. 2 ; Hein. Elem. Pand. Lib. 12, tit. 1, § 3.

* Heineccius uses the same word to express the same things, "res fungibiles." Hein. Elem. Pand. P. 3 ; Lib. 12, tit. 1, § 2.

CHAPTER V.

ON PAWNS OR PLEDGES.

§ 286. HAVING gone through with gratuitous bailments, we next come to the consideration of contracts founded in mutual benefit and interest; and first, of the contract of Pledge, or Pawn, for these words seem indifferently used in our law to express the same idea. Sir William Jones defines a pledge to be "a bailment of goods by a debtor to his creditor, to be kept till the debt is discharged."[1]* Lord Holt defines it thus; "when goods or chattels are delivered to another as a pawn, to be security for money borrowed of him by the bailor; and this is called in Latin (he adds) *vadium*, and in English, a *pawn* or *pledge*."[2] In the civil law, it is properly called *pignus*, and defined thus; " Pignus appellatum a pugno, quia res, quæ pignori dantur, manu traduntur. Unde etiam videri potest, quod quidam putant, pignus proprie rei mobilis constitui."[3] And in the civil law, a pawn (*pignus*) was distinguished from an hypothecation (*hypotheca*) in this, that in the former the possession was delivered to the pawnee; in

---

1 Jones's Bailm. 117; Id. 36; 1 Dane's Abr. ch. 17, art. 4.

2 *Coggs* v. *Bernard*, 2 Ld. Raym. 909, 913.

3 Dig. Lib. 50, tit. 16, 1. 2, § 38; Hein. Pand. Lib. 20, tit. 1, §§ 2, 3, 4, 5.

* My learned friend, Mr. Chancellor Kent, follows the definition of Sir William Jones. 2 Kent Com. 449. See also Halifax's Analysis of the Civil Law, 63; 2 Bell's Com. 20.

the latter it was retained by the pawner.[1]   The words *pignus* and *hypotheca* seem often to have been confounded, for it is said, "Inter pignus autem et hypothecam tantum nomine sonus differt."[2]   Pothier defines a pawn or pledge to be a contract, by which a debtor gives to his creditor a thing to detain as security *for his debt.*[3]   The foregoing definitions are sufficiently descriptive of the nature of a pawn or pledge; but they are, in terms, limited to cases, where a thing is given as a mere security for *a debt;* but a pawn may well be made as security for any *other engagement.*[4]   The definition of Domat is, therefore, more accurate, because it is more comprehensive, viz., that it is an appropriation of the thing given for the security of an engagement.[5]   And in the common law it may be defined to be a bailment of personal property, as security for some debt or engagement.   In our language, the term *pawn* or *pledge* is confined to personal property; and where real or personal property is transferred, by a conveyance of the title, as a security, we commonly denominate it a *mortgage.*

§ 287.   A mortgage of goods is, in the common law, distinguishable from a mere pawn.   By a grant, or conveyance of goods in gage or mortgage, the whole legal title passes conditionally to the mortgagee; and if not redeemed at the time stipulated, the title becomes absolute at law, though equity will interfere

---

1 Dig. Lib. 13, tit. 7, l. 9, § 2; Inst. Lib. 4, tit. 6, § 7; Pothier, De Nantissement, art. prélim. 1.

2 Dig. Lib. 20, tit. 1, l. 5, § 1; Ayliffe's Pand. B. 4, tit. 18, p. 524; Halifax Anal. Civ. Law, 63.

3 Pothier, De Nantissement, art. prélim. 1.

4 *Isaac v. Clark,* 2 Bulst. 306, &c.; Pothier, De Nantissement, n. 11.

5 Domat, B. 3, tit. 1, § 1, n. 1.

to compel a redemption. But in a pledge, a special property only, as we shall presently see, passes to the pledgee, the general property remaining in the pledger.[1]

§ 288. There are few cases, if any, in our law, where an hypothecation, in the strict sense of the civil law, exists; that is, a pledge without possession by the pledgee. The nearest approach is, perhaps, in the case of bottomry bonds, and claims of seamen for wages against ships. But these are rather cases of liens or privileges. There have been some cases of mortgages of chattels, which have been held valid without any actual possession by the mortgagee; but they stand upon very peculiar grounds, and may be deemed exceptions to the general rule.[2] And in those cases the Court have recognised the general distinction, that a mortgage may be without possession; but a pledge cannot be without possession.[3] But of this more hereafter.

§ 289. Let us consider, then, in the first place, what are the essential ingredients in the contract. It may be treated in the common law, as in the civil law, as a contract founded in the law of nature, of reciprocal obligations, and of mutual benefit.[4]

§ 290. And first, as to the things, which may be the subject of it. These are, ordinarily, goods and chattels; but money, negotiable instruments, choses in action, and indeed any other thing valuable of a per-

---

[1] *Ryall v. Quarles*, 1 Atk. 167; *Lickbarrow v. Mason*, 6 East, 25; *Cortelyou v. Lansing*, 2 Cain Err. 200; *Badlam v. Tucker*, 1 Pick. 389, 397; 1 Dane's Abr. ch. 17, art. 4, § 11.

[2] *Ward v. Sumner*, 5 Pick. 59; *Holmes v. Crane*, 2 Pick. 607.

[3] *Ward v. Sumner*, 5 Pick. 59, 60.

[4] Pothier, De Nantissement, n. 13, 14, 15, 16, 17.

sonal nature, such as patent rights and manuscripts, may, by the common law, be delivered in pledge.[1] But in the civil law, and French law, Pothier seems to think, that incorporeal things, such as choses in action, are not deemed to be strictly capable of being conveyed in pledge. However, they are capable, by assignment, of being effectively used for the same purpose.[2] And it may, perhaps, be doubted, if Pothier's opinion is sustained by the civil law in its full extent.[3] In the Scottish law, goods, wares, and commodities are deemed the proper subjects of a pledge. Negotiable securities, also, are deemed capable of becoming a pledge. But, strictly speaking, debts and choses in action are not so; though, by being assigned, and the vouchers delivered, the same benefit is indirectly obtained.[4]

§ 291. It is not indispensable, that the pledge should belong to the pledger; it is sufficient, if it is pledged with the consent of the owner. And even without the consent of the owner, the thing may, as to the parties, be completely deemed a pledge, so that the pledger cannot reclaim it, except on discharging the obligation; for it does not lie in his mouth to assert himself not to be the owner.[5]

---

[1] *McLean* v. *Walker*, 10 Johns. R. 471, 475; *Roberts* v. *Wyatt*, 2 Taunt. R. 268; *Jarvis* v. *Rogers*, 13 Mass. R. 105; 15 Mass. R. 389; *Bowman* v. *Wood*, 15 Mass. R. 534; *Cortelyou* v. *Lansing*, 2 Cain Err. 200; 1 Dane's Abr. ch. 17, art. 4, § 11.

[2] Pothier, De Nantissement, n. 6, & note, ibid.

[3] Domat, B. 3, tit. 1, § 1, n. 23; Ayliffe's Pand. B. 4, tit. 18, pp. 527, 530, 542; Wood's Civ. Law, 219; Cod. Lib. 8, tit. 7, l. 4.

[4] 2 Bell's Com. 20, 23.

[5] Pothier, De Nantissement, n. 7, 27, 28; Ayliffe's Pand. B. 4. tit. 18, p. 53; 1 Dane's Abr. ch. 17, art. 4, §§ 7, 8; *Jarvis* v. *Rogers*, 13 Mass. R. 105.

§ 292. And by the pledge of a thing, not only the thing itself is pledged, but also, as accessory, the natural increase thereof. As, if a flock of sheep are pledged, the young, afterwards born, are also pledged.[1]

§ 293. By the civil law, certain things were prohibited from being put in pawn, such as the necessary apparel and furniture, beds, utensils, &c. of a debtor; his ploughs and other utensils for tillage; things esteemed sacred in the civil law; the benevolence or bounty of a monarch; the pay and emoluments of officers and soldiers.[2] With the exception of the two last, which stand upon general principles of public policy,[3] the common law allows a debtor to pledge any of his property, whether necessaries or otherwise.[4]

§ 294. In the civil law, not only property, of which the party was at the time in possession, or to which he had then a present title, might be pledged; but property, of which he had neither possession nor title, and which should be acquired by him *in futuro*. And when the title was so acquired *in futuro*, the right of the pledgee attached immediately upon it.[5] But, in such cases, it was more properly an hypothecation, than a pledge. In our law, a pledge is strictly confined to property, of which there may be a present possession or title, or in which there is a present vested right.

---

1 Domat, B. 3, tit. 1, § 1, n. 7, 8, 9, 10 ; Dig. Lib. 20, tit. 1, l. 13, 29 ; Ayliffe's Pand. B. 4, tit. 18, p. 530.

2 Domat, B. 1, tit. 1, § 1, n. 24, 25, 26, 27 ; Cod. Lib. 8, tit. 17, l. 8 ; Ayliffe's Pand. B. 4, tit. 18, pp. 527, 530.

3 *McCarthy* v. *Gould*, 1 Ball. & B. 389 ; 2 Anst. 533, 593 ; 1 H. Bl. 627 ; 3 T. R. 681 ; 4 T. R. 248.

4 Ayliffe's Pand. B. 4, tit. 18, p. 542.

5 Domat, B. 3, tit. 1, § 1, n. 2, 5, 6, 20 ; Dig. Lib. 20, tit. 1, l. 1, 15 ; Ayliffe's Pand. B. 4, tit. 18, p. 530.

§ 295. If the pawner has only a limited title to the thing, as for life, or years, he may still pawn it to the extent of his title; but when that expires, the pawnee must surrender it to the person, who succeeds to the ownership.[1]

§ 296. In respect to negotiable instruments for money, the party, who has a lawful possession of them, although not owner, has generally a power of pledging them, as well as of selling them absolutely, so as to bind the rights of the owner.[2] But it seems otherwise in relation to negotiable securities for goods, as bills of lading, where a factor may sell, but he cannot pledge the goods.[3]

§ 297. Secondly. It is of the essence of the contract, that there should be an actual delivery of the thing. Until the delivery of the thing, the whole rests in an executory contract, however strong may be the engagement to deliver; and the pledgee acquires no right of property in the thing.[4] What will amount to a delivery of the thing is matter of law. There need not be an actual manual delivery of the thing. It is sufficient, if there are any of those acts or circumstances, which, in construction of law, are sufficient to pass the possession of the property. Thus, goods at sea may be passed in pledge by a transfer of the muniments of title, as by a transfer of the bill of lading, an assign-

---

[1] *Hoare* v. *Parker*, 2 Term R. 376; 4 Camp. R. 121; *McCombie* v. *Davies*, 7 East R. 5; 1 Dane's Abr. ch. 17, art. 4, § 7; Domat, B. 3, tit. 1, § 3, n. 25.

[2] *Jarvis* v. *Rogers*, 13 Mass. R. 105; S. C. 15 Mass. R. 389.

[3] Abbott on Shipp. P. 3, ch. 9, § 19.

[4] Pothier, De Nantissement, n. 8, 9; *Portland Bank* v. *Stubbs*, 6 Mass. R. 422; *Tucker* v. *Buffington*, 15 Mass. R. 477; *Gale* v. *Ward*, 14 Mass. R. 352; *Cortelyou* v. *Lansing*, 2 Cain Err. 200; 2 Kent Com. 452; Bac. Abr. Bailment B; 2 Roll. R. 439; 6 Pick. R. 59, 60.

ment, &c. So, goods in a warehouse may be transferred by a symbolical delivery of the key thereof.[1]
So, if the pledgee has the thing already in possession,
as a deposit, &c., there the very contract transfers to
him by operation of law a virtual possession, as a
pledge, the moment the contract is completed.[2]

§ 298. In the civil law, although a delivery of the
thing took place in cases of a strict pledge, *pignus*, yet,
as has been already stated, in the case of an hypothecation, no such delivery or possession was necessary.
An hypothecation had a complete effect to transfer and
vest a title in the thing, if that was the intention of the
parties upon the mere execution of the contract, although no possession was given, or it was even stipulated not to be given. This part of the civil law seems
not to have been adopted, in respect to moveables, by
any of the states of Modern Europe; and it was silently suppressed by their anxious desire to promote the
interests of commerce. In none of these states is the
hypothecation of moveables allowed to prevail (as it did
at Rome) against a subsequent *bonâ fide* purchaser;
and in many of these states, it is void even against
personal creditors.[3] This is true in respect to the law
of Scotland, and France; which agrees with the common law of England in making void all hypothecations
of moveables without a delivery, so far as regards creditors.[4]

§ 299. And as possession is necessary to complete
the title by pledge, so, by the common law, the posi-

---

[1] 2 Term R. 462. See also *Jewett* v. *Warren*, 12 Mass. R. 300; *Badlam* v. *Tucker*, 1 Pick. R. 389, 396.

[2] Pothier, Nantissement, n. 9.

[3] 2 Bell's Com. 25, and the authorities there cited.

[4] 2 Bell's Com. 25; Emery on Traité à la Grosse Aventure, ch. 12,
§ 1; 1 Valin. Com. 341.

tive loss, or delivery back, of the possession of the thing with the consent of the pledgee, terminates his title.[1]   However, if the thing is delivered back to the owner for a temporary purpose only, and it is agreed to be redelivered to him, the pledgee may recover it against the owner, if he refuses to restore it after the purpose is fulfilled.[2]   In the civil law it was competent for the creditor, after the constitution of a pledge by delivery, to restore the thing to the possession of the pledger, either on hire, or under any other contract, without impairing his right.   But this principle has not, from its inconvenience, found its way into the modern jurisprudence of continental Europe.[3]

§ 300. Thirdly. It is of the essence of the contract, that the thing should be delivered as a security for some debt or engagement.   But it is of no consequence, whether the debt or engagement, for which the security is given, is that of the pledger or of any other person; for if there is an assent by all the proper parties, it is equally obligatory in each case.[4]   And it may be delivered, as well as security for a future debt or engagement, as for a past; for one, or for many debts and engagements; upon condition or absolutely; for a limited or for an indefinite period.[5]   It may also be implied as well as express;[6] and it matters not, what is

---

1 Per Wilde J. in *Holmes* v. *Crane*, 2 Pick. R. 607; *Jarvis* v. *Rogers*, 15 Mass. R. 389, 397.

2 *Roberts* v. *Wyatt*, 2 Taunt. 268; Domat, B. 3, tit. 1, § 1, n. 30.

3 Dig. Lib. 20, tit. 1, 1. 37; 2 Bell. Com. 22.

4 Pothier, Nantissement, n. 16; Domat, B. 3, tit. 1, § 1, n. 32, 33.

5 *United States* v. *Hooe*, 3 Cranch, 73; *Skirras* v. *Craig*, 7 Cranch, 34; 2 Johns. Ch. R. 309; Pothier, Nantissement, n. 12; Dig. Lib. 13, tit. 7, 1. 11, § 2; 1 Atk. R. 236; Prec. Ch. 419; 2 Vern. R. 691, 698; Gilb. Eq. R. 104; *Stevens* v. *Bell*, 6 Mass. R. 339.

6 Hein. Pand. P. 4, lib. 20, tit. 1, § 7; Domat, B. 3, tit. 1, § 1, n. 2, 3, 4; Ayliffe's Pand. B. 4, tit. 18, p. 528.

the nature of the debt or engagement.[1]   The contract
of pledge is not confined to an engagement for the
payment of money; but it is susceptible of being applied to any other lawful contract whatever.[2]

§ 301. In all cases the pledge is understood to be a
security for the whole and every part of the debt or
engagement.   The payment or discharge of a part,
therefore, still leaves it a perfect pledge for the residue
of the debt or engagement.   " Individua est pignoris
causa," is the language of the civil law.[3]

§ 302. As to the persons, by and between whom
the contract may be made, a few words will suffice.
All persons, having a general capacity to contract, may
enter into this engagement.   But persons under disabilities are affected by a like incapacity in this, as in
other cases of contract.   Married women, idiots, lunatics, and persons *non compos* from age, debility, or otherwise, are wholly unable to make a valid pledge, or
indeed to receive one.   But in respect to minors it
may be otherwise; for their contracts are generally
not void, but voidable only, and are to be avoided only
at their own election.

§ 303. The next inquiry, to which the subject leads,
is that of the rights and duties of the pawnee or
pledgee. (1.) As to his rights.   In virtue of the
pawn, the pawnee acquires, by the common law, a
special property in the thing,[4] and is entitled to the

---

[1] Domat, B. 3, tit. 1, § 2, n. 3, 5.

[2] Domat, B. 3, tit. 1, § 1, n. 2, 3, 4.

[3] Pothier, Nantissement, n. 43, 46; Ayliffe's Pand, B. 4, tit. 18,
p. 533; Domat, B. 3, tit. 1, § 1, n. 18; Pothier, Pand. Lib. 20, tit. 6,
§ 1, art. 1, 2.

[4] 2 Bl. Com. 396; Jones's Bailm. 80; *Moses* v. *Conham*, Owen R.
123, 124; *Ratcliffe* v. *Davis*, 1 Bulst. 29; Yelv. 178; Cro. Jac. 244;
Coggs v. *Bernard*, 2 Ld. Raym. 909, 916; Bac. Abr. Bailment B;
1 Dane Abr. ch. 17, art. 4, §§ 1, 6.

possession of it exclusively, during the time and for the objects, for which it is pledged.   If the owner should wrongfully repossess himself of the pawn, the pawnee may maintain a suit for the restitution of the thing itself, or for damages, at his election.   If it should be taken from his possession by a stranger, he may sue the stranger in the like manner.[1]   And in a suit for damages, the pawnee may recover against a stranger the full value of the thing, although it is pledged to him for less, as he will be answerable over to the owner for the excess.[2]

§ 304.   If there are any subsequent accessorial engagements, which either tacitly or expressly are, by the parties, intended to be attached to the pledge, the pledgee has a title and right of possession co-extensive with the new engagements.[3]   But the mere existence of a former debt due to the pledgee does not authorize him to detain the pledge for that debt, when it has been put into his hands for another debt or contract, unless there is some just presumption, that such was the intention of the parties.[4]   The rule in such cases strictly applies, that the contract is to govern the rights of the parties.   "Modus et conventio vincunt legem."

§ 305.   It has been said in argument, that the rule of the civil law is different; and that the pawnee may insist upon being paid all the debts due to him, whether those debts were secured by the pledge or not, before he can be called upon to deliver it up.   Perhaps it yet

---

[1] 2 Saund. R. 47, Williams's note; *Woodruff* v. *Halsey*, 8 Pick. R. 333.

[2] *Lyle* v. *Barker*, 5 Binn. 457.

[3] Prec. Ch. 419 ; 2 Vern. 691.

[4] *Jarvis* v. *Rogers*, 15 Mass. R. 389, 397, 414; *Green* v. *Farmer*, 4 Burr. 2214 ; 6 T. R. 258 ; 7 East R. 224 ; 15 Mass. R. 490 ; 2 Kent Com. 454 ; Prec. Ch. 419 ; 2 Vern. R. 691.

remains doubtful, whether the rule of the civil law was
intended to apply to any cases, except those, in which
there was an implication, that the subsequent debts
should be tacked to the preceding by the consent of
the parties.[1] Pothier, however, deems the civil law
clear on this point of retainer for other debts, independent of any such consent.   And he states the French
law to concur with the civil law in all cases, where the
claim is certain, and does not sound merely in damages.[2] By the Scottish law, if the precise limits of the
security, and the special appropriation to a particular
debt, are not established by the clearest evidence, the
pledge will be deemed an effectual security for all
debts.[3]

§ 306. The pledge applies not only to the debt or
other engagement, but also to all the incidental charges
and expenses.   If, for instance, a pledge is for a debt,
it covers the interest upon the debt; and if the pawnee is at any expense about the pledge, that also is
covered.[4]

§ 307. In the civil law it should seem, that the
pledgee has not any property in the thing; but a mere
right of detainer.   " Pignus, manente proprietate debitoris, solam possessionem transfert ad creditorem;"[5] or,
as we should say, the pawnee has a mere lien, and no
property.   Strictly speaking, at the common law, a
mere lien may be constituted, without either a *jus in*

---

[1] *Jarvis* v. *Rogers*, 15 Mass. R. 389, 397, 407, 415 ; Cod. Lib. 8, tit.
27 ; Wood, Civ. Law, 222 ; 2 Kent's Com. 455, & note.

[2] Pothier, Nantissement, n. 47.

[3] 1 Bell Com. 684 ; 2 Bell Com. 22.

[4] Domat. B. 3, tit. 1, § 3, n. 4, 19, 20 ; Ayliffe's Pand. B. 4, tit. 18,
p. 531, 532, 537 ; 1 Dane's Abr. ch. 17, art. 4.

[5] Dig. Lib. 13, tit. 7, l. 35, § 1.

re or a *jus ad rem*,[1] though for the most part it is accompanied by a special property.   In the law of Scotland a pledge confers what is called a real right, (that
is, a right in the thing,[2]) but it is not attended with any
other effect, than the power to retain the pledge, and
to apply judicially for a warrant to have it sold
for the debt or engagement.[3]

§ 308. Another right resulting, by the common law,
from the contract of pledge, is the right to sell the
pledge, when there has been a default in the pledger in
complying with his engagement.   Such a default does
not devest the general property of the pawner, but still
leaves in him (as we shall subsequently see) a right
of redemption.   But if the pledge is not redeemed
within the stipulated time by a due performance of the
contract, for which it is a security, the pawnee has
then a right to require a sale to be made thereof, in order to have his debt or indemnity.   And if there is no
stipulated time for the payment of the debt, but the
pledge is for an indefinite period, the pawnee has a
right, upon request, to a prompt fulfilment of the engagement, and if the pawner neglects or refuses to
comply, the pawnee may, upon due demand and notice to the pawner, require the pawn to be sold.[4]

§ 309. By the civil law a right of sale was given to
the same effect as in the common law.   The sale
might be by a judicial order of sale, or by the act of
the party, after due notice to the owner; and in either
case, if the sale was *bonâ fide*, it completely passed
the title to the purchaser.   Justinian, however, direct-

---

1 *Brace* v. *Duchess of Marlborough*, 2 P. Wms. 491.
2 1 Bell Com. 219.
3 2 Bell Com. 20, 21, 22.
4 2 Kent Com. 452.

ed, that if any mode of selling was prescribed by the parties, that should be followed ; but in the absence of any such stipulation the pawnee might sell, after two years from the proper notice to the party, or from a judicial sentence, and not before.[1] The modern nations of continental Europe, and others using the civil law, seem generally to have adopted the rule of requiring a judicial sale.[2]

§ 310. The law of England, existing in the time of Glanville, seems to have required a judicial process to justify the sale, or at least to destroy the right of redemption.[3] But the law, as at present established, leaves an election to the pawnee. He may file a bill in equity against the pawner for a foreclosure and sale ; or he may proceed to sell *ex mero motu*, upon giving due notice of his intention to the pledger. And in the latter case, if the sale is *bonâ fide* and reasonably made, it will be equally as obligatory, as in the first case.[4] But a judicial sale is most advisable in pledges of large value ; as the Courts watch any other sales with uncommon jealousy and vigilance ; and any irregularity may bring its validity into question.[5] With the exception of Louisiana, where the civil law pre-

---

[1] Pothier, Pand. Lib. 20, tit. 5, art. 1, § 6, n. 18, 19 ; Heinecc. Pand. P. 4, Lib. 20, tit. 5, §§ 37, 38, 39, 42 ; Cod. Lib. 8, tit. 3, 1. 3 ; Domat, B. 3, tit. 1, § 3, n. 9, 10 ; Ayliffe's Pand. B. 4, tit. 18, p. 532.

[2] Pothier, Nantissement, n. 24, 25 ; Ersk. Inst. B. 3, tit. 1, § 33 ; Cod. Civ. art. 2078 ; Cod. Louisiana, art. 3132 ; 2 Kent Com. 453 ; Domat, B. 3, tit. 1, § 3, n. 1, 2.

[3] Glanville, Lib. 10, ch. 1, ch. 6 ; 1 Reeve's Hist. 161, 162 ; 2 Bell Com. 20, 21.

[4] *Pothener* v. *Dawson,* 1 Holt, N. P. R. 385 ; *Tucker* v. *Wilson,* 1 P. W. 261 ; 1 Brown, Parl. Cas. 494 ; *Lockwood,* v. *Ewer,* 9 Mod. 278 ; 3 Atk. 303 ; *Cortelyou* v. *Lansing,* 2 Cain Err. 200 ; 2 Kent Com. 453.

[5] 2 Kent Com. 452, 453, 454 ; Prec. Ch. 419 ; Gilb. Eq. R. 104 ; 1 Ves. 278 ; 3 Bro. Ch. R. 21 ; *Hart* v. *Ten Eyck,* 2 Johns. Ch. R. 62.

vails, the English rule seems generally adopted in America.[1]

§ 311. The case of pawns seems distinguishable, in this respect, from the ordinary case of liens ; for a mere right of lien is not understood to carry with it any right of sale to secure an indemnity. The foundation of the distinction rests in this, that the contract of pledge carries an implication, that the security shall be made effectual to discharge the obligation;[2] but in a case of lien, nothing is supposed to be given but a right of retainer.[3]

§ 312. But it may be asked, what are the rights of the pledgee when the pledge is sold, and there are various claims upon the funds produced by the sale? This subject is treated at large in the civil law; and a few of the leading distinctions will here be adverted to. In the first place, those creditors, who have what are called privileged debts in the civil law, that is to say, debts, in respect to which a lien or right of preference exists on the property, enjoy a priority of payment, and are to be paid before the pawnee; and privileged creditors of equal rank are to take *pari passu*. In the next place, those creditors, who, as mortgagees or pawnees, have a specific title to the thing, take according to the priority in point of time of their titles, unless some peculiar circumstances intervene to vary the rule. In the next place, if the pledge is for the joint benefit of several creditors, each of them is entitled to share equally with the others according to his debt. But if

---

1 2 Kent Com. 452, 453; *Cortelyou v. Lansing*, 2 Cain Err. 200; *McLean v. Walker*, 10 Johns. R. 471; *Garlick v. James*, 12 Johns. R. 146; *Hart v. Ten Eyck*, 2 Johns. Ch. R. 62.

2 Gibbs C. J. in *Pottener v. Dawson*, 1 Holt's N. P. C. 385.

3 2 Bell Com. 95, 96.

the thing is pledged severally to two creditors, without
any communication with each other, and one of them
has obtained the possession, he is entitled to a preference, for "In æquali jure melior est conditio possi-
dentis." He therefore, in the case of a sale, is preferred, in receiving compensation, to all the other
creditors, who have entered into a contract of pledge
with the debtor.[1]

§ 313. Few cases have arisen upon this subject in
the common law; and it would be unsafe to rely wholly upon the civil law, as furnishing safe analogies for
our guidance. In the absence, however, of any authority, the Civilians may assist our inquiries; and for
this purpose, Domat, in an especial manner, may be
consulted with advantage.[2]   It had been decided, that
a person, who held a mortgage as security for a debt
due to himself and for another debt due to a third person, and who had agreed to sell the property, whenever
he could realize a sum equal to both debts, and to apply the proceeds to the payment of the debt of the
third person, was entitled, if the proceeds were insufficient to satisfy both debts, to satisfy his own debt
first, and apply the surplus only to the other debt.[3]
The case seems to have turned upon the construction
of the peculiar language of the agreement.   But the
Court said, that as there was no stipulated appropria-

---

[1] Domat, B. 3, tit. 1, § 5, per tot; Heinecc. Pand. P. 4, Lib. 20, tit.
4, §§ 31 to 36; Ayliffe's Pand. B. 4, tit. 18, p. 529; Domat, B. 3, tit. 1,
§ 1, n. 13, 14, § 3, n. 3; Pothier, Pand. Lib. 20, tit. 4, per tot.

[2] Pothier, Nantissement, n. 26; Heinecc. Pand. 4, Lib. 20, tit. 4,
§ 36; Dig. Lib. 20, tit. 1, l. 10; Ayliffe's Pand. B. 4, tit. 18; Domat,
B. 3, tit. 1, § 1, n. 14; Wood Civ. Law, 221; Domat, B. 3, tit. 1, § 5,
per tot; Pothier, Pand. Lib. 20, tit. 4, per tot.

[3] *Marshall* v. *Bryant*, 12 Mass. R. 321.

tion in case the proceeds should fall short of both debts, the party holding the pledge was entitled to satisfy his own demand first, and to pay over the surplus only to the other party. This seems to follow out the rule of the civil law, which, in a like case, considers the possession as entitling the party to a preference.[1]

§ 314. If several things are pledged, each is deemed liable for the whole debt or other engagement. And the pledgee may proceed to sell, until the debt or other dues are completely discharged. And if one thing perishes by accident or casualty without his default, he has a right over all the residue for his whole debt or other duty.[2] And the pledgee may sell not only the things pledged, but all their increments. But when once he has obtained an entire satisfaction, he can proceed no farther; and if there is any surplus, it belongs to the pledger.[3] If the things pawned are insufficient to pay his whole debt or other duty, the surplus constitutes a personal charge on the debtor or other contracting party, and may be recovered accordingly.[4] And the pledgee may release one of the things pawned without affecting any of his rights to the others.[5]

§ 315. The possession of the pawn does not suspend the right of the pawnee to proceed personally

---

[1] Domat, B. 3, tit. 1, § 1, n. 14; Dig. Lib. 20, tit. 1, 1. 10; Dig. Lib. 50, 1. 128; Pothier, Pand. Lib. 20, tit. 4, §§ 20, 31.

[2] Domat, B. 3, tit. 1, § 1, n. 18, § 3, n. 12; *Ratcliffe* v. *Davis*, Yelv. 178; Bac. Abr. Bailment B; Anon, 2 Salk. R. 522.

[3] Domat, B. 3, tit. 1, § 1, n. 29, § 3, n. 12; Bac. Abr. Bailment B; *Stevens* v. *Bell*, 6 Mass. R. 339.

[4] Domat, B. 3, tit. 1, § 1, n. 31; 2 Brown, Ch. R. 125; *South Sea Company* v. *Duncomb*, 2 Str. 919.

[5] Domat, B. 3, tit. 1, § 3, n. 13, 14.

against the pawner for his whole debt or other engagement without selling the pawn ; for it is only a collateral security.[1] If the pawner, in consequence of any
default or conversion of the pawnee, has recovered
back the pawn or its value, still the debt remains and
is recoverable, unless in such prior action it has been
deducted.[2]   And it seems, that by the common law
the pawnee, in such an action for the value, has a right to
have the amount of his debt recouped in the damages.[3]

§ 316. It would seem, that by the civil law the
pawnee could not be forced to commence a personal
suit against the debtor, where there had been an
omission to sell the pledge. The language of the Code
is, " Persecutione pignoris omissâ debitoris actione
personali convenire creditor urgeri non potest." [4]

§ 317. In speaking of sales by the pawnee it has
been assumed, that there is no special agreement
between the parties, as to the time or mode of sale
existing, nor any stipulation wholly interdicting any sale.
If such an agreement should exist, it must ordinarily regulate the rights of both parties ; and neither of
them will be allowed to depart from it with impunity.[5]
But where there was an express prohibition of sale in
the terms of the contract, the civil law authorized the
pledgee to demand his debt, and upon the pledger's
refusal to pay it, enabled him to obtain a judicial de-
cree for a sale ; for it was said, that otherwise the pawn

1 *South Sea Company* v. *Duncomb*, 2 Str. 919 ; Bac. Abr. Bailment B ;
Anon, 12 Mod. 564 ; Holt R. 461 ; 1 Dane's Abr. ch. 18, art. 4, § 9.

2 *Ratcliffe* v. *Davis*, Yelv. 179 ; Bac. Abr. Bailment B.

3 *Jarvis* v. *Rogers*, 15 Mass. R. 389.

4 Pothier, Pand. Lib. 20, tit. 6, § 2, l. 6 ; Cod. Lib. 8, tit. 14, l. 24.

5 *Stevens* v. *Bell*, 6 Mass. R. 339.

might be useless.[1] The common law does not appear
to have made any direct provision in such a case. How
far a Court of Equity might interfere to grant redress,
it is not perhaps easy to say, especially if the pledge
is perishable.

§ 318. But the right of the pledgee is strictly confined to a sale ; for he cannot appropriate the property
to himself upon the default of the pledger; nor can he
so appropriate it (as we shall hereafter see) by any
agreement with the pledger, that upon such default
it shall be irredeemable.[2]

§ 319. In respect to sales also, there is this salutary
restraint upon the pawnee to secure his fidelity and
good faith, that he can never become a purchaser at the
sale.   This rule will be found recognised equally in the
common law and the civil law.[3]

§ 320. Where there is no contract on the part of
the pledgee requiring him to sell the pledge, it has
been said, that at the common law he is not compellable so to do; but he may retain the pledge until the
discharge of his debt or other contract. This doctrine
is true with reference to the case, in which it was used ;
for the point there was, whether a creditor, by a foreign
attachment or execution, could compel the pledgee to
sell; and it was very properly held, that he could not.[4]
But a Court of Equity might, in a fit case, interfere in
favour of the pledger, and compel a sale, if it was
clear, that the property would produce more than sufficient to satisfy the debt, or if it was of a perishable
nature.   The civil law has authorized a compulsive

---

1 Domat, B. 3, tit. 1, § 3, n. 10; Ayliffe's Pand. B. 4, tit. 18, p. 533.

2 Domat, B. 3, tit. 1, § 3, n. 11.

3 Ayliffe's Pand. B. 4, tit. 18, p. 534 ; Cod. Lib. 8, tit. 28, 1. 10.

4 *Badlam* v. *Tucker*, 1 Pick. 389, 400.

sale against the creditor, if not universally, at least in many cases.[1]

§ 321. Where the pledge is a negotiable security, (such as a negotiable note,) the pledgee has a right to recover and receive the money due thereon, and to sue for it in his own name. But he has no right (unless perhaps in a very extreme case) to compromise with the parties to the security for a less sum, than the sum due on the security.[2]

§ 322. In the next place, as to the right of the pledgee to alienate the property. It is very certain, that at the common law he cannot alienate the property absolutely, nor beyond the title actually possessed by him, unless in very special cases.[3] But if the pledge is of mere current coin, or negotiable securities, capable in their own nature of passing by delivery, there, if the pledgee sells to a *bonâ fide* purchaser without notice, the latter acquires an absolute property in the pledge. For in a concurrence of equal rights he, who has trusted the party, and enabled him to impose upon another, shall be bound by his acts. Thus, if the pledge is of certificates of stock, which may pass by delivery, a *bonâ fide* purchaser, or subsequent pledgee, may hold the stock against the real owner.[4] The like rule applies to negotiable securities.[5]

§ 323. But if a negotiable note, or other security, contains on it any intimation, that it belongs to another

---

1 Pothier, Pand. Lib. 20, tit. 5, § 4, n. 16.

2 *Bowman* v. *Wood*, 15 Mass. R. 534; *Garlick* v. *James*, 12 Johns. R. 146.

3 *Demainbray* v. *Metcalfe*, 2 Vern. 691; 1 Eq. Cas. Abr. 324; Prec. Ch. 419; *Hartop* v. *Hoare*, 3 Atk. 43; *Pickering* v. *Busk*, 15 East R. 38.

4 *Jarvis* v. *Rogers*, 13 Mass. R. 105; S. C. 15 Mass. R. 389.

5 *Bowman* v. *Wood*, 15 Mass. R. 534; *Garlick* v. *James*, 12 Johns. R. 146; *Collins* v. *Martin*, 1 Bos. & Pull. 143; *Peacock* v. *Rhodes*, Doug. R. 633; 3 Atk. 56; 1 Burr. 452.

person, or is for his account, there it is incapable of being pledged for the use of the holder.[1]   And the rule, in respect to negotiable securities, seems confined to cases of securities, which pass as money. For although a bill of lading of goods is negotiable, yet if the consignee has a mere lien for advances, he cannot pledge them by indorsing the bill of lading, (though he may sell them,) even if the pawnee is ignorant, that he is not owner; unless indeed the owner should have enabled him so to act by holding him out to the world exclusively as owner; for then he might be bound by the pledge.[2]

§ 324. The pawnee may, by the common law, deliver over the pawn into the hands of a stranger for safe custody without consideration;[3] or he may sell and assign all his interest in the pawn; or he may convey the same interest conditionally, by way of pawn, to another person, without in either case destroying or invalidating his security.[4]   But if the pledgee should undertake to pledge the property (not being negotiable securities) for a debt beyond his own, or to make a transfer thereof to his own creditor, as if he was absolute owner; it is clear, that in such a case he would be guilty of a breach of trust; and his creditor would acquire no title beyond that held by the pawnee.   The only question, which, under such

---

1 *Truetell* v. *Barenden*, 8 Taunt. R. 100.

2 *Newsome* v. *Thornton*, 6 East R. 17 ; *Martini* v. *Coles*, 1 M. & Selw. 140; *Shipley* v. *Kymer*, 1 M. & Selw. 484; *Pickering* v. *Busk*, 15 East R. 38 ; *Queiroz* v. *Trueman*, 3 B. & Cresw. 342.

3 *Ingersoll* v. *Von Bokkelin*, 7 Cowen R. 670.

4 *Moses* v. *Conham*, Owen R. 123; *Ratcliffe* v. *Davis*, 1 Buls. R. 29 ; S. C. Yelv. R. 178; Cro. Jac. 244 ; Jackson J. in *Jarvis* v. *Rogers*, 15 Mass. R. 389, 408 ; *Mann* v. *Shipner*, 2 East, 523, 529 ; *McComb* v. *Davies*, 7 East, 6, 7.

circumstances, would seem to admit of controversy, is, whether the creditor would be entitled to retain the pledge until the original debt was discharged, or whether the owner might recover the pledge, as if the case was a naked tort without any qualified right in the first pledgee.

§ 325. The doctrine of the common law now established in England, after some diversity of opinion, is, that a factor, having a lien on goods for advances, or for a general balance, has no right to pledge the goods; and if he does, he conveys no title to the pledgee.[1] The effect of this doctrine is, in England, to deny to the pledgee any right in such a case to retain the goods, even for the advances or balance due to the factor. In short, the transfer is deemed wholly tortious; so that the principal may sue for and recover the pledge without making any allowance or deduction whatsoever for the debt due by him to the factor. The inconvenience, not to say harshness, of the latter part of the doctrine has been very seriously felt in England. And what renders it somewhat objectionable in principle is, that it is admitted, that the factor has a right to assign or deliver over the goods, as a pledge or security, to the extent of his lien thereon, if he avowedly confines the assignment or pledge to that, and does not exceed his interest.[2] Now, if the right

---

[1] *Daubigny* v. *Duvall*, 5 T. R. 604; *Newsome* v. *Thornton*, 6 East R. 17; *McComb* v. *Davies*, 7 East R. 5; *Martini* v. *Coles*, 1 M. & Selw. 140; *Shipley* v. *Keymer*, 1 M. & Selw. 4 4; *Jolly* v. *Rathbone*, 2 M. & Selw. 298; *Pickering* v. *Busk*, 15 East R. 44; *Queiroz* v. *Trueman*, 3 Barn. & Cresw. 342.

[2] *Mann* v. *Shipner*, 2 East R. 523, 529; *McComb* v. *Davies*, 7 East R. 6, 7; *Kuekein* v. *Wilson*, 4 Barn. & Ald. 443; 1 Bell Com. 483; 2 Bell Com. 95; *Urquhart* v. *McIver*, 4 Johns. R. 103; 2 Kent Com. 489.

or lien of the factor is capable of assignment or transfer at all, as an interest or right adhering to the goods, and entitled to accompany the possession, there seems great difficulty in maintaining, that, because the title to the pledge is infirm in part, upon a general transfer or a general pledge, it shall be bad in toto, notwithstanding the pledgee may be an innocent *bonâ fide* holder. The general denial of the right to pledge by factors does not appear to have approved itself to the minds of Lord Eldon and Lord Ellenborough;[1] and it has been suggested by Mr. Bell, that it probably had its origin in mistake.[2] Parliament, however, has at length interfered, and placed the doctrine on this subject upon a far more rational foundation, than it was placed by the decisions of Westminster Hall.

§ 326. In America the general doctrine, that a factor cannot pledge the goods of his principal, has been frequently recognised.[3] But it does not appear, as yet, to have been carried to the extent of deeming the pledge altogether a tortious proceeding so that the title is not good in the pledgee even to the extent of the lien of the factor; and the principal may maintain an action against the pledgee without discharging the lien, or at least without giving the pledgee a right to recoup the amount of the lien in the damages. Considering the present state of the English law on this point, and the unsatisfactory principle, on which the former doctrine rests, it would perhaps be matter of

---

1 *Pulteney* v. *Kymer,* 3 Esp. R. 182; *Pickering* v. *Busk,* 15 East, 44.

2 1 Bell Com. 486; 2 Kent Com. 491, note (*a.*)

3 *Kinder* v. *Shaw,* 2 Mass. R. 398; *Odiorne* v. *Maxcy,* 13 Mass. R. 178; 2 Kent Com. 455, 456, 487, 488; *Jarvis* v. *Rogers,* 15 Mass. R. 389; *Urquhart* v. *McIver,* 4 Johns. R. 103; *Van Amringe* v. *Peabody,* 1 Mason R. 440.

regret, if the American Courts should feel themselves constrained, by the pressure of authority, to yield to it.[1]

§ 327. But whatever doubt may be indulged as to the case of a factor, it has been decided, that; in case of a strict pledge, if the pledgee transfers the same to his own creditor, the latter may hold the pledge, until the debt of the original owner is discharged.[2] And it has been intimated, that there is, or may be a distinction favourable to the pledgee, which does not apply, or may not apply to a factor, since the latter has but a lien, whereas the former has a special property in the goods.[3] It is not very easy to point out any substantial distinction between the case of a pledgee and the case of a factor. The latter holds the goods of his principal, as a security and pledge for his advances and other dues. He has a special property in them, and may maintain an action for any violation of his possession either by the principal or by a stranger. And he is generally treated, in juridical discussions, as in the condition of a pledgee.[4] But whether the distinction is well or ill founded, it does not materially affect the reasoning, that assigns to the pledgee of a factor a right to detain the pledge until the lien of the factor is discharged. And where, instead of a mere pledge, there is an actual transfer of the goods by a deed or other legal conveyance by way of mortgage, there is no question, that the mortgagee may assign over the goods; and the assignee will be entitled to

---

[1] 2 Kent Com. 491, note (a.)

[2] *Jarvis* v. *Rogers*, 15 Mass. R. 389.   [3] Id. p. 408.

[4] *McComb* v. *Davies*, 7 East R. 5; Whitaker on Liens, 127; 2 Bl. Com. 395, 396; Jones's Bailm. 85, 86; 2 Kent Com. 456; 2 Saund. R. 47, note by Williams; 1 Bell Com. 483; 2 Bell Com. 20, 93; Paley on Agency, ch. 5 & ch. 6, p. 282 to 288.

hold them against the mortgagor, until the mortgage debt, originally contracted, is paid. In such a case a legal, though defeasible title, is vested in the mortgagee, and not a mere lien, and to the extent of that title his assignment is operative and valid, and cannot be disturbed by the mortgagor, even though the mortgagee shall have assumed to convey an absolute title.

§ 328. Upon this subject, the civil law seems to have adopted the following rule. It enabled the pawnee to assign over, or to pledge the goods again, to the extent of his interest or lien on them; and, in either case, the transferree was entitled to hold the pawn, until the original owner discharged the debt, for which it was pledged.[1] But beyond this, the pledge was inoperative, and conveyed no title, according to the known maxim, "Nemo plus juris ad alium transferre potest, quam ipse haberet."[2] A relaxation of the strict rule of the civil law, founded upon the convenience of commerce, has worked its way into the modern jurisprudence of Continental Europe; and the power to pledge has been allowed to factors, so as to bind the goods to the full extent of any advances made upon them, though not for any antecedent debts due from the factor. Mr. Bell, in his Commentaries, has given an interesting view of the origin, progress, and present state of the law of Scotland, as well as of the Continent of Europe, on this subject, which will reward a careful perusal.[3]

§ 329. Another point, usually discussed under this head, is, how far the pawnee is entitled to use the pawn. Much of what properly belongs to this subject

---

1 Cod. Lib. 8, tit. 24, l. 1 ; Domat, B. 3, tit. 3, § 6, n. 1 to 7 ; Ayliffe's Pand. B. 4, tit. 18, p. 539.

2 Dig. Lib. 50, tit. 17, l. 54 ; Cod. Lib. 8, tit. 16, l. 6.

3 1 Bell's Com. 483 to 488.

has been already anticipated under other heads.[1] The
true rules deducible from the common law authorities,
and founded upon the presumed intentions of the
pawner, seem to be the following. (1.) If the pawn is
of such a nature, that the due preservation of it requires some use, there it is not only justifiable, but it is
indispensable to the faithful discharge of the duty of
the pawnee.[2] (2.) If the pawn is of such a nature, that
it will be worse for the use, such, for instance, as the
wearing of clothes, which are deposited, there the use
is prohibited to the pawnee.[3] (3.) If the pawn is of
such a nature, that the keeping is a charge to the
pawnee, as, if it is a cow or a horse, there the pawnee
may milk the cow and use the milk, and ride the
horse by way of recompense (as it is said) for the
keeping.[4]* (4.) If the use will be beneficial to the
pawn, or indifferent, there it seems, that the pawnee
may use it; as, if the pawn is of a setting dog, it may
well be presumed, that the owner would consent to the
dog's being used in partridge shooting, and thus confirmed in the habits, which make him valuable. So
books, which will not be injured by a moderate use,
may be read, examined, and used by the pawnee.[5]

§ 330. (5.) But, if the use will be without any injury,
and yet the pawn will thereby be exposed to extraordinary perils, there the use is impliedly interdicted.

---

[1] Ante, §§ 89, 90.   [2] Jones's Bailm. 81.

[3] 2 Salk. 522; 2 Ld. Ray. 909, 916; Jones's Bailm. 81.

[4] 2 Salk. 522; *Coggs* v. *Bernard*, 2 Ld. Ray. 909, 917; Jones's Bailm.
81; 1 Dane's Abr. ch. 17, art. 4, § 2.

[5] Jones's Bailm. 81 ; *Mones* v. *Conham*, Owen R. 123, 124.

* Mr. Chancellor Kent thinks the profits should belong to the pawner,
and be deducted from the debt; 2 Kent Com. 450.

Sir William Jones, indeed, suggests, that in such a case the goods may be used, (by which he is presumed to mean *lawfully* used,) but at the peril of the pledgee.[1] Thus, he says, "If chains of gold, earrings, bracelets, or other jewels, are pawned to a lady, they may be used by her, but at her peril; for if she is robbed of them, the loss is her own.[2] In another work of considerable authority it is said, that if the goods pawned will be the worse for using, the pawnee must not use them; otherwise he may use them at his peril. As, jewels pawned to a lady, if she keeps them in a bag, and they are stolen, she shall not be charged. But, if she go with them to a party, and they are stolen, she shall be answerable."[3] To the former position, Sir William Jones objects, "because (he says) the bag could hardly be taken, privately and quietly, without her omission of ordinary diligence." And he considers himself well supported in this objection by the authorities.[4] This, however, will be matter of discussion in a subsequent section. But it may well be doubted, whether there is any foundation for the doctrine, which is affirmed, both by Mr. Justice Buller and by Sir William Jones, that in case of a deposit of things, which are not hurt by use, the depositary may, *at his peril*, use them. The language of the authority, which is principally relied on for its support, does not, when properly construed, justify any such conclusion. In *Coggs* v. *Bernard*, (2 Ld. Ray. 909, 916,) Lord Holt says, "If the pawn be such, as it will be worse for using, the pawnee cannot use it, as clothes, &c. But,

---

1 Jones's Bailm. 81.

2 Jones's Bailm. 81.

3 Buller's N. Prius, 72.

4 2 Salk. 522; 2 Ld. Ray. 916, 917.

if it be such as will never be worse, as, if jewels for the
purpose were pawned to a lady, she might use them.
But then she must do it *at her own peril*. For whereas, if she keeps them locked up in her cabinet, if her
cabinet is broken open, and the jewels taken from
thence, she would be excused. If she wears them
abroad, and is there robbed, she will be answerable.
And the reason is, because the pawn is in the nature
of a deposit, *and as such, is not liable to be used.*"
Now, the reason here given, so far from proving, that
the pledgee may lawfully use the jewels, expressly
negatives any such right. And unless the contrary is
expressly agreed, it may fairly be presumed, that the
owner of such a pawn would not assent to the jewels
being used as a personal ornament, and thereby exposed to unnecessary and extraordinary perils.

§ 331. The civil law does not, in respect to the right
of using pawns, seem materially to differ from the common law, unless there is an exception furnished by the
rule of the civil law, that where the pawn is used (as if a
cow is milked) and a profit is obtained thereby, the
pawnee shall be bound to account for the profits, deducting all expenses for the keeping.[1]   Mr. Chancellor
Kent seems to think, that the rule in the common law is,
or, at least, ought to be the same;[2] and his doctrine
certainly carries with it a most persuasive equity.

§ 332. Having considered the rights, the next inquiry
is as to the duties of the pawnee. And here the question naturally presents itself, What is the degree of diligence imposed upon the pawnee, in respect to the
preservation thereof?   As the bailment is for the mu-

---

1 Jones's Bailm. 82 ; Pothier, Dépôt, n 47 ; Id. Nantissement, 35.
2 2 Kent Com. 450.

tual benefit and interest of both parties, the law requires, upon the principles already stated, that the
pawnee should use ordinary diligence in the care of
the pawn; and consequently he is liable for ordinary
neglect in keeping the pawn.[1] This is the rule laid
down by Bracton,[2] and maintained by Lord Holt.[3]
This, too, seems, according to the better opinion, to be
the rule of the civil law.[4] The point of responsibility
is in the civil law stated to be, where there is deceit
and negligence. " Dolum et culpam, &c. pignori ac-
ceptum," [5] says one passage of the Digest; " sed ubi
utriusque utilitas vertitur, ut in empto, ut in locato, ut
in dote, ut in pignore, ut in societate, et dolus et culpa
præstatur," [6] is another passage of the same authority.
A third passage declares, " Ea igitur, quæ diligens pater
familias in suis rebus præstare solet, à creditore exi-
guntur; " [7] and a fourth passage, " Quia pignus utriusque gratiâ datur, &c. placuit sufficere, si ad eam rem
custodiendam exactam diligentiam adhibeat." [8] The
same rule of ordinary diligence is understood to be
adopted in modern times in the civil law countries of
Continental Europe. It has the express sanction of
Pothier, and other writers of acknowledged authority.[9]

---

1 Jones's Bailm. 75 ; 2 Kent Com. 451 ; 1 Dane's Abr. ch. 17, art. 12.

2 Bract. 99 b.

3 2 Ld. Ray. 909, 916.

4 Jones's Bailm. 15, 21, 23, 75 ; Hein. Pand. Lib. 13, tit. 6, §§ 117, 118;
Domat, B. 1, tit. 1, § 4. n. 1.

5 Dig. Lib. 50, tit. 17, 1. 23.

6 Dig. Lib. 13, tit. 6, 1. 5, § 2 ; Id. tit. 7, 1. 13, 14.

7 Dig. Lib. 13, tit. 7, 1. 14.

8 Inst. Lib. 3, tit. 5, § 4 ; Ayliffe's Pand. B. 4, tit. 1, p. 531.

9 Jones's Bailm. 29, 30, 31 ; Pothier, Nantissement, n. 32, 33, 34 ;
Pothier, Obligations, n. 142 ; Domat, B. 3, tit. 1, § 4, n. 1 ; Ersk. Inst. B.
3, tit. 1, § 33 ; 1 Bell's Com. 453.

§ 333. It is under the head of pawns, (though it is often alluded to elsewhere,) that Sir William Jones has principally discussed the question, how far theft (by which he means *private theft*, as contradistinguished from *robbery*) constitutes a valid excuse for bailees, who are responsible for ordinary diligence, and especially, how far it constitutes an excuse for pawnees. We have already had occasion to notice this subject in our Introductory Chapter; and to state, that Sir William Jones holds, that theft is presumptive evidence of ordinary neglect, and of course, that pawnees are liable for losses by theft;[1] unless in cases, where they can, by positive evidence, repel every presumption of such neglect.[2] In this view of the matter he follows the civil law; and, indeed, it seems to have had an undue influence upon his judgment. It may not be unimportant, in this connexion, to review the doctrine of Sir William Jones a little more at large, than has been already done, since he puts himself in direct opposition to Lord Coke, and has bestowed an elaborate criticism on the opinion of the latter.

§ 334. Lord Coke, in his Institutes, said,[3] that "If goods be delivered to one as a gage or pledge, and they be stolen, he shall be discharged, because he hath a property in them, and therefore he ought to keep them no otherwise than his own." To which Sir William Jones, with unusual point, has replied, "I deny the first proposition, the reason, and the conclusion." The first proposition is, that if goods in pledge are stolen, the pawnee is discharged. Sir William Jones asserts the contrary; and says, that a bailee

---

1 Jones's Bailm. 76, 78, 79, 81; Id. 43, 44, 109, 110, 119.
2 Jones's Bailm. 98; *Vere* v. *Smith*, 1 Vent. 121.
3 1 Inst. 89 *a*; 4 Rep. 83 *b*.

cannot be considered as using ordinary diligence, who suffers the goods to be taken by stealth out of his custody. But for this position he cites no common law authority, except a dictum of Mr. Justice Cottesmore, in 10 H. 6, 21, 5, who said, "If I grant goods to a man to keep for my use, if the goods, by my default, [*mesgarde*, i. e. inattention,] are stolen, it should be a charge upon me out of my own goods; but if he is robbed of the same goods, he is excusable by law." [1] Now, the case here put is plainly a mere deposit, where the bailee is responsible only for gross neglect; and if Mr. Justice Cottesmore meant more, he was wrong in point of law. But he was not drawing any distinction between cases of theft, and robbery, as to the presumption of neglect; but between cases of losses by theft by *neglect* of the bailee, and cases of robbery by superior force, as affecting, in opposite manners, the responsibility of the bailee. The dictum, therefore, furnishes no authority to the purpose; and exclusively of this dictum the sole reliance of Sir William Jones is on the civil law, which he cites at large. The purport of the text of the civil law is not disputed; but its application, as an authority in the common law, is not admitted. There is, then, no authority at the common law, which maintains the argument of Sir William Jones.

§ 335. But there are common law authorities, which are entirely the other way. In *Vere* v. *Smith*, (1 Vent. 121,) which was a suit upon a bond to account, the defendant pleaded, that he locked up the money in his master's warehouse, and it was stolen from thence, (not saying without any default on his part,) and it was adjudg-

---

[1] Jones's Bailm. 44, note ; Id. p. 79.

ed, that the plea was a good bar to the action, and a sufficient accounting within the condition of the bond. In the case cited from Fitzherbert's Abridgment, in 8 Edw. 2, (Fitz. Abr. Detinue 59,) where goods were locked in a chest and left with the bailee, and the owner kept the key, and the goods were stolen, the bailee was held to be discharged. The whole reasoning of Lord Holt, in *Coggs* v. *Bernard*, (2 Ld. Ray. 909, 912,) proceeds upon the ground, that theft is not presumptive of negligence. In case even of a gratuitous loan, he says, that "If the bailee puts the horse lent into his stable, and he is stolen from thence, the bailee is not answerable; but if he leaves the stable doors open, and thieves steal the horse, he is chargeable, because the neglect gave the thieves the occasion to steal the horse."[1] The case found in the Book of Assises, [29 Lib. Assisarum, 28,] and cited by Sir William Jones in another page,[2] is directly in point in favour of Lord Coke's opinion. The action was detinue for a hamper, which had been bailed, and the bailee pleaded, that it had been delivered to him in gage for a certain sum of money; that he had put it among his other goods; and that all the goods had been stolen together from him. On that occasion, the Chief Justice said, that "If a man bails me goods to keep, and I put them among my own, I shall not be charged, if they be stolen." And the plaintiff was driven to reply, that "he had tendered the money before the stealing of the goods, and that the bailee (the creditor) refused to accept the money." To this case Sir William Jones gives no other answer than, that he suspects, that by theft in this report was meant robbery, as Brook, in

---

[1] 2 Ld. Ray. 916.   [2] Jones's Bailm. 77, 78.

his Abridgment, had abridged the case with a marginal note, " Quant les biens sont *robbes.*" [1] But, as we have the original case, we have just as good means to judge of its import, as Brook; and the language of the Book of Assises is, that it was a case of theft. It is highly improbable, that in a technical sense, there should have been any robbery, that is, a stealing of the hamper and other goods from the person of the bailee, or in his presence with force, or terror. The language of the case does not lead to any such conclusion; and the nature of the article, as well as the language of the Court, seems to point to it as a case of mere theft. The plea asserts the hamper to have been put among the other goods of the pawnee, which would seem to exclude the notion, that they were in his personal presence. In the modern case of *Finucane* v. *Small,* (1 Esp. R. 315,) Lord Kenyon held, that a bailee of goods kept for hire was not liable for a theft committed by his servants, although there were some prior suspicious circumstances impeaching their fidelity. If, indeed, the circumstances of the case prove, that the theft has been occasioned by negligence, or want of proper caution, there the pawnee may properly be held responsible. [2]

§ 336. The reason given by Lord Coke for his opinion is, that the pawnee has a special property therein. Sir William Jones says, that this is no reason at all; for every bailee has a temporary qualified property in the thing bailed. In this assertion he has, in previous pages of these Commentaries, been shown to be incorrect; for neither depositaries, nor mandataries, nor borrowers, have any special property; though, as they have a

---

[1] Brook. Abr. Bailm. 7.
[2] *Clarke* v. *Earnshaw,* 1 Gow. R. 30.

lawful possession, and they are answerable over, they may maintain an action for any tort done to the thing bailed during the time of their possession.[1] The reason given by Lord Coke is not indeed the true reason; but the true reason is, as Lord Holt says, that the law requires nothing extraordinary of the pawnee, but only that he shall use an ordinary care for restoring the goods.[2]

§ 337. Then, as to the conclusion of Lord Coke, that therefore the bailee ought to keep the goods merely as his own. This is certainly open to the criticism made upon it by Sir William Jones, that it does not express the true rule of law; for the bailee is bound " to take more care of the goods bailed than of his own, unless he in fact be a prudent and thoughtful manager of his own concerns; since every man ought to use ordinary diligence in affairs, which concern another, as well as himself." [3]   But where a bailee takes the same care of the pledge, as he does of his own goods, and both are lost by theft, that furnishes *primâ facie* a presumption of ordinary diligence; for every man will be presumed to exercise such diligence in respect to his own affairs and property, until the contrary is shown. In other words, every man will be presumed to do his duty until the contrary appears. And if the bailee is shown to have taken less care of the bailed goods than of his own, it furnishes a strong, and in many cases a decisive presumption of negligence.[4] Indeed, in some cases Sir William Jones him-

---

1 Ante, §§ 93, 150, 152, 191, 279, 280.

2 *Coggs v. Bernard*, 2 Ld. Raym. 909, 916, 917 ; Jones's Bailm. 82.

3 Jones's Bailm. 82 ; Id. 30, cites Pothier ; Id. 83.

4 Jones's Bailm. 30, 31, 46, 47, 82 ; *Clarke v. Earnshaw*, 1 Gow. R 30.

self admits, that the character of the bailee may enter into the contract, and qualify it, making him, if known to be a very negligent man, not liable, unless the loss is occasioned by more than his habitual negligence; and if he is known to be a very diligent man, making him liable for losses occasioned by less than his habitual diligence.[1] Lord Holt also has proceeded upon the like presumption of due diligence, where a man takes the same care of the bailed goods, that he does of his own.[2] So that, although Lord Coke's conclusion may not be strictly logical, yet it is not, according to the ordinary presumption of law, far from the truth; and at all events it does not leave Sir William Jones in possession of such a victory, as he supposes, since Lord Coke's main proposition remains unshaken.

§ 338. The true principle supported by the authorities seems to be, that theft, *per se*, establishes neither responsibility, nor irresponsibility in the bailee. If the theft is occasioned by any negligence, the bailee is responsible; if without any negligence, he is discharged. Ordinary diligence is not disproved, even presumptively, by mere theft; but the proper conclusion must be drawn from weighing all the circumstances of the particular case. This is the just doctrine, to which the learned mind of Mr. Chancellor Kent has arrived after a large survey of the authorities;[3] and it seems at once rational and convenient.

§ 339. Another duty of the pawnee is to return the pledge and its increments, if any, after the debt or other duty has been discharged.[4] Of course this duty by the common law is extinguished, when the pledge

---

[1] Jones's Bailm. 46, 47.
[2] 2 Ld. Raym. 909, 914, 915.
[3] 2 Kent. Com. 452.
[4] *Isaack v. Clarke*, 2 Bulst. R. 306.

is lost by casualty or other unavoidable accident, or it perishes through its own intrinsic defects, without the default of the pawnee.[1]   And the same rule applies, when the pawn is lost by robbery, or by superior force, or even by theft, if the pawnee has exercised reasonable diligence.   The same rule will be found in the civil law and in the law of Continental Europe.[2]   It is not, however, sufficient for the pawnee to allege, that there has been such a loss.   It must be established by proper proofs.   And it would seem, that in the civil and foreign law the *onus probandi* is on the pawnee to establish the loss to be by such casualty, superior force, or intrinsic defect.   " Sed, si culpæ reus deprehenditur, *vel non probat manifestis rationibus se perdidisse,* quanti debitoris interest, condemnari debet,"[3] is the language of the civil law ; and Pothier implicitly follows it, as requiring, on the part of the pawnee, due proof of the accident, that has caused the loss, and that he was unable to prevent it.[4]   The common law does not probably differ, when a suit is brought for the restitution of the pawn, after a due demand and refusal.   In such a case the demand and refusal would ordinarily be evidence of a tortious conversion of the pawn ; and it would then be incumbent on the pawnee to give some evidence of a loss by casualty, or superior force, independent of his own statement.[5]   But if a suit should be brought against the pawnee for a negligent loss of the pawn, there, it would be incumbent upon the plaintiff

---

1 *Coggs* v. *Barnard*, 2 Ld. Raym. 909.

2 Pothier, Nantissement, n. 29, 30 ;   Domat, B. 3, tit. 1, § 4, n. 2, 7;
Cod. Lib. 8, tit. 14, 1. 19; Ayliffe's Pand. B. 4, tit. 18, p. 541 ; Cod. Lib.
4, tit. 24, l. 5, 1. 9 ; Domat, B. 3, tit. 1, § 4, n. 6.

3 Cod. Lib. 4, tit. 24, 1 5.   4 Pothier, Nantissement, n. 31.

5 2 Salk. 655 ; 7 Cowen R. 500, note (*a.*); 1 T. R. 33 ; *Isaack* v.
Clarke, 2 Bulst. R. 306.

to support the allegations of his declaration by proper proofs, and the *onus probandi*, in respect to negligence, would be on him.[1] And where such an action for a negligent loss was brought against a bailee, it was held by the Court, that his acts and remarks, contemporaneous with the loss, were admissible evidence in his favour, to establish the nature of the loss.[2]

§ 340. If the party, who pledged the goods, was not the owner of them, the pawnee may defend himself by showing, that he has delivered over the goods to the real owner, unless the pledger has a special property, which he is entitled, under the circumstances, to assert against the owner. And if the pledger holds the pledge, merely as a pledge from the owner, the second pledgee may discharge himself from any obligation to the owner, by delivering it up to his own pledger at any time before an offer to redeem is made by the owner.[3]

§ 341. The pawnee makes himself responsible for all losses and accidents, whenever he has done any act inconsistent with his duty, or has refused to perform his duty. If, therefore, the pawner makes a tender of the amount of the debt, for which the pawn is given, and the pawnee refuses to receive it, or to redeliver the pledge, the special property, which he has in the pledge, is determined, and he is henceforth treated as a wrong-doer, and the pawn is at his sole risk.[4]

---

1 *Cooper* v. *Barton*, 3 Camp. R. 5; *Harris* v. *Packwood*, 3 Taunt. 264; *Marsh* v. *Horne*, 5 B. & Cres. 322; but see *Platt* v. *Hibbard*, 7 Cowen, 497; 7 Taunt. R. 403.

2 *Tompkins* v. *Saltmarsh*, 14 Serg. & R. 275.

3 *Jarvis* v. *Rogers*, 15 Mass. R. 389.

4 *Coggs* v. *Bernard*, 2 Ld. Raym. 909, 916, 917; Anon. 2 Salk. 522; Jones's Bailm. 79, 80; Bac. Abr. Bailment B; Id. Trover C; *Ratcliffe* v. *Davis*, Yelv. 178; Bull. N. P. 72; *Parks* v. *Hall*, 8 Pick. 206.

And the same rule applies to all cases of a misuser or conversion of the pawn by the pawnee.[1]

§ 342. And (as has been properly observed) the defaults, by which the pawnee may render himself responsible, are not only those, which consist in acts of commission *(in admittendo)*, but in omissions *(in omittendo)*; for the pawnee is bound to apply all proper care. He is not, therefore, less liable, if by his neglect he suffers a mirror, which is pawned to him, to be ruined, than he would be, if he had broken it by an improper use, or even by a mere wilful act.[2]

§ 343. Another duty of the pawnee at the common law is to render a due account of all the income, profits, and advantages derived by him from the pledge, in all cases, where such an account is within the scope of the bailment. If, for instance, the pawn is a slave, the profits of his labour are to be accounted for.[3] If the pawn consists of cows, horses, or other cattle, the profits of their labour are also to be accounted for, if within the contemplation of the parties. And the civil and foreign law seems, in all cases of this sort, to imply an obligation to account, from the very nature of such a pledge. In rendering an account of the profits the pawnee is at liberty to charge all the necessary expenses and charges, to which he has been put, and to deduct them from the income or profits.[4] If he has sold the pledge, he is bound to account for the proceeds, and to pay over the surplus beyond his debt or other demand, to the

---

1 *De Tollemere* v. *Fuller*, 1 Rep. Const. Ct. So. Caro. 121 ; Domat, B. 3, tit. 1, § 4, n. 1, 2, 3, ; Pothier, Nantissement, n. 51.

2 Pothier, Nantissement, n. 33.

3 *Hinton* v. *Holliday*, 1 N. Carol. Law Journ. 87.

4 Domat, B. 3, tit. 1, § 4, n. 4, 5 ; Pothier, Nantissement, n. 35, 37, 40, 41.

pawner. Pothier thinks, that the duty of the pawnee goes farther; and that he is bound to account for all the profits and income, which he might have received from the pledge.[1] This would doubtless be true in the common law in all cases, where there is an implied obligation to employ the pledge at a profit. As, if there is a pledge of money, and it is agreed, that it shall be let out at interest by the pawnee, and he has neglected his duty.

§ 344. There was a peculiar sort of pledge or mortgage in the civil law, called *Antichresis,* whereby the creditor was entitled to take the profits of the pledge, (as, for instance, of lands or animals,) as a compensation for, and in lieu of, interest. This mode of contract was not held illegal in the Roman law, unless it was made a cover for some illegal act, or for some oppressive usury.[2] But in the modern continental nations, it seems, from its tendency to give the creditor an oppressive power, and to cover usury, to be generally discountenanced; for, in all such cases, the party is bound to account for the profits, deducting expenses, and then is simply allowed his interest.[3] This also seems to be the general rule adopted in England; though Welsh mortgages bear, in many respects, a close resemblance to the contract of antichresis, as the mortgagee is entitled to receive the profits in lieu of interest. But this kind of mortgage, though formerly much in use, is now in a great measure obsolete. It does not seem ever to have been applied to mere personalty.[4]

---

1 Pothier, Nantissement, n. 36; Ayliffe's Pand. B. 4, tit. 18, p. 533.

2 Domat, B. 3, tit. 1, § 1, n. 28, § 4, n. 5; Pothier, Nantissement, n. 20; Ayliffe's Pand. B. 4, tit. 18, p. 525.

3 Id. ibid.

4 1 Powell on Mortgage, by Coventry & Rand, p. 373 *a,* and note (E.)

§ 345. In the natural order of the subject, we are next led to a consideration of the rights and duties of the pawner. And, in the first place, as to his right of redemption. If the pledge is conveyed by way of mortgage, and thus passes the legal title, unless he redeems the pledge at the stipulated time, the title of the pledgee becomes absolute at law ; and the pledger has no remedy at law, but only a remedy in equity to redeem.[1] If, however, the transaction is not a transfer of ownership, but a mere pledge, as the pledger has never parted with the general title, he may, at law, redeem, notwithstanding he has not strictly complied with the condition of his contract.[2] If a clause is inserted in the original contract, providing, that if the terms of the contract are not strictly fulfilled at the time, and in the mode prescribed, the pledge shall be irredeemable, it will not be of any avail. For the common law deems such a stipulation unconscionable, and void upon the ground of public policy, as tending to the oppression of debtors.[3] The civil law treated a similar stipulation (called in that law "lex commissoria") in the same manner, holding it to be a mere nullity.[4] However, the civil law allowed the parties to agree, that upon default in payment the creditor might take the pledge at a stipulated price, provided it was its reasonable value, and the transaction was *bonâ fide*. In both respects the modern continental nations of Europe have adopted the civil law.[5] Whether the same prin-

---

1 *Jones v. Smith*, 2 Vez. jr. 378 ; 2 Cain Err. 200.

2 Com. Dig. Mortgage B ; 1 Powell on Mort. by Coventry & Rand, 401, and notes, ibid.

3 *Cortelyou v. Lansing*, 2 Cain Err. 200 ; 2 Kent Com. 454.

4 Domat, B. 3, tit. 1, § 3, n. 11 ; Pothier, Nantissement, n. 18 ; 2 Kent Com. 434.

5 Domat, B. 3, tit. 1, § 3, n. 11 ; Pothier, Nantissement, n. 19.

ciple exists in the common law, does not appear to have been decided. But there is no doubt, that a subsequent agreement to that effect, or a subsequent waiver of the right to redeem, if made under proper circumstances, would be held binding between the parties.[1]

§ 346. It is clear, by the common law, that in cases of pledge, if a stipulated time is fixed for the payment of the debt, and the debt is not paid at the time, the absolute property does not pass to the pawnee. This doctrine is, at least, as old as the time of Glanville.[2] If the pawnee does not choose to exercise his acknowledged right to sell, he still retains the property as a pledge, and, upon a tender of the debt, he may, at any time, be compelled to restore it; for prescription, or the statute of limitations, does not run against it.[3] However, after a long lapse of time, if no claim for a redemption is made, the right will be deemed to be extinguished; and the property will be held to belong absolutely to the pawnee. Under such circumstances, a court of equity will decline to entertain any suit for the purpose of a redemption. A like rule is adopted in the common law in case of mortgages.[4]

§ 347. The civil law also has declared, that prescription shall not run against the pawner in respect to the pawn; for the pawnee is always considered to hold by his title, as such, until some other title supervenes.[5]

---

[1] *Stevens* v. *Bell*, 6 Mass. R. 339.

[2] Glanville, Lib. 10, ch. 6; 1 Reeves' Hist. 161, 163; 2 Cain Err. 200; Yelv. 178; 1 Buls. 29.

[3] *Kemp* v. *Westbrook*, 1 Vez. 278.

[4] *Lockwood* v. *Ewer*, 2 Atk. 303; Mathews, Presump. Ev. 20, 331; Powell on Mortgages, Coventry's note, 401.

[5] Pothier, Nantissement, n. 53; Cod. Lib. 4, tit. 24, l. 10, 12; Ayliffe's Pand. B. 4, tit. 18, p. 531; Domat, B. 3, tit. 1, § 4, n. 7; Id. tit. 7, § 5, n. 11, 12; Dig. Lib. 44, tit. 3, l. 12; Dig. Lib. 41, tit, 3, l. 13.

But nevertheless, where the title of the pawnee has remained undisturbed for a great length of time, it seems,
that such an extraordinary prescription may be insisted
on as a bar, for the sake of the repose of titles founded
on long possession.[1]

§ 348. But where no time of redemption is fixed by
the contract, there, upon the general principles of law,
the pawner has his whole life to redeem,[2] unless he is
previously quickened, as he may be, by the pawnee,
through the instrumentality of a court of equity, or by
notice *in pais* to the party.[3] A question has arisen,
whether, if the pawner dies without redeeming, the
right survives to his personal representatives. In the
case of *Ratcliffe* v. *Davies*, (Yelv. 178,)[4] it seems to
have been thought by the Court, that the right expired
with the pawner's life. However, there have been cases
in equity, in which the right has been enforced in favour of the representatives of the pawner; and this
seems, according to modern opinions, the true doctrine.[5] If the pawnee dies before redemption, the
pawner may still redeem against his representatives.[6]

§ 349. If at the time, when the pledger applies to
redeem, the pledge has been sold by the pledgee, without any proper notice to the former, no tender of the
debt due need be made before bringing an action; for
the party has incapacitated himself to comply with his

---

1 Ayliffe's Pand. B. 4, tit. 18, p. 531; Cod. Lib 7, tit. 39, l. 4, 9; Domat, B. 3, tit. 7, § 4, n. 14, and note of the Author.

2 Com. Dig. Mortgage B; Yelv. 178, 179; 2 Cain Err. 200; Bac.
Abr. Bailment B; 2 Kent Com. 452.

3 *Cortelyou* v. *Lansing*, 2 Cain Err. 200; *Hart* v. *Ten Eyck*, 2 Johns.
Ch. R. 12; *Garlick*, v. *James*, 12 Johns. R. 146; 2 Kent Com. 452.

4 S. C. 1 Bulst. 29; Noy, 137; Cro. Jac. 244.

5 *Demandray* v. *Melcalfe*, Prec. Ch. 420; 2 Vern. 691, 698; *Vanderzee*
v. *Willes*, 3 Bro. Ch. R. 21; 2 Cain R. 200.

6 Com. Dig. Mortgage B.

contract to return the pledge.[1] And the same rule
applies, where the pledgee dispenses with a tender, as
if he refuses under any circumstances to restore the
pledge.[2]   But, if such an action is brought, the pledgee
may recoup his debt in the damages.[3]

§ 350. Subject to the rights of the pledgee, the owner has a right to sell or assign his property in the pawn;
and in such a case, the vendee will be substituted for
the pledger, and the pledgee will be bound to allow him
to redeem, and to account with him for the pledge, and
its proceeds; and if he refuses, an action at law will lie
for damages, as well as a bill in equity to compel a redemption and account.[4]

§ 351. In every case, where the pledge has suffered
by the default of the pledgee, the owner is entitled to a
recompense in proportion to the damages sustained by
him.   But, in estimating the damages, no compensation is to be made for any injury, which has arisen by
accident, or from the natural decay of the pledge.[5]

§ 352. As the general property of goods pawned remains in the pawner, and the pawnee has a special
property only, the latter (as we have seen) may not
only maintain an action for an injury done to the thing
by a stranger, but the former may also maintain an action against a stranger for any injury done to it, or any
conversion of it.[6]   And where a stranger comes into

---

[1] *Cartelyou* v. *Lansing,* 2 Cain Err. 200; *McLean* v. *Walker,* 10 Johns.
R. 472.

[2] 2 Cain Err. 200, and cases cited, 214.

[3] *Jarvis* v. *Rogers,* 15 Mass. R. 389.

[4] *Ratcliffe* v. *Vance,* 2 Rep. Const. Ct. So. Caro. 239; *Kemp* v. *Westbrook,* 1 Vez. 278.

[5] Pothier, Nantissement, n. 39, 40.

[6] Bac. Abr. Trover C; 2 Roll. Abr. 569, pl. 5; but see *Paine* v. *Middlesex,* 1 R. & M. 99; *Gordon* v. *Harper,* 7 T. R. 9.

possession under a wrongful title from the pawnee, the
owner having a right to consider the bailment, if not for
all, at least for many purposes, at an end, may recover
it against the stranger, and hold him liable for damages.[1]
But, where there is any injury or conversion by a stranger, for which an action lies, both by the pawner and
pawnee, it is said, that a recovery by either ousts the
other of his right to recover; for there cannot be a
double satisfaction.[2] This may be true, as a general
rule. But it deserves consideration, whether the owner can, by his recovery of the pledge, or of damages for
the conversion of it, oust the pledgee of his security in
the pledge or its proceeds. And if the pledgee has recovered damages only to the extent of his lien, it may
farther deserve consideration, whether, upon suitable
proofs, the owner may not be entitled to recover for
the surplus. However, these are propounded merely
as matters open to some doubt. Where the pledgee
is ousted of his possession by a mere stranger, it is said,
that he is entitled to recover the full value of the pledge.
But, where the pledge has been taken possession of,
and retained by the owner, or by one acting under his
authority, or with his assent; there the pledgee is entitled to recover only to the amount of his lien.[3]

§ 353. Goods pawned are not liable to be taken in
execution in an action against the pawner; at least,
not until the bailment is terminated by payment, or

[1] *Newsom* v. *Thornton*, 6 East, 17; *Martini* v. *Coles*, 1 M. & Selw.
140; *Pickering* v. *Busk*, 15 East, 38; *McCombie* v. *Davies*, 6 East, 153;
Dillenbach v *Jerome*, 7 Cowen R. 294; *Smith* v. *James*, 7 Cowen R. 328;
Ante, § 324 325, 326, 327.

[2] Bac. Abr. Trover C; *Rooth* v. *Wilson*, 1 B. & Ald. 59; *Bush* v. *Lyon*,
9 Cowen R. 52; *Smith* v. *James*, 7 Cowen R. 328.

[3] *Ingersoll* v. *Van Bokkelin*, 7 Cowen R. 670, 681, and note; *Lyle* v.
Barker, 5 Binn. R. 457.

other extinguishment of the pawnee's title.[1] This is the rule in cases of execution at the suit of private persons. But it would seem, that in the case of the crown, the pawn might be taken, on satisfaction of the debt to the pawnee, or taken and sold subject to his right.[2]

§ 354. In the next place, as to the duties and obligations of the pawner. By the act of pawning, the pawner enters into an implied engagement or warranty, that he is the owner of the property pawned, and unless he gives notice of a different interest, that he is the general owner, and that he has good right to pass the pawn. If he violates this engagement, either by a tortious or innocent bailment of property, which is not his own, or by exceeding his interest therein, he is liable to the pawnee in an action for damages.[3] And it follows, that the pledger is under an implied engagement not to retake the pledge, or in any manner to interfere with the rights of the pledgee.

§ 355. If the pawn has a defect, unknown to the pawnee, which destroys its value, the civil law gives him a right of action for another pawn in its stead.[4] This seems highly reasonable; the common law, however, gives no such right. But, in such a case, if there is any fraud practised by the pawner, an action for damages will doubtless lie against him, and perhaps, also, the whole contract may, at the option of the pawnee, be rescinded.

---

[1] *Coggs* v. *Bernard*, Holt's Rep. 528, 529; *Badlam* v. *Tucker*, 1 Pick. R. 389; *Bigelow* v. *Wilson*, 1 Pick. 425; *Marsh* v. *Lawrence*, 4 Cowen R. 461; 1 Dane's Abr. ch. 17, art. 4, § 3.

[2] Chitty on Prerog. ch. 12, P 1, § 5, pp. 285, 286.

[3] Pothier, Nantissement, n. 54, 55, 56; Dig. Lib. 13, tit. 7, l. 32; Id. l. 16.

[4] Pothier, Nantissement, n. 57.

§ 356. The pawner, indeed, in all cases of this sort, is bound to good faith, and will be responsible for all frauds, not only in the title, but in the concoction of the contract;[1] for it is a rule of the common law, that fraud vitiates every contract; and that damages, by way of recompense, may be recovered for all losses and injuries occasioned by fraud. But, whenever there is a known defect in the pawn, or in the title to it, there is no pretence to impute fraud, if the pawnee takes it with full knowledge of all the circumstances; for he is bound by his contract, as he has chosen to make it.[2]

§ 357. Another obligation of the pawner, by the civil law, is to reimburse to the pawnee all expenses and charges, which have been necessarily incurred by the latter in the preservation of the pawn,[3] even though, by some subsequent accident, these expenses and charges may not have secured any permanent benefit to the pawner. No decision has been found in the common law upon this point. If there is an express contract to pay such expenses, that would doubtless govern the case. And where the circumstances of the case would naturally lead to an implied agreement to the same effect, it would be equivalent to an express declaration. But whatever might be the rule, as to ordinary expenses and charges, in a case of mutual silence, it would seem reasonable to presume, that extraordinary expenses and charges, which could not have been foreseen, should be at the charge of the pawner. If, for instance, a horse is pawned, and he meets with an injury by accident, the expenses of his cure might be justly deemed

1 Pothier, Nantissement, n. 59.

2 Pothier, Nantissement, n. 58.

3 Pothier, Nantissement, n. 60, 61; Dig. Lib. 13, tit. 7, l. 8; Domat, B. 3, tit. 1, § 3, n. 19.

to be borne by the pawner, as they would be for his ultimate benefit. So, if goods pawned, as, for instance, a ship, be injured by a storm, and expenses are necessary to preserve her from absolute foundering, such expenses would seem properly to fall on the owner.

§ 358. In respect to expenses not necessary, but still useful to the thing pawned, the civil law pursued a middle course, and left them to be allowed or disallowed by the proper judicial tribunal, according to circumstances. If the expenses were very large and onerous, they were not to be allowed. If moderate and beneficial, they might be allowed at its discretion.[1] The common law is not supposed to invest any courts of justice with any such discretion, or to allow to the pawnee any such latitude of expenditure without the approbation of the pawner, either express or implied.

§ 359. We come, in the last place, to the consideration of the manner, in which the contract of pledge or mortgage is or may be extinguished. An extinguishment may arise in several ways. (1.) By the full payment of the debt or the discharge of the other engagements, for which the pledge was given.[2] (2.) By any other satisfaction of the debt, either in fact, or by operation of law ; as, for instance, by receiving other goods in payment or discharge of the debt.[3]

§ 360. (3.) By taking a higher or different security for the debt, without any agreement, that the pledge

---

[1] Pothier, Nantissement, n. 61 ; Dig. Lib. 13, tit. 7, 1. 25 ; Domat, B. 3, tit. 1, § 3, n. 20 ; Ayliffe's Pand. B. 4, tit. 18, pp. 530, 531.

[2] Domat, B. 3, tit. 1, § 7, n. 1 ; Pothier, Pand. Lib. 20, tit. 6, § 1, l. 1, 2, 3, 4, 5 ; Ayliffe's Pand. B. 4, ch. 18, p. 536, 537.

[3] Domat, B. 3, tit. 1, § 7, n. 4 ; Pothier, Pand. Lib. 20, tit. 6, § 4, l. 17, 18 ; Ayliffe's Pand. 536, 537.

shall be retained therefor. This, in the civil law, is
called *novation;* and as the original debt is thereby
extinguished, the contract of pledge, which is but an
accessary, is extinguished also. "Novata autem de-
biti obligatio pignus peremit, nisi convenit ut pignus re-
petatur."[1] But as no novation has the effect, unless
such is the intention of the parties, to extinguish the
prior debt, it follows, that a mere change of the security will not extinguish the right to the pledge against
or without their assent.[2]

§ 361. (4.) So, whatever by operation of law extinguishes the debt, extinguishes the right to the pledge.
Therefore, if in a suit for the debt the pledger has a
judgment in his favour, which bars any future recovery of the debt, that extinguishes the right to the
pledge.[3]

§ 362. (5.) If the right to the debt is barred by
prescription, it is said in the civil law, that the right to
the pledge is gone also.[4] This would be true in the
common law also, when from the length of time there
arises a presumption of the payment of the debt. But
if there is merely a positive bar by the statute of limitations against a personal action for the debt, it may
deserve consideration, how far this will oust the party of his right to retain the pledge towards satisfaction of the debt; for the possession of the pledge may
be the very reason, why the pledgee has omitted to

---

1 Domat, B. 3, tit. 7, § 7, n. 2, 4; Id. B. 4, tit. 3, § 1, n. 1 to 5; Pothier,
Pand. Lib. 20, tit. 6, § 1, l. 6, 7; Ayliffe, Id. 536, 537; Dig. Lib. 13,
tit. 7, l. 11, § 1.

2 Domat, B. 4, tit. 3, § 1, n. 1 to 5; Ayliffe, Id. 536, 537.

3 Domat, B. 3, tit. 7, § 1, n. 3; Pothier, Pand. Lib. 20, tit. 6, § 1, l. 8.

4 Domat, B. 3, tit. 7, § 1, n. 9; Pothier, Pand. Lib. 20, tit. 6, § 5,
l. 37 to l. 40.

bring a personal suit for the debt within the prescribed
time. The pledger is not ordinarily barred of his
right to redeem the pledge, so long as the pledgee
may be presumed to hold it as a pledge. And the
continued possession of the pledgee, under such circumstances, affords proof of the non-extinguishment of
the debt, although the statute of limitations may present a bar to a mere personal action. On the other
hand, if a very long period has elapsed, and the pledge
has continued in the possession of the pledgee, it affords a presumption of an abandonment of it by the
pledger, and if any presumption of an extinguishment
arises in such a case, it is an extinguishment by receiving the pledge in satisfaction. If, then, the statute of
limitations has run against the debt, as a personal
claim, and the pledger seeks to recover back the
pledge, why may not the pledgee avail himself of the
protection of the same statute to bar such suit? And
if the pledger insists, that it is still a pledge, why may
not the other party avail himself of all the fair presumptions arising in the case, that the debt has not been in
fact paid, or that the pledge has been deemed a satisfaction of it? Some of the adjudged cases seem silently to admit the existence of a right in the pledgee
over the pledge, notwithstanding the lapse of a period
exceeding that of the statute of limitations for personal recoveries.[1] This, however, must be considered, in
the absence of direct authority, as a point merely propounded for further consideration. But if the pledger
admits the existence of the debt, and brings a bill to

---

[1] *Kemp* v. *Westbrook*, 1 Ves. 278 ; *Gage* v. *Bulkley*, Ridg. Cas. Temp.
Hard. 278 ; Yelv. 178, 179 ; see also Pothier, Pand. Lib. 20, tit. 6, § 1,
art. 2 ; 1 Powell on Mortg. by Coventry & Rand, 401, and notes, ibid.

redeem, he can do so only upon payment of the debt, although the statute of limitations might otherwise be pleaded as a bar to it.

§ 363. (6.) The right to the pledge is also gone, when the thing perishes. And if it undergoes any permanent and essential transmutation, it would seem, that, by the civil law, the right to it is extinguished.[1] But as far as the property can be traced it will be held still a pledge by the common law, whatever transmutations it may have undergone without the assent of the pledgee.[2]

§ 364. (7.) The right also is extinguished by any act of the pledgee amounting to a release or waiver of the pledge. This may be by a release in solemn form of the debt, or of the right to the pledge. But a release of a part or of an undivided portion of the things pawned will operate as an extinguishment only *pro tanto*.[3] If the pledgee yields up the possession of the pledge to the pledger,[4] or consents, that the latter shall alienate it, or pledge it to another person, either of these acts will amount to a waiver of his right to the pledge.[5]

§ 365. These formal divisions of the modes of extinguishing the right to the pledge have been taken from the civil law, in which they are set down with minute accuracy. The common law, however, is precisely the same as to all the principles, which govern

---

1 Pothier, Pand. Lib. 20, tit. 6, § 3, l. 12, 13 ; Domat, B. 3, tit. 1, § 7, n. 8 ; Ayliffe's Pand. B. 4, tit. 3, p. 536, 537.

2 *Plummer* v. *Wildman*, 3 M. & Selw. 482.

3 Pothier, Pand. Lib. 2, tit. 6, § 4, l. 14.

4 *Homes* v. *Crane*, 2 Pick. R. 607 ; *Runyan* v. *Mercereau*, 11 Johns R. 539.

5 Pothier, Pand. Lib. 20, tit. 6, § 4, l. 21 ; Domat, B. 3, tit. 1, § 7, n. 12, 13, 14.

them, with the exceptions, which have been already incidentally suggested. Indeed, the whole doctrine of
extinguishment is resolvable into the very first elements of justice, founded upon the express or implied
intention of the parties to extinguish the pledge, or upon a virtual extinguishment by the necessary operations of law.

§ 366. It remains to take notice of some peculiari-
ties in the local jurisprudence of Massachusetts, upon
the point now under consideration. · It has been decided, that if a pawnee causes the goods, which are
pawned, to be attached in a personal suit against the
pawner for his debt, by such an attachment his lien or
right to the pledge is extinguished.[1] And it has been
further decided, that the pledgee has no right, in any
such suit, to attach any other property of the pawner,
without first returning the pawn to him.[2] It is to be
observed, that the common process, by which personal
suits are instituted in Massachusetts, is a writ of attachment, which authorizes an attachment of the property,
or, if that cannot be found, of the person of the debtor,
to answer the exigency of the writ. In order to make
the process effectual, it is indispensable, that there
should be either an attachment of property, (nominally
at least) or an arrest. The effect of these decisions,
therefore, is, that the writ of attachment, in all cases of
pledge, is but a writ of capias in favour of the creditor,
and that, however inadequate the pledge may be as a
security, he must abandon it, before he can secure himself by any attachment of the property of his debtor.
What would be the effect of a levy of the execution,

---

[1] *Sweet* v. *Brown*, 5 Pick. R. 178.
[2] *Cleverly* v. *Brackett*, 8 Mass. R. 150.

which should issue upon a judgment in favour of the
creditor for the debt, upon the pledge or other property of the debtor, does not appear to have been decided.
Nor indeed does it appear to have been decided, what
would be the effect of a personal suit brought by the
creditor retaining the pledge.

§ 367. The important head of Pawns or Pledges is
thus brought to a conclusion.   And however minute
some of the details and distinctions may appear to be,
they are far from exhausting the subject.   If the object
of these commentaries had not been rather to present a practical view of the leading principles, than to
introduce nice discussions, there would not be wanting
materials to exercise the subtilty, as well as to employ
the patience of the inquisitive jurist.

CHAPTER VI.

CONTRACTS OF HIRE.

§ 368. THE fifth and last class of Bailments consists
of bailments for hire. A contract of this sort is called
in the Roman law, *locatio,* or *locatio-conductio,* both
words being used promiscuously to signify the same
thing.[1] In the Roman law it may be defined thus:
"Locatio-conductio est contractus quo de re fruendâ vel
faciendâ pro certo pretio convenit."[2] In other words,
it is a contract whereby the use of a thing, or the services and labour of a person, are stipulated to be given
for a certain reward.[3] Pothier defines it to be a contract,
by which one of the contracting parties allows the other to enjoy or use the thing hired during the stipulated
period for a compensation, which the other party engages to pay.[4] A definition substantially the same will
be found in other writers.[5] Lord Holt has defined it
to be, " when goods are left by the bailee to be used
for hire." [6] The objection to this, as well as to the
definition of Pothier, is, that it is incomplete, and covers only cases of the hire of a thing, *(locatio rei,)* and
excludes all cases of the hire of labour and services, and
of the carriage of goods. At the common law it may
properly enough be defined to be a bailment, where a
compensation is to be given for the use of a thing, or for

---

1 Ayliffe's Pand. B. 4, tit. 7, p. 460.

2 Pothier, Pand. Lib. 19, tit. 2, art. 1 ; Inst. Lib. 3, tit. 25 ; Dig.
Lib. 19, tit. 2 ; Heinecc. Pand. Lib. 19, tit. 2, § 307.

3 Wood's Inst. B. 3, ch. 5, p. 235, 236 ; Domat, B. 1, tit. 4, § 1, n. 1.

4 Pothier, Contract de Louage, ch. 1, n. 1.

5 Domat, B. 1, tit. 4, § 1, n. 1 ; see also Cod. Civ. art. 1709, 1710.

6 *Coggs* v. *Bernard,* 2 Ld. Raym. 909, 913.

labour or services about it; or, in other words, it is a hiring or letting of goods, or of labour and services for a reward.[1]

§ 369. We are accustomed, in the common law, to use words corresponding to those of the Roman law, almost in the same promiscuous manner. Thus, letting *(locatio)* and hiring *(conductio)* are precise equivalents, used for the purpose of distinguishing the relative situation of different parties to the same contract. The letter, called in the civil law, *locator*, and in the French law, *locateur, loueur,* or *bailleur,* is he, who, being owner of the thing, lets it out to another for hire or compensation; and the hirer, called in the civil law, *conductor,* and in the French law, *conducteur, preneur, locataire,* is he, who pays the compensation, having the benefit of the use.[2] Both Heineccius and Sir William Jones have taken notice of a nicety in the use of the words *locator* and *conductor* in the Latin language. The employer, who gives the reward, is called *locator operis* (the letter of the work) but *conductor operarum* (the hirer of the labour and services); while the party employed, who receives the pay, is called *locator operarum* (the letter of the labour and services) but *conductor operis* (the hirer of the work.[3]) The nicety, though not as much felt in the English language, is yet not a total stranger to it.*

---

1 2 Kent Com. 456; 1 Bell Com. 451.

2 Wood's Inst. B. 3, ch. 5, p. 236; Pothier, Louage, n. 1; Domat, B. 1, tit. 4, § 1, n. 2; Heinecc. Pand. Lib. 19, tit. 2, § 318; Jones's Bailm. 90; Wood's Inst. Civ. Law, 236.

3 Hein. Pand. Lib. 19, tit. 2, § 320 note; Jones's Bailm. 90, note (r); Pothier, Pand. Lib. 19, tit. 2, p. 2, art. 1, § 1, 15; Pothier Louage, n. 392.

* Mr. Gibbon, in common with many other writers, has complained of the poverty of our language, in regard to terms expressive of some

§ 370. The contract of letting and hiring is usually divided into two kinds; (1.) *Locatio*, or *locatio-conductio rei*, the bailment of a thing to be used by the bailee for a compensation to be paid by him. (2.) *Locatio operis*, or the hire of the labour and services of the bailee, for a compensation to be paid by the bailor.[1] And this last kind is again subdivided into two classes, (1.) *Locatio operis faciendi*, or the hire of labour and work to be done, or care and attention to be bestowed, on the goods bailed by the bailee for a compensation; or (2.) *Locatio operis mercium vehendarum*, or the hire of the carriage of goods from one place to another for a compensation.[2] Each of these heads will be severally treated of in its order; and for the sake of brevity we shall often call the bailor the letter, and the bailee the hirer. Lord Holt has called the former the lender, and the latter the borrower;[3] but this language is equivocal, and may lead to some confusion, since it is usually appropriated to cases of gratuitous loans.

§ 371. Before proceeding to the consideration of the different species of contracts of bailments for hire, it may be proper to state some things, which are applicable to them all. Pothier, as well as other foreign jurists, who have treated the subject with systematic

---

1 Cod. Civ. art. 1709, 1710; Pothier, Louage, art. prélim; Merlin, Repert. art. Louage, art. Bailm.

2 Jones's Bailm. 85, 86, 90, 103; Id. 118; 2 Kent Com. 456; Cod. Civ. art. 1709, 1710, 1711.

3 *Coggs* v. *Bernard*, 2 Ld. Raym. 909, 913.

---

of the different classes of bailments, and especially of the difference between a *mutuum* and a *commodatum*. He has not hesitated to adopt the term "location," to signify the contract of hire. One might almost be tempted to follow him in this naturalization of the Roman word. Gibbon's Rome, vol. 8, ch. 44. p. 84.

accuracy, has remarked, that it is a contract, which arises from the principles of natural law; that it is voluntary and founded in consent; that it involves mutual and reciprocal obligations; and that it is for mutual benefit.[1] In some respects it bears a strong resemblance to the contract of sale *(emptio-venditio)*; the principal difference between them being, that in cases of sale the owner parts with the whole proprietary interest in the thing; and in cases of hire, the owner parts with it only for a temporary use or purpose.[2]

§ 372. From what has been observed, it is obvious, that three things are of the essence of the contract. (1.) That there should be a thing to be let; (2.) a price for the hire; and (3.) a contract possessing a legal obligation.[3] If, for instance, the thing, which is the subject of the contract, has perished, as, if a horse, the subject of the hire, is dead, the contract becomes a nullity.[4]

§ 373. (1). As to the thing to be let. In the common law, where the bailment of a thing is spoken of, it is confined to personal property;[5] though, in the civil and continental law, it is equally applicable to real estate, and to incorporeal hereditaments.[6] There seems no difficulty in the common law in applying the contract of bailment to choses in action and securities, as

---

1 Pothier, Louage, n. 2; Wood's Civ. Law, B. 3, ch. 5, pp. 235, 236; Ayliffe's Pand, B. 4, tit. 7, p. 460.

2 Pothier, Louage, n. 2, 3, 4; Jones's Bailm. 86; Dig. Lib. 19, tit. 2, 1. 1, 2; Pothier, Pand. Lib. 19, tit. 2, art. 1, §§ 2, 9, 10.

3 Pothier, Louage, n. 6.

4 Ibid. n. 7.

5 *Coggs* v. *Bernard*, 2 Ld. Ray. 909, 913; Jones's Bailm. 89, 90.

6 Pothier, Louage, n. 9; Domat, B. 1, tit. 4, § 1, n. 4, 9; Id. § 4; Cod. Civ. art. 1713; Ayliffe's Pand. B. 4, tit. 7, p. 464; 1 Bell's Com. 451.

well as to goods and chattels. Though the use of the former on hire is probably rare, the carriage of them is a very common business of bailees for hire. Nor is there any intrinsic difficulty in applying it to land and immovable property. But, wherever land or immovable property is the subject of the contract, it passes under another denomination, and embraces many different considerations. We never hear of the bailment of a house or farm, although we often do of the demising and renting of houses and lands. The thing must not only be personal property, but it must be let. There must be a right in the bailee to use the thing, or to have the possession or enjoyment of it for certain purposes, express or implied, during the contemplated period of the bailment.[1]

§ 374. (2.) As to the price or recompense. This, also, is of the essence of the contract, for if no hire is to be paid, it becomes a gratuitous loan.[2] And according to the civil and foreign law, the price must not be merely nominal, but intended to be a substantive compensation.[3] It ought to be certain and determinate, or be capable of certainty and estimation, in contradistinction to being contingent or conditional in its nature. As, if the contract is to pay such price as A shall decide, and A is dead, or he refuses to name any price, the contract will be void.[4] But, in cases of this sort, Pothier thinks, that it would be just to interpret the intention of the parties to be, that, at all events, a reasonable compensation should be made; and since it

---

1 Pothier, Louage, n. 22, 23, 27, 31.

2 Pothier, Louage, n. 32, 33, 34; Inst. Lib. 3, tit. 25; Pothier, Pand. Lib. 19, tit. 2, art. 1, l. 4, 5, 6.

3 Ibid.

4 Pothier, Louage, n. 37.

could not be in the manner prescribed, that it ought to be ascertained by other persons, especially if the bailment has already taken effect.[1]

§ 375. It is not necessary, that a specific price should be expressly agreed on; for it may be tacitly implied. When the labour is to be performed by an artisan, if no express price is agreed on, he is tacitly presumed to engage for the usual price paid for the like services at the same place, according to the general custom; or, what is the same thing, what they are fairly worth there.[2] For, "Id certum est, quod certum reddi potest." So, in cases of hiring the use of a thing, in the absence of all positive engagements the customary price is presumed to be given; and if no price is fixed by custom, then a reasonable price.

§ 376. According to the civil and foreign law, the price ought to be payable in money; for, if it is not, it is not strictly a *locatio-conductio;* but it passes into another class, that of innominate contracts. However, this was not very important even in the civil law; for the innominate contract was equipollent; and governed by the same rules and obligations as a *locatio-conductio.*[3]

§ 377. Sir William Jones, whose close adherence to the civil law marks every page of his treatise, has also confined his definition of letting to hire to cases, where a pecuniary compensation is given; and he has classed all other cases as innominate contracts.[4] But, there

---

1 Pothier, Louage, n. 37.

2 Pothier, Louage, n. 40.

3 Pothier, Louage, n. 38; Id. Appx. Louage, n, 45S, 491; Inst. Lib. 3, tit. 25, § 2; Pothier, Pand. Lib. 19, tit. 2, art. 1, 1. 5.

4 Jones's Bailm. 118; Id. 93; 2 Bl. Com. 444; Halifax's Anal. Civ. Law, 62.

seems no reason for any such distinction in the common law, since no difference, either in responsibility or remedy, exists between the cases of pecuniary and any other sort of recompense;[1] and they are all treated indiscriminately as cases of bailment for hire.* Lord Holt's definition (2 Ld. Raym. 909, 913,) suggests nothing as to the hire being pecuniary. If A permits B to use his pleasure-boat for a day, in consideration, that B will permit him to use his chariot for the same time, this is a case of double or reciprocal bailments for use on hire. So, if A gives B a pair of pointers for the use of B's hunter during the season, it is a grant of the absolute property on one side, for the temporary bailment of property for use on the other side. These cases belong to the innominate contract of the civil law, *do ut des*.[2] The same rule applies to the innominate contract, *facio ut facias*, where two persons agree to perform reciprocal work; as, if A, a cabinet-maker, agrees to repair B's side-board, if B, who is a carrier, will carry A's bureau to Boston; this is a case of double or reciprocal bailments, *operis faciendi*. And similar illustrations may be given of the other innominate contracts, *do ut facias*, and *facio ut des*. All these, then, being strictly cases of bailments for hire at the common law, and governed by similar obligations, without any of the set forms of remedy known to the civil law, it seems, at best, useless to retain dis-

---

[1] Jones's Bailm. 93.   [2] Jones's Bailm. 93.

* Mr. Chancellor Kent has followed Sir William Jones in describing it as a bailment for a pecuniary recompense, apparently from deference to the authority of the latter. 2 Kent Com. 456.

tinctions borrowed from the civil law, which involve no differences of principle, and may embarrass without instructing us.

§ 378. (3.) As to the legal obligation of the contract. To produce this result, it is necessary, (1.) that the bailment should not be prohibited by law; (2.) that it should be between persons competent to contract; and (3.) that there should be a voluntary consent between the parties.

§ 379. (1.) Certain bailments are prohibited by law, either from their repugnance to sound morals, or their being against public policy, or their being positively forbidden. A bailment of furniture to be used in a brothel is an example of the first kind; a bailment of goods for the purpose of supplying a public enemy is one of the second kind; and a bailment of goods for the purpose of smuggling is one of the third kind.[1] Pothier has put a question, How far the letting of masks and dresses for masquerades and balls is matter of a valid civil contract, seeing, that by the severe discipline of the Catholic church these amusements are not permitted? He thinks, that as they are not prohibited by the secular law, they have an obligatory force in the secular forum; but, that in point of conscience, they are a dishonest traffic, by which the parties ought not to profit; and therefore, *in foro conscientiæ*, and perhaps in the ecclesiastical courts, the parties might be compelled to renounce them.[2]

§ 380. (2.) The parties must be competent to contract. And in this respect the general principles of the common law, as to the capacity of contracting parties, apply to this in common with other contracts.[3] Thus,

---

[1] Pothier, Louage, n. 24, 25, 26. [2] Pothier, Louage, n. 26.
[3] Pothier, Louage, n. 42, 46.

married women, idiots, lunatics, and persons *non compos*, by reason of age, infirmity, or sickness, are unable to contract. Minors, also, are incapable of contracting, unless the contract is clearly for their benefit. And where a minor carries on trade, work done for him in the course of his trade is not the subject of an action against him; for the law will not suffer him to engage in trade.[1] And a party is not permitted, by bringing an action *in tort* against a minor, which is founded on a contract with him, to charge him, if he would not otherwise be liable. Therefore, if a minor hires a horse, and rides him immoderately, he is not responsible in an action, laying the grievance *in tort*, as he would not be, if it were an action brought upon the contract.[2]

§ 381. (3.) There must be a voluntary consent. But upon this we need not enlarge. If there is any substantial mistake between the parties, as to the thing to be hired, or price to be paid; as to the use to be had, or the act to be done; or any fraud or imposition; or any concealment injurious to either party; the contract has not any legal obligation.[3]

§ 382. The next consideration is, as to the rights, duties, and obligations of the parties, resulting from the contract of bailment for hire.

ART. I.   HIRE OF THINGS.

§ 383. FIRST. In cases of LOCATIO REI, or hiring of a thing. What are the rights and duties of the letter to hire (*locator rei*). According to the foreign and

---

1 *Dilk* v. *Keighley*, 2 Esp. R. 480; *Green* v. *Greenbank*, 2 Marsh. R. 485.
2 *Jennings* v. *Rundall*, 8 T. R. 335.
3 Pothier, Louage, n. 48 to 52; Pothier, Pand. Lib. 19, tit. 2, art. 1, l. 7.

civil law, in virtue of the contract the letter impliedly engages to allow to the hirer the full use and enjoyment of the thing hired, and to fulfil all his own engagements and trusts in respect to it, according to the original intention of the parties; ("Præstare, frui licere, uti licere.") This implies an obligation to deliver the thing to the hirer; to refrain from every obstruction to the use of it by the hirer during the period of the bailment; to do no act, which shall deprive the hirer of the thing; to warrant the title and possession to the hirer, to enable him to use the thing or to perform the service; to keep the thing in suitable order and repair for the purposes of the bailment; and, finally, to warrant the thing free from any fault inconsistent with the proper use or enjoyment of it. These are the main obligations deduced by Pothier from the nature of the contract; and they seem generally founded in unexceptionable reasoning.[1]

§ 384. (1.) The delivery of the thing (unless otherwise agreed) should be with its proper accompaniments; as, if a horse is let to ride, with a suitable saddle and bridle; and the delivery should be at the expense of the letter, and at the place, where the thing is, and at the time specified. However, these things are generally regulated by the customs and usages of business at the place, where the hiring takes effect, which are thus silently adopted into the contract. " In contractibus tacite veniunt ea, quæ sunt moris et consuetudinis." [2]

---

[1] Pothier, Louage, n. 53; Id. n. 277; Domat, B. 1, tit. 4, § 3; Pothier, Pand. Lib. 19, tit. 2, p. 2, art. 2, § 3, n. 42 to 73; Cod. Civ. art. 1719; Heinec. Pand. L. 19, tit. 2, § 324; 1 Bell Com. 452.

[2] Pothier, Louage, n. 54 to 58; Domat, B. 1, tit. 4, § 3, n. 1; Dig. Lib. 19, tit. 2, l. 15, § 1; Cod. Civ. art. 1720.

§ 385. (2.) The refraining from every obstruction of the hirer in the use of the thing or in performing his own engagements respecting it. This results from the first principles of justice. The only point of a practical nature worth consideration is, what amounts to an obstruction. If a chattel is let, the resumption of the possession by the letter is a clear case of violation of duty. But whenever the letter is impliedly bound to keep it in repair during the time of the bailment, he may for a temporary purpose of this sort, if necessary, resume the possession. Thus, if a coach is let for a month, and it requires repairs, the owner may take possession for such a time, as is necessary to complete the repairs; but he must then return it.[1]

§ 386. (3.) The like remark applies to the doing of any act, which will deprive the hirer of the thing. As, if the letter sells the thing bailed, or suffers it to be rightfully attached, so that the hirer is deprived of the use of it. In such cases, there is a clear violation of his implied obligation.[2]

§ 387. (4.) The implied warranty of the title and possession to the hirer. This of course applies only against the legal claims of third persons to disturb the enjoyment and use of the thing; for tortious acts on their part furnish no just foundation for a remedy over against the letter; much less do torts, occasioned by the default of the hirer himself.[3]

---

[1] Pothier, Louage, n. 77, 106; Dig. Lib. 19, tit. 2, l. 15, 25; Domat, B. 1, tit. 4, § 3, n. 1, 7; Cod. Civ. art. 1719, 1725.

[2] Pothier, Louage, n. 86, 87; Domat, B. 1, tit. 4, § 3, n. 4; Dig. Lib. 19, tit. 2, l. 25; 1 Bell Com. 452.

[3] Pothier, Louage, n. 81 to 89; Domat, B. 1, tit. 4, § 3, n. 2; Dig. Lib. 19, tit. 2. l. 9; Cod. Civ. art. 1719, 1725, 1726, 1727.

§ 388. (5.) The obligation to keep the thing in suitable order and repair for the purpose of the bailment. This is considered by Pothier, as an obligation arising by operation of law from the fact, that the enjoyment or use, contemplated by the contract, cannot otherwise be obtained. Thus, if a loom is let to hire for a number of years, the letter is bound to keep it in suitable repair during the period, unless the necessity of repairs arises from the fault of the hirer.[1] But however correct this may be as a general principle, it is affected by all the contrary implications, which may arise from the usages of trade and the customs of the place, as well as from positive compact.[2] Thus, (says Pothier,) when a horse is let to one on hire, to be kept by him for a certain period, the hirer is to pay for his shoeing during that time. But it is otherwise, if a person lets his coach and horses to another for a journey, to be driven by his own servants.[3]

§ 389. In respect, however, to necessary and extraordinary expenses incurred upon the thing, the foreign law obliges the letter to pay them to the hirer. Thus, if a hired horse is taken sick on the journey agreed on, without the fault of the hirer, his cure is at the expense of the letter.[4] But the letter is never liable for expenses, which are not necessary, though they may be useful.[5] Mr. Bell says, that in the Scottish law to ground a claim for expenses, it is necessary to show, (1.) that the occasion of the expense was not ascribable to the hirer ; (2.) that the expense was

---

[1] Pothier, Louage, n. 77, 106, 129, 130, 219, 325; Domat, B. 1, tit. 4, § 3, n. 1, 7 ; Id. § 2, n. 9, 14 ; Dig. Lib. 19, tit. 2, l. 25, § 2 ; Cod. Civ. art. 1769, 1724, 1725.

[2] Pothier, Louage, n. 107, 132. [3] Pothier, Louage, n. 107, 129.

[4] Pothier, Louage, n. 129. [5] Pothier, Louage, n. 131.

indispensably necessary; (3.) that the letter had due notice as soon as circumstances permitted.[1]

§ 390. (6.) The obligation of warranty against faults and defects, which prevent the due enjoyment or use of the thing. In respect to these, the rule of the foreign law is, that the warranty extends to all faults and defects, which go to the total prevention of the use or enjoyment of the thing; but not to those, which render the use or enjoyment less convenient. Thus, if a horse is let, which is wholly unfit to perform the journey from his vices or defects, as from blindness, it goes to the very foundation of the bailment, and the warranty attaches upon it. But it will be otherwise, if he has some slight vices or defects, such as being restive or starting, or not being sure footed; these defects do not come within the reach of the warranty.[2] The warranty extends not only to vices and defects, which are known, but to those, which are unknown to the letlet; to those, which exist at the time of the contract, and to those, which supervene afterwards; to those, which exist in the accessory, as well as to those, which exist in the principal.[3] Where the vice or defect is known to the letter, he is liable for all damages on account of the deceit. But where it is unknown to him, it goes simply in discharge of the contract, so that he is not entitled to the hire.[4]

§ 391. Besides these there are other implied obligations in the civil law. Such are the duties of disclosing the faults of the thing hired, and practising no artful

---

[1] 1 Bell Com. 453.

[2] Pothier, Louage, n. 110, 114; Dig. Lib. 19, tit. 2, 1. 19, 45; Cod. Civ. art. 1721.

[3] Pothier, Louage, n. 111, 112, 115; Cod. Civ. art. 1719, 1721.

[4] Pothier, Louage, n. 118, 119, 120; Domat, B. 1, tit. 4. § 3, n. 8, 10

concealment; of charging only a reasonable price; and
of indemnifying the hirer for all expenses, which are
payable by the letter. These, though enlarged upon
by Pothier, seem to require but this brief notice, as
they are self-evident.[1]

§ 392. Such are some of the more important obligations, deduced in the civil and foreign law on the part
of the letter. It is difficult to say, how far (reasonable
as they are in a general sense) they are recognised in
the common law. In some respects the common law
certainly differs. The civil law treats leases of real
estates as bailments on hire, and indeed emphatically as
bailments;[2] and, as we have seen, the owner or lessor
is, in the absence of all other stipulations or customs,
bound to repair. The common law is different in such
cases; for the landlord, without an express agreement,
is not bound to repair; and the tenant may and ought
to repair at his own expense.[3] Lord Mansfield, in
Taylor v. *Whitehand,* (Doug. R. 744, 748,) said, that
by the common law he, who has the use of a thing,
ought to repair it. It is true, that the remark was applied to the case of a grant of a way, which was out of
repair; but the remark was general. Lord Hale is
also reported to have said, that if plate is let, and is
worn out in the service, the letter is not liable to any
action, unless he has been guilty of some default.[4] It
has also been decided, that tenants are bound to repair fences during their occupancy.[5] In the absence of

---

1 Pothier, Louage, n. 121, 201, 202, 203; Domat, B. 1, tit. 4, § 4,
n. 7, 10.

2 Jones's Bailm. 90.

3 *Pomfret* v. *Ricroft,* 1 Saund. R. 321, 322, note; Id. 323, n. 7; *Countess
of Shrewsbury's Case,* 5 Rep. 13; 2 Esp. R. 590; Holt's N. P. R. 7;
2 Saund. R. 422; *Fowler* v. *Bott,* 6 Mass. R. 63.

4 *Pomfret* v. *Ricroft,* 1 Saund. 321, 323, & ibid. note 7.

5 *Cheetham* v. *Hampson,* 4 T. R. 318.

any direct authority upon the other points above stated from the foreign law, they must be propounded as still open to controversy in our law. Cases may easily be put of a practical nature, and of frequent recurrence. Suppose a coach is hired for a journey, and it is injured, and requires repairs, without any fault of the hirer during the journey; who is to bear the expense of these repairs? If the repairs are very great, and are permanently beneficial to the owner, are they to be borne exclusively by the owner, or by the hirer, or jointly by both in proportion to the benefit received by each? A tenant is not obliged to make permanent or general repairs.[1] Is a like rule applicable to chattels? Suppose a ship, let for a voyage, should from accidents require repairs, and the contract contains no clause relative to repairs; are they to be paid for ultimately by the hirer, or by the owner? Is there a difference between temporary and permanent repairs; between slight and beneficial repairs; between such as merely make good the old work, and such as increase the value of the ship? These questions are put; but they can be satisfactorily answered only, when they shall have undergone a judicial decision.

§ 393. In respect to animals hired the common understanding is, that the hirer is bound to provide them with suitable food during the time of such hiring, unless there is some agreement to the contrary.[2]

§ 394. As to the rights and duties of the hirer. First. As to his rights. In virtue of the bailment the hirer acquires a special property in the thing during the continuance of the contract, and for the purposes

---

[1] 2 Esp. R. 590; Holt's N. P. R. 7.

[2] *Handford v. Palmer*, 2 Brod. & Bing. 359; S. C. 5 Moore R. 74.

expressed or implied by it.[1] Hence he may maintain
an action for any tortious dispossession of it, or any injury to it during the existence of his right.[2] But since,
in such case, the owner has also a general property,
unless he has, by virtue of his agreement, parted with
it for a term, he also may maintain a like suit against
the stranger.[3] But in such case a recovery by either,
it seems, bars, or at least may bar, the action of the
other.[4]

§ 395. The hirer also acquires the right, and the exclusive right to the use of the thing during the time of
the bailment ; and the owner has no right to disturb
him in the lawful enjoyment of it during the time of the
user. And if during that time the thing is re-delivered to the owner for a temporary purpose, he is
bound to deliver it back afterwards to the hirer.[5]

§ 396. It has also been decided, that where a thing,
as, for instance, a horse is let to hire for a particular
object or journey, and the hirer wrongfully uses it for
another object or journey, there the owner has no right
to retake it by force.[6] But it seems, that such a misuser amounts to a virtual determination of the bailment, and destroys the hirer's special property therein ; and the owner may maintain trover therefor.[7]

---

1 Jones's Bailm. 85, 86 ; Bac. Abr. Bailment C ; Yelv. 172 ; 2 Bl.
Com. 395, 396 ; 2 Kent Com. 456 ; 2 Saund. 47, and note by Williams.

2 *Croft* v. *Alison*, 4 Barn. & Ald. 590 ; 2 Saund. R. 476 ; Id. 47 *c* ;
Bac. Abr. Trespass C ; Id. Trover C ; 9 Mass. R. 104, 265 ; 3 Camp.
R. 187.

3 Bac. Abr. Trespass C ; Id. Trover C ; 2 Bl. Com. 396 ; *Gordon* v.
Harper, 7 T. R. 9 ; *Paine* v. *Middlesex*, 1 R. & M. 99 ; 2 Saund. R. 47,
notes by Williams, &c. ; 2 Bl. Com. 396.

4 Bac. Abr. Trespass C ; Id. Trover C ; 1 Buls. 69 ; 1 Barn. & Ald
59 ; 2 Saund. 47, and note.

5 *Roberts* v. *Wyatt*, 2 Taunt. R. 268.   6 *Lee* v. *Atkinson*, Yelv. 172.

7 *Wilkinson* v. *King*, 2 Camp. R. 335 ; *Loeschman* v. *Machin*, 2 Stark.
311 ; *Youle* v. *Harbottle*, Peake R. 49 ; 2 Saund. R. 47 *f*, and notes of
Williams and Patterson ; see also 2 Salk. 655.

§ 397. In respect to the duties of the hirer, they are very succinctly stated by Domat. The engagements (says he)[1] of the person, who takes any thing to hire, are, to put the thing to no other use, than that, for which it is hired; to use it well; to take care of it; to restore it at the time appointed; to pay the rent or hire; and, in general, to observe whatever is prescribed by the contract, by law, and by custom.

§ 398. In the first place, let us consider what is the degree of care or diligence to be employed by the hirer of the thing generally; for the exceptions to the rule will require a separate consideration. And here the degree of care exacted by the civil law has been matter of some disputation. The language of that law is, *Dolum et culpam recipit locatum.* And again, *Ubi utriusque utilitas vertitur, ut in empto, ut in locato, &c. et dolus et culpa præstatur.*[2] These passages point only to the rule, that the hirer is liable not only for fraud, but for negligence. The degree of negligence is not stated. But in the Institutes (Lib. 3, tit. 25, § 5,) it is said, "Ab eo [the hirer] custodia talis desideratur, qualem diligentissimus pater familias suis rebus adhibet." And the question is, in what sense the word *diligentissimus* is here used. Does it signify a diligent father of a family, or a *very* diligent father of a family; or, in other words, does it import ordinary, or extraordinary diligence? Heineccius seems to consider the hirer liable, not only for fraud, but for slight and ordinary, as well as for gross negligence: "Culpam latam et levem."[3] Sir William Jones has maintained,

---

1 Domat, B. 1, tit. 4, § 2, art. 1; Pothier, Louage, n 133, 188.

2 Dig. Lib. 50, tit. 17, l. 23; Dig. Lib. 13, tit. 6, l. 5, § 2; Cod. Lib. 4, tit. 65, l. 28.

3 Heinec. Pand. Lib. 19, tit. 2, § 324; Domat, B. 1, tit. 4, § 2, art. 4.

with great force and ability, that the word *diligentissimus*
in the text imports no more than ordinarily diligent.[1]
Lord Holt, obviously founding himself upon Bracton,[2]
supposed, that it imported *very* diligent. And, accordingly, Lord Holt held, that " At the common law, a
hirer was bound to very great diligence." " If (said he)
goods are let out for a reward, the hirer is bound to the
utmost diligence, such as the *most* diligent father of a
family uses."[3] And in Buller's Nisi Prius (72) it is
laid down, that the hirer is to take all *imaginable* care.
Sir William Jones, on the contrary, has contended, that
the case being one of mutual benefit, the hirer is bound
only for ordinary diligence, and of course is responsible
only for ordinary negligence.[4] And his opinion appears
to be now settled upon principle to be the true exposition of the common law.[5] And the rule laid down by
Pothier is in exact conformity to that of the common
law. " The hirer (says he) is bound to take the same
care to preserve the thing, which a good and prudent
father of a family would take of his own;[6]* and this
also is the rule of the Scottish law.[7]

---

1 Jones's Bailm. 87, 88; Vinn. ad Inst. Lib. 3, tit. 15, l. 2, comm. § 13.

2 Bract. 62 *b.*

3 *Coggs* v. *Bernard*, 2 Ld. Ray. 909, 916.

4 Jones's Bailm. 86, 87, 120.

5 1 Dane's Abr. ch. 17, art. 3, 12; 2 Kent Com. 456, and note (c);
Dean v. *Keate*, 3 Camp. R. 4; *Miller* v. *Salisbury*, 13 Johns. R. 211;
2 Brod. & Bing. R. 359; *Platt* v. *Hibbard*, 7 Cowen R. 497.

6 1 Bell's Com. 453, 455.

7 Pothier, Louage, n. 190, 192; Domat, B. 1, tit. 4, § 2, art. 4; Cod.
Lib. 4, tit. 65, l. 28; Cod. Civ. B. 3, tit. 8, art. 1728; Ayliffe's Pand. B. 4,
tit. 7, p. 463; Ersk. Inst. B. 3, tit. 3, §§ 14, 15.

* Pothier has examined this whole subject of responsibility for diligence with great ability in some general observations on the Treatise
of Monsieur Le Brun, to which Sir William Jones has referred in his
Essay (p. 30, note (*t*,)) as printed " at the end of his Treatise on the Mar-

§ 399. Hence, the hirer of a thing being responsible only for that degree of diligence, which all prudent men, that is, which the generality of mankind use in keeping their own goods of the same kind,[1] it is very clear, that he can be liable only for such injuries, as are shown to come from an omission of that diligence. If a man hires a horse, he is bound to ride it moderately, and to treat it as carefully, as any man of common discretion would his own, and to supply it with suitable food.[2] And if he does so, and the horse in such reasonable use is lamed or injured, he is not responsible for any damages.[3] If two persons jointly hire a horse and chaise on joint account, both are answerable for any misconduct or negligence of either in driving, or in any other want of proper care. But it would be otherwise, where one is the sole hirer, and the other merely invited to ride, the hirer, in such a case, alone being responsible.[4]

§ 400. And the hirer is not only liable for his own personal default and negligence, but for the default and negligence of his servants and domestics about the thing hired. If, therefore, a hired horse is ridden by the servant of the hirer so immoderately, that he is injured or killed thereby, the hirer is personally responsible.[5] So,

---

[1] Jones's Bailm. 88 ; 2 Brod. & Bing. R. 359.

[2] Jones's Bailm. 88, 89.

[3] *Miller* v. *Salisbury*, 13 Johns. R. 211 ; 1 Bell's Com. 453.

[4] *Davy* v. *Chamberlain*, 4 Esp. R. 229.

[5] Jones's Bailm. 89 ; 1 Bl. Com. 430, 431 ; Domat, B. 1, tit. 4, § 2, n. 5 ; 1 Bell's Com. 455.

riage Contract." I did not find it in that place in my own edition of Pothier's works. But while the present work was passing through the press, in the course of other researches, I discovered, that it was printed in the later editions of Pothier's works, at the end of his Treatise on Obligations, though it is (strangely enough) altogether omitted in Sir William D. Evans's Translation of that work ; to which it is properly an appendage. See also Pothier, Pand. De Regulis Juris. § 981.

if the servant of the hirer carelessly and improperly leaves open the stable door of the hirer, and the horse is stolen by thieves, the hirer is responsible therefor.[1] So, if ready furnished lodgings are hired, and the hirer's servants negligently injure or deface the furniture.[2]

§ 401. The Roman law seems to have been relaxed a little from this severe but important rule; for it made the master responsible only, when he was culpably negligent in admitting careless guests or servants into his house.[3] It has been observed, both by Pothier[4] and Sir William Jones,[5] that this distinction must have been sufficiently perplexing in practice; and the rule of the common law, which is like that of the foreign law in modern times, is not only more safe, convenient, and uniform in its application; but it imposes upon the hirer a salutary diligence and caution in regard to those, who are admitted into his house, or kept in his service. The letter can otherwise have no sufficient security against losses from the misconduct of guests or servants.

§ 402. But the master is not universally liable for the misdeeds of his servants; and therefore we are to distinguish, whether the act complained of has been done in the service of the master, or in obedience to his orders, or not; for in the former cases only is the master responsible. The master is not responsible for any wilful or malicious injury done by his servant without his knowledge or consent; but only for injuries, which are done by the servant in the master's service in the course of his employment. Thus, if a servant in driv-

---

[1] Jones's Bailm. 89; 2 Ld. Ray. 909, 916; *Salem Bank* v. *Gloucester Bank*, 17 Mass. R. 1.

[2] Jones's Bailm. 89.

[3] Dig. Lib. 19, tit. 2, l. 11; Dig. Lib. 9, tit. 2, l. 27, § 11.

[4] Pothier, Louage, n. 193; Domat, B. 1, tit. 4, § 2, n. 5.

[5] Jones's Bailm. 89, 90.

ing his master's coach by his negligence runs against, and injures another coach, his master is responsible for the injury to the owner of the injured coach. But it is otherwise, if the servant wilfully and wantonly drives against the other coach, and thus does the injury without the connivance or consent of his master.[1] So, if the servant of a blacksmith in shoeing a horse negligently injures him, the master is responsible.[2] But it will be otherwise, if he maliciously drives a nail into the horse's foot in order to lame him.[3]

§ 403. And the hirer is not responsible for any injury by negligence of servants, who are not actually in his employ. If a person hires a coach and horses of a stable-keeper for a journey, and the horses are driven by the servant of the latter, he and not the hirer is responsible for any injury done by the negligence of the servant in the course of the journey.[4] And generally, if a person hires a carriage and horses, and the owner sends a postillion or coachman with them to drive them, the hirer is discharged from all attention to the horses; and he remains liable only to take ordinary care of the glasses and inside of the carriage, while he sits in it.[5]

§ 404. But though the master is responsible for the misfesances and negligent acts of his servants, it does not follow, that the servant is not himself also responsible to the bailor. The distinction furnished in some decisions is this, that servants are responsible to the bailor for misfesances but not for nonfesances; and in

---

1 *McManus* v. *Cricket*, 1 East R. 106; *Croft* v. *Alison*, 4 Barn. & Ald. 590; 6 T. R. 651, 659; 8 T. R. 188.

2 1 Bl. Com. 431.

3 2 Salk. 440, 441.

4 *Sammel* v. *Wright*, 5 Esp. R. 263; Pothier, Louage, n. 196.

5 Jones's Bailm. 88, 89; Pothier, Louage, n. 196.

the latter case the remedy of the bailor is solely against the master.[1]

§ 405. It is the duty of the hirer to supply a horse, hired by him, with suitable food during the time of hiring; and, therefore, any neglect on his part in this particular will make him responsible to the owner.[2] And if a hired horse is exhausted, and refuses its feed, the hirer is bound to abstain from using the horse; and if he pursues his journey with the horse, he is liable for all the injury.[3] If a hired horse falls sick during a journey, the hirer ought to procure the aid of a farrier, if one can be obtained; and if he does, he is not responsible for any mistakes of the farrier in the treatment of the horse. But if, instead of procuring the aid of a farrier, when he can, he prescribes himself unskilfully for the horse, and thus causes his death, he will be responsible for the damages, although he acts *bonâ fide*.[4]

§ 406. What shall, and what shall not be deemed negligence on the part of a hirer is sometimes a matter of considerable nicety. It has already been stated, that Sir William Jones holds, that a loss by theft is *primâ facie* evidence of negligence;[5] and reasons have been offered to prove, that no such rule exists in the common law, however it may exist in the civil law.[6] But even if there is such a rule, it is but a bare presumption, and capable of being rebutted by proof, that the theft was by no negligence of the hirer.[7]

---

1 12 Mod. R. 488; Sayer R. 41; *Cameron* v. *Reynolds*, Cowp. R. 403; *Renning* v. *Goodchild*, 3 Wilson R. 454; 5 Burr. R. 2721; 1 Vent. 238.
2 *Handford* v. *Palmer*, 3 Bro. & Bing. 359; S. C. 5 Moore R. 74.
3 *Bray* v. *Mayne*, 1 Gow. R. 1; 1 Bell Com. 455.
4 *Dean* v. *Keate*, 3 Camp. R. 4; 1 Bell Com. 455.
5 Jones's Bailm. 43, 44, 76, 78, 98, 110; Ante, § 333 &c. & 1 Vent. 121.
6 Pothier, Louage, n. 429.
7 Jones's Bailm. 96, 98; 2 Ld. Raym. 909, 918.

§ 407. In respect to thefts by the servants of a hirer, generally speaking, he is not liable therefor, unless there are some circumstances, which impute to him a want of due diligence. Thus, where a trunk was deposited with an upholsterer for a reward, the contents of which were stolen by his servants, notwithstanding reasonable care in the custody of it by him, he was held not responsible for the loss.[1] But if he had used greater precaution in respect to like property of his own, he would have been liable for the loss. Thus, if a watch is deposited with a watch-maker for repairs, and it is left in his shop in a less secure repository than that, in which he keeps his own, and it is stolen by his servants, he will be responsible for the loss.[2] So, if an agister of cattle for a reward leaves open the gates of his field, or allows the fences to be defective, so that the cattle escape, he is liable for the loss.[3] And in like manner, the proprietors of a dry dock are responsible for any injury to a vessel undergoing repairs there, occasioned by the bursting of the dock gates, if by reasonable care the bursting might have been prevented.[4]

§ 408. But if the thing hired is lost or injured by inevitable casualty, or by superior force, and without any fault of the hirer, he is exonerated from all risk.[5] So, if the loss be not strictly inevitable, but there has been no omission of reasonable diligence on the part of the hirer. Thus, a warehouseman is not responsible for destruction of goods by rats, if he has used the or-

---

1 *Finucane* v. *Small*, 1 Esp. R. 314.

2 *Clarke* v. *Earnshaw*, 1 Gow. R. 30.

3 *Broadwater* v. *Blot*, Holt N. P. R. 547; Jones's Bailm. 91, 92; 1 Bell Com. 458.

4 *Leck* v. *Maestaer*, 1 Camp. R. 138.

5 *Menotone* v. *Athawes*, 3 Burr. 1592 ; *Longman* v. *Galini*, Abbott on Shipp. P. 3, ch. 4, § 8; p. 259, note (*d*) ; 1 Bell Com. 453, 455, 458.

dinary precautions to guard against the loss.[1] So, if the owner of slaves lets them to a master of a vessel for a voyage, and they run away in a foreign port, the master is not responsible therefor, if he has acted in good faith and with reasonable care, although he might perhaps have exercised a higher power of confinement over them.[2]

§ 409. Pothier puts a case, which he deems clear, in proof of the position, that the hirer may be responsible for a loss, where his misconduct is not the *cause*, but the *occasion* of the loss. If the bailee is prohibited by the terms of the bailment from keeping combustible materials in the place, where the thing is, and the thing is destroyed by fire, even through mere casualty, he holds him responsible, because it is a breach of his engagement.[3] And so in the civil law. " Si hoc in locatione convenit, *ignem ne habeto,* et habuit, tenebitur, etiamsi fortuitus casus admisit incendium." [4] It seems, that by the civil law the hirer is made liable for all losses and injuries to the thing hired, occasioned by the private enmity of persons hostile to the hirer, if by his own fault he has provoked that enmity. But Pothier justly doubts, how far this rule ought to be followed in practice.[5]

§ 410. The question may here arise, as in many other cases of bailments, on whom lies the burthen of proof of negligence, or of repelling it. With certain

---

1 *Cailiff* v. *Danvers,* Peake R. 114; *Moore* v. *Mourgue,* Cowp. R. 479; *Miller* v. *Salisbury,* 13 Johns. R. 211; Abbott on Shipp. P. 3, ch. 3, § 9, p. 244.

2 *Beverly* v. *Brook,* 2 Wheat. R. 100.

3 Pothier, Louage, n. 195; see also 1 Bell Com. 458.

4 Dig. Lib. 19, tit. 2, l. 11, § 1.

5 Pothier, Louage, n. 195; Domat, B. 1, tit. 4, § 2, n. 6; Dig. Lib. 19, tit. 2, l. 27, § 4.

exceptions, which will hereafter be taken notice of, as to innkeepers and carriers,[1] it would seem, that the burthen of proof of negligence is on the bailor; and proof merely of the loss is not sufficient to put the bailee on his defence. This has been ruled in a case against a depositary for hire, where the goods bailed were stolen by his servants;[2] and also in the case of a horse hired and injured during the term of the bailment, positive proof was required on the part of the owner to sustain his action.[3] There seem, however, to be some discrepancies in the authorities on this subject, which invite the attention of the learned reader.[4]

§ 411. According to the French law, as laid down by Pothier, in every case of loss the hirer is bound to prove, that the loss was without any default on his part; for the law makes no presumption in his favour. And in case of a loss by fire, if the fire is in the house of the hirer, Pothier seems to think, that that circumstance alone raises a presumption of negligence.[5] The Code of France [6] throws the burthen of proof upon the hirer of leased property to show, that the loss has not been by his default; and it makes him responsible for losses occasioned by fire, unless the fire is by inevitable casualty, or superior force, or communicated by the burning of a neighbouring house. By the Scottish

---

[1] 5 T. R. 276; Jones's Bailm. 96.

[2] *Finucane* v. *Small,* 1 Esp. R. 314.

[3] *Cooper* v. *Barton,* 3 Camp. R. 5, note; *Newton* v. *Pope,* 1 Cowen R. 109.

[4] *Platt* v. *Hibbard,* 7 Cowen R. 497, 500, note (a); *Harris* v. *Packwood,* 3 Taunt. R. 264; *Marsh* v. *Horne,* 5 B. & Cresw. 322; 2 Salk. 655.

[5] Pothier, Louage, n. 194, 199, 200.

[6] Cod. Civ. art. 1732, 1733, 1734.

law, if any specific injury has occurred, not manifestly accidental, the *onus probandi* lies on the hirer to justify himself by proving the accident.[1]

§ 412. In cases of robbery, the hirer is not chargeable, unless it has been occasioned by his own fault or negligence; for (as has been stated in another place) robbery is deemed an accident by superior force *(vis major.)*[2] If, however, the hirer travels by roads dangerous for robbery, or at an unseasonable hour of the night, or if in any other manner, by his own negligence, he exposes the property to an undue risk of robbery, he will be bound to make good the loss.[3] But if he takes another road, because the common highway is impracticable or dangerous, and other travellers are accustomed to do the same, he will be justified in so doing.[4]

§ 413. As to the use of the thing hired. There is, on the part of the hirer, an implied obligation, not only to use the thing with due care and moderation, but not to apply it to any other use than that, for which it is hired. Thus, if a horse is hired as a saddle horse, the hirer has no right to use the horse in a cart, or to carry loads, or as a beast of burden.[5] If a carriage and horses are hired for a journey to Boston, the hirer has no right to go with them on a journey to New York.[6]

---

1 1 Bell Com. 454.

2 Jones's Bailm. 44, 78, 79, 88, 98, 103, 122; 2 Ld. Raym. 909, 916; Id. 1087; Id. 918; Pothier, Louage, n. 195.

3 Jones's Bailm. 81, 88, 98, 103; Pothier, Louage, n. 195; 2 Ld. Raym. 909, 917.

4 Pothier, Louage, n. 195.

5 Pothier, Louage, n. 189; Domat, B. 1, tit. 4, § 2, art. 2, 3; Jones's Bailm. 68; Id. 88; 2 Saund. 47 g, and note; 1 Bell Com. 454; *Lockwood* v. *Bull*, 1 Cowen R. 322.

6 Jones's Bailm. 68; 2 Ld. Raym. 915.

So, if they are hired for a week, he has no right to use them for a month.[1]   And if the thing is used for a different purpose from that, which was intended by the parties, or in a different manner, or for a longer period, the hirer is not only responsible for all damages, but if a loss occurs, although by inevitable casualty, he will be responsible therefor.[2]   In short, such misuser is deemed a conversion of the property, for which the hirer is deemed responsible.[3]

§ 414. Another implied obligation of the hirer is to restore the thing hired, when the bailment is determined.[4]   He is of course to restore it in as good condition as he received it, unless it has been injured by some internal decay, accident, or other means, wholly without his default.[5]   If it has sustained any injury by his neglect, he is liable in damages, notwithstanding the owner has received it back.[6]   If the hirer, instead of delivering back the thing, pays its full value to the owner, on account of the injury sustained by his negligence, he becomes henceforth the proprietor of the thing; and the letter has no longer any title to it.[7]

§ 415. The time, the place, and the mode of restitution of the thing hired, are governed by the circumstances of each particular case, and depend upon rules

---

1 Jones's Bailm. 68; 2 Ld. Raym. 915; *Wheelock* v. *Wheelwright*, 5 Mass. R. 104.

2 *De Tollemere* v. *Fuller*, 1 Rep. Const. C. So. Carol. 121; Jones's Bailm. 68, 69, 121; 2 Ld. Raym. 909, 917.

3 Bac. Abr. Bailment C; Id. Trover C, D, E; 2 Saund. R. 47 *g*; *Isaacs* v. *Clarke*, 2 Bulst. R. 306, 309.

4 *Syeds* v. *Hay*, 4 T. R. 260, per Buller J.

5 Pothier, Louage, n. 197, 198, 200; Domat, B. 1, tit. 4, § 2, n. 11; *Cooper* v. *Barton*, 3 Camp. R. 5, n.; *Miller* v. *Salisbury*, 13 Johns. R. 211.

6 *Reynolds* v. *Shuler*, 5 Cowen R. 323.

7 Pothier, Louage, n. 198.

of presumption of the intention of the parties, like those in other cases of bailments.

§ 416. Another implied obligation on the part of the hirer is to pay the hire or recompense.[1]   This is a natural result from the contract, and requires no reasoning to support it.   Pothier, however, has thought it worthy of a separate discussion, principally with reference to leases of real estates on rent, in respect to which there are many points entitled to grave consideration, which cannot properly find a place in the more limited view of bailments at the common law.[2]

§ 417. In general, it may be said, that the whole hire is not due, unless the hirer has had the use and enjoyment of the thing in the manner contemplated by the parties.[3]   If he has had the use or enjoyment for a part of the time only, or it has been from unforeseen circumstances greatly diminished, he ought not to be required to pay more than a proportionate hire, *pro tanto*.[4]   If various things are hired, and the use and enjoyment of a part only has been realized, the hirer ought, in like manner, to be liable only *pro tanto*.[5]   But in both these cases it is to be understood, that the deficiency in the use and enjoyment has not been by the default of the hirer, but has arisen from accident, or from the default of the letter; and that the obligation to pay the whole hire is not either expressly or impliedly stipulated for by the contract, notwithstanding any deficiency in the use or enjoyment.[6]

---

[1] Pothier, Louage, n. 134; Domat, B. 1, tit. 4, § 2, n. 11; Cod. Civ. art. 1728.

[2] Pothier, Louage, n. 134 to 164.   [3] Pothier, Louage, n. 139.

[4] Pothier, ibid, n. 139, 140, 143, 144.   [5] Pothier, ibid, n. 141.

[6] Pothier, Louage, n. 141, 142, 143, 144; Id. n. 165, 168; Id. 178.

§ 418. The next consideration is, as to the manner, in which the contract of hire may be dissolved or extinguished. And, from what has been already said, it follows, that as to liabilities *in futuro* it is extinguished by the loss or destruction of the thing by any inevitable casualty; by a voluntary dissolution of the contract by the parties; and by operation of law, as where the hirer becomes proprietor, by purchase or otherwise, of the thing hired.[1]

§ 419. Whether the contract is dissolved by the death of either party depends upon the intention of the parties, and the rules of law applicable to contracts in general. Where the use is to be for a specific time, it generally remains in force during that period. Where it is during pleasure, it is dissolved by the death of either party.[2]

§ 420. The principles stated in the few last sections, it will be perceived, are derived altogether from the civil law. The common law does not furnish any direct recognitions of them. But it may be safely affirmed, that they are so consonant with general justice, and with the nature of the contract, that in the absence of authority they may be used as guides to assist our general reasoning.

ART. II.   HIRE OF LABOUR AND SERVICES.

§ 421. WE are next led to the consideration of the rights, duties, and obligations of the parties in the second class of Bailments for Hire, LOCATIO OPERIS, or the Hiring of Labour and Services. This (as has been already observed) is divisible into two branches:

---

[1] Pothier, Louage, n. 198, 309, 310; Cod. Civ. art. 1741.

[2] Pothier, Louage, n. 317; 1 Bell's Com. 452.

(1.) LOCATIO OPERIS FACIENDI; (2.) LOCATIO MER-
CIUM VEHENDARUM. Each of these will be treated
separately, as each is of very extensive influence in
the business of civil life,[1] and in some respects involves,
or may involve, distinct principles.

§ 422. And first, as to LOCATIO OPERIS FACIENDI.
This may again be divided into two kinds; (1.) the
Hire of Labour and Services, or *Locatio operis faciendi*, strictly so called, such as the hire of tailors to make
clothes, and of jewellers to set gems, and of watch-
makers to repair watches; (2.) *Locatio custodiæ*, or
the receiving of goods on deposit for a reward, which
is properly the hire of care and attention about the
goods; and the bailee may well enough be called *locator operæ*, since the care and attention, which he lets
out for pay, are in truth principally a mental operation,
though the custody generally includes some physical
labour.[2]   Of this last class are warehouse-men and
wharfingers, and other depositaries for hire.   And as
these differ from mere depositaries principally in receiving a compensation for their services;[3] so another
class of hirers, viz. agents, factors, commission merchants, bailiffs,[4] and other persons acting for a compensation, differ from mandataries principally in the
same circumstance.[5]   The undertaking of the latter
lies in fesance; that of the former in custody.[6]   Innkeepers seem to partake of the character of both; but
they will be reserved for a separate consideration.[7]

---

1 Jones's Bailm. 90 ; 2 Kent Com. 457 ; Merlin. Repért. art. Louage.
2 Jones's Bailm. 90, 96, 97 ; Merlin. Repért. art. Louage.
3 Jones's Bailm. 49.   4 2 Ld. Ray. 909, 918.
5 Jones's Bailm. 98.   6 Jones's Bailm. 98.
7 Jones's Bailm. 49, 92, 93, 94.

§ 423. In the civil and foreign law all agencies for hire, and all sorts of labour and services, are sometimes treated of under the head of bailments for hire.[1] In the common law, such agencies and labour and services only are included, as are employed about personal property entrusted by the owner to the bailee. But, in strictness, both laws concur in the same general doctrine; for, where the workman is not only to do the work, but is to furnish the materials, it is deemed in the civil law rather a case of sale, than a case of *locatio operis*.[2] And in the common law, it would be treated as a case of bailment, only when the stock or materials belong to the employer. And, where the principal materials belong to the employer, the case would still be treated as a bailment, although the workman might furnish some accessorial materials or ornaments.[3] Thus, if A sends cloth to a tailor to be made into a garment, and the tailor furnishes buttons and twist to complete it, it will be a mere case of *locatio operis faciendi*.

§ 424. In cases of hire of things, the bailee is to pay the hire; but in cases of hire of work, the bailor is to pay it. In many other respects, these contracts involve the like or corresponding obligations between the parties.[4] According to the systematical mode of treating them in the foreign law, both may be said to arise from natural law; to be founded in consent; and to involve reciprocal engagements.[5] In contracts for

---

[1] Domat, B. 1, tit. 4, § 7, n. 2, 3, 4; Pothier, Louage, n. 392.

[2] Pothier, Louage, n. 392, 394; Domat, B. 1, tit. 4, § 7, n. 1, 2, 3, 4; Dig. Lib. 19, tit. 2, l. 2, § 1; Inst. Lib. 4, tit. 25, § 4; Merlin. Repért. art. Louage; 1 Bell's Com. 455.

[3] Pothier, Louage, n. 394; 1 Bell's Com. 455.

[4] Pothier, Louage, n. 393.

[5] Pothier, Louage, n. 393.

work, it is of the essence of the contract, (1.) that there should be work to be done; (2.) for a price or reward; and (3.) a lawful contract between parties capable and intending to contract.[1]

§ 425. The obligations or duties on the part of the employer, as deduced in the foreign law, are principally these; (1.) to pay the price or compensation; (2.) to pay for all proper new and accessorial materials; (3.) to do every thing on his part to enable the workman to execute his engagement; (4.) and finally, to receive the thing when finished. But care is to be taken, that the materials are not extravagant, nor the claims beyond the fair scope of the engagement.[2] Besides these, the employer is bound to good faith and honesty in his conduct. He must not conceal defects, or impose upon the other party; and he must conform to all the special stipulations contained in his contract.[3] These duties are formally treated of by Pothier; and they seem so clear upon principles of general justice, that the common law could hardly be deemed a rational science, if it did not recognise them.

§ 426. If, while the work is doing, the thing perishes by internal defect, by accident, or by superior force, without any default of the workman, the latter is, or may be entitled to compensation, to the extent of the labour actually performed on it; for the maxim is, "Res perit domino."[4] And if the workman has been at any charge in preserving the thing, beyond what his under-

---

1 Pothier, Louage, n. 395, 396, 397, 398, 399, 400, 401, 403.

2 Pothier, Louage, n. 405, 406, 407 to 409, 410, 436; Domat. B. 1, tit. 4, § 9, n. 1 to 8.

3 Pothier, Louage, n. 411 to 417.

4 Dig. Lib. 19, tit. 2, l. 59; Domat, B. 1, tit. 4, § 9, n. 4; Pothier, Louage, n. 433, ch. 3, *Menetone* v. *Athawes*, 3 Burr. 1592; *Gillet* v. *Mawman*, 1 Taunt. R. 137.

taking implies, the civil law in such a case decreed him compensation.[1] The common law in a case of clear necessity would probably adopt the like rule, as a fair presumption of the intention of the parties. Thus, if the thing were carried away by an inundation, the expenses of recovering it would be deemed a fair charge on the bailor.

§ 427. But although, upon the general principles of law applicable to the contract, if a thing perishes, while it is yet in the hands of the workman, and before the work is completed, without any default on his part, he is entitled to compensation for his labour; yet it must be admitted, that the rule has not obtained universal favour. The modern Code of France declares, that in such a case, there shall be no compensation to the workman; but, that the thing perishes to the loss of the employer and the workman respectively.[2]

§ 428. The obligations or duties on the part of the workman or undertaker are thus summed up in the foreign law; to do the work; to do it at the time agreed on; to do it well; to employ the materials furnished by the employer in a proper manner; and lastly, to exercise the proper degree of care and diligence about the work.[3] It seems unnecessary to enter upon any inquiry as to any particulars embraced under any, but the last head, since they are the plain results of the undertaking.

§ 429. What, then, is the degree of care, which bailees of work for hire are responsible for? The gen-

---

[1] Domat, B. 1, tit. 4, § 9, n. 8.

[2] Cod. Civ. art. 1790 ; 2 Pardes. Droit Commer. P. 2, tit. 7, ch. 2, art. 526 ; 1 Bell's Com. 456.

[3] Pothier, Louage, n. 419 to 433; Pardes. Droit Commer. P. 2, art. 523 to 525, and 528.

eral rule is, (as has been often observed,) that where
the contract is of mutual benefit, there ordinary diligence only is required.   And this is the degree of diligence, therefore, which applies to contracts of this sort,
as well by the common law, as by the civil and foreign
law.[1]   Thus, a watch-maker, having a watch left with
him for repairs, is obliged to use ordinary diligence in
keeping it; and if he omits it, and the watch is lost, he
is liable for the value in damages.[2]   And a workman is
not only bound to guard the thing bailed against ordinary hazards, but likewise to exert himself to preserve
it from any unexpected danger, to which it may be exposed.[3]   It has been very correctly observed, that different things may require very different care.   The care
required in building a common door-way, is quite different from that required in raising a marble pillar, but
both come under the description of ordinary care.[4]

§ 430.   Pothier considers, that in cases of theft the
bailee of work is liable to his employer for the loss of
the thing.   It is probable, that he holds this doctrine
upon the general ground of the civil law, that it is presumptive evidence of ordinary negligence.[5]   It has been
already seen, that at the common law the rule is different; for, whether the bailee would in such a case be
liable or not, would depend, not upon the fact of theft,
but upon the question, whether the loss had been occasioned by the ordinary negligence of the bailee.

§ 431.   But, where skill, as well as care, is required
in performing the undertaking, there, if the party pur-

---

1 Jones's Bailm. 91, 94; Pothier, Louage, n. 429; 2 Kent Com. 457,
458; 1 Bell's Com. 453, 455.
2 *Clarke* v. *Earnshaw*, 1 Gow. R. 30.
3 *Leck* v. *Maestaer*, 1 Camp. R. 138.
4 1 Bell's Com. 458.   5 Pothier, Louage, n. 4.

port to have skill in the business, and he undertakes for
hire, he is bound, not only to ordinary care and diligence in preserving the thing, but also to the exercise
of due and ordinary skill in the employment of his art or
business about it; or, in other words, to perform it in a
workmanlike manner.[1] In cases of this sort he must
be understood to have engaged to use a degree of diligence, and attention, and skill, adequate to the performance of his undertaking.[2] *Spondet* (say the Roman lawyers) *peritiam artis.*[3] And it is his own fault,
if he undertakes without sufficient skill, or applies less
than the occasion requires. Thus, if a farrier undertakes the cure of a diseased or lame horse, he is bound
to a reasonable exercise of skill; and if through his
ignorance or bad management the horse dies, he is
liable for the loss.[4] So, if a ship-carpenter undertakes
to build a ship, he engages for reasonable skill, as well
as care in building it.

§ 432. And the degree of skill and diligence, which
is required, rises in proportion to the value, the delica-
cy, and the skill of the operation. Thus, an artisan,
employed to repair a very delicate mathematical instrument, is expected to exert more care and skill, than he
would about common instruments. The case put by
Gaius is of this nature. The removal or raising of a fine
pillar of granite or porphyry requires peculiar care and
skill; and the law exacts, therefore, more than ordinary diligence and skill in the undertaker of such a work

---

1 Jones's Bailm. 91; 2 Kent Com. 458, 463; 1 Bell's Com. 459.

2 Jones's Bailm. 22, 53, 62, 97, 98, 120, 121; *Coggs* v. *Bernard,* 2 Ld.
Ray. 909, 918; Domat, B. 1, tit. 4, § 8, n. 1; Pothier, Louage, n. 425.

3 Jones's Bailm. 23, note (*m*), 98, note (*l*); Pothier, Louage, n. 425 to
428; Pardes. Droit Comm. P. 2, art. 528; Ayliffe's Pand. B. 4, tit. 7, p.
466; Ersk. Inst. B. 3, tit. 3, § 16; 1 Bell's Com. 459.

4 Jones's Bailm. 62, 99, 100; 1 Roll. Abr. 10; 1 Bell's Com. 459, 461.

for a stipulated compensation, that is, more diligence and skill than is required of workmen in removing ordinary things of the same kind. But if all things are done by the undertaker, which a quite diligent and skilful workman would observe, ("quæ diligentissimus quisque observaturus fuisset,") and there is no negligence, he will be exonerated, although the column should be fractured.[1] * So, if a gem is delivered to a jeweller to be set or engraved, and it is broken; if this arises solely from the defect of the material, the jeweller is not responsible; but it is otherwise, if it arises from the unskilfulness, or negligence, or rashness of the artisan.[2] So, if clothes are delivered to a fuller to be dressed, and he suffers them to be eaten by mice, he will be reponsible, if it is by his negligence; and the Roman law imputed negligence to him in such a case.[3]

§ 433. But in all these cases, where skill is required, it is to be understood, that it means ordinary skill in the business or employment, which the bailee undertakes for. For he is not presumed to engage for the extraordinary skill, which belongs to a few men only in his business or employment, or for extraordinary endowments or acquirements. Reasonable skill constitutes the measure of the engagement in regard to the thing undertaken.[4]

---

[1] Jones's Bailm. 98; Dig. Lib. 19, tit. 2, 1. 25, § 7; Ayliffe's Pand. B, 4, tit. 7, p. 463.

[2] Dig. Lib. 19, tit. 2, 1. 13, § 5; Pothier, Louage, n. 428.

[3] Dig. Lib. 19, tit. 2, 1. 13, § 6; Jones's Bailm. 105.

[4] *Moore* v. *Morgue,* Cowp. R. 497; Jones's Bailm. 94; 1 Bell Com. 458, 459.

* Mr. Bell, in his Commentaries, has laid down some rules on the subject of professional skill, which may assist the learned inquirer in his efforts to arrive at a just criterion. 1 Bell Com. 459, 460.

§ 434. Sir William Jones, however, while he admits the general rule, seems to intimate in one place a more stringent doctrine. " When (says he) a person, who, if he were wholly uninterested, would be a man-datary, undertakes for a reward to perform any work, he must be considered as bound still more strongly to use a degree of diligence adequate to the performance of it. His obligation must be rigorously construed; and he would perhaps be answerable for *slight neglect*, where no more would be required of a mandatary, than *ordinary exertions*." [1] Now, this seems incon-sistent with the general principles applicable to such bailments for hire. In such cases the bailee is liable only for ordinary neglect, and not for slight neglect; for ordinary neglect of skill, and not for slight neglect of skill. In short, as a workman, he undertakes for the ordinary diligence of a workman in business of that sort; and he is responsible only for the omission of it.[2] And the very case, put by Sir William Jones, of com-missioners, [commission merchants,] factors, and bailiffs, when their undertaking lies in fesance,[3] shows his mis-take; for it is clear, that they are responsible only for ordinary diligence and skill.[4] Sir William Jones may have been misled by considering, that, as the rule of the civil law as well as the common law made the bailee answerable for a skill in his business adequate to the undertaking, he was answerable at all events, if there was the slightest neglect in applying that skill. Domat

---

1 Jones's Bailm. 98.

2 2 Kent Com. 453, 463; 1 Bell Com. 459, 460, 461.

3 Jones's Bailm. 98.

4 *Russell* v. *Palmer*, 2 Wils. R. 325; *Denew* v. *Daverell*, 3 Camp. R. 451; *Shiels* v. *Blackburn*, 1 H. Bl. 159; *Leave* v. *Prentice*, 8 East R. 348.

seems to have adopted a similar mode of reasoning; and perhaps that is the doctrine of Pothier.[1]

§ 435. But even where the business or employment requires skill, if the bailee is known not to possess it, or he does not exercise the particular art or employment, to which it belongs, and he makes no pretension to skill in it; there, if the bailor, with full notice, trusts him with the undertaking, the bailee is only bound for a reasonable exercise of the skill, which he possesses, or of the judgment, which he can employ; and if any loss ensues, he is not chargeable.[2]   As if (to put a case from the Mahomedan law) a person will knowingly employ a common mat-maker to weave or embroider a fine carpet, he must impute the bad workmanship to his own folly.[3]   So, if a man, who has a disorder in his eyes, should employ a farrier to cure the disease, and he should lose his sight by using the remedies prescribed, he would certainly have no legal ground of complaint.[4]

§ 436. In case of hire of work the bailee is liable, not only for misfesance, but also for nonfesance; and in this respect the contract differs from that of a mere gratuitous bailee.[5]

§ 437. From what has been said it follows, that a workman is not chargeable, if the thing perishes while in his custody without his default, either by inevitable casualty, by internal defect, by superior force, by robbery, or by any other peril not to be guarded against

---

[1] Domat, B. 1, tit. 4, § 8, n. 3; Pothier, Louage, n. 425.

[2] Jones's Bailm. 53, 98, 99, 100; 2 Ld. Raym. 909, 914, 915; 1 Bell Com. 459.

[3] Jones's Bailm. 100.   [4] Jones's Bailm. 99, 100.

[5] Jones's Bailm. 101; 3 Bl. Com. 157; *Elsee* v. *Gatward*, 5 T. Rep. 143; *Thorne* v. *Dias*, 4 Johns. R. 83.

by ordinary diligence;[1] unless indeed he should take such risks upon himself by a special contract.

§ 438. And here it may not be unimportant to take notice of a distinction between cases, where the workman is to make a thing out of materials owned by his employer, and cases, where he is to make it out of his own materials. In the former case, if the thing perishes without his default, before it is completed or delivered to his employer, he is, or may be (as we have seen) entitled to a compensation to the extent of his work actually done.[2] But in the latter case the whole loss is his own, if the thing perishes before a delivery of it to his employer, and he is entitled to no recompense. In each case, however, the same rule of law applies, "Res perit domino." The only difference being, that in the one case the employer is the owner; and in the other the workman. In the one case it is a bailment; in the other a sale of a thing *in futuro.*[3]

§ 439. The distinction, too, between cases of *mutuum* and cases of bailment on hire deserves mention in this place, although much of what would properly apply here has been already suggested under the head of *commodatum,* or gratuitous loans. The distinction between an obligation to restore the specific things, and a power of returning other things equal in value, holds in cases of hiring, as well as in cases of deposits and gratuitous loans. In the former case it is a regular bailment; in the latter, it becomes a debt. Thus,

---

[1] Jones's Bailm. 88, 98, 119, 120; Pothier, Louage, n. 428; Id. ch. 3, n. 434; Pardessus, Droit Comm. Part. 2, art. 526; Domat, B. 1, tit. 4, § 8, n. 4, 9; Cod. Civ. art. 1789, 1792.

[2] Domat, B. 1, tit. 4, § 8, n. 4, 9; Pothier, Louage, ch. 3, art. 434; 1 Bell Com. 455.

[3] Domat, B. 1, tit. 4, § 7, n. 3; Id. § 8, n. 10.

according to the famous law of Alfenus, if an ingot of silver is delivered to a silversmith to make an urn, the whole property is transferred, and the employer is only a creditor of metal equally valuable, which the workman engages to pay in a certain shape, unless it is agreed, that the specific silver shall be wrought up into the urn.[1] So, where A delivered to B some cotton yarn on a contract to manufacture the same into cotton plaids, and B was to find the filling, and was to weave so many yards of plaids at eighteen cents per yard, as was equal to the value of the yarn at sixty-five cents per pound, it was held, that it was a sale of the yarn, and that by the delivery of it to B it became his property, and he was responsible for the delivery of the plaids, notwithstanding a loss of the yarn by an accidental fire.[2] But if A and B had agreed to have the particular yarn, with filling to be found by B, made into plaids on joint account, and the plaids, when woven, to be divided according to their respective interests in the value of the materials, and the plaids, before the division, had been burnt by an accidental fire, the loss would have been (it should seem) mutual, each losing the materials furnished by himself.

§ 440. There are some other obligations implied on behalf of the bailee of work on a thing; such as the duty of observing good faith, and practising no fraud, deceit, or imposition on the bailee, either as to the quality, quantity, or nature of his services.[3] He is also bound to conform to any special stipulations, constituting a part of his contract.[4] And when the work is done, he is

---

1 Jones's Bailm. 102; Id. 64; Dig. Lib. 19, tit. 2, 1. 31; Ersk. Inst. B. 3, tit. 1, § 18; Domat, B. 1, tit. 4, § 1, n. 4; 2 Kent Com. 463.

2 *Buffum* v. *Merry*, 3 Mason R. 478.

3 Pothier, Louage, n. 432.   4 Pothier, Louage, n. 433.

bound to return the thing in good order to his employer. But this duty of returning the thing requires some qualification. For every bailee of this sort has a lien on the thing for the amount of his compensation ; and therefore is not, unless he specially agrees otherwise, bound to restore the thing bailed, until that compensation is paid. Thus, a tailor, who has made a suit of garments out of the cloth delivered to him, is not bound to deliver the suit to his employer, until he is paid for his services ; nor a ship-carpenter, the ship, which he has repaired ; nor a jeweller, the gem, which he has set, or the seal, which he has engraved ; nor an agistor, the horse, he has taken on hire ; until their compensations are respectively paid.[1]

§ 441. Questions of a very embarrassing nature sometimes arise upon contracts of this nature at the common law ; as, for instance, how far a workman is entitled to receive compensation, when his work has been left incomplete ; or he has done it improperly ; or he has deviated from the directions of his employer. If there is a special contract in the case, generally speaking, according to the rules of the common law, no compensation can be recovered, unless the contract has been entirely fulfilled. If, therefore, a carpenter has undertaken to build a building according to a particular plan, and for a specified price, and he deviates from that plan, or does not complete the work, or does it imperfectly or unskilfully, it seems, that he cannot recover any part of the stipulated compensation ; for he has not brought himself within the terms of the contract.[2] So, if he has done any extraordinary work on

---

[1] 2 Roll. Abr. 92, M. 1; *Blake* v. *Nicholson*, 3 M. & Selw. 167; *Chase* v. *Westmore*, 5 M. & Selw. 180; *Ex parte Deese*, 1 Atk. 228.

[2] *Ellis* v. *Hamlen*, 3 Taunt. 52 ; 1 Bell Com. 455, 456.

it beyond his contract, he is not entitled to recover for such extraordinary work.[1] But if, in either case, the deviation from the contract has been with the assent or acquiescence of the employer, then he may recover upon the original contract, so far as it can be traced in the execution, and on a *quantum meruit* for the residue of his services.[2] And if the work has, with the express assent or acquiescence of the employer, been left incomplete, or he has knowingly dispensed with a perfect and skilful performance of it, in like manner a compensation can be recovered.[3] Where the work has been done on the property of the employer, it is sometimes difficult to deduce any just inference of such assent, or acquiescence, or dispensation ; because he is often compellable to use it, as it is, with all its imperfections, especially if it is of an immovable nature. But where the article is of a movable nature, and might be rejected, if unsatisfactory, as a bureau, made out of a log of mahogany belonging to the employer, or a silver urn, out of old silver furnished by the employer, there the receipt of the article without objection might perhaps furnish a ground to presume a waiver of the objections, notwithstanding the unskilfulness or incompleteness of the workmanship. The rule in Scotland seems in all cases to be, that balancing the inconvenience and damage arising from the imperfect or faulty performance against the benefit actually derived from the work, the workman is entitled to demand, or bound to make up the difference.[4]

---

1 1 Bell Com. 455, 456.

2 1 Bell Com. 455, 456 ; *Patterson* v. *Bank of Columbia*, 7 Cranch R. 299 ; S. C. 2 Peters's Cond. R. 501.

3 *Linnongdale* v. *Livingston*, 10 Johns. R. 36.

4 1 Bell Com. 456.

ART. III.　HIRE OF CUSTODY.

§ 442. We are next led to the consideration of bailments of LOCATIO CUSTODIÆ, or Deposits for Hire.
A contract of this sort may be properly deemed, as has
been already stated, a hiring of care and attention.[1]
St. German seems to make no distinction, at least not
in one part of his work, between a gratuitous depositary and a depositary for hire, as to the degree of diligence exacted of him.[2]　But Sir William Jones, with
great propriety, insists, that there is a great difference
between them; and that bailees of this sort (like other
interested bailees) are bound to ordinary diligence, and
of course are responsible for losses by ordinary negligence.[3]　To this class belong Agisters of cattle, Warehouse-men, and Wharfingers, whose obligations would
therefore seem to fall within the general rule.

§ 443. (1.) As to AGISTERS OF CATTLE, it has been
decided, that they are within the rule. They do not en-
sure the safety of the cattle agisted, but are merely
responsible for ordinary negligence.[4]　And it will be
such negligence for him or his servants to leave open
the gates of his field, in consequence of which neglect
the cattle stray and are stolen.[5]

§ 444. (2.) As to WAREHOUSE-MEN, it has also been
decided, that they come within the general rule, and are
bound only to take reasonable and common care of any

---

[1] Jones's Bailm. 96, 97 ; 1 Bell's Com. 458.

[2] Doct. & Stud. Dial. 2, ch. 38.

[3] Jones's Bailm. 97 ; 1 Bell's Com. 458.

[4] Jones's Bailm. 91, 92 ; *Broadwater* v. *Blot*, Holt N. P. R. 547; 1
Bell's Com. 458.

[5] Jones's Bailm. 92 ; 1 Bell's Com. 458.

commodity entrusted to their charge.[1] And, therefore, if the commodity is injured or destroyed by rats, while in his custody, he is not responsible, if he has exercised ordinary care in preserving them.[2] And a person, who receives goods in his store standing upon a wharf, for the purpose of forwarding them, is deemed but a mere warehouse-man, and responsible for ordinary diligence only, even though he holds himself out as a general or public store-keeper of goods.[3] Warehouse-men are not liable for thefts, unless occasioned by their want of proper care; and their care is not to be governed by that required of common carriers.[4]

§ 445. The most important practical question, which arises in respect to warehouse-men, is to ascertain, when their liability, as such, begins and ends; or, in other words, when their duty of custody commences and finishes. And it has been decided, that as soon as the goods arrive, and the crane of the warehouse is applied to raise them into the warehouse, the liability of the warehouse-man commences; and it is no defence, that they are injured by falling into the street from the breaking of the tackle, even if the car-man, who brought them, has refused the offer of slings for further security.[5]

§ 446. But suppose, (which is not an uncommon case,) that a person acts both as a common carrier and as a warehouse-man, it sometimes becomes a matter of great nicety to decide, in which character he is charge-

---

1 *Cailiff* v. *Danvers*, Peake R. 114; *Finucane* v. *Small*, 1 Esp. R. 315; Jones's Bailm. 49, 96, 97.

2 Peake R. 114.

3 *Platt* v. *Hibbard*, 7 Cowen R. 497; *Roberts* v. *Turner*, 12 Johns. R. 232; *Brown* v. *Denison*, 2 Wendell R. 593.

4 Ibid.   5 *Thomas* v. *Day*, 4 Esp. R. 262.

able; for, as the responsibilities of the two characters are very different, he may in one character be liable for a loss, from which he would be exempt in the other. For example, a common carrier is liable for losses by fire, not occasioned by inevitable casualty; [1] whereas a warehouse-man is not liable for any losses by fire, unless he has been guilty of ordinary negligence. Thus, a common carrier from Stour-point to Manchester undertook to carry goods from the former to the latter place, and to forward them from thence to Stockport. Upon arrival at Manchester the goods were deposited in his warehouse, to await an opportunity of sending them on to Stockport by the Stockport carrier, there being none there at that time, by whom they could be sent on. Before he had an opportunity of forwarding them, they were destroyed by an accidental fire. And the question was, whether he was liable for the loss or not. And it was held, that he was not liable, because his duty as carrier had terminated, and his duty as warehouse-man had commenced before the loss. It was not thought to make any difference in the case, that he received no distinct compensation as warehouse-man.[2]

§ 447. However, if the carrier's duty had not been completed at the time of the loss, it would have been otherwise. As, if the deposit in the warehouse had been at some intermediate place in the course of his own route; [3] or if, after the arrival at the place of destination, he was still bound to deliver the goods to the owner; and before such delivery he had put them into his

---

[1] *Forward* v. *Pittard,* 1 T. R. 27 ; 1 Bell's Com. 464.

[2] *Garside* v. *Trent. & Mersey Navigation Co.,* 4 T. R. 581 ; 1 Bell's Com. 464, 465.

[3] *Forward* v. *Pittard,* 1 T. R. 27.

own warehouse for safe custody, where they were consumed by fire, he would nevertheless have been liable for
the loss.[1] In these and other like cases, which may
be easily put, his proper duty as carrier not being ended, he is still considered as acting in the character of
carrier, although he makes a distinct charge for warehouse room, and also for cartage of the goods after their
arrival at the place of destination from the warehouse
to the owner's house. And in such cases it will make
no difference, whether the warehouse rent and cartage
is paid by the carrier to a third person, or it is paid on
his own personal account and profit; so, always, that
the delivery of the goods to the owner is by the usage
a part of his proper duty as carrier.[2]

§ 448. But, when the goods have arrived at their
place of destination, and are there deposited in the
carrier's warehouse, to await the owner's convenience
in sending for them; there the duty as carrier ends on
the arrival of the goods at the warehouse; and the
duty as warehouse-man commences.[3] If a carrier undertakes to forward goods beyond the line of his own
carriage, and on arrival at the termination of his route
he puts them into a proper vehicle for the further conveyance, having no interest therein, nor hire therefor,
he is not responsible for any subsequent loss.[4]

§ 449. And where a person is at the same time a
wharfinger, warehouse-man, forwarding merchant, and
carrier, and receives goods into his warehouse to be
forwarded, the warehouse being on his wharf, and the

1 *Hyde* v. *Trent. Nav. Co.* 5 T. R. 389 ; 1 Bell's Com. 464, 465.
2 *Hyde* v. *Trent. Nav. Co.* 5 T. R. 389.
3 *In re* v. *Webb*, 8 Taunt. R. 443 ; S. C. 2 Moore R. 500; 2 Kent Com.
469 ; 1 Bell's Com. 464, 465.
4 *Ackley* v. *Kellogg*, 8 Cowen R. 223.

goods are not yet put upon their transportation, he is liable only in his character as warehouse-man, for his duty as such has not ceased.[1]

§ 450. Care should be taken by warehouse-men to make deliveries to the parties properly entitled; for, if by mistake they deliver the goods to a wrong person, they will be responsible for the loss, as upon a wrongful conversion.[2] And a warehouse-man, who has received goods from a consignee to be kept for his use, may refuse to redeliver them, if they are the property of another, if the latter prohibits the re-delivery.[3]

§ 451. (3.) As to WHARFINGERS. Upon principle, their case is not distinguishable from that of other depositaries for hire; and therefore they are responsible only for ordinary diligence.[4] An attempt, however, has been made to extend their liability to that of common carriers, founded upon some general expressions of Lord Mansfield and Lord Ellenborough, which, however, upon close examination, will be found not to justify the conclusion. Lord Mansfield, in *Ross* v. *Johnson*, (5 Burr. 2827,) said, "It is impossible to make a distinction between a wharfinger and a common carrier. They both receive goods upon a contract. Every case against a carrier is like the same case against a wharfinger." Now, it is most material to consider, that the sole point before the Court was, whether trover would lie against a carrier, when the goods had been lost or stolen by his negligence, and not converted by him; and a case was cited of a wharfinger, in which it was

---

1 *Platt* v. *Hibbard*, 7 Cowen R. 497 ; *Roberts* v. *Turner*, 12 Johns. R. 232 ; *Roskell* v. *Waterhouse*, 2 Stark. R. 461.

2 *Lubbock* v. *Inglis*, 1 Stark. R. 104.

3 *Ogle* v. *Atkinson*, 5 Taunt. R. 759.

4 Jones's Bailm. 49, 96, 97.

held, that case, and not trover, under such circumstances, was the proper action. And in this view, Lord
Mansfield's language was most accurate and appropriate; for there could, in such a case, be no difference
between a wharfinger and a carrier, as to the form of
the action.[1] In *Maving* v. *Todd*, (1 Stark. R. 72,)
which was an action against the defendants, who were
wharfingers and lighter-men, for not safely keeping a
quantity of goods entrusted to them in London, to be
shipped to the vendees of the plaintiff at Newcastle, it
appeared, that the goods had been accidentally destroyed by fire, while on the defendant's premises;
and the question was, whether the defendants, whose
duty it was to convey the goods from the wharf in
their own lighter to the vessel in the river, were liable
for the loss. Lord Ellenborough is reported to have
said, that "The liability of a wharfinger, while he has
possession of the goods, was similar to that of a carrier." Now, it does not appear at what time the goods
were destroyed by fire; whether, when they were in
the warehouse, or on the wharf of the defendants, or in
their progress to be put on board of the lighter. If the
goods were on the wharf in their transit to go on board
of the lighter, the remark of Lord Ellenborough, though
not accurate in expression, would, in substance, have
been justifiable in the particular case, for his duty as
lighter-man would then have commenced. But, if his
lordship meant to say, (according to the dictum in Starkie,) that the liability of a wharfinger and carrier were
universally the same, he was certainly incorrect. Indeed, the case is perfectly explicable on another
ground; and that is, that the goods were in the hands

---

[1] 1 Bell's Com. 467, & note (6); *Packard* v. *Getman*, 6 Cowen R. 757.

of the defendants, as lighter-men (who are deemed common carriers) for carriage, and not as mere wharfingers.   And the only point, worthy of consideration, is, whether, as the defendants united both characters, they were, in point of fact, acting in one character or the other at the time of the loss by the fire.   In another report of the same case,[1] the action is said to have been brought against the defendants "as wharfingers;" and the goods were burnt, while on the wharf, before any opportunity of shipping them.   But in this report, no notice is taken of the above dictum of Lord Ellenborough; which may, therefore, justly raise a doubt as to the accuracy of the other report.

§ 452. The case of a wharfinger is in no respect distinguishable from a warehouse-man; and it has, in fact, not been distinguished in any solemn adjudication.[2]   On the other hand, the case of a carrier has always been treated as an excepted case, turning upon peculiar principles of public policy.   In fact, the case before Lord Ellenborough was decided on another point in favour of the defendants, that of a special contract excluding losses by fire, and therefore never called for any revision; and if it is to be understood as containing any general proposition, not qualified by the particular circumstances of the case, it is opposed by better and well considered opinions.[3]

§ 453. At what time the responsibility of a wharfinger begins and ends, depends upon the question, when

---

[1] 4 Camp. R. 225.

[2] *Sideaways* v. *Todd*, 2 Stark. R. 400 ; 1 Bell's Com. 467, & note (6).

[3] *Garside* v. *Trent. Nav. Co.* 4 T. R. 581 ; *Hyde* v. *The Same*, 5 T. R. 581 ; *In re* v. *Webb*, 8 Taunt. R. 443 ; *Platt* v. *Hibbard*, 7 Cowen R. 497, 502; The Reporter's Note ; *Roberts* v. *Turner*, 12 Johns. R. 232 ; *Brown* v. *Denison*, 2 Wend. R. 593 ; 2 Ld. Ray. 909, 918 ; *Sideaways* v. *Todd*, 2 Stark. R. 400.

he acquires, and when he ceases to have the custody of
the goods in that capacity.   This is generally governed
by the usages of the business.   Where goods are in the
wharfinger's possession to be sent on board of a vessel
for a voyage, as soon as he delivers the possession and
care of them to the proper officers of the vessel, although
they are not actually removed, he is, by the usages of
trade, deemed exonerated from any further responsibility; and the goods are deemed in the constructive possession of the officers of the ship.[1]   A mere delivery of
goods at a wharf is not necessarily a delivery of them
to the wharfinger; and there must be some act or assent on his part to the custody, before he becomes the
custodee.[2]

§ 454. In respect to depositaries for hire, there seem
some discrepancies in the authorities, whether the *onus
probandi* of negligence lies on the plaintiff, or of excul-
pation on the defendant, in a suit brought for the loss.
In England the former rule is maintained.[3]   In America an inclination the other way has been expressed.[4]

§ 455. (4.) FACTORS AND OTHER BAILIFFS to man-
age for hire.   They are generally held liable only for
a reasonable exercise of skill, and for ordinary diligence in their vocation.   They are, consequently, not
liable for any losses by theft, robbery, fire, or other accident, unless it is connected with their own negligence.[5]   Factors have, generally, a right to sell goods;

---

[1] *Corbin* v. *Downe*, 5 Esp. R. 41; Dig. Lib. 4, tit. 9, l. 3.

[2] *Buckman* v. *Levi*, 3 Camp. R. 414; *Gibson* v. *Inglis*, 4 Camp. 72;
Packard v. *Getman*, 6 Cowen R. 757.

[3] *Finucane* v. *Small*, 1 Esp. R. 316; *Harris* v. *Packwood*, 3 Taunt.
267; *Marsh* v. *Horne*, 5 Barn. & Cresw. 322, 327.

[4] *Platt* v. *Hibbard*, 7 Cowen R. 497, 500.

[5] Jones's Bailm. 98; *Vere* v. *Smith*, 1 Vent. 121; *Coggs* v. *Bernard*,
2 Ld. Ray. 909, 918.

but no right to pawn them.[1]　They are at liberty to act according to the general usages of trade, and to give credit on sales, wherever that is customary.　They are bound, however, in all cases, to follow the lawful instructions of their principals.[2]　If they act with reasonable diligence and good faith, they are protected. And in cases of unforeseen emergency and necessity, they may even act contrary to the general tenor of the instructions of their principal, if those instructions are manifestly applicable to ordinary circumstances only. But good faith alone is not sufficient.　There must be reasonable skill, and a fixed obedience to orders; and if there is any loss occasioned by negligence, or mistake, or inadvertence, which might fairly have been guarded against by ordinary diligence, the factor is responsible; and *a fortiori*, where he is guilty of any misfesance.[3] The rights, duties, and responsibilities of factors, however, more properly belong to a treatise on agency; and therefore it is sufficient to make these brief remarks in this place.[4]

§ 456. Although factors and other depositaries for hire are thus bound to ordinary diligence, they are not under any obligation to suggest to their principals wise precautions against inevitable accident; and therefore they are not obliged to advise insurance against fire, much less to insure the thing bailed without an authority from their employer.[5]

---

1 Ante, § 305, 306.　　　　　2 *Sheeter* v. *Hurlock*, 1 Bing. R. 34.

3 *Ulmer* v. *Ulmer*, 2 Nott & McCord, 489.

4 Livermore on Agency & Paley on Agency ; Com. Dig. Merchant B ; Bac. Abr. Merchants & Merchandise.

5 Jones's Bailm. 102.

§ 457. The next class of bailments for hire, which is entitled to attention, is LOCATIO MERCIUM VEHEN-DARUM, or the carriage of goods for hire. In respect to contracts of this sort entered into by private persons, not exercising the business of common carriers, there does not seem to be any material distinction, varying the rights, obligations, and duties of the parties, from those of other bailees for hire. Every such private person is bound to ordinary diligence, and a reasonable exercise of skill; and of course he is not responsible for any losses not occasioned by ordinary negligence, unless he has expressly, by the terms of his contract, taken upon himself such a risk.[1] Thus, a private person, who has undertaken the carriage of goods for hire, and warranted, that they shall go safe, will be held upon his undertaking for any loss within the scope of his contract, but not as a common carrier.[2]

§ 458. In respect to carriers for hire generally, it would not seem, that they were originally by the civil law put under any peculiar obligations not belonging to other bailees for hire.[3] A special edict, however, was passed, (as we shall see hereafter,) by which ship-masters, innkeepers, and stable-keepers, ("nautæ, caupones, stabularii,") were put under peculiar responsibility, and made liable for all losses not arising from inevitable casualty, or overwhelming force, (" damno fa-

---

[1] *Coggs* v. *Bernard*, 2 Ld. Raym. 909, 917, 918 ; *Hodgson* v. *Fullarton*, 4 Taunt. R. 787 ; *Hatchwell* v. *Cooke*, 6 Taunt. R. 577 ; 2 Marsh R. 293 ; Jones's Bailm. 103, 106, 121 ; 1 Bell Com. 461, 463, 467.

[2] *Robinson* v. *Dunmore*, 2 Bos. & Pull. 417.

[3] Domat, B. 1, tit. 4, § 8, n. 5 ; 1 Bell Com. 465.

tali.")[1]　And the modern nations of Continental Europe seem to have incorporated the same general obligations into their jurisprudence with exceptions of a like nature.[2]　The Roman edict, it will be at once perceived, did not extend in terms to carriers on land; though in most countries it has been practically expounded, so as to include them.[3]

§ 459. The common law, however, upon the subject of carriers, who are common carriers for hire, extends their liability beyond that, which is supposed to exist in the civil law; and as this subject is of great importance and interest, it will be extensively examined under the succeeding head of inquiry.

ART. V.　EXCEPTED CASES.

§ 460. We now come to the consideration of those cases of hire, which constitute EXCEPTIONS from the general rule, as to rights, duties, and responsibilities, in bailments of this nature. These are the cases of POST-MASTERS, INNKEEPERS, and COMMON CARRIERS. Each of these exceptions stands upon grounds of peculiar public policy, and therefore requires a separate discussion.

---

[1] 1 Bell Com. 465, 466; Pothier, Pand. Lib. 4, tit. 9; Ersk. Inst. B. 3, tit. 1, § 28; Dig. Lib. 4, tit. 9, l. 1, 5; Domat, B. 1, tit. 16, § 1, 2.

[2] Pardessus, Droit Comm. Part. 2, art. 516, 542, 545, 553; Cod. Civ. art. 1782 to 1786; Domat, B. 1, tit. 16, §§ 1, 2; Merlin Répertoire, art. Voiturier; Ersk. Inst. B. 3, tit. 1, § 28, tit. 3, §§ 15, 16; Moreau & Carlton's Partidas, Part. 5, tit. 8, l. 26.

[3] Ersk. Inst. B. 3, tit. 1, § 28 & note; Domat, B. 1, tit. 16, §§ 1, 2; 1 Bell Com. 467.

ART. VI.   POSTMASTERS.

§ 461. (1.) And first as to POSTMASTERS. When
the mail was carried for hire by private persons, on
their own account, from town to town, their case was
not different, in point of right and responsibility, from
that of other carriers; for there does not seem any
sound distinction between the carriage of letters and
the carriage of other goods or packages.[1] In the reign
of Charles the Second,[2] in pursuance of the policy of
the government during the Commonwealth, a general
post-office was established under the authority of Parliament, and a postmaster-general and subordinate
post-offices and postmasters were created, with appropriate salaries and compensations; and by these
and by later acts the carrying of letters by private persons has been prohibited.[3]

§ 462. In the year 1699 an action was brought
against the postmaster-general for the loss of a letter,
containing exchequer bills, by the negligence of his servants and deputies; and three judges against Lord
Holt held, that the plaintiff was not entitled to recover.[4]
The ground of the opinion of the three judges appears
to have been, that the post-office establishment is a
branch of the public police, created by statute for purposes of revenue, as well as for public convenience, and
that the government have the management and control
of the whole concern. It is, in short, a government

---

[1] Jones's Bailm. 109, 110; *Whitfield* v. *Despencer*, Cowp. 754, 765;
Lane v. *Cotton*, 2 Ld. Raym. 646.

[2] Stat. 12 Charles 2, ch. 35.

[3] Jones's Bailm. 109; 1 Bell Com. 468.

[4] *Lane* v. *Cotton*, 1 Ld. Raym. 646; S. C. 12 Mod. 482.

instrument, established for its own great purposes. The postmasters enter into no contract with individuals, and receive no hire, like common carriers, in proportion to the risk and value of the letters under their charge, but only a general compensation from government.[1] The same question was again still more elaborately discussed in a case in the time of Lord Mansfield, brought against the postmaster-general, to recover the amount of a bank note, stolen out of a letter by one of the sorters of letters, when the Court adhered to the doctrine of the three judges against the opinion of Lord Holt.[2] Upon that occasion Lord Mansfield said, "The ground of Lord Holt's opinion in that case is founded upon comparing the situation of the postmaster to that of a common carrier, or the master of a ship taking goods on board for freight. Now, with all deference to so great an opinion, the comparison between a postmaster and a carrier or a master of a ship seems to me to hold in no particular whatever. The postmaster has no hire, enters into no contract, carries on no merchandise or commerce. But the post-office is a branch of revenue and a branch of police, created by act of parliament. As a branch of revenue there are great receipts ; but there is likewise a great surplus of benefit and advantage to the public arising from the fund. As a branch of police, it puts the whole correspondence of the country (for the exceptions are very trifling) under government, and entrusts the management and direction of it to the crown, and the officers appointed by the crown. There is no analogy, therefore, between the case of the postmaster

---

1 2 Kent Com. 474; 1 Bl. Com. 323.
2 *Whitfield* v. *Despencer*, Cowp. R. 754.

and a common carrier." In truth, in England and in America the postmasters are mere public officers, appointed by the government; and the contracts made by them officially are public and not private contracts, binding on the government, and not on themselves personally.

§ 463. But although the posmaster-general is not liable as a common carrier, or for any negligence or delinquency of his deputies or servants in the office, it does not follow, that these deputies and servants are not liable for losses occasioned by their own negligence and delinquency. On the contrary, it is clear, that they are liable for all losses and injuries occasioned by their own default in office.[1] Whether a deputy postmaster is liable for the neglect of his clerks and servants has not as yet been decided in our Courts.[2] But it was held in one case, that if it is intended to charge any postmaster with the default of his clerk or servant the declaration should state the case according to the fact; and that, upon a general charge of negligence by the postmaster himself, it is not competent to give evidence of the negligence of his clerk or servant.[3] * In a case properly made up, charging the postmaster with the default of his clerk or servant, it was said, that his liability would only result from his own neglect in not properly superintending the discharge of the duties of his office.[4]

---

[1] *Renning* v. *Goodchild*, 3 Wilson R. 443; *Whitfield* v. *Despencer*, Cowper R. 754; 2 Kent Com. 474; *Stork* v. *Harris*, 5 Burr. R. 2709; 1 Bell Com. 468.

[2] 1 Bell Com. 468, 469.

[3] *Dunlap* v. *Munroe*, 7 Cranch, 242, 269; S. C. 2 Peters's Cond. R. 484.

[4] Ibid. p. 242, 269.

* This position seems irreconcilable with the general doctrine in *Brucker* v. *Fromont*, 6 T. Rep. 659.

ART. VII.   INNKEEPERS.

§ 464. (2.) As to INNKEEPERS. The soundness of the public policy of subjecting particular classes of persons to extraordinary responsibility, in cases where an extraordinary confidence is necessarily reposed in them, and there is an extraordinary temptation or danger of plunder, can hardly admit of question; and has been recognised in the jurisprudence of many countries. Hence arose the Prætor's Edict in the Roman law, which declared, that ship-masters, innkeepers, and stable-keepers, if they did not restore what they had received to keep safe, he would give judgment against them. "Nautæ, caupones, stabularii, quod cujusque salvum fore receperint, nisi restituent, in eos judicium dabo." [1] And the reason assigned by Ulpian for this edict is, that it is necessary to place confidence in such persons, and to commit the custody of things to them; that no person ought to complain of the severity of the rule; for it is in his own choice to receive the goods of persons, or not; and unless the rule was thus established, an opportunity would be afforded of combining with thieves against those, who trusted them; whereas now they had an inducement to abstain from such combinations. [2] And Gaius observed, that although neither shipmasters, nor innkeepers, nor stable-keepers receive a compensation for mere custody; but ship-masters for carriage of goods; and innkeepers for entertainment of their guests, and

---

[1] Dig. Lib. 5, tit. 9; Pothier, Pand. Lib. 4, tit. 9; Domat, B. 1, tit. 16, §§ 1, 2; Heinecc. Pand. Lib. 4, tit. 8, § 544 to 545, § 547.

[2] Dig. Lib. 4, tit. 9, l. 1, § 1; Heinecc. Pand. Lib. 4, tit. 8, § 545.

stable-keepers for the keeping of cattle ; yet that they
were bound for custody of the thing, in like manner as a fuller and tailor are bound ' for custody of the
thing, *ex locato*, although they receive their compensation, not strictly for custody, but for the exercise of
their art.[1]

§ 465. The construction put upon this edict was,
that the bailees were liable in all cases of loss or damage, although happening without any default, unless it
was by what was called a *fatal damage ;* " At hoc edicto
omni modo qui recepit, tenetur, etiamsi sine culpâ
ejus res periit, vel damnum datum est, nisi si quid
damno fatali contingit ; " and among fatal damages
were included losses by shipwreck, by lightning, or
other casualty, by pirates, and by superior force.[2]
Losses by fire, burglary, and robbery, seem also to
have been deemed losses by fatal damage.[3] Mr. Bell,
indeed, seems to think, that they ought not to be ; but
he admits, that the opinion of many jurists is against
him.[4] But theft was not numbered among such casualties.[5] And the bailees were liable not only for
themselves, but for their servants and other persons
employed in their service and under their protection.
Thus, ship-masters were liable for the acts of their under officers and other persons employed in their service ; innkeepers for the acts of their servants and
guests ; and stable-keepers for the acts of persons in
their service.[6]

---

[1] Dig. Lib. 4, til. 9, l. 5 ; Jones's Bailm. 94.

[2] Dig. Lib. 4, tit. 9, l. 3, § 1 ; Domat, B. 1, tit. 16, § 1, n. 4, 5 ;
Heinecc. Pand. Lib. 4, tit. 8, § 551.

[3] Ersk. Inst. B. 3, tit. 1, § 28 ; 1 Voet ad Pand. 301.

[4] 1 Bell Com. 469, 470, & note, ibid.

[5] Dig Lib. 4, tit. 9, l. 5, § 1 ; Pothier, Pand. Lib. 4, tit 9, § 8.

[6] Dig. Lib. 4, tit. 9, l. 1, § 8, l. 2, 3 ; Domat, B. 1, tit. 16, §§ 1, 2 ;
Heinec. Pand. Lib. 4, tit. 8, §§ 546, 551, 552 ; 1 Bell Com. 469, 471.

§ 466. In respect to innkeepers, although they were thus made responsible for the acts and misdeeds of persons in their service, it was not an unlimited responsibility. The guest or traveller was bound to deliver his baggage into the proper custody; and if he chose to trust his baggage to one not employed in such a service, as if he gave a bag of money to a child or to a scullion, the innkeeper was not responsible.[1] So the innkeeper was responsible only for the acts of his servants done in his own house; and not for their acts done elsewhere, as for a theft in another place.[2]

§ 467. The doctrine thus asserted in the Roman law in respect to innkeepers has been generally incorporated into the jurisprudence of Continental Europe. It will be found in the law of Spain,[3] of France,[4] of Scotland,[5] and probably in that of every other nation, whose jurisprudence had its origin in the civil law.

§ 468. Pothier [6] deduces from the text of the civil law the doctrine, that the innkeeper is not only bound for good faith, as in the case of ordinary deposits, but also for exact care, (" un soin exact,") and that, consequently, he is responsible for ordinary neglect (" de la faut legere.") [7] He therefore holds him liable for losses by theft of his domestics and of his guests, and of persons coming and going to and from the inn; for the theft is imputed to his negligence, if the goods are put

---

[1] Domat, B. 1, tit. 16, § 1, n. 3, 4; 1 Yeates R. 34.

[2] Domat, ibid, n. 7.

[3] Moreau & Carlton, Partid. 5, tit. 8, law 26.

[4] Pothier, Depôt, n. 77 to 81; Merlin, Repértoire, art. Hotelier, N. 4; Cod. Civ. art. 1952, 1953, 1954; Pardessus, Comm. P. 2, tit. 6, ch. 3, art. 516.

[5] Ersk. Inst. B. 3, tit. 1, 1. 28.

[6] Pothier, Depôt, n. 75 to 81.   [7] Pothier, Depôt, n. 96.

into his custody. But if the goods are not put into his custody, he is responsible only in case the theft is proved to have been by his domestics or other persons in his service, and not by other guests or travellers. And the burthen of proof, in such case, is on the guest, whose goods are stolen. If the guest chooses to keep the goods in his own custody, or if he confides them to another person, not authorized by the innkeeper to receive them, the latter is discharged of all responsibility. In this class of deposits, according to Pothier, parol evidence of the contract by witnesses is admissible, contrary to the general rule of the French law, which requires a written contract, where the value of the thing deposited exceeds one hundred livres.

§ 469. The general principles of the civil law upon this subject have been stated somewhat more at large, because they form a proper introduction to those of the common law, in which the responsibility of innkeepers is said to be founded on the custom of the realm. In point of fact its origin may be clearly traced up to the civil law, from which the common law without any adequate acknowledgments has from time to time borrowed many of the important principles, which regulate the subject of contracts.

§ 470. By the common law innkeepers are bound to take, not (as Lord Holt has said [1]) ordinary care, but uncommon care of the goods and baggage of their guests ; and they are responsible for the acts of their servants and domestics, as well as for the acts of other guests. The Register Brevium asserts their responsibility in these terms. That by the custom of the realm innkeepers are obliged to keep the goods and chattels of their guests, which are within their inns, without sub-

---

[1] 12 Mod. 487 ; 2 Kent Com. 458.

traction or loss day and night, so that no damage shall come to them from the negligence of the innkeeper or his servants.[1]   And though an innkeeper is not paid in money for securing a traveller's trunk ; yet the guest *facit, ut faciat,* and alights at the inn, not solely for his own refreshment, but also that his goods may be safe.   And indeed the custody of the goods may be considered as accessary to the principal contract; and the money paid for the apartments as extending to the care of the box or portmanteau.[2]   If, therefore, the goods or baggage of his guest are damaged in his inn, or are stolen from it by his servants or domestics, or by another stranger guest, he is bound to make restitution.[3]   And the innkeeper cannot exonerate himself from this responsibility by a refusal to take any care of the goods, because there are suspected persons in his house, for whose conduct he cannot be answerable, for the law will not permit him thus to escape from his proper duty.[4]   It might indeed be otherwise, if he refused admittance to a traveller, because he really had no room for him, and the traveller nevertheless should insist upon entering and placing his baggage in a chamber without the innkeeper's consent.[5]   But by the common law (which in this respect differs from the civil law) an innkeeper is not, if he has suitable room, at liberty to refuse to receive a guest, who is ready and able to pay him a suitable compensation.   On the contrary he is bound to receive him, and if upon false pretences he refuses, he is liable to an action.[6]

---

1 *Calye's case,* 8 Rep. 32.   2 Jones's Bailm. 94 ; 12 Mod. R. 487.

3 Jones's Bailm. 94, 95; 1 Bl. Com. 430; 2 Kent Com. 458 to 463; *Calye's case,* 8 Rep. 32.

4 Jones's Bailm. 94 ; Moore R. 78.

5 Jones's Bailm. 94 ; Dyer, 158 *b*; 1 Ander. R. 29.

6 1 Roll Abr. 3, F ; Bac. Abr. Inn & Innkeepers C ; *Bennett* v.

§ 471. It is not necessary to prove, that the goods have been lost by the negligence of the innkeeper; for it is his duty to provide honest servants and honest inmates, and to exercise an exact vigilance over all persons coming into his house as guests or otherwise. Nor is it necessary, that the goods should be in his special keeping; but it is generally sufficient, that they are in the inn.[1] It has been observed by Sir William Jones,[2] that "rigorous as this rule may seem, and hard as it may actually be in one or two particular instances, it is founded on the great principle of public utility, to which all private considerations ought to yield. For travellers, who must be numerous in a rich and commercial country, are obliged to rely almost implicitly on the good faith of innholders, whose education and morals are none of the best, and who might have frequent opportunities of associating with ruffians and pilferers, while the injured guest would seldom or never obtain legal proof of such combinations, or even of their negligence, if no actual fraud had been committed by them." This is the very reasoning of the civil law on the same subject, founded on motives of public policy.

§ 472. But innkeepers are not responsible to the same extent as common carriers. The loss of the goods, while at an inn, will be presumptive evidence of negligence on the part of the innkeeper or of his domestics. But he may, if he can, repel this presumption, and show, that there has been no negligence whatsoever; or, that the loss is attributable to the

---

Mellor, 5 T. R. 274; *Thompson* v. *Lacy*, 3 B. & Ald. 285; 3 Bl. Com. 166; *Newton* v. *Trigg*, 1 Shower R. 270; 1 Saund. R. 312 *c*; 1 Bell Com. 472.

1 Jones's Bailm. 95; 1 Bl. Com. 450; 2 Kent Com. 459; *Calye's case*, 8 Rep. 32.

2 Jones's Bailm. 95, 96.

proper negligence of the guest, or that it has been occasioned by inevitable casualty or by superior force.[1]
Thus, although a common carrier is liable for all losses
occasioned by an armed mob, (not being public enemies,) an innkeeper would not be liable for such a loss;[2]
nor would he be liable (it should seem) for a loss by
robbery and burglary by persons from without the inn.[3]
However, this doctrine should be now stated with some
hesitation, for in a very recent case Mr. Justice Bailey
said, "It appears to me, that the innkeeper's liability
very closely resembles that of a carrier. He is *primâ
facie* liable for any loss not occasioned by the act of
God or the king's enemies; although he may be exonerated, where the guest chooses to have his goods under his own care."[4] From which language, it may
perhaps be inferred, that the learned Judge would hold
him responsible in cases of burglary and robbery. The
case, however, did not call for the dictum.

§ 473. And the innkeeper will be exonerated, also,
by showing, that the guest has been robbed by his own
servant, or by one, who came to the inn as the com-
panion of the guest.[5] But it will be no excuse for the
innkeeper in case of a loss by theft, that he was sick
or insane, or absent from home at the time; for he is
bound, in such cases, to provide faithful domestics and
agents.[6]

---

[1] Jones's Bailm. 96 ; *Burgess* v. *Clements*, 4 M. & Selw. 619 ; *Calye's
case*, 8 Rep. 32.

[2] *Morse* v. *Slue*, 1 Vent. 190, 238 ; Hob. R. case 30 ; *Rich* v. *Kneeland*,
Cro. Jac. 330 ; 12 Mod. 480 ; Jones's Bailm. 109.

[3] Jones's Bailm. 96 ; *Burgess* v. *Clements*, 4 M. & Selw. 306 ; 12 Mod.
487 ; 8 Rep. 32.

[4] *Richmard* v. *Smith*, 8 B. & Cres. 9.

[5] *Calye's case*, 8 Rep. 32 ; Bac. Abr. Inns & Inkeepers, C. 4.

[6] *Calye's case*, 8 Rep. 32.

§ 474. Having thus seen, what is the general responsibility imposed upon innkeepers by the common law, it may be proper to consider; (1.) who are deemed innkeepers in the sense of that law; (2.) what are their general rights and duties ; (3.) who are to be deemed properly guests; (4.) in respect to what goods, and under what circumstances, the liability of innkeepers attaches; (5.) and lastly, under what circumstances they are exonerated by operation of law, or by the acts of the parties.

§ 475. (1.) Who are deemed innkeepers. An innkeeper may be defined to be the keeper of a common inn for the lodging and entertainment of travellers and passengers, their horses and attendants, for a reasonable compensation.[1] It must be a common inn, or *diversorium*, that is, an inn kept for travellers generally, and not merely for a short season of the year, and for select persons, who are lodgers.[2] But it is not necessary, that the party should put up a sign as keeper of an inn. It is sufficient, if in fact he keeps one.[3] In a recent case it was said, that "The true definition of an inn is a house, where the traveller is furnished with every thing, which he has occasion for whilst on his way."[4] And where a house of entertainment was kept in London, in which the keeper provided lodgings and entertainment for travellers and others, it was held to be an inn, although it had no stables, and no stage-coaches or wagons stopped there.[5] But the keeper of

---

[1] Bac. Abr. Inns & Innkeepers, C.

[2] *Calye's case*, 8 Rep. 32; Carth. 417 ; 5 Mod. R. 427 ; 1 Salk. 387 ; Bac. Abr. Inn, B ; 1 Bell's Com. 469.

[3] Bac. Abr. Inn, B.

[4] *Thompson* v. *Lacy*, 3 Barn. & Ald. 283.

[5] Id. ibid.

a mere coffee-house is not deemed an innkeeper.[1] And a person, who keeps a mere private boarding house, or lodging house, is in no just sense an innkeeper.[2]

§ 476. (2.) As to the rights and duties of inkeepers. An innkeeper is bound (as has been already said) to take in all travellers and wayfaring persons, and to entertain them, if he can accommodate them, for a reasonable compensation; and he must guard their goods with proper diligence.[3] But he is not bound by law to furnish his guests with rooms to show their goods, but only with convenient lodging rooms and lodging.[4] And the law invests him with some peculiar privileges; for he has a lien upon the goods, and also, as it should seem, upon the person of his guest, for his compensation.[5] But the horse of a guest can be detained only for his own meal, and not for the meal and expenses of the guest.[6]

§ 477. (3.) Who are to be deemed guests. As inns are instituted for passengers and wayfaring men, a neighbour or friend, who is no traveller, but comes to the inn at the request of the innkeeper, and lodges there, is not deemed a guest. But where a traveller comes to the inn, and is accepted, he becomes instantly a guest.[7] And it was held by three Judges against Lord Holt, that if a traveller leaves his horse at an inn, and lodges elsewhere, he is to be deemed a guest. But not, if he leaves goods, for which the innkeeper receives no com-

---

1 *Doe* v. *Laming*, 4 Camp. 77.   2 1 Bell's Com. 469.

3 *Thompson* v. *Lacy*, 3 Barn. & Ald. 283; 1 Bell's Com. 472.

4 *Burgess* v. *Clements*, 4 M. & Selw. 306; S. C. 1 Stark. R. 251, n.

5 *Thompson* v. *Lacy*, 3 Barn. & Ald. 287; *Jones* v. *Thurloe*, 8 Mod. 172; *Newton* v. *Trigg*, 1 Shower 270; Bac. Abr. Inns, D.

6 Bac. Abr. Inns, D.

7 *Calye's case*, 8 Rep. 32; Bac. Abr. Inns, C. 5.

pensation.[1] And where a person came to an inn with
a hamper of hats, and went away, and left them there
for two days, and in his absence they were stolen, it
was held, that he was not to be deemed a guest.[2] The
length of time, that a man is at an inn, makes no difference ; whether he stays a week, or a month, or longer ;
so always, that, though not strictly *transeuns,* he retains his character as a traveller.[3] But if a person
comes upon a special contract to board, and sojourn at
an inn, he is not in the sense of the law a guest ; but a
boarder.[4]

§ 478. (4.) As to their liability. Innkeepers are
liable only for the goods, which are brought within the
inn (*infra hospitium.*) If, therefore, an innkeeper at
the request of his guest sends his horse to pasture, and
the horse is stolen, the innkeeper is not, as such, liable
for the loss.[5] But if the guest does not request it, but
the innkeeper does it of his own accord, he is liable for
the loss.[6] However, it has been said, that this rule requires some qualifications ; for if it is the common custom of the country (as it is, in the summer season, in
some parts of America,) to put the horse in such a case
to pasture, the implied consent of the owner may be
fairly presumed, if he knows of the custom.[7] And the
common usage of the country must have great weight
in all such cases. In the country towns in America, it
is very common to leave chaises and carriages under
open sheds all night at inns ; and also to leave the stable doors open or unlocked. Under such circumstan-

---

1 *York* v. *Grindstone,* 1 Salk. 388 ; 2 Ld. Ray. 866.
2 *Jelly* v. *Clarke,* Cro. Jac. 188 ; Bac. Abr. Inn, C. 5.
3 Bac. Abr. Inns, C. 5.   4 Bac. Abr. Inns, C. 5.
5 *Calye's case,* 8 Rep. 32 ; Jones's Bailm. 91.
6 Ibid.   7 2 Kent Com. 453.

ces, if a horse or chaise should be stolen, it would deserve consideration, how far the innkeeper would be liable, as the traveller might be presumed to consent to the ordinary custom.

§ 479. A delivery of the goods into the custody of the innkeeper is not necessary to charge him with them; for although the guest doth not deliver them, or acquaint the innkeeper with them, still the latter is bound to pay for them, if they are stolen, or carried away; even though the person, who stole them or carried them away, is unknown.[1] Nor is it any excuse for the innkeeper, that he delivered to the guest the key of the chamber, in which he is lodged, and that the guest left the chamber door open.[2] But if the innkeeper requires of his guest, that he should put his goods into a particular chamber under lock and key, and that then he will warrant their safety, and otherwise not; and the guest, notwithstanding, leaves them in an outer court, where they are taken away, the innkeeper will be discharged.[3] And although an innkeeper refuses to take charge of goods for a party until another day; yet, if he admits him as a guest into his inn for temporary refreshments, and the goods are stolen, while he is there, the innkeeper will be responsible for the loss.[4] If, indeed, the innkeeper had received the goods, and the party had gone away, and afterwards the loss had occurred, the innkeeper would have been liable only as a bailee or depositary; and if he had refused to receive

---

1 *Calye's case*, 8 Rep. 32; *Quinton v. Courtney*, Hayw. N. C. R. 41; *Chute v. Wiggins*, 14 Johns. R. 175; 1 Bell's Com. 469.

2 *Calye's case*, 8 Rep. 32.

3 *Calye's case*, 8 Rep. 32.

4 *Bennet v. Mellor*, 5 T. Rep. 273.

the party as a guest, he would not have been liable at all.[1]

§ 480. Where the goods are delivered at the usual place for such goods at the inn, the innkeeper is chargeable with them, although not strictly within the inn; as, if wheat in a sleigh is put into the outer house appurtenant to the inn, and used for such purposes, and afterwards is stolen, the innkeeper is liable for the loss.[2]

§ 481. Although the general language of the Writ in the Register is, that the innkeeper is liable for the *goods* and *chattels* of the guest, which would seem not to extend to deeds, obligations, and choses in action; yet the latter are held movables within the custom to bind the innkeeper.[3] But the innkeeper is liable only for the safe custody of personal property of his guest. He is not responsible for any tort or injury done by his servants or others to the person of his guest, without his own co-operation or consent.[4]

§ 482. (5.) What circumstances will exonerate the innkeeper. By the common law, as laid down in Calye's case, (8 Rep. 32,) an innkeeper is not chargeable, unless there is some default in him, or in his servants, in the well and safe keeping and custody of his guest's goods and chattels within his common inn; but he is bound to keep them safe without any stealing or purloining. This doctrine, however, is to be understood with this qualification, that the loss will be deemed *primâ facie* evidence of negligence; and that the innkeeper cannot exonerate himself but by positive proof,

---

1 Ibid.; 1 Bell's Com. 4f9.

2 *Chute* v. *Wiggins*, 14 Johns. R. 175.

3 *Calye's case*, 8 Rep. 32.   4 Ibid.

that the loss was not by means of any person, for whom he is responsible.[1]

§ 483. The innkeeper, however, may be exonerated in divers other ways; as, for example, by showing, that the guest has taken upon himself exclusively the custody of his own goods, or has, by his own neglect, exposed them to the peril.[2] Thus, where a traveller had some boxes of jewelry, and desired a room to himself for the purpose of opening and showing it to customers; and he had the room assigned to him, and the key delivered to him, with directions about locking the door; and he used the room accordingly, and unpacked his jewelry; and he afterwards went away, and left the room for some hours, leaving the key in the lock on the outside of the door, and some of his boxes of jewelry were stolen; it was held, that the innkeeper was not liable, and that the guest, by accepting the key of the room under the circumstances, had superseded the liability of the innkeeper to take care of the goods.[3] So, where a guest at an inn deposits his goods in a room, and makes use of it as a warehouse for them, having the exclusive possession of it, he is understood to take upon himself the exclusive charge of his own goods.[4] The same principle will apply, where a guest at an inn, instead of confiding his goods to the innkeeper, of choice commits them exclusively to the custody of another person, who is living at the inn.[5]

§ 484. But, if the habit of the servants at an inn is to place the guest's goods in their bed-rooms; and a

---

[1] *Bennet* v. *Mellor,* 5 T. R. 273; *Burgess* v. *Clements,* 4 M. & Selw. 306.

[2] *Calye's case,* 8 Rep. 32.

[3] *Burgess* v. *Clements,* 4 M. & Selw. 306; S. C. 1 Stark. R. 251, n.

[4] *Farnworth* v. *Packwood,* 1 Stark. R. 249; 2 Kent Com. 461.

[5] *Sneider* v. *Geiss,* 1 Yeates R. 34.

guest should request his to be carried into the common commercial room, to which travellers in general resort, and they are there stolen, the innkeeper will nevertheless be held responsible for the loss, unless the innkeeper has given notice to the guest, that he will not be responsible, unless the goods are put into the bed-room.[1] The mere exercise of a choice by the guest, not objected to, though for his own convenience, if he does not acquire an exclusive possession thereby, will not discharge the innkeeper from his general responsibility.

§ 485. In many of the states of America, inns and taverns are governed by special statute regulations, and no persons are permitted to assume the business of keeping them, unless by particular license from the public authorities.[2] The common law, respecting the duties and liabilities of innkeepers, is understood, however, to prevail in all the United States, except Louisiana, in which state the civil law constitutes the basis of its jurisprudence;[3] and in so far as that law differs from the common law, it furnishes the rule for the government of all questions arising therein.

§ 486. There is one peculiarity of the civil law, which has no place in ours. If an innkeeper entertained a traveller gratis, he was still liable to him as a guest in the same manner, as if he received compensation.[4] But in our law it is apprehended, that he would not be so liable, unless he is to receive a compensation.[5]

---

1 *Rickmond* v. *Smith*, 8 Barn. & Cres. 9.

2 2 Kent Com. 462.

3 Code of Louisia. B. 3, tit. 11, § 4, art. 31, 32, 33.

4 Dig. Lib. 4, tit. 9, l. 6.

5 Bac. Abr. Inns, C. D.; *Calye's case*, 8 Rep. 32; *Thompson* v. *Lacy*, 3 B. & Ald. 285.

§ 487. The present head of inquiry may be closed by adding, that innkeepers are responsible for the loss of goods, only when they have been received by them in that character. If they have become bailees generally, they are then liable only according to the nature of the particular bailment or contract.[1] There is a decision in the Scottish law, quoted by Mr. Bell, which seems at variance with this doctrine. There, a parcel containing money was given to an innkeeper to be sent by a carrier or coach going from his house; and it was subsequently missing, and the money stolen; and the innkeeper was held responsible; but upon what ground does not distinctly appear.[2]

ART. VIII.   COMMON CARRIERS.

§ 488. (3.) In the next place as to COMMON CARRIERS. It has been already stated, that the civil law imposed by the Prætor's Edict the same responsibility upon innkeepers, ship-masters, and stable-keepers. Whatever, therefore, has been said under the preceding head, as to the rights, duties, and obligations of innkeepers by the civil law, applies with equal force to the rights, duties, and obligations of carriers by water under the same law.[3] In the modern countries governed by the civil law the same rule is generally, if it is not invariably, adhered to. It may be clearly traced in the jurisprudence of France, Spain, Holland, Scot-

---

[1] Dig. Lib. 4, tit. 9, l. 3, § 2; *Hyde* v. *Mersey & Trent. Nav. Co.* 5 T. R. 389.

[2] 1 Bell's Com. 469, and note (5).

[3] Dig. Lib. 4, tit. 9, l. 1 to 7; Pothier, Pand. Lib. 4, tit. 9; Domat, B. 1, tit. 16, § 1 & 2 per tot.

land, and the German states.[1]   And the case of carriers by land, at least in modern times, seems not to
have been distinguished from that of carriers by water.[2]
So that the responsibility of common carriers may be
summed up in the pithy language of the Code of
France, which declares, that they are responsible for
theft and damage caused by their servants, or others
in their employ and confidence; but they are not responsible for thefts committed with armed force or superior power; and, of course, they are exempted from
losses by mere casualty.[3]

§ 489. By the common law, as understood in the
reign of Henry the Eighth, a responsibility of a like extent and nature seems to have existed; for it is said,
that at that time a common carrier was held chargeable
in cases of a loss by robbery, only when he had trav-
elled by roads dangerous for robbery, or driven by
night, or at any inconvenient hour.[4] However this may
be, it is certain, that in the commercial reign of Elizabeth a different rule prevailed; [5] and the doctrine has
been firmly established for a great length of time, that
a common carrier is responsible for all losses, except
those occasioned by the act of God, or of the king's
enemies. By the act of God, a phrase, which perhaps

---

1 Pardessus, Droit Comm. P. 2, tit. 7, ch. 5, art. 537 to 555; Cod.
Civ. art. 1782, 1786, 1952; Moreau & Carlton, Partidas 5, tit. 8, 1. 26;
Ersk. Inst. B. 3, tit. 1, § 28; 1 Bell Com. 465, 466; Abbott on Shipp.
P. 3, ch 3, § 3, note (l); 1 Voet. ad Pand. Lib. 4, tit. 9.

2 Ibid, Merlin Repértoire, Voiture, Voiturier; 1 Bell Com. 467.

3 Cod. Civ. art. 1782, 1784, 1952, 1953, 1954; *Elliot* v. *Russell,*
10 Johns. R. 1.

4 Jones's Bailm. 103 ; Doct. & Student, Dial. 2, ch. 38; Abbott on
Shipp. P. 3, ch. 3, § 3, note (l); Noy's Maxims, ch. 43, p. 93.

5 1 Inst. 89 ; Moore, 462 ; 2 Roll. Abr. 2 ; Jones's Bailm. 103; *Proprietors of Trent. Navig.* v. *Wood,* 3 Esp. R. 127.

habit has rendered too familiar to us, is meant inevitable accident; [1] and by the king's enemies are meant public enemies, with whom the nation is at open war.[2]

§ 490. The reason assigned by Lord Holt for this doctrine is as follows : " The law (says he) charges this person, thus intrusted to carry goods, against all events, but acts of God and of the enemies of the king. For though the force be never so great, as if an irresistible multitude of people should rob him, nevertheless he is chargeable. And this is a politic establishment, contrived by the policy of the law for the safety of all persons, the necessity of whose affairs obliges them to trust these sorts of persons, that they may be safe in their dealings. For else these carriers might have an opportunity of undoing all persons, that had any dealings with them, by combining with thieves, &c.; and yet doing it in such a clandestine manner, as would not be possible to be discovered. And this is the reason the law is founded upon in that point." [3] The ground of the resolution is (as Sir William Jones has justly observed) not the reward of the carrier, upon which Sir Edward Coke lays much stress; but the public employment exercised by the carrier, and the danger of his combining with robbers to the infinite injury of commerce, and extreme inconvenience to society.[4] He is treated as an insurer against all but the excepted perils,[5] upon that distrust, which an ancient writer has called the *sinew of wisdom.*[4]

---

1 Jones's Bailm. 104, 105.

2 Abbott on Shipp. P. 3, ch. 4, § 3; Ante, § 25.

3 *Coggs* v. *Bernard*, 2 Ld. Raym. 909, 918; *The Maria & Vrow Johanna*, 4 Rob. R. 348, 352.

3 Jones's Bailm. 103, 104.   4 *Forward* v. *Pittard*, 1 T. R. 27.

5 Jones's Bailm. 107; 1 Bell Com. 461, 464, 466, 467.

§ 491. The subject is discussed with great force and point in the case of *Riley* v. *Horne,* (5 Bing. R. 217,) where Mr. Chief Justice Best has elaborately examined it in all its bearings upon the commercial interests of the country. His language is as follows :

" When goods are delivered to a carrier, they are usually no longer under the eye of the owner ; he seldom follows, or sends any servant with them to the place of their destination. If they should be lost or injured by the grossest negligence of the carrier or his servants, or stolen by them, or by thieves in collusion with them, the owner would be unable to prove either of these causes of loss ; his witnesses must be the carrier's servants, and they, knowing, that they could not be contradicted, would excuse their masters and themselves.

" To give due security to property, the law has added to that responsibility of a carrier, which immediately rises out of his contract to carry for a reward, namely, that of taking all reasonable care of it, the responsibility of an insurer.

" From his liability as an insurer, the carrier is only to be relieved by two things, both so well known to all the country when they happen, that no person would be so rash as to attempt to prove, that they had happened when they had not, — namely, the act of God and the king's enemies."

§ 492. In questions, therefore, as to the liability of a carrier, the point ordinarily is not so much, whether he has been guilty of negligence or not, as whether the loss comes within either of the excepted cases.[1] Not

---

[1] Abbott on Shipp. P. 3, ch. 4, § 1 ; *Gosling* v. *Higgins,* 1 Camp. R. 451.

but that, if the carrier is actually guilty of negligence, he will be liable for a loss, which otherwise might be deemed a loss by an inevitable casualty.[1] Thus, if a bargemaster should rashly shoot a bridge, when the bent of the weather is tempestuous, and a loss should ensue, he would be chargeable on account of his temerity and imprudence. But it would be otherwise, if using all proper precautions he should shoot a bridge at a proper time, and the barge should be driven by the force of the current or by the wind against a pier, and thereby the goods should be lost; for then it would be esteemed a loss by mere casualty.[2] The consideration of questions of this sort, however, will find a more proper place hereafter.

§ 493. The rigour of the common law, as to carriers, has in several cases been relaxed in England by statutes, and especially in the case of the owners of ships.[3] None of these statutes are known to have been adopted in America; and the common law responsibility, therefore, is considered as our only guide on the present subject.[4]

§ 494. Let us then consider, (1st.) Who are deemed common carriers. (2dly.) What are their duties and obligations. (3dly.) What are the risks, for which they are liable at the common law. (4thly.) The commencement and termination of their risks. (5thly.) The effect of special contracts and notices. (6thly.) What

---

[1] Abbott on Shipp. P. 3, ch. 4, § 1; Jones's Bailm. 122; *Lyon* v. *Wells*, 5 East R. 428; *Goff* v. *Clinckard* cited 1 Wils. R. 282; *Elliot* v. *Rossel*, 10 Johns. R. 1; 1 Bell Com. 463.

[2] Jones's Bailm. 107; *Amies* v. *Stevens*, 1 Str. 128.

[3] 7 Geo. 2, ch. 15; 26 Geo. 3, ch. 86; 53 Geo. 3, ch. 159; 6 Geo. 4, ch. 125.

[4] 2 Kent. Com. 470.

will excuse or justify a non-delivery of the goods. (7thly.) The doctrine of average and contribution. (8thly.) And lastly the general rights of carriers.

§ 495. First. Who are deemed common carriers. It is not (as we have seen) every person, who undertakes to carry goods for hire, that is deemed a common carrier. A private person may contract with another for the carriage of his goods, and incur no responsibility beyond that of any ordinary bailee for hire, that is to say, the responsibility of ordinary diligence.[1] To bring a person within the description of a common carrier, he must exercise it as a public employment; he must understake to carry goods for persons generally; and he must hold himself out as ready to engage in the transportation of goods for hire as a business, not as a casual occupation, *pro hac vice*.[2] A common carrier has, therefore, been defined to be one, who undertakes for hire or reward to transport the goods of such, as choose to employ him, from place to place.[3]

§ 496. Common carriers are generally of two descriptions. (1.) Carriers by land. (2.) Carriers by water. Of the former description are the proprietors of stage-wagons and stage-coaches, which ply between different places, and carry goods for hire.[4] So truckmen, teamsters, cartmen, and porters, who under-

---

[1] Bac. Abr. Carrier A; *Robinson* v. *Dunmore*, 2 Bos. & Pull. 417; *Hodgson* v. *Fullarton*, 4 Taunt. 787; *Hutton* v. *Osborne*, Selw. N. P. 382, n.; Jones's Bailm. 121; *Satterlee* v. *Groat*, 1 Wend. R. 272; *Hatchwell* v. *Cooke*, 6 Taunt. R. 577.

[2] 1 Salk. 249; *Satterlee* v. *Groat*, 1 Wend. R. 272; 1 Bell Com. 467.

[3] *Dwight* v. *Brewster*, 1 Pick. 50, 53; *Gisbourne* v. *Hurst*, 1 Salk. 249, 250.

[4] 2 Ld. Raym. 909, 918; Jones's Bailm. 104, 106; 4 T. R. 389; 5 T. R. 389; *Forward* v. *Pittard*, 1 T. R. 27; 2 Kent Com. 464, 465; 8 Serg. & Rawle, 500; Id. 533; Bac. Abr. Carriers A.

take to carry goods for hire, as a common employment, from one part of a town or city to another. Of the latter description are the owners and masters of ships and steam-boats engaged in the transportation of goods for persons generally for hire. So are lightermen, hoymen, barge-owners, ferry-men, canal-boatmen, and others employed in like manner.[1]

§ 497. The rule in respect to carriers by water, established in England, seems to be generally understood to be the rule in America. It has been recognised in an ample manner in several of the states.[2] Recently, however, in New York, it has been adjudged, that the owners of a vessel bringing goods from New Orleans to New York for hire were not to be deemed common carriers.[3] But this decision is in direct repugnance to prior decisions made on the same point in the same state.[4] An effort also has been made in Pennsylvania to relax the general rigour of the rule, and to take a distinction between carriers on inland waters and carriers on land; but it does not seem yet to be settled.[5] In respect to carriers on land, the rule of the common law seems every where admitted in its full rigour [6] in the states governed by the jurisprudence

---

[1] Jones's Bailm. 106, 107, 108; 2 Kent Com. 464, 465; Bac. Abr. Carriers A; *Mors* v. *Slue*, 1 Mod. 85; 1 Vent. 190, 238; T. Raym. 220; 2 Lev. 69; *Allen* v. *Sewall*, 2 Wend. R. 327, 340; 1 Bell Com. 467.

[2] *Richards* v. *Gilbert*, 5 Day R. 415; 2 Kent Com. 471, 472; *Clarke* v. *Richards*, 1 Connect. R. 54; *Williams* v. *Grant*, 1 Connect. R. 487; *Emery* v. *Henry*, 4 Greenl. 407; *Mc Clure* v. *Hammond*, 1 Bay. R. 99, 101; *Harrington* v. *Lyles*, 2 Nott & McCord, 88.

[3] *Aymar* v. *Astor*, 6 Cowen R. 266.

[4] 2 Kent Com. 471, 472; *Elliot* v. *Rossell*, 10 Johns. R. 1; *Kemp* v. *Contrey*, 11 Johns. R. 107.

[5] *Gordon* v. *Little*, 8 Serg. & R. 533; *Bell* v. *Read*, 4 Binn. R. 127.

[6] 2 Kent Com. 471, 472; 8 Serg. & Rawle, 533; *Dwight* v. *Brewster*, 1 Pick. R. 50.

of the common law. Louisiana follows the doctrine of the civil law in her own code.[1]

§ 498. But the proprietors of stage-coaches, whose employment is solely to carry passengers, (such as hackney coachmen,) are not deemed common carriers.[2] They are not responsible for mere accidents happening to the persons of passengers, but only for want of that due care, which is required of bailees for hire ordinarily.[3] But, if they are accustomed to carry the baggage of passengers, although they receive no specific compensation therefor, and receive simply their fare for the passage of the travellers; yet they are responsible (even if not as common carriers) at least for due and reasonable care of such baggage; since the passengers are thus induced to travel in the coach, and the custody of the baggage may be properly deemed, as in the case of an innkeeper, an accessary to the principal contract.[4]

§ 499. And in modern times it seems not quite settled, whether as to passengers' baggage, without any distinct compensation, the coach proprietors are not liable as common carriers. The language of those cases, which are supposed to intimate a liability of this sort, may perhaps be explicable upon the ground of the ordinary responsibility for ordinary care.[5] In a late

---

1 Code of Louisiana, B. 3, tit. 8, ch. 3, § 2.

2 Bac. Abr. Carriers A ; 2 Kent Com. 466; 1 Bell Com. 468, 475.

3 *Aston* v. *Heaven*, 2 Esp. R. 533 ; *Christie* v. *Griggs*, 2 Camp. R. 79 ; *Dudley* v. *Smith*, 1 Camp. 167 ; *White* v. *Boulton*, Peake R. 81 ; *Robinson* v. *Dunmore*, 2 Bos. & Pull. 417.

4 Lord Holt, 12 Mod. 487; Jones's Bailm. 94; Dig. Lib. 4, tit. 9, l. 5; 2 Kent. Com. 466; *Middleton* v. *Fowler*, 1 Salk. 282 ; *Upshare* v. *Aidee*, Comyns R. 25 ; but see Selwyn, N. P. 323, note (*d*).

5 Selwyn N. P. 4 edit. p. 323 and note ; 4 Esp. R. 177 ; 2 Bos. & Pull. 419, per Chambre J. ; 2 Kent Com. 466 ; 5 Petersd. Abr. Carriers, 59, note ; Jeremy on Carriers, 12.

case Mr. Chief Justice Best seems to have placed the responsibility of coach proprietors, carrying passengers, and their baggage, upon the ordinary footing of common carriers, as to their baggage.[1]   And Mr. Bell deduces this as the true modern doctrine on the subject.[2]

§ 500. But if the proprietors of a stage-coach for passengers carry goods also for hire, they are in respect to such goods to be deemed common carriers.[3] The like reasoning applies to packet-ships and steamboats, which ply between different ports, and are accustomed to carry merchandise, as well as passengers.

§ 501. When it is said, that the owners and masters of ships are deemed common carriers, it is to be understood of such ships, as are employed as general ships, or for the transportation of merchandise for persons in general; such as vessels employed in the coasting trade, or in foreign trade, for all persons offering goods for the port of destination.[4]   But if the owner of a ship employs it on his own account generally, or if he lets the tonnage with a small exception to a single person, and then for the accommodation of a particular individual he takes goods on board for freight, (not receiving them for persons in general,) he will not be deemed a common carrier; but a mere private carrier; for he does not hold himself out as engaged in a public business or employment.[5]

---

[1] *Brook* v. *Pickwick*, 4 Bing. R. 218, 222; *Allen* v. *Sewall*, 2 Wend. R. 327, 341; *Clarke* v. *Gray*, 6 East R. 564.

[2] 1 Bell Com. 467, 468, 475.

[3] Bac. Abr. Carriers A; *Lovett* v. *Hobbs*, 2 Shower R. 128; 1 Salk. 282; *Upshare* v. *Aidee*, Comyns R. 25; *Dwight* v. *Brewster*, 1 Pick. 50.

[4] Abbott on Shipp. P. 3. ch. 2, §§ 1, 2.

[5] See, however, *Walter* v. *Brewer*, 11 Mass. R. 99; *King* v. *Lenox*, 19 Johns. R. 235; *Reynolds* v. *Tappan*, 15 Johns. R. 370; *Allen* v. *Sewall*, 2 Wend. R. 327, 342; *Boucher* v. *Lawson*, Cas. T. Hard. 194.

§ 502. A person, who receives and forwards goods, taking upon himself the expenses of transportation, for which he receives a compensation from the owners, but who has no concern in the vessels or wagons, by which they are transported, and no interest in the freight, is not to be deemed a common carrier; but a mere warehouse-man and agent.[1]

§ 503. We have had already occasion to notice, that notwithstanding wharfingers are sometimes asserted to be liable as common carriers; yet that, properly speaking, there is at present no sufficient authority, on which to rest that doctrine.[2]

§ 504. In the case of *Dale* v. *Hall*, (1 Wils. R. 281,) it would seem to have been held, that a person, who undertakes to carry goods by water, is liable as a common carrier, notwithstanding the declaration does not allege him to be a common carrier, but is founded upon a special contract. That case was in fact against a common hoyman for the negligent loss of goods; and the Court was of opinion, that as he was a common hoyman, evidence to show, that he was in fact guilty of no negligence, was improperly admitted in his defence. It is difficult to perceive, how upon the actual frame of the declaration any general responsibility as a common carrier could be inferred. And the case, if it proceeded upon the notion, that every carrier by water for hire was to be deemed a common carrier, and responsible as such, is inconsistent with later decisions.[3]

---

1 *Roberts* v. *Turner*, 12 Johns. R. 232; *Platt* v. *Hillard*, 7 Cowen R. 497.

2 Ante, §§ 451, 452.

3 *Hutton* v. *Osborne*, 1 Selwyn N. P. 4th edition, p. 327, note (6); *Robinson* v. *Dunmore*, 2 Bos. & Pull. 417; *Saterlee* v. *Groat*, 1 Wend. R. 272; *Boucher* v. *Lawson*, Cas. Temp. Hard. 194.

§ 505. In order to charge a person as a common carrier it is not necessary, that a specific sum should be agreed on for the hire; for if none is agreed on, he is entitled to a reasonable compensation.[1]

§ 506. Where several persons are engaged as partners in the business of common carriers on land, and by contract between them one finds horses and drivers for certain stages, and the other supplies them for the remaining stages, they are, notwithstanding, to be treated as partners, and jointly responsible throughout the whole course of their route.[2] And the same principle applies to different partners in a coach-office, who are owners or partners in different coaches employed at the same office on the common business; though they have not a common interest in each coach. All of them will be held responsible as partners for any contract made by the keeper of the office for any loss of a package sent by either of the coaches, in which the keeper is a partner.[3]

§ 507. Common carriers are not only responsible for their own acts, but for those of their servants and other persons in their employment.[4] And any arrangements made between the carriers and their servants or agents, so that the latter may exclusively receive the compensation for the carriage of particular packages (as money), will not exempt the carriers from responsibility for the loss, unless it is known to the

---

[1] *Bastard* v. *Bastard*, 2 Shower R. 81; 2 Shower 129; 2 Ld. Raym. 909, 918; *Allen* v. *Sewall*, 2 Wend. R. 327.

[2] *Weyland* v. *Elkins*, Holt N. P. 227; 1 Starkie R. 272.

[3] *Helsby* v. *Mears*, 5 Barn. & Cresw. 504.

[4] *Cavenagh* v. *Such*, 1 Price R. 328; *Williams* v. *Cranston*, 2 Stark. R. 82; *Middletown* v. *Fowler*, 1 Salk. 282; 1 Bell Com. 455, 465, 471; *Hyde* v. *Trent & Mersey Navig. Co.* 5 T. R. 397; *Ellis* v. *Turner*, 8 T. R. 531.

party, so that he contracts exclusively with the servants and agents.[1]

§ 508. Secondly. What are the duties and obligations of common carriers. One of the duties of a common carrier is to receive and carry all goods offered for transportation upon receiving a suitable hire. This is the result of his public employment as a carrier; and by the custom of the realm, if he will not carry goods for a reasonable compensation, upon a tender of it, and a refusal of the goods, he will be liable to an action, unless there is a reasonable ground for the refusal.[2] If a carrier refuses to take charge of goods, because his coach is full; or because the goods are of a nature, that will at the time expose them to extraordinary danger or to popular rage; or because the goods are not of a sort, which he is accustomed to carry; or because he has no convenient means of carrying such goods with security; or they are brought in an unseasonable time; these will furnish reasonable grounds for his refusal; and will, if true, be a sufficient legal defence to a suit for the non-carriage of the goods.[3] A carrier is not obliged to receive goods, until he is ready to set out on his accustomed journey.[4]

§ 509. Another duty of carriers is, to take the utmost care of the goods from the moment of receiving them; to obey the directions of the owner in

---

[1] *Allen* v. *Sewall*, 2 Wend. R. 327; 1 Bell Com. 464, 465,

[2] Bac. Abr. Carriers B; *Boulston* v. *Sandiford*, Skin. 279; *Jackson* v. *Rogers*, 2 Show. R. 328; 1 Saund. 312 c; *Riley* v. *Horne*, 5 Bing. R. 217, 224.

[3] *Jackson* v. *Rogers*, 2 Show. R. 327, 328, 1 Saund. 312, note; *Lane* v. *Cotton*, 1 Ld. Ray. 646; *Batson* v. *Donovan*, 4 B. & Ald. 32; *Lovett* v. *Hobbs*, 2 Show. R. 128; 12 Mod. 3; *Edwards* v. *Sharratt*, 1 East R. 604.

[4] *Lane* v. *Cotton*, 1 Ld. Ray. 652; 1 Com. R. 105.

respect to them;[1] to carry them safely to the proper place of destination; and to make a right delivery of them there, according to the usage of trade, or the course of business.[2] They are also bound to provide suitable vehicles for the transportation, with all reasonable equipments, and servants to take care of them. If the carriage is to be by water, they are bound to provide a ship tight, staunch, and strong, and suitably equipped for the voyage, with proper officers, and a proper crew;[3] to proceed without deviation to the proper port; to expose the goods to no improper hazards; and to guard against all injuries, incident to the property, by reasonable care in preserving the goods from the effects of storms, of bad air, of leakages, and of embezzlements.[4] In short, every carrier is bound to all the diligence, which prudent and cautious men, in the like business, usually employ for the safety and preservation of the property confided to his charge. If the carrier deviates from the voyage, he is responsible for all losses, even from inevitable casualty; for under such circumstances the loss is traced back through all the intermediate causes to the first departure from duty.[5]

§ 510. Thirdly. What are the risks, for which they are liable by the common law. These have been

---

1 *Streeter* v. *Hurlock*, 1 Bing. R. 34.

2 Selw. N. P. Carriers, p. 323; *Streeter* v. *Hurlock*, 7 Moore R. 283; S. C. 1 Bing. R. 34; *Hyde* v. *Trent & Mersey Nav. Co.* 5 T. R. 389; *Forward* v. *Pittard*, 1 T. R. 27; *Ellis* v. *Turner*, 8 T. R. 531; *Davis* v. *Garrett*, 6 Bing. R. 716.

3 *Lyon* v. *Mells*, 5 East R. 428; *Amies* v. *Stevens*, 1 Str. 128; *Bell* v. *Reed*, 4 Binn. 127.

4 Abbott on Shipp. P. 3, ch. 3, § 1 to 12; *Lyon* v. *Mells*, 5 East R. 527.

5 *Davis* v. *Garrett*, 6 Bing. R. 716.

already stated to be the risks of all losses, except by
the act of God, or of the king's enemies.[1]   But, as it is
a matter of some nicety to decide, what cases fall
within the exception, and the point has undergone repeated adjudications, it is proposed here to collect the
result of the principal authorities.

§ 511. (1.) What are, and what are not, losses by
the act of God.   The expression, *act of God*, denotes
(as has been stated in another place) natural accidents,
such as lightning, earthquakes, and tempests ; and not
accidents arising from the negligence of man.[2]   Under
this expression are said to be comprehended all misfor-
tunes and accidents arising from inevitable necessity,
which human prudence could not foresee or prevent.[3]
Lord Mansfield said in one case, The act of God
means something in opposition to the act of man.[4]

§ 512. Many questions arising under this head have
been discussed in cases of carriers by sea, where there
has been a bill of lading, containing the common exception of the "perils of the sea."   What is the precise
import of this phrase is not, perhaps, very exactly settled.   In a strict sense, the words, "perils of the sea,"
denote the natural accidents peculiar to that element ;
but in more than one instance they have been held to
extend to events not attributable to natural causes.[5]
Thus, they have been held to include a capture by
pirates on the high sea ; and a case of loss by collision

---

1 1 Dane Abr. ch. 17, art. 5.

2 Ante, § 25 ; Jones's Bailm. 103 to 107 ; Id. 122 ; Co. Litt. 89, (*a*) ;
Coggs v. *Bernard*, 2 Ld. Ray. 909, 917 ; 12 Mod. R. 480 ; Abbott on
Shipp. P. 3, ch. 4, § 1 ; Park. Insur. ch. 3 ; Phillips on Insur. ch. 13, § 7.

3 *Williams* v. *Grant*, 1 Connect. R. 487.

4 *Forward* v. *Pittard*, 1 T. R. 33.

5 Abbott on Shipp. P. 3, ch. 4, §§ 1, 2, 3, 4, 5, 6 ; Park. Insur. ch. 3 ;
Marsh. Insur. B. 1, ch. 7, p. 214 ; 1 Bell Com. 579.

by two ships, where no blame is imputable to either, or at all events not to the injured ship.[1] It has indeed been said, that by "perils of the sea" are properly meant no other than inevitable perils or accidents upon that element, and, that by such perils or accidents common carriers are, *primâ facie*, excused, whether there is a bill of lading, containing the express exception of "perils of the sea," or not.[2] If the law is so, then the decisions upon the meaning of these words become important in a practical view in all cases of maritime and water carriage.

§ 513. It seems, that a loss occasioned by a leakage, which is caused by rats, gnawing a hole in the bottom of the vessel, is not in the English law deemed a loss by a peril of the sea, or by inevitable casualty.[3] * But if the master had used all reasonable precautions to prevent such a loss, as by having a cat on board, by the general consent of the writers upon the foreign maritime law, it would be held a peril of the sea, or inevitable accident.[4] In conformity to this

---

[1] Id. Ibid. 3 Kent Com. 251, note (*a*); Abbott on Shipp. P. 3, ch. 8, § 12; *Buller* v. *Fisher*, 3 Esp. R. 67.

[2] Per Gould J. *Williams* v. *Grant*, 1 Connect. R. 487; but see Marsh. Insur. B. 1, ch. 7, p. 214.

[3] *Dale* v. *Hall*, 1 Wills. R. 281; *Hunter* v. *Potts*, 4 Camp. R. 203; see Marsh. Insur. B. 1, ch. 7, § 4, p. 242.

[4] Abbott on Shipp. P. 3, ch. 3, § 9; Roccus De Navibus, n. 58; Id. De Assecur. n. 49; 1 Emerig. Assecur. 377, 378; Marsh. Insur. B. 1, ch. 7, § 4, p. 242; but see 3 Kent Com. 243, and note (*c*).

---

* Sir William Jones (Jones's Bailm. 105) says, that the true reason of this decision is not mentioned by the reporter, viz. that it was in fact at least ordinary negligence to let a rat do such mischief in the vessel, and the Roman law had so decided in an analogous case. But it is impossible to explain the case on this ground, since the defendant positively proved, that he had taken all possible care, and was guilty of no negligence ; and on this ground the jury gave a verdict in his favour.

rule, the destruction of goods at sea by rats has in Pennsylvania been held a peril of the sea, where there has been no default of the carrier.[1]   On the other hand, the destruction of a ship's bottom by worms in the course of a voyage has been deemed not to be a peril of the sea both in England and America, upon the ground, (it would seem,) that it is a loss by ordinary wear and decay.[2]

§ 514. We have already had occasion to notice, that losses by collision of ships at sea, without any negligence on the part of the injured or lost vessel, are deemed losses by perils of the sea, or by inevitable casualty.[3]

§ 515. The general rule in cases of insurance is, that the immediate and not the remote cause of the loss is to be considered. "Causa proxima, non remota spectatur." And this rule may in some cases apply to carriers.[4]

§ 516. But it is not every loss proceeding directly from natural causes, which is to be deemed, as happening by a peril of the sea ; and questions of this sort often turn upon very nice distinctions. Thus, if a carrier-ship should perish in consequence of striking against a rock or shallow, the circumstances, under which that event has taken place, must be ascertained, in order to decide, whether it happened by a peril of the sea, or by the fault of the owner, carrier, or master.

---

[1] *Garrigues* v. *Coxe*, 1 Binn. R. 592 ; but see *Aymer* v. *Astor*, 6 Cowen R. 266, and 3 Kent Com. 248, note (*c*).

[2] Park. Insur. ch. 3, *Rohl* v. *Parr*, 1 Esp. R. 444 ; *Martin* v. *Salem Ins. Co.* 2 Mass. R. 429 ; but see *De Peyster* v. *Columbian Insur. Co.* 2 Cain. R. 85.

[3] *Buller* v. *Fisher*, 3 Esp. R. 67 ; Abbott on Shipp. P. 3, ch. 4, §§ 2, 5 ; *Smith* v. *Scott*, 4 Taunt. 126.

[4] Abbott on Shipp. P. 3, ch. 4, §§ 5, 6.

If the situation of a rock or shallow is generally known, and the ship is not forced upon it by adverse winds or tempests, the loss is to be imputed to the fault of the master. And it matters not in such a case, whether the loss arises from his own rashness in not taking a pilot, or from his own ignorance or unskilfulness.[1] On the other hand, if a ship is forced upon such a rock or shallow by adverse winds or tempests, or if the shallow is occasioned by a sudden and recent collection of sand in a place, where ships before could sail with safety; or if the rock or shallow is not generally known; in all these cases the loss is to be attributed to the act of God, and it is deemed a peril of the sea.[2]

§ 517. A remarkable case illustrative of this doctrine occurred. An action was brought against the master of a carrier-vessel, navigating the river Ouse and Humber from Selby to Hull. At the trial it appeared, that at the entrance of the harbour of Hull there was a bank, on which vessels used to lie with safety; but of which a part had been swept away by a great flood some short time before the misfortune in question; so, that it had become perfectly steep, instead of shelving towards the river. A few days after this flood a vessel sunk by getting on the bank, and her mast, which was carried away, was suffered to float in the river, tied to some part of the vessel. The defendant's vessel, upon sailing into the harbour, struck against the mast, which, not giving way, forced the defendant's vessel towards the bank, where she struck, and would have remained safe, had the bank been in its former situation. But upon the tide's ebbing

---

[1] *The William,* 6 Rob. 316.
[2] Abbott on Shipp. P. 3, ch. 4, § 6; *Elliot v. Rossell,* 10 John. R. 1; *Kemp v. Coughtry,* 11 Johns. R. 107.

her stern sunk into the water, and the goods were spoiled. Evidence was offered to show, that there was no negligence; but it was rejected. The Judge, who tried the cause, ruled, that the act of God, which would excuse the carrier, must be immediate, and not remote; and a verdict having been found for the defendant, on a motion for a new trial, the doctrine of the Judge at the trial was confirmed.[1] But if the mast, which was the immediate cause of the loss, had not been in the way; but the bank had been suddenly removed by an earthquake, or the removal of the bank had been unknown, and the vessel had gone on the bank in the usual manner, the decision would have been otherwise.[2]

§ 518. In the case above stated, it does not appear, that a collision with the mast might not have been guarded against by extraordinary precautions, as it must have been visible on the approach of the vessel; and the masters and owners are certainly responsible for every injury, which might have been prevented by human foresight and care. Thus, where in a voyage from Hull to Gainsborough a carrier-vessel was sunk by striking against the anchor of another vessel, which anchor lay under water, and without a buoy, whereby some goods were injured, the carriers were held responsible for the loss.[3] The ground of this decision seems to have been, that both parties were guilty of negligence; the one in leaving his anchor without a buoy; the other in not avoiding it, as, when he saw the vessel in the river, he must have known, there was an anchor near at hand.[4] If, however, the anchor had

---

1 Abbott on Shipp. P. 3, ch. 4, § 1; Id. ch. 3, § 9; *Hahn* v. *Corbett*, 2 Bing. R. 205.

2 Abbott on Shipp. P. 3, ch. 4, § 6.

3 Abbott on Shipp. P. 3, ch. 3, § 9.

4 Abbott on Shipp. P. 3, ch. 4, § 5.

been left by the vessel, and she had departed, and there were no means of distinguishing its situation, the result (it should seem) would have been otherwise.

§ 519. In a case against a carrier for an injury done to a cargo by steam, it appeared, that the steam escaped through a crack in the steam-boiler, occasioned by the frost; and the Court held, that at the season of the year, in which such injuries by frost are likely to occur, it is gross negligence in the carrier to fill up his boiler with water over night, without keeping up a suitable fire to prevent such accidents.[1]

§ 520. If a carrier-ship is properly moored in a harbour having a hard, uneven bottom, and on the reflux of the tide, in consequence of a considerable swell, she strikes hard on the bottom, and her knees are injured, and thereby her cargo is damaged; such a loss is to be deemed a loss by the peril of the sea.[2]

§ 521. So, if a carrier-ship is taken in tow by a ship of war, and in order to keep up she is obliged to use an extraordinary press of sail in a gale of wind, and thereby her cargo is injured, it is a loss by the perils of the sea.[3]

§ 522. And if, in moving a ship from one part of a harbour to another, it becomes necessary to send some of the crew on shore to make fast a new line, and to cast off a rope, by which she is made fast, and these men are impressed immediately, before casting off the rope, and thereby the ship goes on shore, it is a loss by the perils of the sea.[4]

---

[1] *Siordet* v. *Hall*, 4 Bing. R. 607; *Coggs* v. *Bernard*, 2 Ld. Ray. 909, 911.

[2] *Fletcher* v. *Inglis*, 2 Barn. & Ald. 315.

[3] *Hagedorn* v. *Whitmore*, 1 Stark. R. 157.

[4] *Hodgson* v. *Malcolm*, 5 Bos. & Poll. 336.

§ 523. And where a carrier-vessel is beating up a river against a light and variable wind, if, while changing her tack, the wind suddenly fails or changes, and she goes ashore, and her cargo is injured, this also is to be deemed a loss by the act of God, and will excuse the carrier.[1]

§ 524. If the carrier-vessel is reasonably sufficient for the voyage, and is lost by a peril of the sea, the carrier will not be chargeable by its being shown, that a stouter vessel would have outlived the storm. Nor, if a hoy is sunk by being driven by a sudden gust against a pier, will the hoy-man be made liable by its being shown, that a stronger vessel would have sustained the injury without sinking.[2]

§ 525. The case of a jettison at sea, to save the vessel from foundering, and to preserve the lives of the crew, is (as we shall presently see) a loss by the act of God, though accomplished by the immediate agency of man.[3] But it would be otherwise, if occasioned by the vessel's being overloaded; as, if a ferry-man should overload his boat, and the passengers' goods should be thrown overboard.[4]

§ 526. (2.) What are, and what are not, losses by the king's enemies. By enemies is to be understood public enemies, with whom the nation itself is at open war; and not merely robbers, thieves, or other private depredators, however much they may be deemed in a moral sense at war with society. Losses, therefore, which are occasioned by robbery on the highway, or by

---

1 *Cost* v. *McMechan*, 6 Johns. R. 160.

2 *Amies* v. *Stevens*, 1 Str. 128; Abbott on Shipp. P. 3, ch. 4, § 7.

3 *Bird* v. *Astcock*, 2 Bulst. 280; Jones's Bailm. 108; 1 Caines R. 43; 3 Connect. R. 9.

4 2 Ld. Ray. 909, 911.

the depredations and violence of mobs, rioters, and in-
surgents, and other felons, are not deemed losses by
enemies within the meaning of the exception.[1] But
losses by pirates on the high seas are deemed within
it; for they are universally treated as the enemies of all
mankind, and are subjected to punishment accordingly.[2] And here the question may often become material, whether we are to look to the immediate, or to the
remote cause of the loss; for in some instances (as
under the common American bills of lading) the perils
of the seas are excepted, and not the acts of the king's
enemies. Suppose a carrier-ship should be driven by
a storm on an enemy's coast, and she should there be
captured by the enemy, before she should be stranded;
is this a loss by perils of the sea, or by capture? It
seems, that it is a loss by capture; for, that is the proximate cause.[3] But suppose, that she should be first
stranded on the coast by the gale, and in consequence
thereof should be afterwards captured by the inhabit-
ants? In that case, it seems, that it would be deemed
a loss, not by capture, but by the perils of the sea, upon
the same principle; for the gale is the proximate cause
of the stranding.[4]

§ 527. The case of a loss by jettison, made by com-
pulsion of an enemy to gratify his revenge, or from an
apprehension (well or ill founded) of danger, would, it
is presumed, be deemed an act of the enemy, although

---

1 *Moss* v. *Slue*, 1 Vent. 190, 238; *Prop's of Trent Nav.* v. *Wood*,
3 Esp. R. 127; *Barclay* v. *Heyguin*, cited 1 T. R. 38; Marshall Ins. B.
1, ch. 7, § 5, p. 242, \ c.; Jones's Bailm. 103 to 107; Id. 122; *Coggs* v.
Bernard, 2 Ld. Ray. 909, 918; 12 Mod. 480; T. Raym. 220; *Woodleiffe*
v. *Curteis*, 1 Roll. Abr. 2.

2 Ante, § 25.

3 *Green* v. *Elmslie*, Peake R. 212.

4 *Hahn* v. *Corbett*, 2 Bing. R. 205.

done by the immediate agency of the ship's crew or officers.

§ 528. In all cases, where the common carrier cannot make out a defence upon some one of the grounds already stated, which form exceptions to his liability, he must pay the loss, although there has been no negligence whatsoever on his part. Hence, (as we have seen,) he is liable for all thefts, robberies, and embezzlements by any of the crew, or by any other persons, although he may have exercised every possible vigilance to prevent the loss.[1] In like manner he is liable for a loss occasioned by an accidental fire wholly without any negligence on this part;[2] and by an accident arising from any unseen nuisance in the course of his navigation.[3]

§ 529. In all cases of loss it seems, that the *onus probandi* is on the carrier to exempt himself from liability; for *primâ facie*, the law imposes the obligation of safety on him.[4] And it seems, that the breaking down or overturning of a stage-coach is *primâ facie* evidence of negligence on the part of the proprietor and his servants.[5]

§ 530. In respect to the property carried, it matters not, whether it be money or goods, or other moveable merchandise.[6] The carrier is equally responsible for

---

1 Abbott on Shipp. P. 3, ch. 3, § 3; Jones's Bailm. 107, 109, 122; *Schieffelin* v. *Harvey*, 6 Johns. R. 170; *Watkinson* v. *Laughton*, 8 Johns. R. 213; *Gibbon* v. *Paynton*, 4 Burr. 2298.

2 *Forward* v. *Pittard*, 1 T. R. 33; see Salk. 143.

3 *Prop's. Trent Navig.* v. *Wood*, 3 Esp. R. 127.

4 *Forward* v. *Pittard*, 1 Term R. 27, 33; *Murphy* v. *Slaton*, 3 Munf. R. 239; *Bell* v. *Read*, 4 Binn. 127; *Colt* v. *McMechan*, 6 Johns. R. 160; see *Whalley* v. *Wray*, 3 Esp. R. 74; see 7 Cowen, 500, and note (*a*); *Riley* v. *Horne*, 5 Bing. R. 217, 226.

5 *Christie* v. *Griggs*, 2 Camp. R. 79.

6 *Kemp* v. *Coughtry*, 11 Johns. R. 107.

each. But in respect to goods in a carrier-vessel, which are shipped to be stowed on deck, as they are from their situation peculiarly liable to be thrown overboard to lighten the vessel in cases of disress, if they are necessarily so thrown overboard, the carrier is exonerated, and the owner of the goods must bear the loss without contribution.[1] But if such goods are without the consent of the owner, or a general custom binding him, stowed on deck, and on that account ejected in tempestuous weather, the carrier will be chargeable with the loss.[2]

§ 531. The case of Barcroft, as cited by Lord Chief Justice Rolle, would seem to imply a responsibility of the carrier even in cases of jettison. It is stated thus : " A box of jewels had been delivered to a ferryman, who knew not what it contained, and a sudden storm arising in the passage he threw the box into the sea. Yet it was resolved, that he should answer for it." [3] Sir William Jones suspects, that there must have been some proof of culpable negligence in the case, and that probably the casket was both small and light enough to have been kept longer on board than other goods. Even then the case would be sufficiently hard ; as the ferryman did not know the contents, and might have acted for the best. But if the doctrine of the case be, that jettison will not in a clear case of necessity discharge the carrier, it is not law ; for it was expressly decided in Lord Coke's time, in the case of a bargeman, that where goods were thrown overboard in a great storm to save the lives of the passengers by

1 *Smith* v. *Wright*, 1 Cain R. 43 ; *Lenox* v. *United Ins. Co.* 3 Johns. Cas. 178 ; Abbott on Shipp. P. 3, ch. 8, § 13.

2 *Barber* v. *Bruce*, 3 Connect. R. 9 ; 1 Cain R. 48.

3 Aleyne R. 22 ; Jones's Bailm. 107, 108.

lightening the barge, the bargeman was exonerated; for the storm was the act of God, and the occasion of throwing them overboard.[1]

§ 532. Fourthly. As to the commencement and termination of the risk of common carriers. (1.) The commencement of the risk. To render a carrier responsible there must be an actual delivery to him, or to his servants, or to some other person authorized to act in his behalf; and as soon as such delivery is complete, the responsibity of the carrier as such commences.[2] But it is often a matter of great nicety to decide upon the circumstances of the case, whether there has been such a delivery or not. Thus, where goods were left in the yard of an inn, where the carrier and other carriers put up, but no actual delivery to the carrier or his servant was proved, it was deemed not a complete delivery to the carrier, so as to charge him with the custody.[3] So, where goods were delivered at a wharf to an unknown person there, and no knowledge of the fact was brought home to the wharfinger or his agents, this was held not to be a sufficient delivery to charge him, either as wharfinger or as a carrier, with the custody of the goods.[4] And where, by the usage of the business, a delivery of goods on the dock near the carrier-boat (as in the case of a carrier canal-boat) is a good delivery, so as to charge the carrier, it must be understood with this qualification, that due notice is given to him of the fact; for otherwise he will not be chargeable, since, until he has knowledge, that the

---

[1] Cited by Lord Coke in *Bird* v. *Astcock*, 2 Bulst. R. 280; Jones's Bailm. 108.

[2] 1 Bell Com. 464.

[3] *Solway* v. *Holloway*, 1 Ld. Raym. 46; 1 Bell Com. 464.

[4] *Buckman* v. *Levi*, 3 Camp. 414; 1 Bell Com. 464.

goods are on the dock for the purpose of being carried, he has no right to assume any custody of them.[1]

§ 533. The liability of carriers attaches from the time of their acceptance of the goods, whether that acceptance is in a special manner, or according to the usage of their business.[2]　But an acceptance in some way, either actual or constructive, is indispensable.[3] And where goods are actually put into the wagon or barge of a carrier, he will not be chargeable, if it appears, that there is no intention to trust him with the custody; as if the owner is uniformly in the habit of placing his own servant on board as a guard, who exclusively takes upon himself the management and custody of them.[4]　But the mere fact, that the owner or his servant goes with the goods, if the other circumstances of the case do not exclude the custody of the carrier, will not of itself exempt him from responsibility.[5]

§ 534. It is in many cases the usage of the masters and owners of ships to receive goods on the quay, or beach, or in their boats, or at the wharf, or warehouse of the shipper or his agent; or to take them, at other special places, into the custody of the mate or other proper officer of the ship.　In all such cases their liability as carriers commences at the instant of such acceptance of the goods.[6]

---

1 *Packard* v. *German*, 6 Cowen R. 757.

2 *Dale* v. *Hall*, 1 Wils. 281; *Boehm* v. *Combe*, 2 M. & Selw. 172.

3 Abbott on Shipp. P. 3, ch. 3, § 2; *Packard* v. *Getman*, 6 Cowen R. 757; 1 Bell Com. 464.

4 *East India Co.* v. *Pullen*, 1 Str. R. 690; *Robinson* v. *Dunmore*, 2 Bos. & Pull. 419; *Shieffelin* v. *Harvey*, 6 Johns. 170; Marshall Insur. B. 1, ch. 7, § 5, p. 252 &c.; *Rucker* v. *London Assur. Co.* Ibid.

5 Abbott on Shipp. P. 3, ch. 3, § 3; *Cobban* v. *Downe*, 5 Esp. R. 41; Marshall Insur. B. 1, ch. 7, § 5, p. 252 &c.; 1 Bell Com. 464.

6 *Robinson* v. *Dunmore*, 2 Bos. & Pull. 419; Marshall Inst. B. 1, ch. 1, § 5, p. 252, &c.

§ 535. But it sometimes happens, that a party is at once a warehouse-man or an innkeeper, and a carrier, and that, after a receipt of the goods and before their being put *in itinere,* they are lost or destroyed.   In such cases the question often arises, whether the receiver is liable in the one capacity or another ; for the responsibility of each (as we have seen) is not, or at least may not be, co-extensive.[1] In the case of *Maving* v. *Todd,* (1 Stark. R. 72,) (which has been already under notice in another place,) where goods were received by a wharfinger, who was at the same time a lighterman, for the purpose of being shipped from London to Newcastle, and the wharfinger was at the same time a lighterman, whose duty it was to convey the goods from the wharf to the ship in his own lighter to the vessel in the river, and the goods while on the premises were accidentally destroyed by fire, Lord Ellenborough is reported to have held, that while the wharfinger was in possession of these goods, his liability was similar to that of a carrier.   The case, however, went off upon another ground ; and in another report of the same case [2] the dictum is not even alluded to.

§ 536. In all such cases the material point, upon which the controversy hinges, is, whether the one, or the other character predominates in the particular stage of the transaction.[3] If a common carrier receives goods into his own warehouse for the accommodation of himself and his customers, so that the deposit there is a mere accessary to the carriage, and for the purpose of facilitating it, his liability as a carrier begins with the receipt of the goods.[4] So, if an innkeeper is at the

---

[1] 1 Bell Com. 469.   [2] 4 Camp. R. 225.
[3] Ante, § 430 to 433.   [4] *Foward* v. *Pittard,* 1 T. R. 27.

same time a carrier, and goods are sent to his inn and received by him for transportation, he is liable, as carrier, for any loss, before they are put upon their transit.[1]

§ 537. On the other hand, if a person is at the same time a common carrier, and a forwarding merchant, and he receives goods into his warehouse to be forwarded, according to the future orders of the owners; if the goods are lost by fire before such orders are received, or the goods are put in transit, he is not chargeable as a common carrier, but only as a warehouse-man.[2]

§ 538. (2.) The termination of the carrier's risk. As soon as the goods have arrived at their proper place of destination, and are deposited there, and no further duty remains to be done by the carrier, his responsibility, as such, ceases.[3] We have already had occasion to consider some cases illustrative of this doctrine, under another head. If a carrier between A and B receives goods to be carried from A to B, and thence to be forwarded by a distinct conveyance to C; as soon as he arrives with the goods at B, and deposits them in his warehouse there, his responsibility as carrier ceases; for that is the terminus of his duty as such. He then becomes, as to the goods, a mere warehouse-man, undertaking for their further transportation.[4]

§ 539. And the like result would be, if the goods were destined to B only, if it is not by the custom of

---

[1] Buller J.'s opinion in *Hyde v. Trent & Mersey Nav. Co.* 5 T. R. 389; 1 Bell's Com. 469.

[2] *Platt v. Hibbard*, 7 Cowen R. 497; *Roskell v. Waterhouse*, 2 Stark. R. 461; *Ackley v. Kellogg*, 8 Cowen R. 223; Ante, § 430 to 433; 1 Bell's Com. 469.

[3] Ante, § 424 to 428, 432.

[4] *Garside v. Trent & Mersey Nav. Co.* 4 T. R. 581; *Ackley v. Kellogg*, 8 Cowen R. 223.

the business the carrier's duty to deliver the goods to the consignees there, but simply to deposit them in his warehouse.[1] But if it is his duty to deliver the goods to the consignees at B, then his liability as carrier does not cease by such a deposit; but he is chargeable for any loss, which occurs, until an actual delivery to the party.[2] So, he is chargeable, in like manner, for any loss during a deposit in any warehouse, at an intermediate state of the journey between A and B.[3]

§ 540. And if, notwithstanding any custom to the contrary, the carrier specially undertakes to deliver the goods to the owner, he is chargeable for any loss before such delivery, although, in all respects, he has followed the general custom of the place.[4]

§ 541. On the other hand, however universal the custom may be, to deliver the goods to the owner, at the place of destination; still the parties may, by their contract, waive it; and if they do, the carrier is discharged.[5] As, if the owner, after the arrival of the goods, requests the carrier to let them remain in his warehouse until the owner can conveniently send for them; and they are there deposited, and are afterwards destroyed by fire; the duty of the carrier being at an end, he is not responsible for the loss in that character.[6] So, if a man, having no warehouse of his own, directs the carrier to leave his goods at the wagon-office, until

---

[1] *In re v. Webb,* 8 Taunt. R. 443; S. C. 2 Moore, 560; 2 Kent Com. 469.

[2] *Hyde v. Trent Nav. Co.* 5 T. R. 389; *Golden v. Manning,* 3 Wils. R. 429; S. C. 2 Black. R. 916; *Catley v. Witherington,* Peake R. 202.

[3] Ibid.

[4] *Wardell v. Mourillyan,* 2 Esp. R. 693.

[5] *Strong v. Natally,* 4 Bos. & Pull. 16; Marshall Insur. B. 1, ch. 7, § 5, p. 252, &c.; *Sparrow v. Carruthers,* 2 Str. R. 1236.

[6] *In re v. Webb,* 8 Taunt. 443; 2 Moore R. 500.

he should find it convenient to remove or sell them, the carrier's responsibility will terminate with the deposit.[1]

§ 542. In all cases of this sort, the material consideration is, whether the owner of the goods has taken any exclusive possession of them, or has terminated the custody of the carrier by any act or direction, which does not flow from the duty of the carrier. So long as the carrier retains the possession of the goods, or is to perform any farther duty, either by custom or contract, as carrier, he is responsible for their safety. But, when the transit is ended, and the delivery is either completed or waived by the owner, then the responsibility of the carrier ceases.[2] So, if the goods, after their arrival, are put on board of a lighter in the customary way, and the owner then takes an exclusive custody of them, before they are landed, the carrier is discharged from any subsequent loss.[3]

§ 543. A question often arises in practice, whether the carrier is bound to make a personal delivery of the goods to the owner, or not. This may admit of different answers, according to circumstances. The manner of delivering the goods, and consequently the period, at which the responsibility of the carrier will cease, may, in many instances, depend upon the custom of particular places, and the usage of particular trades, or upon a special contract between the parties. If there is any special contract between the parties, or any local custom or usage of trade on the subject, that will govern;

---

1 *Richardson* v. *Goss*, 3 Bos. & Pull. 119 ; *Scott* v. *Petit*, 3 Bos. & Pull. 472; *Dixon* v. *Baldwin*, 5 East R. 151 ; *Rowe* v. *Pickford*, 1 Moore R. 526; Abbott on Shipp. P. 3, ch. 9.

2 Marshall Insur. B. 1, ch. 7, § 5, p. 252, &c. ; Abbott on Shipp. P. 3, ch. 3, § 12.

3 *Strong* v. *Natally*, 4 Boss. & Pull. 16.

the former as an express, and the latter as an implied term in the contract.[1] But, in the absence of any special contract, or custom, or usage, probably no general rule can be laid down. There seems a strong inclination of opinion at present to hold, (though there is some diversity of judicial opinion,) that the carrier is bound, generally, to make a personal delivery to the owner, unless there is some custom of trade, or some contract to the contrary. Lord Kenyon was strenuously the other way; but three other Judges, on that occasion, differed from him.[2] And on more recent occasions, the opinions of other distinguished Judges have settled down in favour of the doctrine of the three Judges against him.[3] However this may be, it seems clear, that carriers are bound to give notice of the arrival of the goods to the persons, to whom they are directed, if they are known to them, and within a reasonable time; they must take care, at their peril, that the goods are delivered to the right person; for, otherwise, they will become responsible.[4]

§ 544. It was said in one case by Mr. Justice Buller, that when goods are brought into England from foreign countries, they are brought under a bill of lading, which is merely an undertaking to carry them from port to port. A ship, trading from one port to another, has not

---

1 *Hyde* v. *Trent Nav. Co.* 5 T. R. 389; *Catley* v. *Wintringham*, Peake R. 150; *Golden* v. *Manning*, 3 Wils. R. 429; *Wardell* v. *Mourillyan*, 2 Esp. R. 693; *In re* v. *Webb*, 8 Taunt. 443; Abbott on Shipp. P. 3, ch. 3, § 12.

2 *Hyde* v. *Trent Nav. Co.* 5 T. R. 389; 2 Kent Com. 469.

3 *Duff* v. *Budd*, 3 Bro. & Bing. 177; 6 Moore R. 469; *Bodenham* v. *Bennett*, 4 Price R. 34; *Birkett* v. *Willan*, 2 Barn. & Ald. 356; *Garnett* v. *Willan*, 5 Barn. & Ald. 58; *Storrs* v. *Crowley*, 1 McClel. & Young, 129; *Stephenson* v. *Hart*, 4 Bing. R. 476; 2 Kent Com. 469.

4 *Golden* v. *Manning*, 3 Wils. R. 429; *Garnett* v. *Willan*, 5 Barn. & Ald. 58.

the means of carrying goods on land; and therefore, according to the established course of trade, a delivery on the usual wharf is such a delivery, as will discharge the carrier.[1] If, however, the consignee of goods requires the goods to be delivered to himself on board of the ship, and directs them not to be landed on a wharf, it is said, that the master must obey the request; for the wharfinger has no right to insist upon the goods being landed at his wharf, although the vessel be moored against it.[2]

§ 545. How far the above rule, as to foreign voyages, has been adopted in America, does not appear from any decided cases.   In respect to goods transported coastwise, it has been decided in one case in New York, that a delivery of goods upon the wharf at the port of unlivery is no discharge of the carrier; and, that evidence of a usage so to deliver goods is immaterial.   And, that the carrier does not, by sending the goods to the consignee by a cartman, without the orders of the consignee, discharge himself from responsibility, even though it is a common practice.[3] If the consignee is unable, or refuses to receive the goods, the carrier is not at liberty to leave them on the wharf; but it is his duty to take care of them for the owner.[4]

§ 546. Cases may often occur, where a person is at once a carrier of goods, and an agent or factor for the sale of them; and the inquiry may present itself, when, under such circumstances, his liability as carrier terminates.   Suppose the owner of a ship is master, and

---

[1] *Hyde* v. *Trent Nav. Co.* 5 T. R. 389; Abbott on Shipp. P 3, ch. 3, § 12.

[2] *Syeds* v. *Hay*, 4 T. R. 260; Abbott on Shipp. P. 3, ch. 3, § 12.

[3] *Ostrander* v. *Brown*, 15 Johns. R. 39; 2 Kent Com. 469.

[4] Ibid.; *Mayell* v. *Potter*, 2 Johns. Cas. 371; *Stephenson* v. *Hart*, 4 Bing. R. 476.

also is consignee of the goods of shippers, which were put on board for sale. When do his rights and responsibility commence and terminate in each capacity? It has been decided, that during the voyage he retains the character of owner and master, and of course, during the voyage, he is responsible as carrier.[1] But, after his arrival at the port of destination, and the landing of the goods there, it would seem, that his duty as carrier is at an end. Suppose a case, in which the master is consignee and not owner of the goods; is the owner of the ship, as carrier, responsible for the acts of the master, after the landing of the goods at the port of destination, either before or after the sale? If, by the course of a particular trade, or the dealings between the particular parties, it is the usage for the master to take the consignment of the goods shipped, and to sell the same, and to receive, on behalf of the owner of the ship, a compensation for the whole service in the name of freight, which compensation is divisible between the owner and the master, according to their private agreement; in such a case, the owner of the ship may be responsible for the acts of the master throughout, because the latter, in such a case, acts as his agent; though it might be otherwise, if the master acted as factor solely for the shipper, and received a distinct compensation from him. But in such a case, the owner of the ship would seem to be liable, not in the character of a common carrier, but merely as a factor; and the responsibility of the one is (as we have seen) materially different from that of the other.[2]

---

1 *Kendrick* v. *Delafield*, 3 Cain. R. 67; *Cook* v. *Com. Ins. Co.* 11 Johns. R. 40; *Earl* v. *Rowcroft*, 8 East. R. 126, 140; *Crousillat* v. *Ball*, 4 Dall. R. 294.

2 *Emery* v. *Hersey*, 4 Greenleaf R. 407; *Kemp* v. *Coughtry*, 11 Johns.

§ 547. The case of *Kemp* v. *Coughtry* (11 Johns. R. 107) may seem to countenance a different doctrine. There, the master of a coasting vessel was employed to carry goods from Albany to New-York, and the usual course of the trade was, for the master to sell the goods at New York, without charging any thing more than the ordinary freight, and to account to the owner of the goods for the proceeds, and not to the owners of the vessel. The master, after receiving the goods, carried them to New York and sold them there; and brought the money (the proceeds of the sale) on board, and put it into his trunk; and he and his crew having left the vessel a short time after locking the cabin, upon his return the cabin and trunk were found broken open, and the money stolen. It was resolved, upon this state of facts, that the owners (the master being one) were responsible for the loss. The Court appear to have treated the case as one arising against them solely in the character of common carriers. The reasoning was, that the money, when on board, was to be considered exactly the same as a return cargo, purchased with the proceeds of the goods; and in such a case it would be clear, that the liability of common carriers would attach on the owners.

§ 548. But, upon the posture of the facts, the very question was, whether the specific money on board was to be treated as cargo, or was to be carried back for hire; and whether the master was bound to carry back the specific money received by him, or was only bound to pay over and account to the shipper for the amount and value of the proceeds in any money whatsoever. Now, it is certainly no part of the duty of a

---

R. 107; *Kendrick* v. *Delafield*, 3 Cain R. 67; Abbott on Shipp. p. 98, n. (3); Id. p. 134, n. (1.)

common carrier to sell goods and to account for the
proceeds. If he sells, it is not as a carrier, but as a
factor. The owners of the vessel may be liable for
his acts as factors, if the course of trade makes him
their agent in the business of selling. But when there
is a right delivery of the goods at the place of destination, the duties of the carrier as such, would seem
to cease ; and the duty of factor to commence. If the
specific money received, or any other goods bought
with it, are to be returned in the same vessel to the
original port, and the freight paid contemplates that
course of trade, then, as soon as the goods or money
are put on board for the purpose of the return carriage, the liability of the carrier certainly re-attaches.
But the evidence in the case went to show, not that
there was to be any such return of the particular
money or goods in the vessel, but merely, that there
was a liability of the master to account for the proceeds to the owners of the goods, and not to the owner of the vessel. Perhaps the application of the law
to the facts, rather than the law itself, as laid down in
the case, would deserve farther consideration.

§ 549. Fifthly. We come next to consider the
effect of special contracts and notices of carriers. It
was formerly a question of much doubt, how far common carriers on land could by contract limit their
responsibility upon the ground, that exercising a public employment they are bound to carry for a reasonable
compensation, and had no right to change their common law rights and duties.[1] And it was said, that,
like innkeepers, they were bound to receive and accommodate all persons, as far as they may, and could not

---

[1] 1 Bell Com. 472, 473.

insist upon special and qualified terms. The right, however, of making such qualified acceptances by common carriers seems to have been asserted in early times. Lord Coke declared it in a note to *Southcote's case*, (4 Rep. 84;) and it was admitted in *Mors* v. *Slue*, (1 Vent. 238.) It is now fully recognised, and settled beyond any reasonable doubt.[1] Still, however, it is to be understood, that common carriers cannot by any special agreement exempt themselves from all responsibility so as to evade altogether the salutary policy of the common law. They cannot, therefore, by a special notice exempt themselves from all responsibility in cases of gross negligence and fraud; or, by demanding an exhorbitant price, compel the owner of the goods to yield to unjust and oppressive limitations of their rights.[2] And the carrier will be equally liable in case of the fraud or misconduct of his servants, as he would be in case of his own personal fraud or misconduct.[3]

§ 550. In respect to carriers by water, and especially on foreign voyages, there has prevailed from a very early period a practice of accompanying the shipment with a bill of lading, which specifies the risks, from which the carrier is to be exempted. He

---

[1] *Nicholson* v. *Willan*, 5 East R. 507; *Clay* v. *Willan*, 1 H. Bl. 298; *Harris* v. *Packwood*, 3 Taunt. 264; *Evans* v. *Soule*, 2 M. & Selw. 1; *Smith* v. *Horne*, 8 Taunt. 146; *Batson* v. *Donovan*, 4 Barn. & Ald. 39; *Riley* v. *Horne*, 5 Bing. R. 217; *Bodenham* v. *Bennett*, 4 Price R. 34; *Down* v. *Fromont*, 4 Camp. 41; *Lowes* v. *Kermode*, 8 Taunt. 146.

[2] Jones's Bailm. 48; Doct. & Stud. Dial. 2 ch. 38; Noy. Maxims, ch. 43, p. 93; *Lyon* v. *Mells*, 5 East R. 430, 438; *Harris* v. *Packwood*, 3 Taunt. R. 264, 272; 1 Williams' Saund. 312, note; *Batson* v. *Donovan*, 4 Barn. & Ald. 21, 32; *Hyde* v. *Trent Navig.* 1 Esp. R. 36; *Maving* v. *Todd*, 1 Stark. 72; *Bodenham* v. *Bennett*, 4 Price R. 34; *Brooke* v. *Pickwick*, 4 Bing. R. 218; *Harris* v. *Packwood*, 3 Taunt. 264.

[3] *Ellis* v. *Turner*, 8 T. R. 531; *Garrett* v. *Willan*, 5 Barn. & Ald. 57.

engages, according to the old form of the bill of lading, to make a right delivery of the goods, "the dangers of the seas only excepted." It is observable, that the acts of the king's enemies are not included in the exception;[1] and therefore a question has arisen, how far the express exception of the perils of the sea excludes the other exception of the common law, acts of the king's enemies, upon the well known maxim, that "Expressio unius est exclusio alterius."[2] But the point has been left undecided. We have, however, seen, that a loss by pirates is deemed a peril of the seas; and that furnishes one strong analogy in regard to captures by enemies.[3] In England the form of the bill of lading has lately been changed, and the exception now is in the following terms, "The act of God, of the king's enemies, fire, and all and every other dangers and accidents of the seas, rivers, and navigation of whatever nature and kind soever, save risk of boats, as far as ships are liable thereto, excepted."[4] In America, it is believed the old form of the bill of lading, generally, if not universally, prevails in practice.

§ 551. In respect to special contracts, they may be divided into two classes; first, such as are express; secondly, such as are implied. The latter class is the most frequent in cases of carriage of goods on land. It sometimes arises from the particular dealing between the parties, either generally, or in the given case; sometimes from the general course of trade or business; and sometimes, and most usually, from the

---

1 Abbott on Shipp. P. 3, ch. 2, § 3.
2 Abbott on Shipp. P. 3, ch. 4, § 4.
3 Abbott on Shipp. P. 3, ch. 4, § 2, 3, 4.
4 Abbott on Shipp. P. 3, ch. 4, § 3; Id. ch. 4, § 1, and note.

public advertisements and notices, given by carriers, stating the terms and limits of their responsibility.

§ 552. Few questions have arisen upon the interpretation of express contracts, entered into by parties for the transportation of goods. The terms of the exception in the modern bill of lading in England, it has been remarked by Mr. Abbott,[1] have given rise to but one judicial decision. In a contract by a bill of lading, however, it furnishes no excuse to the carrier, that the goods have been seized for a violation of the revenue laws, unless that seizure is in fact for a legal cause of forfeiture.[2]

§ 553. Many of the questions, which of late years have engaged the attention of courts of justice, have been upon the validity, obligation, and effect of the notices given by common carriers and others in the course of their business. Upon this subject it will be proper to bestow a particular examination.

§ 554. First, then, as to the VALIDITY OF NOTICES by common carriers. Mr. Chief Justice Best, in a judgment already alluded to, expressed a strong opinion in favour of their validity and the reasonableness of giving them full effect. After adverting to the fact, that the common law makes them liable for every loss, except by the act of God, and the king's enemies, he proceeds to say, "As the law makes the carrier an insurer, and as the goods he carries may be injured or destroyed by many accidents, against which no care on the part of the carrier can protect them, he is as much entitled to be paid a premium for his insurance of their delivery at the place of their destination, as for the

---

1 Abbott on Shipp. P. 3, ch. 4, § 1.
2 *Gosling* v. *Higgins*, 1 Camp. R. 451.

labour and expense of carrying them there. Indeed,
besides the risk, that he runs, his attention becomes
more anxious, and his journey is more expensive, in
proportion to the value of his load. If he has things
of great value contained in such small packages, as to
be objects of theft, or embezzlement, a strong and
more vigilant guard is required, than when he carries
articles not easily removed, and which offer less temptation to dishonesty. He must take what is offered to
him, to carry to the place, to which he undertakes to
convey goods, if he has room for it in his carriage.
The loss of one single package might ruin him. By
means of negotiable bills, immense value is now com-
pressed into a very small compass. Parcels containing these bills are continually sent by common carriers.
As the law compels carriers to undertake for the security of what they carry, it would be most unjust, if
it did not afford them the means of knowing the extent of their risk. Other insurers, whether they
divide the risk, which they generally do, amongst
several different persons, or one insurer undertakes
for the insurance of the whole, always have the amount
of what they are to answer for specified in the policy
of insurance.[1]" On the other hand, Mr. Bell in his
Commentaries has presented an elaborate argument
against the validity of these notices, and upon the inconveniences, to which they give rise. His remarks
will be found worthy of a perusal by every lawyer,
who desires to examine the subject with philosophical
accuracy.[2] However, the validity of these notices

---

1 *Riley* v. *Horne*, 5 Bing. R. 217, 220, 221; see also Ld. Ellenborough's Remarks in *Leeson.* v. *Holt*, 1 Stark. R. 187.
2 1 Bell Com. 473, 474, 475.

seems now established beyond all controversy in the common law; though many learned judges have expressed some regret, that they ever were recognised in Westminster Hall.

§ 555. In further examining this subject it will be proper to consider, first, the nature and effect of these notices; secondly, upon whom they are obligatory; thirdly, the rights and duties of each party in respect to them; fourthly, the effect of fraud and concealment in respect to the goods; fifthly, the degree of liability imposed by law upon the carrier, notwithstanding such notices; and sixthly, what amounts to a waiver, or discharge, on either side, of the obligation of such notices.

§ 556. First. The nature and effect of these notices. It is impossible to lay down any universal rule, as to the construction of them, because they are not generally conceived in the same terms; and each must, therefore, be governed by its own peculiar language, and by the limitations, which are engrafted into it. The general tenor of these notices is to declare, that the carrier will not be responsible for any loss of goods beyond a certain value, unless entered and paid for accordingly. In case there is not such an entry, and payment, it will depend upon the true construction of the terms of the particular notice, whether the carrier will be liable, even to the extent of the fixed value, in case of a loss of goods of greater value and not paid for. Thus, in one case, where the terms of the contract were, that "cash, plate, jewels, &c. would not be accounted for, if lost, of more than £5 value, unless entered as such" and paid for, the Court were of opinion, that the carrier was not liable for any loss whatever, in case the goods exceeded the specified

value, and no entry or payment of the increased value
had been made.[1] And in another case, where the words
were, that " no more than £5 will be accounted for,
for goods," &c. unless the special terms are complied
with, it was decided, that in case of a loss the carrier
might still be held responsible to the value of £5.[2]
It is of great practical importance, therefore, to carriers to fix the terms of their notices in such a manner
as to avoid all ambiguities of this sort; as in all cases
of doubt, they will be construed unfavourably to the
carrier.[3]

§ 557. But the notice in all cases, where it is
brought home to the parties, is, in the absence of all
contravening circumstances, deemed proof of the contract actually subsisting between them; and of course
it varies, *pro tanto*, the general liabilities of the common
law in respect to common carriers. And neither party can under such circumstances be permitted to escape from the obligatory force of the terms of the
notice. It is, then, to be construed like every other
written contract; and so far as its exceptions extend,
they convert the general law into a qualified responsibility.[4] Where a carrier gives notice, that he will not
be liable for goods lost beyond £5, unless paid for,
such notice extends as well to goods of passengers
going by the conveyance, as to goods alone sent by
the same conveyance.[5]

---

1 *Clay* v. *Willan*, 1 H. Black. 298 ; *Izett* v. *Mountain*, 4 East R. 371 ;
Nicholson v. *Willan*, 5 East R. 507 ; *Harris* v. *Packwood*, 3 Taunt. 264 ;
Marsh v. *Horne*, 5 Barn. & Cresw. 322 ; 1 Bell Com. 475.

2 *Clarke* v. *Gray*, 6 East R. 564 ; *Cobden* v. *Bolton*, 2 Camp. R. 108.

3 *Butler* v. *Heane*, 2 Camp. R. 415.

4 *Nicholson* v. *Willan*, 5 East R. 507 ; *Maving* v. *Todd*, 1 Stark. 72 ;
Harris v. *Packwood*, 3 Taunt. R. 271, 272.

5 *Clarke* v. *Gray*, 4 Esp. R. 177 ; S. C. 6 East R. 564 ; but see *Brooke*
v. *Pickwick*, 4 Bing. R. 218.

§ 558. Secondly. Upon whom such notices are obligatory. The mere advertisement by the carrier of the terms and limitations of his responsibility, however public it may be, will have no effect, except upon those, to whom knowledge of it is brought directly or constructively home.[1] Thus it will not be sufficient, that the notice has been publicly posted up in the carrier's office in writing or in print, unless the party, who is to be affected by it, is proved to have read it; or other circumstances are adduced, establishing his knowledge of it.[2] And if the notice is published in a newspaper, it is not sufficient proof, unless accompanied by some evidence, that the party is accustomed to read the newspaper, so as to lay a foundation of implied knowledge.[3] If a carrier has published two different notices, each of which is before the public at the time of the carriage, that will bind him, which is least beneficial to himself; and if at the time of the carriage he delivers a written notice without any limitation of responsibility, that nullifies his prior notice containing a limitation.[4] A notice known to the principal, binds him in respect to all his agents, who send goods by the same carrier; and on the other hand, a notice known to the particular agent, who sends goods, binds the principal in respect to such goods, notwithstanding the principal is personally ignorant of the notice.[5] A notice suspended

---

1 *Davis* v. *Willan*, 2 Stark. 279; *Gibbon* v. *Paynton*, 4 Burr. 2302; *Evans* v. *Soule*, 2 M. & Selw. 1; *Roskell* v. *Waterhouse*, 2 Stark. 462; 1 Bell Com. 475.

2 *Keer* v. *Willan*, 2 Stark. 53; *Davis* v. *Willan*, 2 Stark. 279; *Clayton* v. *Hunt*, 3 Camp. R. 27; *Butler* v. *Heare*, 2 Camp. R. 415; *Evans* v. *Soule*, 2 M. & Selw. 1; *Gibbon* v. *Paynton*, 4 Burr. 2302.

3 *Leeson* v. *Holt*, 1 Stark. R. 186; *Rowley* v. *Horne*, 3 Bing. R. 2; *Munn* v. *Baker*, 2 Stark. 255.

4 *Munn* v. *Baker*, 2 Stark. R. 255; *Cobden* v. *Bolton*, 2 Camp. 108.

5 *Mayhew* v. *Eames*, 3 Barn. & Cres. 601; 1 Car. & Payne 550; *Maving* v. *Todd*, 1 Stark. 72; *Clarke* v. *Hutchins*, 14 East R. 475.

at the offices at the *termini* of the journey will not bind persons, who deliver goods at intermediate places on the route, unless notice is brought home to them.[1]

§ 559. Where several persons are carriers, as partners, and publish a notice, and one of the partners afterwards undertakes, without any communication with, or knowledge of the others, to carry packages for a particular person free from expense, it seems, that such a contract is not binding on the partnership in derogation of their notice, if such act is not within the scope of his authority, or done by connivance in fraud of their rights.[2]

§ 560. In all cases, where the notice cannot be brought home to the person interested in the goods directly or constructively, it is a mere nullity, and the carrier is responsible according to the general principles of the common law.[3]

§ 561. Thirdly. The rights and duties of each party growing out of notices. It may be stated generally, that a carrier, who undertakes to carry goods, is, like every other person, bound to perform his contract in the mode and to the extent involved in his contract. Wherever he undertakes to carry and deliver, he cannot exempt himself from responsibility by transferring the goods to another carrier, or by sending them by another conveyance. His contract is deemed a contract for personal care and diligence by himself or his own servants. If, therefore, the goods are sent by a different conveyance from that implied by the under-

---

[1] *Gouger* v. *Jolly*, Holt N. P. R, 317; *Clayton* v. *Hunt*, 3 Camp. 27.

[2] *Bignold* v. *Waterhouse*, 1 M. & Selw. 255; *Helsby* v. *Mears*, 5 B. & Cresw. 504.

[3] *Brooke* v. *Pickwick*, 4 Bing. R. 218, 222; 1 Bell Com. 475.

taking, or in a different manner, and they are lost, the carrier will be liable for the loss, although otherwise he might have been exonerated from it by the terms of a notice.[1] And the carrier is in like manner responsible if he carried the goods beyond the place of destination and they are lost, although otherwise his notice would protect him.[2]

§ 562. It is also (as has been already stated) a part of the implied contract of every carrier to employ a vehicle suitable for the transportation; and if by water, to employ a vessel reasonably stout, strong, and well equipped for the voyage. And he is not at liberty to tranship the goods in any other vessel in the course of the voyage, except from mere necessity, when his own ship becomes incapable by inevitable casualty from performing it. The existence of the common notice will not in any respect change this implied duty.[3]

§ 563. On the other hand the owner of the goods is bound to observe good faith towards the carrier, (of which more will be said hereafter,) and to pack his goods, and put them in a fit condition for the journey; and if he does not, he must bear any loss arising from his own neglect. But the carrier may himself by implication dispense with an exact performance of part of this duty, and assume upon himself the proper care of securing the property in a fit state for the journey.[4]

---

[1] *Garnett* v. *Willan*, 5 Barn. & Ald. 53; *Sleat* v. *Fagg*, 5 Barn. & Ald. 342; *Nicholson* v. *Willan*, 5 East R. 507; 1 Roll. Abr. 2; C. Pl. 3; *Barnwell* v. *Hussey*, 1 Const. Rep. So. Car. 114.

[2] *Ellis* v. *Turner*, 8 T. R. 531.

[3] Abbott on Shipp. P. 3, ch. 3, §§ 1, 8; *Lyon* v. *Mells*, 5 East, 428; *Evans* v. *Soule*, 2 M. & Selw. 1; Marsh. Insur. B. 1, ch. 7, § 5, p. 249.

[4] *Beck* v. *Evans*, 16 East R. 245; *Stuart* v. *Crawley*, 2 Stark. R. 324.

§ 564. Thus much may suffice in this place as to the general rights and duties of the parties under notices, as the subject will be resumed under the succeeding heads.

§ 565. Fourthly. The effect of concealment or fraud. It is the duty of every person sending goods by a carrier to make use of no fraud or artifice to deceive him, whereby his risk is increased or his care and vigilance may be lessened.[1] And if there is any such fraud or unfair concealment, it will exempt the carrier from responsibility under the contract, or rather it will make the contract a nullity.[2] Thus, where notes, to the amount of £100, were packed in an old mail-bag and stuffed with hay to give it a mean appearance, and in this state were delivered to a carrier, and the bag arrived safe, but the notes were stolen; this concealment was held to be such a fraud upon the carrier, as to discharge him from all responsibility for the loss.[3] In this case there was an artifice made use of in order to mislead the carrier. The doctrine is not confined to mere cases of concealment or suppression of facts for the purpose of misleading; but it applies to all cases of false affirmations having the same object.[4] And wherever the owner represents the contents of the package to be of a particular value, he will not be permitted, in case of a loss, to recover from the carrier any amount beyond that value.[5]

§ 566. How far a bare concealment of the value of a package, without any other circumstances of a sus-

---

1 *Edwards* v. *Sherrath*, 1 East R. 604.

2 *Batson* v. *Donovan*, 4 B. & Ald. 21; 2 Kent Com. 468.

3 *Gibbon* v. *Paynton*, 4 Burr. 2298; 2 Kent Com. 468.

4 *Titchburne* v. *White*, 1 Str. 145.

5 *Tyly* v. *Morrice*, Carth. R. 485; *Batson* v. *Donovan*, 4 B. & Ald. 21; *Riley* v. *Horne*, 5 Bing. R. 217.

picious nature, ought to be deemed of itself an unfair
or fraudulent concealment in cases of carriage generally, or under notices of the nature we have been considering, has been much discussed; and there has not
been a perfect uniformity of judicial opinion upon the
point. Indeed, a question of the same nature has engaged the attention of learned jurists and casuists in
ancient as well as in modern times. In relation to
contracts it has been often mooted, how far a man may
innocently be silent as to any matters, which might
form ingredients in directing the judgment of the other
contracting party. We have already had occasion to
notice a diversity of judgment among the Roman law-
years on a case, where a question of this sort was
incidentally presented.[1] Cicero and Pothier contend
for a liberal good faith and a frank disclosure in all
cases of this sort, and found themselves upon principles of a pure and sublime morality. Sir William
Jones, although he gives no express opinion on the
point, evidently maintains the necessity of a full disclosure of all the facts in the case of a deposit.[2] The
question, however, has more commonly arisen in discussion upon contracts of sale; and it is in those
cases, that Cicero and Pothier have spoken with so
much zeal and persuasive force.* In the forum of con-

---

[1] Ante, § 75.   [2] Jones's Bailm. 38, 39.

* This subject was a good deal discussed in *Laidlow* v. *Organ*,
(2 Wheaton R. 178, 185); and Mr. Wheaton has, in his valuable report of that case, appended a long note, containing the substance of Pothier's remarks on the subject. Mr. Verplank has thought the subject
worthy of a particalar examination in his able " Essay on the Doctrine of
Contracts " (in 1825.) Mr. Chancellor Kent has discussed the subject
with his usual fullness of learning and accuracy of research, and vin-
dicated the present state of the law from any just reproach, as founded
in practical sense and general convenience. 2 Kent Com. 377 to 386.

46

science the question might not perhaps admit of so many doubts. But law, as a practical science, is compelled to stop short of enforcing every moral duty; and aims only at that justice, which, in the business of human life, has general convenience and certainty in its administration. In relation to sales the doctrine now generally maintained is, (as Pothier admits,) that the vendor may be innocently silent, as to any extrinsic circumstances equally open to both parties, which might influence the price of the commodity; but at the same time he must take care not to do or say any thing, which shall tend to mislead or impose upon the other party. [1]

§ 567. In cases of common carriers, where there is no notice, the better opinion seems to be, that the party, who sends the goods, is not bound to disclose their value, unless he is asked. [2] But the carrier has a right to make the inquiry and to have a true answer; and if he is deceived, and a false answer given, he will not be responsible for any loss. If he makes no inquiry, and no artifice is made use of to mislead him, then he is responsible for any loss, however great the value may be. [3]

§ 568. There has been much more doubt, whether the same rule applies to cases of notices. Mr. Justice Best, in *Batson* v. *Donovan*, (4 Barn. & Ald. 17,) was of opinion, that the same rule does apply in cases

---

1 *Laidlow* v. *Organ*, 2 Wheat. R. 178; 2 Kent Com. 377; see also *Etting* v. *Bank of U. S.* 11 Wheat. R. 59; *Pidcock* v. *Bishop*, 3 B. & Cresw. 605; *Smith* v. *Bank of Scotland*, 1 Dav. Parl. R. 272.

2 Jones's Bailm. 105; 2 Kent Com. 468.

3 *Kening* v. *Eggleston*, Aleyn. R. 93; *Morse* v. *Slue*, 1 Vent. 238; *Tyley* v. *Morris*, Carth. 485; *Titchburne* v. *White*, 1 Str. 145; *Gibbons* v. *Paynton*, 4 Burr. 2298; *Riley* v. *Horne*, 5 Bing. R. 217; *Batson* v. *Donovan*, 4 Barn. & Ald. 21.

of notices, and to that opinion he has ever since strenuously adhered.[1]   On the contrary the three other
Judges, who sat in that case, thought, that in cases of
notices the party, who sends the goods without payment for the extraordinary value, holds them out impliedly as articles of ordinary value, and consequently
perpetrates a fraud upon the carrier, who is thus induced not to bestow upon them the care and diligence,
which their extraordinary value would require ; and
under such circumstances the contract itself becomes
a nullity. A distinction, however, has since been suggested by the Court in another and later case, viz. that
the carrier would notwithstanding be liable for malfesance, or for a wrong delivery, although he would not
be liable for any negligence, however gross.[2]   In the
latest case on the subject,[3] in which a very elaborate
judgment was pronounced by Lord Chief Justice Best
for the Court, the inclination of the Court in its general
reasoning seems to be, that the carrier is bound to
make the inquiry, although there is a notice. The
point, however, was not directly in judgment. In
another case [4] the Court of Common Pleas thought,
that a passenger in a coach was not bound to disclose
the value of his baggage, notwithstanding the carrier
had published a notice.

§ 569. However then the doctrine may be in cases
of notices, as to the duty of inquiry on the one side,

---

[1] *Garnet* v. *Willan,* 5 B. & Ald. 53, 63 ; *Riley* v. *Horne,* 5 Bing. R.
217 ; *Brooke* v. *Pickwick,* 4 Bing. R. 218 ; *Sleat* v. *Fagg,* 5 B. & Ald.
342 ; *Bignold* v. *Waterhouse,* 1 M. & Selw. 261.

[2] *Sleat* v. *Fagg,* 5 Barn. & Ald. 342 ; see also *Nicholson* v. *Willan,*
5 East R. 507 ; *Dwight* v. *Brewster,* 1 Pick. R. 50.

[3] *Riley* v. *Horne,* 5 Bing. R. 217.

[4] *Brooke* v. *Pickwick,* 4 Bing. R. 218.

and of non-concealment on the other, all the authorities are agreed, that, if any deception is intentionally practised, the fraud avoids the contract. But a case may exist, where the goods are of an extraordinary value, and not paid for as such; and yet the circumstances may lead to the conclusion, that the carrier has either a direct or presumptive knowledge, that they exceed the common value, and therefore no fraud is in fact perpetrated upon him. Under such circumstances the inquiry is presented, whether the terms of the notice not being complied with, the carrier is answerable for their loss. The Court of King's Bench have held, that the carrier is not under such circumstances responsible for any loss by theft, the goods not having been exposed to more than the ordinary risk. On that occasion the Court said, that there is no incongruity in a carrier's engaging to place goods in a course of conveyance and declaring at the same time, that he will not be answerable for the loss of them; and upon the terms of the notice, if the carrier had delivered the goods in question, he would not have been entitled to more than the common compensation for the carriage of goods exclusive of the risk of loss.[1] There are antecedent cases, which seem to look the other way.[2] Whether those cases are now to be deemed wholly overruled, may perhaps be thought to deserve further inquiry. The doctrine, however, clearly does not apply to any case, where there has been a waiver of the notice.

---

[1] *Marsh* v. *Horne*, 5 B. & Cresw. 322; see also *Harris* v. *Packwood,* 3 Taunt. 264; *Levi* v. *Waterhouse,* 1 Price R. 280; *Thoroughgood* v. *Marsh*, 1 Gow. R. 105; *Alfred* v. *Horne*, 3 Stark. 136.

[2] *Beck* v. *Evans,* 16 East R. 244; S. C. 3 Camp. R. 267; *Doun* v. *Fromont,* 4 Camp. R. 40; but see *Brooke* v. *Pickwick,* 4 Bing. R. 218; 1 Bell Com. 475.

§ 570. Fifthly. The degree of liability, which is imposed upon the carrier notwithstanding such notices. In the first place, it is clear, that such notices will not exempt the carrier from any losses by the malfesance, misfesance, or gross negligence of himself or his servants. If, therefore, he or they convert the goods to a wrong use ; if he or they make a wrong delivery to a person not entitled to them ; or if he or they are guilty of gross negligence in the carriage or care of them, the loss must be borne by the carrier, notwithstanding his notice, for the terms are uniformly construed not to exempt him from such losses.[1]

§ 571. But an inquiry may be made, whether he will not also be liable for ordinary as well as for gross negligence. That point does not appear to have been settled by any positive adjudication. There are *dicta* by various judges indicating, that the common rule of ordinary diligence in the common cases of hire is applicable to the case of carriers under notices.[2] But until some more solemn decision it can hardly be deemed settled, especially as the declarations of the judges at *nisi prius*, as well as in *banc*, are almost uniformly pointed to the question of gross negligence or not.[3] One of the latest cases on the subject seems to hold, that gross negligence must be established to affect the carrier with the loss.[4]

---

[1] *Beck* v. *Evans*, 16 East 244 ; *Smith* v. *Horne*, 8 Taunt. 144 ; *Bodenham* v. *Bennett*, 4 Price, 31 ; *Birkett* v. *Willan*, 2 B. & Ald. 356 ; *Garnett* v. *Willan*, 5 B. & Ald. 53 ; *Sleat* v. *Fagg*, 5 B. & Ald. 342 ; *Ellis* v. *Turner*, 8 T. R. 531 ; *Lyon* v. *Mells*, 5 East R. 439 ; *Duff* v. *Budd*, 3 Bro. & Bing. 177 ; 1 Bell Com. 475.

[2] *Bodenham* v. *Bennett*, 4 Price R. 31 ; *Smith* v. *Horne*, 8 Taunt. R. 144 ; *Batson* v. *Donovan*, 4 B. & Ald. 21 ; Best J. 1 Bell Com. 475.

[3] *Riley* v. *Horne*, 5 Bing. R. 217 ; *Batson* v. *Donovan*, 4 B. & Ald. 21 ; *Brooke* v. *Pickwick*, 4 Bing. R. 218.

[4] *Lowe* v. *Booth*, 13 Price R. 329.

§ 572. Sixthly. What amounts to a waiver of the notice. In some of the cases cited under a former head[1] it seems to have been thought, that the mere receipt of goods, whose apparent value was beyond the sum in the notice, without any extra-payment therefor, was a waiver of the notice.[2] But the later doctrine seems to exclude any presumption founded merely upon the knowledge of that fact, and requires some auxiliary circumstance to support it.[3] If, however, the carrier is told what is the value of the goods, and is directed to charge what he pleases, and he chooses to charge only the ordinary hire, it is a waiver of the notice as to the goods.[4] So an express agreement to carry a package of extraordinary value for the common hire will be a waiver of the notice, even if made by one partner only, if it be within the scope of his authority.[5]

§ 573. This head respecting notices may be concluded by stating, that in cases of notice the burthen of proof of negligence is on the party, who sends the goods, and not of due diligence on the part of the carrier; which is contrary to the general rule in cases of carriers, where there is no notice.[6]

§ 574. Seventhly. The next inquiry is, what will excuse or justify a non-delivery of the goods by a common carrier. From what has been said it is a sufficient excuse or justification for him to show, that, without

---

[1] Ante, § 567.

[2] 16 East R. 244 ; 4 Camp. 40 ; 4 Bing. R. 218.

[3] *Marsh* v. *Horne*, 5 Barn. & Cres. 322.

[4] *Evans* v. *Soule*, 2 M. & Selw. 1 ; *Wilson* v. *Freeman*, 3 Camp. 527.

[5] *Helsby* v. *Mears*, 5 B. & Cres. 504.

[6] *Marsh* v. *Horne*, 5 B. & Cresw. 322, 327 ; *Riley* v. *Horne*, 5 Bing. R. 217, 226.

any negligence on his part, the goods have been lost by the act of God or of the king's enemies; and in cases of special limitations of responsibility by notices or otherwise, that the loss has been by other perils, against which he did not insure, or under circumstances, which do not affect him with the imputation of undue negligence. Under the ordinary contract of common carriers the burthen of proof of the excuse or justification lies on him; but in cases of notices (as has been already seen [1]) the burthen of proof of negligence rests on the party, who delivers the goods.

§ 575. But there are also cases, where the carrier's own agency is concerned in the loss, which however is by law deemed excusable. Thus, in cases of throwing overboard goods to lighten a ship or boat, and preserve life, the carrier will be excused, if it has arisen from necessity.[2] Thus, if a ferryman was, in a storm, to throw overboard even a box of jewels, if it was done from absolute necessity to save life, he would stand excused.[3] But if it was done without necessity, or rashly and imprudently, it would be otherwise.[4]

§ 576. A carrier may also show in his defence, that the goods have perished by some internal defect without any fault on his side; for his warranty does not extend to such cases. And if, from the nature of the goods carried, they are liable to peculiar risks, and the carrier takes all reasonable care, and uses all proper

---

1 Ante, § 573.

2 Abbott on Shipp. P. 3, ch. 8, § 2, 3, 4; 2 Kent Com. 468.

3 *Mouse's case*, 12 Co. R. 63; *Smith* v. *Wright*, 1 Cain R. 43; 2 Kent Com. 468.

4 *Bancroft's case*, Aleyn. R. 93; Jones's Bailm. 107; 2 Bulst. 280; 2 Roll. Abr. 567.

precautions to prevent injuries, and notwithstanding if they are destroyed by such risks, he is excusable. Thus, if horses or other animals are carried by water, and in consequence of a storm they break down the partitions between them, and by kicking each other some are killed, the carrier will be excused; and it will be deemed a loss by perils of the sea.[1]

§ 577. In respect to the carriage of slaves, a question has been made, how far the carrier incurs the common law responsibility. A slave has volition and has feelings, which cannot be entirely disregarded. These properties cannot be overlooked in conveying him from place to place. He cannot be stowed away like a common package. Not only does humanity forbid this proceeding, but it might endanger his life and health. Consequently this rigorous mode of proceeding cannot be safely adopted, unless stipulated for by express contract. The slave being at liberty to escape may escape. The carrier has not and cannot have the same absolute control over him, that he has over inanimate matter. In the nature of things and in his character he resembles a passenger, and not a package of goods. It would seem reasonable therefore, that the responsibility of the carrier should be measured by the law, which is applicable to passengers, rather than by that, which is applicable to the carriage of common goods. For these reasons it has been held, that the doctrine of common carriers as to goods does not apply to the case of slaves, and that the carrier is liable for ordinary neglect only.[2] Therefore, where certain slaves in the

---

1 *Gabay* v. *Lloyd*, 3 Barn. & Cresw. 793; *Lawrence* v. *Aberdeen*, 5 Barn. & Ald. 107.

2 *Boyce* v. *Anderson*, 2 Peters's Sup. Ct. R. 150.

yawl of a steam-boat carrier were upset and drowned, it was decided, that the carrier was not responsible for the loss, unless it was caused by the negligence or un-skilfulness of himself or his agents.[1]

§ 578. A non-delivery will also be excused by any act of the shipper, which discharges the carrier from any further responsibility.[2] As, if with the consent of the shipper he delivers them over to another carrier, or deposits them at an intermediate place to await the future orders of the shipper; or if the shipper takes them into the exclusive custody of himself or his own servants.[3] But it will be otherwise, if he merely ac-companies them in their transit, not exercising any ex-clusive custody.[4]

§ 579. In like manner the carrier will be excused for a non-delivery, if it has been occasioned by the il-legal act of the shipper. Thus, if the goods have been forfeited by the illegal act of the shipper, and are seized for the forfeiture, the carrier is discharged. But a mere seizure for a supposed forfeiture, if in fact without cause, leaves the carrier still bound by his contract.[5]

§ 580. But an excuse, which in a practical sense is much more important and extensive, is that resulting from the right of the shipper to stop the goods in the possession of the carrier, while they are still in transit.

---

[1] *Boyce* v. *Anderson*, 2 Peters's Sup. Ct. R. 150.

[2] Ibid ; *Gregson* v. *Gilbert*, Park. Insur. 83.

[3] Ante, p. 341 ; *Sparrow* v. *Carruthers*, 2 Str. R. 1236 ; *Hurry* v. *Royal Exc. Assur. Co.* 2 Bos. & Pull. 430 ; *Rucker* v. *London Assur.* Marsh. Insur. B. 1, ch. 7, § 5, p. 252, &c.; *Bamvall* v. *Hussy*, 1 Cons. R. So. Car. 114 ; *East India Co.* v. *Pullen*, 1 Str. 690 ; *Saunderson* v. *Lamberton*, 6 Binn. R. 129 ; *Strong* v. *Natally*, 4 Bos. & Pull. 16.

[4] *Robinson* v. *Dunmore*, 2 Bos. & Bull. 419 ; Roll. Abr. 2. C. Pl. 3 ; Marshall Insur. B. 1, ch. 7, § 5, p. 252, &c.

[5] *Gosling* v. *Higgins*, 1 Camp. R. 451.

This right is commonly called in common law the right of stoppage *in transitu*. When it arises, and is properly exercised, the carrier is completely discharged from all further responsibility.

§ 581. This is not the place for a full discussion of this subject, as it belongs more appropriately to another branch of commercial and maritime jurisprudence. It may, however, be useful to state some few particulars, which respect it. When goods are shipped on a credit by a seller or consignor, and the consignee or buyer becomes insolvent, or has failed before their arrival, the law, in order to prevent the loss, that would happen to the seller or consignor, allows him in many cases to countermand the delivery before the arrival of the goods at the place of destination, and to cause them to be re-delivered to himself, or to some other person appointed to act for him. In such a case the delivery to the carrier is supposed to vest the title to the property in the buyer, subject only to this right of devestment *in transitu*. The right, however, is (as will be at once perceived) not an unlimited right. It exists only in cases, where all the following circumstances concur; where the goods are sold on a credit; where the consignee is insolvent; where the goods are still in transit; and where the buyer has not yet parted with his ownership to any *bonâ fide* purchaser under him. Each of these requisites is important enough to deserve a separate discussion in its proper place; and especially the question, under what circumstances the transit is or is not at an end, which is full of nice distinctions and curious learning. At present no more is necessary than to bestow this hasty glance upon them.[1]

---

[1] Abbott on Shipp. P. 3, ch. 9, per tot.

§ 582. Another excuse is, when the goods are demanded or taken from the possession of the carrier by some person having a superior title to the property. It is generally true, that the carrier cannot dispute the title of the person, who delivers the goods to him, or set up an adverse title to defeat his right of action growing out of the contract.[1]   But this is true only, when that adverse claim is not asserted by the superior claimant himself, but merely by the carrier of his own motion.   Where the adverse title is made known to the carrier, if he is forbidden to deliver the goods to any other person, he acts at his peril; and if the adverse title is well founded, and he resists it, he is liable to an action for the recovery of the goods.[2]

§ 583. Eighthly. The doctrine of average and contribution. This principally arises in cases of jettison and other accidents in the transportation of goods by sea. In such cases, where goods are thrown overboard for the common benefit, or other positive sacrifices are made, or expenses incurred for the same purpose, the law allows a compensation to those, who have made the sacrifice, and have incurred the loss or expense, and they may demand a *pro ratâ* contribution from all other persons deriving a benefit therefrom, according to their interest, towards the loss or expense. This, in cases of accidents at sea, is called a general average, or general contribution, in which ship, cargo, and freight are compelled to contribute according to their value to repay the common loss.   But the

---

[1] 3 Esp. R. 115.
[2] *Taylor* v. *Plummer*, 3 M. & Selw. 562; *Wilson* v. *Alderton*, 1 Barr. & Adolp. 450.

full discussion of this subject properly belongs to a treatise on the law of shipping.[1]

§ 584. Carriers on land may also entitle themselves, if not to a common contribution in the nature of a general average, at least to a compensation for expenses necessarily incurred about the preservation of the goods from extraordinary perils, not properly belonging to themselves as carriers. Thus, if a sudden flood or storm should do injury to the goods, and require some immediate expense for their preservation, the carrier would be bound to incur it, and would be entitled to a reimbursement.

§ 585. Ninthly. The general rights of carriers. In virtue of the delivery of the goods they acquire a special property in them, and may maintain an action against any person, who displaces that possession or does any injury to them. This right arises from their general interest in conveying the goods, and their responsibility for any loss or injury to them during their transit.[2] And having once acquired the lawful possession of the goods for the purpose of carriage, the carrier is not obliged to restore them to the owner again, even if the carriage is dispensed with, unless upon being paid his due remuneration ; for by the delivery he has already incurred risks.[3]

§ 586. A carrier is in all cases entitled to demand the price of carriage before he receives the goods, and

---

[1] Abbott on Shipp. P. 3, ch. 8; Stevens on Average, Bencoke on Insurance, Park on Insurance, and Marshall on Insurance, in their chapters on General Average.

[2] Bac. Abr. Carrier C ; Jones's Bailm. 80 ; *Goodwin* v. *Richardson*, Roll. Abr. 5; 1 Ld. Raym. 278; *Wilhusan* v. *Snow*, 1 Vent. 52 ; 2 Saund. R. 476 ; 2 Saund. R. 47 c, note.

[3] *Bradstreet* v. *Columbian Ins. Co.* 9 Johns. R. 17 ; *Herbert* v. *Hallett*, 3 Johns. Cas. 93.

if not paid, he may refuse to take charge of them. If, however, he takes charge of them without the hire being paid, he may afterwards recover it.[1]

§ 587. The compensation, which becomes due for the carriage of goods by sea, is commonly called *freight;* and the circumstances, under which the whole or a part only of the freight is earned, forms a head of great practical importance under the law of shipping. It will accordingly be found treated at large in professed treatises on that subject.[2]

§ 588. The carrier is also entitled to a lien on the goods for his hire, and is not compellable to deliver them until he receives it, unless he has entered into some special contract, by which it is waived.[3] His lien may also be defeated by giving up the possession of the goods ; and if it is once waived, it cannot afterwards be resumed.[4]

§ 589. The consignor or shipper is ordinarily bound to the carrier for the hire or freight of the goods.[5] But whenever the consignee engages to pay it, he also may become responsible. It is usual for bills of lading to state, that the goods are to be delivered to the consignee or to his assigns, he or they paying freight ; in which case the consignee and his assigns by accept-

---

[1] *Wright* v. *Snell,* 5 Barn. & Ald. 353; *Jackson* v. *Rogers,* 2 Show. 327; *Morse* v. *Slue,* 1 Vent. 238; *Batson* v. *Donovan,* 4 Barn. & Ald. 32; 1 Saund. R. by Will. 312 *a.*

[2] Abbott on Shipp. P. 3, ch. 7.

[3] *Skimer* v. *Upsham,* 1 Ld. Raym. 752; *Sodergren* v. *Flight,* 6 East R. 662; *Hutton* v. *Bragg,* 2 Marsh. R. 345; *Stevenson* v. *Blacklock,* 1 M. & Selw. 543; *Chase* v. *Westmore,* 5 M. & Selw. 186; *Crawshay* v. *Homfrey,* 4 B. & Ald. 50; *Rushforth* v. *Hadfield,* 6 East 522; 2 Kent Com. 497, 498.

[4] *Kinloch* v. *Craig,* 3 T. R. 119; *Sweet* v. *Pym,* 1 East R. 4; *Yates* v. *Railston,* 8 Taunt. 293; 2 Kent Com. 497, 498.

[5] *Moore* v. *Wilson,* 1 T. R. 659.

ing the goods become by implication bound to pay the freight.[1] And the fact, that the consignor is also liable to pay the freight, will not in such a case make any difference.[2]

ART. IX.   CARRIERS OF PASSENGERS.

§ 590. Having considered the rights, duties, and obligations of carriers of goods for hire, we may now pass to the consideration of those of CARRIERS OF PASSENGERS. It has been already stated, that carriers of passengers merely for hire are not subject to the same responsibility as carriers of goods for hire at the common law.[3] Attempts have been made to extend their responsibility to all losses and injuries, except those arising from the act of God, or public enemies. But it has been uniformly resisted by the Courts, though a strict responsibility is imposed on them.[4] It may be useful, however, to consider somewhat more at large, than has yet been done, their duties, liabilities, and rights. And first, of PASSENGER CARRIERS ON LAND.

§ 591. (1.) Their duties in the commencement of the journey. The first and most general obligation on their part is to carry passengers whenever they offer themselves and are ready to pay for their transportation. This results from their setting themselves up, like innkeepers, farriers, and other carriers, for com-

---

[1] Abbott on Shipp. P. 3, ch. 7, § 4; *Dougal* v. *Kemble,* 3 Bing. R. 383.

[2] Abbott, ibid; *Dougal* v. *Kemble,* 3 Bing. R. 383; *Moorsom* v. *Kymer,* 2 M. & Selw. 303; *Barker* v. *Haven,* 17 Johns. R. 234.

[3] Ante, § 498; 1 Bell Com. 468, 475.

[4] *Aston* v. *Heaven,* 2 Esp. R. 533.

mon public employmeñt.   They are no more at liberty to refuse a passenger, if they have sufficient room and accommodation, than an innkeeper has a guest.[1] If several persons have contracted to go in company inside, the carriers have no right to separate them into different parts of the coach outside and inside.[2]

§ 592. In the next place they are bound to provide coaches reasonably strong and sufficient for the journey, with suitable harness, trappings, and equipments; and to make a proper examination thereof previous to each journey.[3]

§ 593. In the next place they are bound to provide careful drivers of reasonable skill and good habits for the journey; and to employ horses, which are steady, and not vicious, or likely to endanger the safety of the passengers.[4] In the pithy language of an eminent Judge it may be said, that " the coachman must have competent skill; he must be well acquainted with the road he undertakes to drive; he must be provided with steady horses, a coach and harness of sufficient strength and properly made, and also with lights by night. If there is the least failure in any of those things, the duty of the coach-proprietors is not fulfilled, and they are responsible for any injury or damage, that happens."[5]

---

[1] *Bretherton* v. *Wood*, 3 Brod. & Bing. 54; 9 Price R. 408; 6 Moore R. 141; *Ansell* v. *Waterhouse*, 2 Chitty R. 1; *Mersiter* v. *Cooper*, 4 Esp. R. 260; 1 Bell Com. 462.

[2] *Long* v. *Horne*, 1 Carr. & Payne, 610.

[3] *Bremner* v. *Williams*, 1 Carr. & Payne, 144; *Crofts* v. *Waterhouse*, 3 Bing. 321; *Jones* v. *Joyce*, 1 Stark. 493; *Christie* v. *Griggs*, 2 Camp. R. 80; 1 Bell Com. 462.

[4] *Waland* v. *Elkins*, 1 Stark. R. 272; *Christie* v. *Griggs*, 2 Camp. R. 79; *Harris* v. *Costar*, 1 Carr. & Payne, 636; *Crofts* v. *Waterhouse*, 3 Bing. R. 321.

[5] Per Best C. J. in *Crofts* v. *Waterhouse*, 3 Bing. R. 314, 321; 1 Bell Com. 462.

§ 594. In the next place they are bound not to overload the coach either with passengers or luggage; and to take care, that the weight is suitably adjusted, so that the coach is not top-heavy and made liable to overset.[1]

§ 595. In the next place they are bound to receive and to take care of the usual luggage, which it is customary to allow every passenger to carry for the journey.[2]

§ 596. And in all these cases they are not only personally bound for their own acts, but for the acts of their servants and agents in their employ, and also, in cases of partnership, for the acts of their partners.[3]

§ 597. (2.) Their duties on the progress of the journey. Passenger-carriers are bound to stop at the usual places, and allow the usual intervals for refreshment of the passengers; and they cannot at their mere caprice vary or annul these accommodations; for every passenger is understood to contract for the usual reasonable accommodations.[4]

§ 598. They are bound to make use of all the ordinary precautions for the safety of passengers on the road.[5] This involves a consideration of the duties of the coachman in driving on the road. If he is guilty of any rashness, negligence, or misconduct, or is unskilful, or deviates from the acknowledged custom of the road, the proprietors will be responsible for any injury resulting from his acts. Thus, if the driver drives

---

1 *Long* v. *Horne,* 1 Carr. & Payne, 612; *Israel* v. *Clark,* 4 Esp. R. 259; *Aston* v. *Heaven,* 2 Esp. R. 533; *Heard* v. *Mountain,* 5 Petersd. Abr. Carriers, p. 54; 1 Bell Com. 462.

2 *Robinson* v. *Dunmore,* 2 Bos. & Pull. 419; 4 Esp. 177; 6 East, 564.

3 *Waland* v. *Elkins,* 1 Stark. R. 272; Holt's N. P. 227.

4 5 Petersd. Abr. Carriers, p. 48, note.

5 1 Bell Com. 462.

with reins so loose, that he cannot govern his horses, the proprietors of the coach will be answerable.[1] So, if there is danger in a part of the road, or in a particular passage, and he omits to give due warning to the passengers.[2] So, if he takes the wrong side of the road, and an accident happens from want of proper room.[3] So, if by any incaution he comes in collision with another carriage.[4] In short, he must in all cases exercise a sound and reasonable discretion in travelling on the road, to avoid dangers and difficulties, and if he omits it, his principals are liable.[5] And the liability of the coach proprietors will be the same, although the injury to the passenger is caused by his own act, as by leaping from the coach, if there is real danger, and it arises from the careless conduct of the driver.[6]

§ 599. There are in England three customary rules or directions for driving; first, that in meeting each party shall bear or keep to the left. The rule in America is the reverse, that each party shall bear or keep to the right. Secondly, that in passing, the foremost person bearing to the left, the other shall pass on the off side. Thirdly, that in crossing, the driver shall bear to the left hand and pass behind the other carriage.[7] But the rule in England is not inflexible, that the driver shall in all cases pass another carriage on the

---

[1] *Aston* v. *Heaven*, 2 Esp. R. 533.

[2] *Dudley* v. *Smith*, 1 Camp. R. 167.

[3] *Wordsworth* v. *Willan*, 4 Esp. R. 273; *Waland* v. *Elkins*, 1 Stark. 272.

[4] *Mayhew* v. *Boyce*, 1 Stark. R. 423; *Dudley* v. *Smith*, 1 Camp. R. 167.

[5] *Jackson* v. *Tollett*, 2 Stark. R. 37.

[6] *Jones* v. *Boyce*, 1 Stark. R. 493; *Crofts* v. *Waterhouse*, 3 Bing. R. 321.

[7] 5 Petersd. Abr. Carrier, p. 55, note; and see *Wayde* v. *Carr*, 2 Dow & Ryl. 255.

off side.   He may, if the street or road is very broad,
go on the near side.[1]   So, if there is no other carriage
on the road, whose passage may be interrupted, the
driver is not bound to keep the left side of the road
according to the rule of the road.   In such cases he
may go on either side of the road, as he pleases.[2]   And
if the driver is on the wrong side of the road, the carrier is not answerable for any accident, unless there is
some negligence on the part of the driver.[3]

600. (3.) The termination of the journey.   In all
cases the coach proprietors are bound to carry the
passengers to the end of the journey, and to put them
down at the usual place of stopping ; and if that is an
inn-yard, it is not sufficient to put them down on the
outside of the gateway of the inn.[4]   If they agree to
take a passenger to a particular place, this also becomes obligatory on them.[5]   And if the custom of the
coach is to carry the passengers to their own houses
or lodgings in a particular place, that must be conformed to.

§ 601. Next, as to the liabilities of passenger-carriers.
These naturally flow from their duties.   As they are
not, like common carriers of goods, insurers against all
injuries except by the act of God, or public enemies,
the inquiry is naturally presented, what is the nature
and extent of their responsibility.   It is certain, that
their undertaking is not an undertaking absolutely to
convey safely.   They are bound only to *due* care and

---

1 Ibid ; *Wordsworth* v. *Willan*, 4 Esp. R. 273.
2 *Aston* v. *Heaven*, 2 Esp. R. 533 ; *Mayhew* v. *Boyce*, 1 Stark. R.
423.
3 *Crofts* v. *Waterhouse*, 3 Bing. R. 319, 321.
4 *Dudley* v. *Smith*, 1 Camp. R. 167.
5 *Ker* v. *Mountain*, 1 Esp. R. 27.

diligence in the performance of their duty.[1] But in what manner are we to measure this due care and diligence? Is it ordinary care and diligence, which will make them liable only for ordinary neglect? Or is it extraordinary care and diligence, which will render them liable for slight neglect? As they undertake for the carriage of human beings, whose lives and limbs and health are of great importance as well to the public as to themselves, the ordinary principles in criminal cases, where persons are made liable for personal wrongs and injuries arising from slight neglect, would seem to furnish the true analogy and rule. It has been accordingly held, that the passenger-carrier binds himself to carry safely those, whom he takes into his coach, *as far as human care and foresight will go*,[2] that is, for the utmost care and diligence of very cautious persons.

§ 602. But passenger-carriers, not being insurers, are not responsible for accidents, where all reasonable skill and diligence has been employed. When every thing has been done, which human prudence can suggest, accidents may happen. The lights may in a dark night be obscured by fog; the horses may be frightened; the coachman may be deceived by the sudden alteration of objects on the road; the coach may be upset accidentally by striking another vehicle or meeting with an unexpected obstruction; in all these and the like cases, if there is no negligence, the coach proprietors are exonerated.[3]

---

1 *Harris* v. *Costar*, 1 Carr. & Payne, 636; *Crofts* v. *Waterhouse*, 3 Bing. R. 321.

2 *Aston* v. *Heaven*, 2 Esp. R. 533; *Christie* v. *Griggs*, 2 Camp. R. 79; *White* v. *Boulton*, Peake R. 80; 1 Bell Com. 562.

3 *Crofts* v. *Waterhouse*, 3 Bing. R, 319, 321; *Christie* v. *Griggs*, 2 Camp. R. 79; *Aston* v. *Heaven*, 2 Esp. R. 533.

§ 603. The rights of passenger-carriers. As they
are under obligations to carry passengers, and cannot
properly refuse them, when they have accommodations, so on the other hand they are entitled to be secure of their reward or compensation. They have,
therefore, a right to demand and to receive their fare
at the time when the passenger engages his seat; and
if he refuses, they may fill up the place with other passengers, who are ready to make the proper deposit.[1]

§ 604. The passenger-carrier also has a lien upon
the baggage of the passenger for his fare or passage-
money; but not on the person of the passenger, or
the clothes he has on.[2]

§ 605. Secondly, The rights, duties, and liabilities
of PASSENGER CARRIERS BY WATER. In the preceding remarks our attention has been principally drawn
to the conduct of passenger-carriers on land. But
there are some rules of an analogous nature, which
have been adopted for the regulation and government
of PASSENGER AND CARRIER VESSELS in inland navigation, as well as upon the ocean, which deserve notice, as they may furnish grounds of responsibility or
excuse for losses, which have arisen in the course of
their voyages, from the accidents or collisions or ri-
valries of navigation.

§ 606. Thus, in New York various positive regulations have been adopted by the legislature in regard
to the conduct of canal boats; and if the master of any
boat deviates from them and any injury occurs, he and
the owners will not only be liable to the statute penalties, but they will also be bound to make good all

---

[1] *Ker* v. *Mountain*, 1 Esp. R. 27.
[2] Abbott on Shipp. P. 3, ch. 3, § 11; *Wolf* v. *Sumners*, 2 Camp. R.
631.

losses and injuries sustained thereby. It seems to be
a general regulation, that freight-boats shall afford every facility to the passage of packet or passenger boats,
as well through the locks as every where else on the
canal.   Therefore, if a packet-boat arrives at a lock
while a freight-boat is waiting for it to be emptied, the
freight-boat is bound to yield the first passage into the
lock to the packet-boat.   And if, by any undue resistance on the part of the freight-boat, an injury occurs,
it must be borne by the master and owners of the
latter.[1]

§ 607. The conduct of carrier-vessels on the ocean
has in several instances come under the examination of
judicial tribunals; and a law of the sea, as well as a
law of the road, has been recognised, as to their rights
and duties.   The Court of Admiralty has a general
jurisdiction in what are technically called cases of collision, that is, cases, where damages have been occasioned by the running foul or collision of two vessels
on the ocean.   And as the Court of Admiralty is the
only tribunal sitting in countries under the jurisprudence of the common law, which can ordinarily administer a remedy *in rem*, and hold the offending vessel itself liable for the payment of the damages, questions of this nature have been of more frequent occurrence in that Court than elsewhere.[2]

§ 608. According to Lord STOWELL, there are
four possibilities, under which accidents of this sort
may occur. In the first place it may happen without
blame being imputed to either party; as where the

---

[1] *Farnsworth* v. *Groot*, 6 Cowen R. 698.

[2] *The Thames*, 5 Rob. 308; *The Neptune*, 1 Dodson R. 467; *The Woodrop Sims*, 2 Dodson R. 83; *The Dundee*, 1 Hagg. R. 109; *Gale* v. *Laurie*, 5 B. & Cres. 156.

loss is occasioned by a storm or any other *vis major*. In that case the loss must be borne by the party, on whom it happens to light; the other not being responsible to him in any degree. Secondly, a misfortune of this kind may arise, where both parties are to blame, where there has been a want of due diligence or of skill on both sides. In such a case the rule of law is, that the loss must be apportioned between them, as having been occasioned by the fault of both of them. Thirdly, it may happen by the misconduct of the suffering party only; and then the rule is, that the sufferer must bear his own burthen. Lastly, it may have been the fault of the ship, which ran down the other; and in this case the injured party would be entitled to an entire compensation from the other.[1] The ancient general maritime law exacted a full compensation out of all the property of the owners of the guilty ship, upon the common principle applying to persons undertaking the conveyance of goods, that they were answerable for the conduct of the persons, whom they employed; and of whom the other parties, who suffered damage, knew nothing, and over whom they had no control. To this rule England for a long time conformed; but Holland having for the protection of its own navigation limited the remedy to the value of the ship, freight, apparel, and furniture, England has recently followed the example, and established by statute a like limitation.[2] In America, no positive enactment has been made; and therefore the responsibility of the

---

[1] I quote the very language of Lord Stowell in *The Woodrop Sims*, 2 Dodson R. 83, 85; see also 1 Bell Com. 579, 580, 581.

[2] Statute 53 Geo. 3, ch. 159; *The Dundee*, 1 Hagg. Adm. R. 109; *Gale v. Laurie*, 5 B. & Cres. 156; *The Catharine of Dover*, 2 Hagg. Adm. R. 145.

vessel and its owners stands upon the general maritime law.

§ 609. Another case has been put by a learned commentator upon commercial law.[1] It is where there has been some fault or neglect; but on which side the blame lies is inscrutable, or left by the evidence in a state of uncertainty. In such cases, many of the maritime states of continental Europe, have adopted the rule to apportion the loss between the two vessels.[2] In the Scottish law this point seems left undetermined; although one of her early jurists has considered .the rule to be the same as the rule of apportionment on the continent.[3] The English law, at the time when Mr. Bell published the last edition of his Commentaries, had not furnished any authority either for or against the rule.[4] In a recent case of collision, however, Sir Christopher Robinson, in summing up the facts to the masters of Trinity House, whom he had called to his assistance, made the following remarks: "The result of the evidence will be one of three alternatives; either a conviction on your mind, that the loss was occasioned by accident, in which case it must be sustained by the party, on whom it has fallen; *or a state of reasonable doubt as to the preponderance of evidence, which will have nearly the same effect;* or third, a conviction, that the party charged with being the cause of the accident is justly chargeable with the loss of this vessel, according to the rules of navigation, which ought to have governed them."[5] It is not perhaps quite certain, whether the learned

---

1 Mr. Bell; 1 Bell Com. 579.
2 1 Bell Com. 579 to 582, and the authorities there cited.
3 Ibid.   4 Ibid.
5 *The Catherine of Dover*, 2 Hagg. R. 145, 154.

Judge had in his mind at the moment a case, where there was a collision by some fault, but it was uncertain by which party, when he speaks of "a state of reasonable doubt, as to the preponderance of evidence," or whether he applied that language to a doubt, whether it was a loss by *accident* or not; though the former would seem to be the natural construction. If his language was meant to apply to a case of inscrutable fault or blame, then the rule in England would seem to be not to apportion in a case of loss by inscrutable fault or blame. If it was meant to apply merely to the question of accident, then the rule is still open to controversy in England. If the question is still open to controversy, there is great cogency in the reasoning of Mr. Bell in favour of adopting the rule of apportioning the loss between the parties.[1] Many learned jurists support the justice and equity of such a rule; and especially it has the strong aid of Pothier and Emerigon.[2]

§ 610. In the civil law, in cases of loss by pure accident, or by the act of God, the same rule existed as in the common law, that the loss must be borne by the sufferer according to the maxim, that it falls, where it lights.[3] Mr. Bell seems in his text to incline to the opinion, that the same rule pervades and has pervaded the maritime and municipal codes of all nations; and that the rule of apportionment to be found in any of those codes, applied only to cases of mutual fault, or of inscrutable fault.[4] That the rule of the civil law was adopted into the maritime codes of many nations,

1 1 Bell Com. 581.
2 Pothier, Avaries, n. 155; 1 Emerig. Assur. ch. 12, § 14.
3 Dig. Lib. 9, tit. 2, l. 29, §§ 2, 4; 1 Bell Com. 580.
4 1 Bell Com. 580, 581, and notes.

cannot admit of a doubt. That it was adopted into all, or that it now pervades all, is by no means clear. Mr. Abbott entertains a different opinion on this point from Mr. Bell, and says, that by the law of most of the continental nations of Europe the injury done by one vessel to another or its cargo, without fault in the persons belonging to either ship, is to be equally borne by the owners of the two vessels;[1] and Mr. Marshall expresses the same opinion.[2] Mr. Bell, however, has the support of many learned jurists on his side.[3]

§ 611. In all these cases of collision the essential question is, whether proper measures of precaution are taken by the vessel, which has unfortunately run down the other. This is partly a question of nautical usage, and partly a question of nautical skill. If all the usual and customary precautions are taken, then it is treated as an accident, and the vessel is exonerated. If otherwise, then the offending vessel and its owners are deemed responsible. Some rules, however, which probably had their origin in the customs of navigation, are now adopted as positive rules of law. Thus, the law imposes upon the vessel, having the wind free, the obligation of taking proper measures to get out of the way of a vessel, that is close hauled, and of showing, that it has done so ; otherwise the owners will be responsible for any loss, which ensues.[4] Therefore, a vessel sailing *with* the wind must give way to one sailing *by* the wind ; and the vessel sailing *by* the wind

---

[1] Abbott on Shipp. P. 3, ch. 8, § 12.

[2] Marshall on Insur. B. 1, ch. 12, § 2.

[3] 1 Bell Com. 580, 581, and notes, ibid. ; Pothier, Avaries, n. 155 ; 1 Emerig. Assur. ch. 12, § 14 ; 3 Kent Com. 184.

[4] *The Woodrop Sims*, 2 Dodson R. 83; 3 Kent Com. 184; *The Thames*, 5 Rob. 345 ; 1 Bell Com. 580.

is not obliged to alter her course.[1]   Another rule is,
that the master of a vessel entering a port or river,
where other vessels are lying at anchor, is bound to
make use of all proper checks to stop the head-way
of his vessel in order to prevent accidents; and if
from want of such precautions a loss ensues, he and
his owners will be responsible.[2]   Another rule is, that
when vessels are crossing each other in opposite
directions, and there is the least doubt of their going
clear, the vessel on the starboard tack is to persevere
in her course, while that on the larboard is to bear up,
or keep more away before the wind.[3]   And in respect
to steam-boats, as they do not receive their impetus
from sails, but from steam, they are capable of being
kept under better command; and therefore it seems,
from their greater power, they ought always to give
way in favour of a vessel using sails only.[4]   There
are some other rules laid down by Emerigon, and other
foreign jurists; but as they do not appear to be expressly recognised in the common law, it may be
questionable how far they constitute a part of the
general law of the sea.[5]

§ 612. Some statute regulations have been made
by the congress of the United States for the regulation
of passenger-ships in voyages to or from foreign ports.
They require, that the number of passengers, which
shall be taken on board of any ship, bound to or from
the United States, to or from any foreign port, shall
not exceed two for every five tons of the ship's custom-
house measurement; and, that the quantity of water

---

1 Angell's Law Intelligencer for 1829, p. 20.
2 *The Neptune* 2d, 1 Dodson R. 467; 3 Kent Com. 184.
3 *The Shannon,* 2 Hagg. R. 174.   4 Ibid.
5 Emerig. Assur. ch. 12, § 14.

and provisions, which shall be taken on board and secured under deck, by every ship bound from the United States to any port on the continent of Europe, shall be sixty gallons of water, one hundred pounds of salted provisions, one gallon of vinegar, and one hundred pounds of wholesome ship-bread. It is also made necessary for the master to have a manifest or list on board of all the passengers taken on board at any foreign port. These enactments are enforced by suitable penalties and forfeitures.[1]

ART. X.   SPECIAL OR QUASI BAILEES FOR HIRE.

§ 613. There is a class of bailments not exactly falling under any of the heads already examined, which bears some analogy to cases of deposits for hire, or *locatio custodiæ ;* and to judicial deposits under the French law.[2] Such are cases of POSSESSION OF PROPERTY BY CAPTORS, BY REVENUE OFFICERS, BY PRIZE AGENTS, BY OFFICERS OF COURTS, AND BY SALVORS, who have preserved property, and are entitled to salvage. All these seem quasi bailees, or depositaries for hire.

§ 614. First, in respect to CAPTORS. If the capture is tortious and without reasonable cause in the exercise of belligerent rights, the captors are bound for all losses and damages whatsoever. If on the other hand the capture is originally justifiable, the captors are deemed possessors *bonâ fide,* and the law is clear, that a *bonâ fide* possessor is not responsible for casualties. But he may by subsequent misconduct forfeit

---

1 Statute of 1819, ch. 170 ; 3 Story U. S. Laws, 1722.
2 Pothier, Dépôt, n. 84 to 118.

the protection of his fair title, and render himself liable
to be considered as a trespasser from the beginning.[1]
But mere irregularities will not charge the captors, unless they produce an irreparable loss, or justly prevent
a restitution of the property.[2]   If there has been any
embezzlement, the captors must answer for that, if it
occurred while the property was in their custody,
whether it was done by themselves, or by any persons
acting under them.[3]

§ 615. The first question in all cases of this nature
is, what is the degree of care or diligence, to which
the captors are bound.   An attempt has been made to
charge them with the same degree of responsibility as
innkeepers and common carriers ; but this doctrine has
been constantly repudiated.[4]   On the other hand an
attempt has been made to bring down their responsibility to the same degree as that, which the captors
take, or may be presumed to take, of their own property.
This doctrine has also been overruled.[5]   The true
rule deducible from the nature of their rights and duties seems to be, that they are bound to the same degree of diligence, which prudent persons exercise in
keeping their own property ; that is, they are bound to
ordinary diligence.[6]

§ 616. The reasoning of Lord Stowell on this subject seems entirely convincing. When goods are taken
justifiably, *jure belli*, the captors have a right to bring
them in for adjudication ; and if in so doing any accident happens, they will be excusable, except for want of

---

[1] *The Betsey*, 1 Rob. 93, 96.   [2] *The Betsey*, 1 Rob. 93, 99, 100.
[3] *The Concordia*, 2 Rob. 102 ; *The Dermohr*, 3 Rob. 129, 130.
[4] *The Maria & Vrow Johanna*, 4 Rob. 348, 350 ; *The Rendsberg*,
6 Rob. 142, 146.
[5] *The William*, 6 Rob. 316.   [6] *The Maria, &c.* 4 Rob. 348, 350.

due care on the part of themselves or their agents. But however justifiable the original seizure may be, still the captors hold but an imperfect right. The property may turn out to belong to others; and if the captors put it into an improper place, or keep it with too little attention, they are liable to the consequences, if the goods are not kept with the same caution, with which a prudent person would keep his own property.[1] The position sometimes taken, that captors are answerable only for the same care, as they would take of their own property, is not a just criterion in a case of this sort. In cases of capture there is no confidence reposed, nor any voluntary election of the person, in whose care the property is left. It is a compulsory act of justifiable force; but still of such force, as removes from the owner any responsibility for the imprudent or incautious conduct of the prize-master. It is not enough, therefore, that a person in that situation uses as much caution, as he would use about his own affairs. The law requires, that there should be no deficiency of due diligence.[2]   And if a loss occurs, the *onus* is on the captors to show, that due diligence has been used, and that the loss was not from any fault or misconduct on the part of themselves or their agents.[3] If there has been any loss by the wilful negligence of the prize-master, by not taking a pilot at the proper place, or by not placing the vessel in a proper situation for quarantine, the captors will be responsible, as much as in cases of embezzlement.[4]

---

[1] *The Maria, &c.* 4 Rob. 348, 351, 352; *The Catharine & Anna,* 4 Rob. 39.

[2] *The William,* 6 Rob. 316, 318.   [3] Ibid.

[4] *The Die Fire Damer,* 5 Rob. 357; *The Freya,* 5 Rob. 75; *The William,* 6 Rob. 316.

§ 617. If the goods have been unlivered by a de-cree of the Prize Court, and placed under the joint locks of the officers of the revenue and of the captors in a warehouse, and are stolen from thence by burg-lars without any want of due care by the bailees, the unlivery being under the direction of the Court, and the possession of the captors the possession of the Court, the captors are not liable for the loss.[1]

§ 618. Secondly. The same rules, which apply to captains, would seem to apply to REVENUE OFFICERS and others, who seize property for supposed forfeitures. If the seizure is without justifiable cause, they are re-sponsible for all losses and damages; if for justifiable cause, they are responsible only for losses and damages occasioned by the want of ordinary diligence.[2]

§ 619. Thirdly. As to PRIZE AGENTS, the same prin-ciples upon the like reasoning would seem to prevail. Indeed, they do not seem essentially to differ from other agents acting for hire.[3]

§ 620. Fourthly. As to OFFICERS OF COURTS. In respect to property in the custody of the officers of a Court pending process and proceedings, such officers are undoubtedly responsible for good faith and reason-able diligence. If the property is lost or injured by any negligent or dishonest execution of the trust, they are liable in damages; but they are not, as of course, liable because there has been an embezzlement or theft. They must be affected with culpable negligence or fraud. And it seems, that the Court places such confidence in its officers, that it will require some proof at least of negligence or fraud, before it will

---

1 *The Maria, &c.* 4 Rob. 348.
2 *Burke v. Trevitt,* 1 Mason R. 96, 101.
3 *The Rendsberg,* 6 Rob. 142, 154 to 158.

throw the burthen of proof upon them to exonerate themselves.[1]   The degree of diligence, which officers of the Court are bound to exert in the custody of the property, seems to be such ordinary diligence, as belongs to a prudent and honest discharge of their duties, and such as is required of all persons, who receive compensation for their services.[2]   That is the rule of the French law ; and it is founded upon the neutrality of interest and benefit in the parties.[3]

§ 621.   And generally a like rule applies to RE-CEIVERS and other depositaries appointed by the Court.[4]   Pothier, however, thinks, that the general receiver of a Court, ("Receveur des consignations,") who in virtue of his office receives the property brought into Court, becomes bound to all possible diligence, and is liable for the slightest neglect.[5]   He founds his reasoning, however, upon circumstances peculiar to the French law, or at least upon circumstances not applicable to receivers in general either in England or America.

§ 622.   Fifthly. As to SALVORS.   Wherever a ship and cargo, or any part thereof, are saved at sea by the exertions of any persons from impending perils, or are recovered after an actual abandonment or loss, such persons are denominated Salvors ;   and they are entitled to a compensation for their services, which is known by the name of *salvage*.[6]   As soon as they take possession of the property for the purpose of preserving it, as if they find a ship derelict at sea, or if they re-

---

[1] *Burke* v. *Trevitt*, 1 Mason R. 96, 101 ; *The Hoop*, 4 Rob. 145 ; *The Rendsberg*, 6 Rob. 142, 157.

[2] *The Rendsberg*, 6 Rob. 142, 154, 156, 169 ; *Burke* v. *Trevitt*, 1 Mason R. 96, 100, 101.

[3] Pothier, Dépôt, n. 92, 96.

[4] 3 Atk. 480 ; 2 Ch. R. 9 ; 2 Vez. 85 ; 3 Vez. jr. 566 ; 11 Vez. 377.

[5] Pothier, Dépôt, n. 111.   [6] Abbott on Shipp. P. 3, ch. 10.

capture it, or if they go on board a ship in distress, and take possession with the assent of the master or other persons then in possession, they are deemed *bonâ fide* possessors, and their possession cannot be lawfully displaced.[1] They have a lien on the property for their salvage, which the laws of all maritime countries will respect and enforce.

§ 623. Persons thus undertaking to act as salvors are responsible not only for good faith, but for reasonable diligence in their custody of the salvage property. If they are guilty of gross negligence, or embezzlement, or fraud, they certainly forfeit all their claims to salvage.[2] But whether, besides a forfeiture of their claims for salvage, they may not also in a case of gross negligence be positively responsible to the owners of the property for loss occasioned by such negligence, does not appear ever to have been the subject of any judicial determination. Indeed it does not any where appear, what is the degree of diligence, to which they are bound; whether it is, like bailees for hire, to ordinary diligence, or to slight diligence, like a depository in a case of *miserabile depositum.* The closest analogy is that of a mere finder of goods on land, who incurs (as has been seen) the responsibility of a mere depositary without hire.[3] But the finder of goods on land is not entitled to receive any compensation, as the salvor at sea is; and this may furnish a distinction fit for consideration in a case, which shall call for a decision upon this point.

§ 624. Where salvage property has been brought in port, and pending a suit for compensation a part of

---

1 *The Blandenhade*, 1 Dodson R. 414.
2 *The Blaireau*, 2 Cranch, 240; 1 Peters's Cond. R. 397.
3 Ante, §   Doct. & Stud. ch. 38.

it perishes by accident, as by fire, without any default on either side, if the property remains in the custody of the Court, the loss is to be borne by the owners and salvors as a common loss. But if the property has been delivered to either party upon an appraisement, the loss is then to be borne exclusively by such party, for he takes upon himself the risk.[1] The consideration of the subject of salvage generally belongs more appropriately to the Law of Shipping; and therefore will not be further enlarged upon in this place.

§ 625. These Commentaries upon the Law of Bailments are now brought to a conclusion. Upon a review of the whole subject it will at once occur to the reader, what a great variety of topics, discussed in the civil and foreign law, remains wholly unsettled in the common law. He will also be struck with the many ingenious and subtile distinctions, singular cases, refined speculations and theoretical inquiries, to which the free habits of the civilians conduct them in the course of their reasoning. Let it be remembered, however, that if some of these distinctions and speculations and inquiries seem remote from the practical doctrines of the common law, they may yet be of great utility in the investigation and illustration of elementary principles. They employed the genius and exhausted the learning of many of the greatest jurists of all antiquity; and were thought worthy of being embodied in the texts of Justinian's immortal Codes. In modern times the noblest minds have felt a life of laborious diligence well rewarded by gathering together illustrative commentaries in aid of these texts. What, indeed, was juridical wisdom in the best days of imperial Rome;

---

1 *The Three Friends*, 4 Rob. 268.

what is yet deemed the highest juridical wisdom in the most enlightened and polished nations of continental Europe ; ought not to be, and cannot be, matter of indifference to any, who study the law, not as a mere system of arbitrary rules, but as a rational science. The common law has silently borrowed many of its best principles and expositions of the law of contracts, and especially of commercial contracts, from the Continental jurisprudence. To America may yet be reserved the honour of still further improving it by a more intimate blending of the various lights of each system in her own administration of civil justice.

INDEX.

B.

C.

E.

F.

G.

H.

M.

52

W.

www.ingramcontent.com/pod-product-compliance
Lightning Source LLC
Chambersburg PA
CBHW031427180326
41458CB00002B/474